Get Certified and Get Ahead

5/4/2002 Cam, USA 9.99

Get Certified and Get Ahead

Anne Martinez

McGraw-Hill

New York   San Francisco   Washington, D.C.
Auckland   Bogotá   Caracas   Lisbon   London
Madrid   Mexico City   Milan   Montreal   New Delhi
San Juan   Singapore   Sydney   Tokyo   Toronto

Library of Congress Cataloging-in-Publication Data

Martinez/ Anne.
    Get certified and get ahead / Anne Martinez.
        p. cm. — (Certification series)
    Includes index.
    ISBN 0-07-041127-1
    1. Electronic data processing personnel—Certification.
  I. Title II. Series.
  QA76.3.M325 1998
  004'.023—dc21   98-9328
                                    CIP

McGraw-Hill

A Division of The McGraw-Hill Companies

The views expressed in this book are solely those of the author, and do not represent the views of any other party or parties.

   4 5 6 7 8 9 0 DOC/DOC 9 0 3 2 0 1 9 8

ISBN 0-07-041127-1

The sponsoring editor for this book was Judy Brief and the production supervisor was Pamela Pelton. It was set in New Century Schoolbook by Patricia Wallenburg.

Printed and bound by R. R. Donnelley & Sons Company.

McGraw-Hill books are available at special quantity discounts to use as premiums and sales promotions, or for use in corporate training programs. For more information, please write to the Director of Special Sales, McGraw-Hill, 11 West 19th Street, New York, NY 10011. Or contact your local bookstore.

 This book is printed on recycled, acid-free paper containing a minimum of 50% recycled, de-inked fiber.

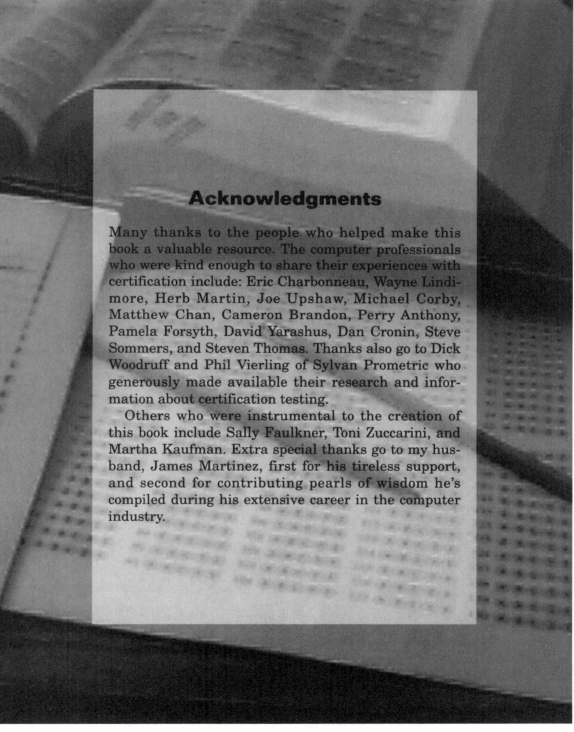

Acknowledgments

Many thanks to the people who helped make this book a valuable resource. The computer professionals who were kind enough to share their experiences with certification include: Eric Charbonneau, Wayne Lindimore, Herb Martin, Joe Upshaw, Michael Corby, Matthew Chan, Cameron Brandon, Perry Anthony, Pamela Forsyth, David Yarashus, Dan Cronin, Steve Sommers, and Steven Thomas. Thanks also go to Dick Woodruff and Phil Vierling of Sylvan Prometric who generously made available their research and information about certification testing.

Others who were instrumental to the creation of this book include Sally Faulkner, Toni Zuccarini, and Martha Kaufman. Extra special thanks go to my husband, James Martinez, first for his tireless support, and second for contributing pearls of wisdom he's compiled during his extensive career in the computer industry.

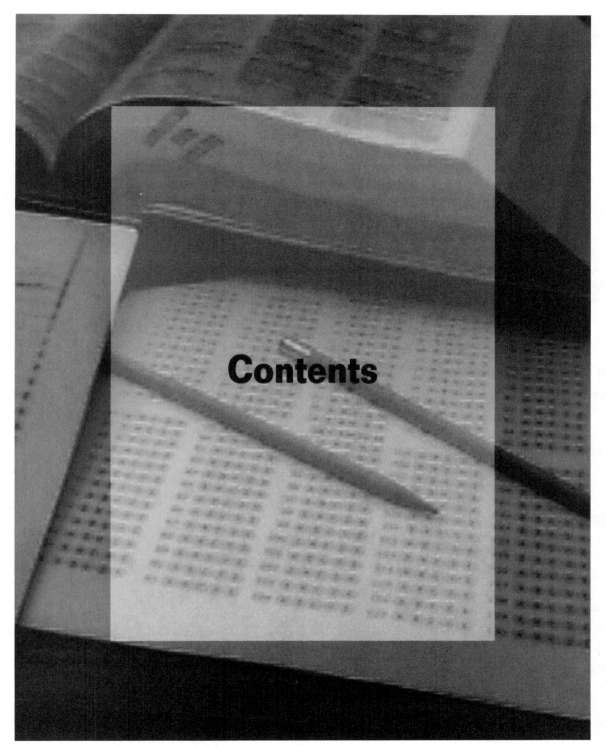

Contents

Section 1
Why Certify?   1

Chapter 1

Chapter 2

Section 2
How to Get (Happily) Certified 73

Chapter 8
Which Certification is Best for You? 131

Chapter 9
Learning Alternatives 149

Chapter 10
Your Personal Training and Certification Road Map 171

Chapter 11
Study Secrets 187

Section 3
Utilize Your Certification to the Max   219

Chapter 17
Another Certification? 323

Section 4
Resources   331

Certification Programs 333

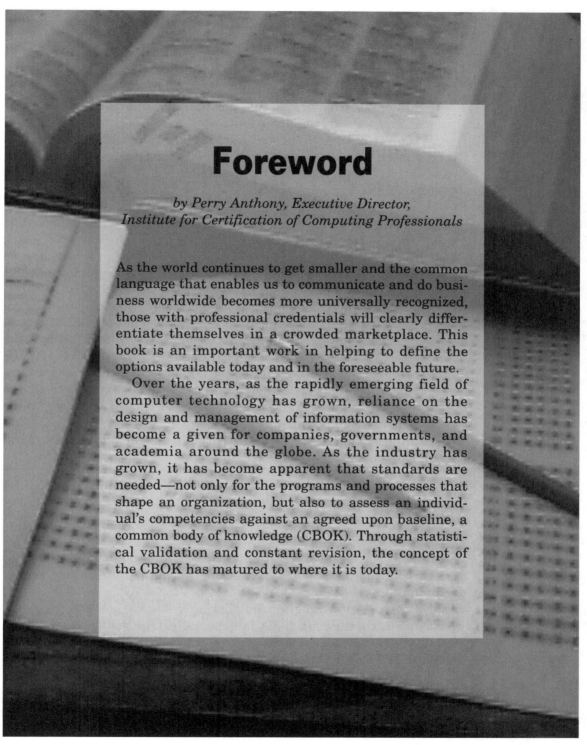

Foreword

by Perry Anthony, Executive Director,
Institute for Certification of Computing Professionals

As the world continues to get smaller and the common language that enables us to communicate and do business worldwide becomes more universally recognized, those with professional credentials will clearly differentiate themselves in a crowded marketplace. This book is an important work in helping to define the options available today and in the foreseeable future.

Over the years, as the rapidly emerging field of computer technology has grown, reliance on the design and management of information systems has become a given for companies, governments, and academia around the globe. As the industry has grown, it has become apparent that standards are needed—not only for the programs and processes that shape an organization, but also to assess an individual's competencies against an agreed upon baseline, a common body of knowledge (CBOK). Through statistical validation and constant revision, the concept of the CBOK has matured to where it is today.

Unlike hundreds of other industries from hairdressers to engineers, accountants to lawyers, the computing profession has asserted its desire to remain self-regulated. Adherence to standards in purely voluntary. Whether or not this position endures is of considerable importance for the computing industry.

It is precisely due to the maturation of the computing industry that there is an increasing demand for the establishment of standards, and for certification programs that define a CBOK, measure performance, and recognize competence with professional certification.

Among federal and state legislators, there is growing concern about the lack of agreed-upon computer-industry standards. The multitude of technical problems resulting from the Year 2000 issue, and the resulting impact on the everyday life of nearly everyone worldwide, is likely to attract considerable focus by regulatory bodies regarding the standards issue.

The explosion of technological advancements has also created an explosion in technical certification programs. The handful of certifications sponsored by computer societies in the 1960s through the 1980s has evolved to a mind-boggling and growing number. By the year 2000, there will be approximately 200 different certifications. Computing professionals and the organizations they represent are faced with a complex and confusing array of choices for determining and demonstrating competence.

A professional certification process should include three critical components:

1. Exam-based testing statistically demonstrating mastery of a CBOK.
2. Adherence to a code of conduct and ethics.
3. Mandatory continuing education.

However, successful navigation of the examination track that leads to certification is only one part of the overall and continuing certification process.

No certification program has listing value without a continuing education component. This is especially true for the computing industry, due to the explosive nature of technology. If certificate holders are not required to demonstrate that they're in a program of continuing education, their certificates will quickly be rendered meaningless by progress.

Sometimes called *recertification* or *professional development*, a formal, structured continuing education program must be in place and complied with in order to retain a meaningful professional certificate. A continuing education program should include a definition of areas (or disciplines) in which continuing education credits can be earned; a mechanism for submitting, retaining, and reporting; and a clearly defined time frame in which this is to be accomplished.

In addition, a process for terminating or otherwise invalidating a certificate for noncompliance should be clearly articulated, and an independent appeals process established.

To an employer or hiring entity, a recognized designation communicates a commitment by an employee that they are a professional in their field and have demonstrated competence in a defined area that is relevant and important. The computer professional has demonstrated that his or her competency applies to a specific vendor product or to the mastering of broader concepts and principles that frame the industry.

Today, both individuals and their organizations recognize the technical and marketing importance of demonstrating competence in a particular discipline. Computing professionals have an increasing responsibility to establish their credentials in the marketplace through their own initiatives. Due to the rampant downsizing and "rightsizing" in most organizations, the individual can no longer look solely to their employer for career development. More of the responsibility to take initiative in career advancement has fallen on the individual.

In response to this change, many education and training organizations have evolved to meet the growing need for continuing education. Many offer certificates at the conclusion of a course or series of courses. These organizations in many instances are better equipped than colleges to respond quickly to the marketplace demands for current and topical programs that validate knowledge.

The ICCP was pleased to provide a foreword for this important publication. The ICCP legacy of standards development and independent certification of knowledge has its roots in the early 1960s. Current combined membership exceeds 250,000 IT professionals, and a numerous constituent organizations include many leading international industry societies.

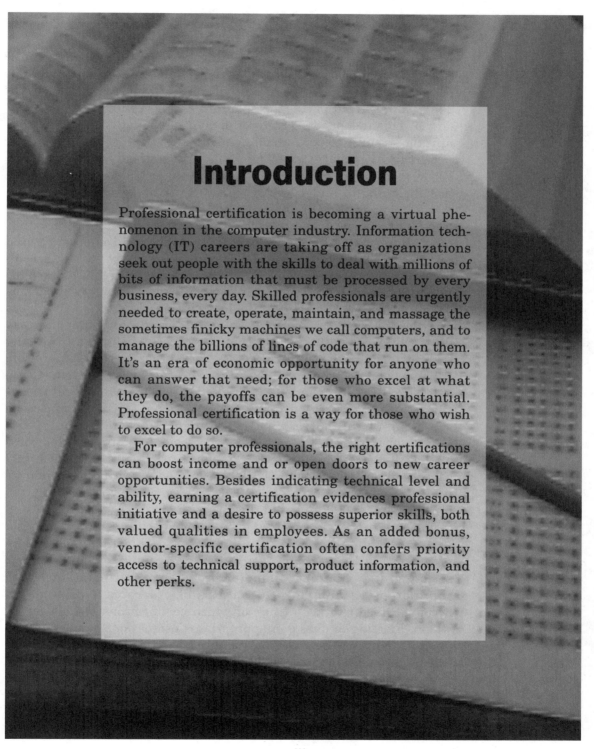

Introduction

Professional certification is becoming a virtual phenomenon in the computer industry. Information technology (IT) careers are taking off as organizations seek out people with the skills to deal with millions of bits of information that must be processed by every business, every day. Skilled professionals are urgently needed to create, operate, maintain, and massage the sometimes finicky machines we call computers, and to manage the billions of lines of code that run on them. It's an era of economic opportunity for anyone who can answer that need; for those who excel at what they do, the payoffs can be even more substantial. Professional certification is a way for those who wish to excel to do so.

For computer professionals, the right certifications can boost income and or open doors to new career opportunities. Besides indicating technical level and ability, earning a certification evidences professional initiative and a desire to possess superior skills, both valued qualities in employees. As an added bonus, vendor-specific certification often confers priority access to technical support, product information, and other perks.

Certification provides an external validation and measurement of technical qualifications. When you're certified, that demonstrates to potential employers that not only do you say you know what you're doing; an external party (the sponsor of your certification) says you do too. This independent support of your qualifications can lend significant strength to your professional credibility.

Certification is also a way to distinguish yourself from your peers. When going after choice assignments, that extra credential can be just the thing to nudge your resume to the top of the pile. In fact, certification is such an effective route to career advancement that professionals are flocking to certification programs. Consider that more than 20,000 people are currently enrolled in computer-related certification programs through Learning Tree International, a leading industry trainer. Alan Salisbury, president of Learning Tree International, reports that enrollment in the company's programs has jumped 30-40% a year for the last several years.

Although certification has been around in the computer industry for a while, it's only recently that the concept has begun to really take off. One of the early successes came from Novell Corporation, which pioneered vendor-sponsored certifications with its CNE (Certified Novell Engineer) and CNA (Certified Novell Administrator) certifications. The Microsoft Certified Professional (MCP) certifications are some of the hottest at the moment, especially the MCSE (Microsoft Certified Systems Engineer designation). More than 58% of the MCPs responding to Microsoft Corporation's second annual salary survey, dated Jan/Feb 1997, reported a certification-induced income boost, often exceeding 10%. MCSEs, of which there are currently about 15,000, reported the largest increases.

Although there are study guides for specific certification programs, including the Novell and Microsoft designations and the A+ program, until now there hasn't been any comprehensive guide to selecting and obtaining computer professional certifications. With the increasing number of certification programs available, it's become difficult to keep track of which certifications are offered by whom. Electing to pursue inappropriate designations can be a costly mistake; earning the right ones a shrewd career move. This book is intended to help you make that shrewd move.

In Section 1, *Why Certify?*, you'll gain a full understanding of the many benefits of certification and just what it can and can't do for you. You'll hear from other computer professionals who've achieved certification, and learn what it has helped them accomplish.

Section 2, *How To Get (Happily) Certified*, walks you through the process of choosing the certification that will best support your goals, and guides you step-by-step through the process of earning it. You'll find advice on cutting your costs and boosting your study efficiency. If you find you'll need additional training to qualify for the certification of your choice, there are many learning options available to you, and they are explained in detail in this section. You'll also learn about mistakes others have made while pursuing certification so that you can avoid them yourself.

Section 3, *Utilizing Your Certification To The Max*, shows you what you can do with your certification once you've obtained it. You'll learn how to advertise your new status, ask for a raise, or go after that new job.

The final section contains a valuable collection of resources to help you achieve your goals. Details of over a hundred certifications are included, including how to get them, what you'll need to qualify, and what it will cost. You'll also find an array of additional resources, from books to Web sites to self-study software tools, that can provide additional support. Whatever your career dreams are, this book is designed to help you explore and apply professional certification as a tool to obtaining them.

SECTION 1

Why Certify?

CHAPTER 1

Getting Ahead By Getting Certified: 20 Quick FAQs

1. What Does "Certified" Mean?

Certification provides independent verification of certain levels of expertise in a particular area. Basically, it means you've completed the steps required to receive a particular designation. But this basic definition comes with a weakness—in some cases, individuals can become "certified" simply by paying a particular membership fee or by attending the required seminar. Such certifications are meaningless and a waste of time and money. They are not what this book is about.

This book is concerned with certifications that *mean something*. It's about achieving designations that demonstrate to your employer and/or clients that you are, indeed, an expert in a particular area or areas, and that a reputable, recognizable organization is willing to attest to that.

Such certifications typically arise from a scenario like this: a computer-related organization, vendor, or consortium has identified a particular function that requires specific skills, knowledge, and expertise—for example, intranet security. They detail just what those skills are and what knowledge is critical. Most likely, they also identify a series of steps that will enable you to obtain the targeted level, and implement methods of assessing your progress. Certification is conferred when you prove that you have, in fact, obtained the specified abilities and knowledge.

With many certifications, you'll also be granted a privileged relationship with the program's sponsor. The relationship can include priority technical support, early product updates, access to special forums, or other perks that will enable you to perform at a higher level.

This book is meant to be an informative source that enables you to take advantage of professional certification opportunities. The included resources, advice, and tools will help you select and obtain a certification to best serve your personal and career goals; and the book teaches you how to utilize certification as a powerful career advancement tool.

2. What Certifications are There?

You've probably heard of certifications granted by Microsoft, Novell, and maybe a few others. But most (Information Systems) IS pros don't realize that there are currently more than 170 technical certification programs up and running. You can become a 3COM 3Wizard, Certified Network Expert (CNX), or an IBM Certified AS/400 Professional System Administrator, just to name a few.

With so many certifications out there, it's helpful to divide them into categories by type of sponsor. The largest chunk of the certification list is taken up by vendors who offer certifications related to their product lines. Cisco Systems, IBM, Digital Equipment Corp (DEC), Adobe, and Bay Networks are examples. In fact, the vendor-sponsored category of certifications is so expansive that everything else can reasonably be grouped into one additional category: nonvendor certifications.

Nonvendor certifications include those sponsored by professional groups. As examples, the Institute for Certified Computing Professionals (ICCP) developed the Certified Computing Professional (CCP) designation; the A+ Service Technician Certification is overseen by the Computing Technology and Industry Association (CompTIA); and the Network Professional Association (NPA) has come out with the Certified Network Professional (CNP) program. Learning Tree International, a well-known training company, has developed its own certification programs covering a variety of technologies.

Certifications can have a broad focus, such as open systems, or hone in on the details of a particular technology, such as the UNIX operating system or TCP/IP. There are many to choose from, depending on your goals and needs. A few certifications enjoy much wider recognition than most, but that doesn't mean the others won't prove valuable to you. It's all a matter of matching your work goals, time availability, and financial resources to a certification program. If you choose one of the lesser-known certifications, you may have to take greater pains in explaining and promoting it, but if it's in line with your goals, it's a better choice than an instantly recognized certification that doesn't relate to what you really want to accomplish.

3. Who Benefits from Certification Programs?

Certification programs can benefit people and organizations that work in the computer field, sell to the computer market, or employ technical people to perform computer-related tasks. Those with the most to gain are:

- Computer professionals
- Certification sponsors
- Employers
- Clients and customers

Virtually any IS professional can get *something* (in addition to the official piece of paper) by pursuing a well-chosen certification. Most will reap many benefits. The payoffs may come in the form of a salary increase, better job, added confidence, or additional skills that allow you to move into a new area. Course work often includes hands-on exercises with up-to-the-minute software and/or equipment, exposure you might not otherwise have.

This is not to claim that every certification program is equally valuable. But when the urge strikes to branch into something new or simply to escalate your level of expertise in something you already know, certification is a good way to go.

Certification sponsors benefit from the deal too. In addition to revenue from training courses and materials, certification programs generate product and company recognition. Every 3Wizard WAN Solutions Master is a confirmation of the power and importance of 3COM, every Certified Banyan Instructor an endorsement of Banyan. By establishing the A+ Technician Certification and the Certified Document Imaging Architech (CDIA) designation, the Computing Technology and Industry Association (CompTIA) has enhanced its own value and reputation.

The more people vendors can teach to master their product, the more likely it is that the product will be successfully utilized to its fullest extent, an added plus for both.

To employers, certification serves as independent evidence that you have demonstrated the skills and abilities required to complete the program. It also offers a method for bringing employees up to speed on the latest technologies, and a way to provide for the continuing education computer people often crave. Certification training can reasonably be billed as an employee benefit.

Customers benefit, too, because a certification gives them additional evidence of your qualifications and suitability for the task at hand. Nontechnical clients in particular find that reassuring.

4. Will Certification Help Me Earn More?

Although increasing income isn't the only reason for obtaining certification, it's certainly a frequently cited motivator. In some cases, certifications can translate directly into increased rates. According to Seattle area recruiter Maurice Fuller of SDC Computer Services, a Microsoft Certified System Engineer Certification (MCSE) is hard to get but really pays for itself. "They're worth $5 extra an hour," he estimates.

But even when a certification doesn't translate readily into a pay increase, it can be used as an effective tool to accomplish the same thing. Even if you're not a consultant or contractor, you can command a higher paycheck as your technical skills grow. That's a fundamental of the job market. Your current employer can be "encouraged" to face up to your greater value, an issue that's discussed later in the book. Or perhaps you might discover that to get that salary increase, you'll have to move on to another position. Advice addressing that possibility can be found between these covers too.

If you don't parlay your certification into a raise in the short term, it will, nonetheless, add to your base of knowledge and qualifications, which should pay off in the long term.

5. How Will Certification Affect My Marketability?

As long as you choose a certification with your career goals in mind, it should serve admirably as a marketability booster. First, certification training listed on your resume demonstrates your ability and your desire to stay current; this is no small task in an industry where skills can become obsolete as quickly as they became cutting edge. Second, it shows that you take initiative, a trait many employers look for.

The computer field continues to be a worker's market. Almost anyone who's any good at all is able to get work. But when it comes to landing just the position you're after, you'll always benefit by differentiating yourself from your competitors, especially when it comes to the more desirable positions. Usually those with higher salaries and cutting edge work will have plenty of applicants lining up for consideration. Picture a hiring manager sorting through a pile of resumes, searching for clues that elevate one candidate above another. She may have six resumes that indicate the desired experience level and qualifications. Yours includes a certification in just the technology used in the position she's hiring. It's a no-brainer to slide your resume into the "schedule an interview" pile. That's a successful competitive edge.

Although technical recruiters report few requests specifying a desire for individuals with a specific certification, such positions are beginning to show up with increasing regularity. So far, employers only ask for the more widely known certifications, such as Novell's Certified Novell Engineer (CNE) title. But as more individuals obtain certification and employers become aware of the availability of professionals with specific certifications, demand is likely to grow. By starting a certification program now, you won't have to play catch-up later.

6. Can Certification Compensate for Inexperience?

Not entirely. Hands-on experience is still a key criteria in determining your qualifications for a particular position. And in some ways, tests have gotten a bad rap; some think good test scores only prove that you're a good test taker, so the fact that you passed a particular exam may be taken with a grain of salt. That's the bad news.

The good news is that certification absolutely *does* supplement experience. If you have some experience and a related certification, you'll come out ahead of the person with only the experience, and you may be considered at least equally as qualified as a person with slightly more work experience.

On top of that, certification is something you can earn now, starting today. Work experience requires time to accrue and there is little you can do to speed the process.

Many certification sponsors are addressing concerns about the meaning of exam scores by adding experience requirements and/or hands-on training as part of their certification process. Completing one of these certification programs will give you the professional designation *and* that invaluable practical experience.

7. Can Certification Help Me Move Into Something New?

Most definitely. Although certification can't completely replace experience (see Question 6), it can effectively serve as a bridge to a new specialty. Suppose you're an experienced intranet or Internet developer and want to get into systems security consulting. Although it might be possible for you to talk your way into a first entry-level security-related position, it would be difficult at best. But if you first complete one of the applicable certification programs, suddenly you will have something exactly on target to add to your resume. Not only that, but there are several programs to choose from, depending on the depth of knowledge you seek and the time and money you're willing to invest.

For example, you could enroll in Learning Tree International's System Security Certified Professional program, which promises that by the time you graduate you'll able to design and implement an organization's security strategy, expound upon threats from Internet hackers, secure an operating system, implement firewalls, and perform other security tasks. You'll have to complete five courses (averaging four days each) and their related exams. Most of the courses are hands-on, so you won't just read about configuring a firewall—you'll do it. Other possibilities include the Certified Information Systems Security Professional (CISSP) program overseen by the International Information Systems Security CertificationConsortium (ISC²), or the Internet Security Engineer certification from Net Guru Technologies.

Want to slide into a Java opening? You can go right to the source and become a Sun Certified Java Programmer or Developer. Learning Tree offers a Java certification, too.

Technical training is another hot area to which you might aspire. Again, there are several certifications to choose from, depending upon your goals. Many vendors, including Adobe, Banyan, Corel, Microsoft, and Novell will certify you to teach their products. Or, you can go with a vendor-independent certification like the Certified Technical Trainer (CTT) from Educational Testing Service. The possibilities for this kind of bridging are wide open.

It's true that there are other classes you could enroll in to learn new software or hardware skills, but a single course listed on your resume is much less impressive than a completed certification. And if you go with individual courses, you'll have to figure out which classes appear best suited to your goals, which can be difficult when moving into an area with which you are less familiar. Certification programs offer a complete curriculum developed with the intent of providing skills that have been identified as critical to success in a particular area. That's not as rigid as it sounds, because most programs include a choice of electives in addition to core courses. Why build your own bridge when you can cross one already constructed by a cadre of expert architects?

Certification programs offer a good way to learn a new area *and* obtain a credential at the same time. That's a combination that's hard to beat.

8. Which Program Is Best For Me?

You could just pick a certification based on a gut feeling, but if you want to be certain of the best match, it's going to take a bit of homework. First, you'll have to identify just what it is you're trying to accomplish, which can be more difficult than it sounds. It's like deciding what to major in at college, but at least this time you'll have the advantages of perspective and experience, which allow you to visualize the options more clearly.

Once you've managed that, you'll have to pin down the details of your current skills and experience and see where the bridge needs to be built, or maybe just the foundations strengthened, to get where you'd like to be. These two steps come easily to some people, but take quite a bit of thought for others. Completing them will put you halfway there.

Next comes the research part. Because there are more than 160 certifications to choose from, and more are being added all the time, you'll want to browse through the options until you identify the ones that might suit your purposes. The exhaustive reference sections included in this book, along with other resources, can help you to do this. Don't stop when you uncover the first possible program because there may be several that make the first cut. Then you'll want to find out as much as you can about the certifications on your tentative list before settling on one.

Again, this process will cost you some time and effort, but putting in the work up front will be time and effort well spent if it lands you in the right certification program. The extensive resources in this book will guide and support you through the decision-making process and provide you with plenty of other references you can turn to, if necessary.

9. How Much Will it Cost?

The price of certification is difficult to pin down in advance. There are many variables, the first and largest of which is your choice of certification to pursue. In some cases, the sole requirement for initial certification is that you pass the exam. An example is the Certified Information Systems Auditor (CISA) program from the Information Systems Audit and Control Association (ISACA). In 1997, the exam fee was $275 for ISACA members and $355 for nonmembers. The fees are expected to remain the same during 1998.

You might be able to pass a qualifying exam strictly by drawing on expertise you already have, but that's risky. Most likely you'll want to study the relevant material first. A study guide may be all you need, or a series of hands-on courses might be more in order. Your needs will probably fall somewhere in between. A manual is obviously drastically less expensive than instructor-led training.

Most certifications require some degree of continuing education over the years to retain the certification. Generally there's a lot of freedom about the exact nature of the training—a community college class, a professional seminar, an employer run seminar (which costs you nothing), or an online course might all qualify. So the cost of your continuing education can vary greatly, depending on how you choose to accomplish it.

In some instances, you'll have to pay an annual maintenance fee to the sponsoring organization. The annual CISA maintenance fee, for example, is $35 for ISACA members and $45 for nonmembers.

Word on the street is that an MCSE certification (one of the hottest at the moment) can run you ten thousand dollars by the time you complete the necessary classes and requirements. There's no denying that's a serious chunk of change, but it's alleged to have a major impact on future earnings that begins *before you even complete the certification*. Apparently you can gain value in the eyes of some employers simply by being in the process of earning an MCSE. A similar effect probably applies to other designations as well.

Monetary expenses aren't the only costs of earning certification. You'll also have to devote time and effort, often a substantial amount.

As you can see, it's impossible to state that certification will cost X dollars or will take every candidate Y months to obtain. The uncertainty can be very annoying, but the payoff is the flexibility that allows each person, to a large degree, to map out their own path and their own pace. Only after you've decided which certification to go after and figured out which learning alternatives are most attractive to you will you be able to come up with a reasonably close cost estimate. This book will help you evaluate your potential costs so you don't encounter unexpected financial surprises down the line.

10. Is Financial Assistance Available for Certification Training?

Absolutely. If you are on a company payroll, there may well be dollars in the budget that can be funneled your way. If you can convince your employer that the training will benefit the company as well as yourself, then the company's training budget may cover part or all of your expenses. Another employer source to look into is the tuition reimbursement program, which may refund part or all of your tuition fees, provided you meet the company's requirements. This book will tell you how to approach your employer to find out just what's available (or can be made available) to you.

Uncle Sam is sympathetic to students, too. Funds you expend on education (in some cases, including related transportation costs) in your current field can be deducted on your federal income tax return, either on Form 2106, "Employee Business Expenses," or on Schedule C, "Profit or Loss from Business". This book includes specific advice explaining how to take advantage of education-related tax breaks and clarifying related tax return intricacies.

Judicious selection of learning alternatives and a little shopping around can save you money too. For example, some community technical colleges have begun offering some of the *same exact classes* you'll find at Novell Authorized Education Centers at a fraction of the cost. You'll often have the option of purchasing a package deal that includes several courses at a discounted rate that is more affordable than purchasing each course individually. It's the certification version of bulk discounting. And then there's the ultra-condensed version, where you travel to a learning center, bury yourself in theory and technology for two weeks, and emerge certified (or nearly so), though perhaps a bit dizzy as well.

Another somewhat less desirable alternative is to finance your certification by paying for it in installments rather than large lump sums. Alternatively, you can extend your chosen program over time, enrolling in courses as you feel financially able to do so.

You may also be able to get your (or your employer's) training money to serve double duty by parlaying your classes into college credits. To help you get the most (training) for the least (money), these options and others are laid out in detail in this book.

11. How Long Does Earning CertificationTake?

How long it takes is largely up to you. If you choose a route that includes one four-day class followed by an exam, then you'll finish in less than a week. But to do this, you'll either have to have a depth of knowledge in the relevant technologies or select a certification that's very narrowly focused.

There's also the cram course version (see Question 10), where you basically put the rest of your life on hold and completely immerse yourself in training for an extended period. For many people this isn't practical because it would interfere with their home and work obligations. It can be physically and emotionally exhausting. Of course, it can also be exciting if you're learning technologies you're passionate about. But not all certification programs offer condensed training regimens.

The most common path is less frantic: you sign up or self-study for the first course, complete it, take the exam. Then you move on to requirement number two, and so on. This method isn't as likely to consume all your spare time and allows for less rushed learning.

Most certification programs specify a time limit within which you must meet all the requirements. Such deadlines are particularly helpful for procrastinators, but can help anyone determine a workable pace.

The bottom line is that earning certification can take a week, or it can span several years. It's basically up to you.

12. Where Will I Have to Go for Certification Training?

You can go back to school or travel to a training site if you want to, but these days there are so many alternatives that it's unlikely you'll have to. You may have to attend some courses at a training center or school if equipment you don't have (such as an Internet server) is used as part of a required, hands-on course. But most of your learning can be done from home, work, nearby independent training centers, or anywhere you can haul your notebook computer or printed study guide. You can thank your own career field for that—computers and technology have freed classes from the classroom. Today, training can be completed in many ways. Learning alternatives include:

- Self-study texts and workbooks
- Computer-based training (CBT)
- Online classes
- Classes at an authorized training center
- Community college programs

These aren't all available for every certification, but usually there are several options to choose from. You'll have to decide which ones will work best for you by analyzing your learning style, degree of self-motivation, and other factors. This book includes an exploration of the ins and outs of various training methods.

13. Do I Need a College Degree?

Absolutely not. In fact, there are generally no educational prerequisites. Even the lack of a high school diploma won't bar your entrance to computer certification programs.

That's always been one of the great things about computer work—there's room for everyone who is capable and often even for those with marginal skills but burning passion for the field. Good educational credentials, however, will often smooth the way into the upper ranks of computer professionals and are listed as a requirement in many job postings. Larger companies, especially, seem to automatically expect candidates to hold a Bachelor of Computer Science degree. Startups are often more flexible.

But we've all heard of the self-taught hacker who founded a company in his garage and moved on to become an industry mover and shaker.

It seems pretty much a continuation of that tradition that certification programs basically work like this: you fill out the paperwork and pay your money—you get in. You complete the requirements, which often include exams and sometimes a record of related work history, and you get certified.

14. How Do I Decide Between an MBA or Certification?

You'll have to undertake a difficult task: nailing down your goals. If working in a management capacity is important to you, the MBA might be the way to go, especially if you like to work for large corporations. Keep in mind, however, that an MBA doesn't command as much respect as it used to. That's probably because it's become a more widely held and widely available credential, perhaps losing some of its value in the process.

If, on the other hand, you're seeking increased pay and responsibility but aren't necessarily attracted to the management route, an MBA might not do you a whole lot of good, and certification might be just what you're looking for. People with top technical skills can command a premium in the job market because companies desperately need them to keep up with technology.

The bottom line is that the only person who can decide what sort of career move is best for you is you. Ranking one opportunity above another is meaningless without doing so in the context of your personal goals and aspirations. You'll have to figure out just what those are, research your options with an open mind, and decide for yourself.

15. What if I Don't Remember How to Study?

Going back to studying after a long hiatus is rather like programming in a language you haven't used in a while. At first you may feel hesitant and keep double-checking your syntax, function calls and so on, but as you write line after line, your hesitation shrinks and your fingers begin to fly over the keyboard. It's as though an unused section of your brain dusts itself off and clicks back online. Study habits come back the same way.

But what if you never had very good study habits in the first place? Don't worry, it's never too late to learn how to learn. In fact, you may be among the many people who find studying much easier this time around simply because there are specific reasons and personal goals driving your effort. But whether your study brain cells never developed much muscle, or if they're simply a little "dusty," the tips and techniques in this book will help you brush up on efficient and effective study habits.

16. What Resources are Available to Help Me with Certification?

You'll find information on the more popular (and better funded) certifications all over the Internet and on the shelves of your nearest mega bookstore. Materials covering lesser-known and newer programs require more detective work, but frequently available resources include:

- Internet forums and discussion groups
- Study guides and text books
- Self-assessment tests and computer programs
- Expert instructors
- Materials provided by the certification sponsor
- World Wide Web sites
- And, of course, this book.

Thanks largely to the Internet, you'll be able to access many powerful and useful learning aides right from your computer. If you're not already set up with an Internet connection, this is a good reason to get yourself a modem and sign up for service. You'll be giving yourself virtually twenty-four-hour access to others who've obtained your certification already, are in the process of doing so, or who write or teach about it or about related technologies.

There are plenty of offline resources, too. You may have to special-order books and study guides, but your certification sponsor will be able to tell you which materials you need and how to obtain them. A set of HTML pages on the companion Web site will enable you to click and link immediately to the home page of a particular certification.

17. What Resources Provide Current Certification News?

Once you've chosen your certification program, you may be able to make use of one of the many books that hone in on a single certification, such as:

- *Novell's CNA Study Guide for Netware 4.1*, by David James Iv Clarke and Kelley J. P. Linberg
- *A+ Certification Success Guide: For Computer Technicians*, by Sarah T. Parks and Bob Kalman
- *MCSE Study Guide: Windows NT Server and Workstation 4*, by Joe Casad (Editor), Wayne Dalton, Ken Rosen and Steven Tate
- *Webmaster Administrator Certification Handbook*, by Net Guru Technologies

Industry magazines such as *LAN Times*, *Information Week*, and *Contract Professional* periodically run articles about certification. If you're in the computer field, you should already be reading one or more of these on a regular basis just to keep up with the industry.

There are a number of excellent sites on the Web that cater to people in various stages of obtaining certification. Here are two top general certification sites:

- **www.diac.com/~wlin/cpcert.html**—an excellent computer professional certification resource with links to many certification pages, study aids, user groups, and mailing lists.

✏ **www.arrowweb.com/Echarbon/cert.html**—another bounty of links and information on numerous vendor and nonvendor certifications as well as exam preparation tools and advice.

You'll also find certification news on the sponsors' individual sites. The reference sections included in this book and on the companion Web site contain Web addresses for each certification, as well as details on many more books, learning aids, and certification resources.

18. How Can I Promote Myself And My Certification?

To make the most of your certification, you'll want to learn how to maximize its value as a career tool. Filing it away in a cabinet won't do that. The most obvious thing to do is advertise your new status by adding it to your resume and business cards, but don't stop there. You can also learn to be your own PR person. With a little effort you can get your name out in the world as an expert in your field. The Internet is an excellent tool for this purpose. Through well-planned use of web pages, forums, and other Internet resources, you can get your name to pop up in association with your area of certification. But be careful to abide by Internet etiquette (often called *netiquette*); indiscriminate self-promotion will annoy other Internet users and ultimately work against you. You can also establish expert status by providing useful information to media outlets such as newspapers and television.

There are also techniques you can use to move up in the ranks at your current company or in billing rates if you're an independent. These include finding ways to demonstrate your enhanced value, and simply asking your boss for a raise or promotion.

After you obtain a certification, you might also decide that it's time to move on to a new company or perhaps become an independent contractor or consultant. If you decide to go this route, the directory of major recruiting firms included with this book may come in handy. You'll find specific advice on this important topic in several chapters of this book.

19. What's the Future of Computer Certification?

The value of computer professional certifications appears to be on the rise. Judging by the rapid emergence of new programs, big business and professional organizations seem eager and able to fuel the market.

More than 20,000 people are currently enrolled in computer-related certification programs through Learning Tree International, a leading industry trainer. Alan Salisbury, president of Learning Tree, reports that enrollment in the company's programs has jumped 30 to 40% each year for the past several years. No wonder their catalog continues to grow thicker.

Consider too, that in excess of 100,000 Microsoft Certified Professionals (MCPs) are already in the job market, along with more than 75,000 Novell CNEs and 50,000 ICCP Computer Certified Professionals (CCPs), and those are just a few of the biggies.

Nonetheless, there is reason to believe that the certification marketplace is still in its infancy—or perhaps toddlerhood—and like a toddler, charging ahead at great speed but not necessarily in a straight line. Many factions—professional associations, software and hardware vendors, nonprofit organizations, and consortiums—are working themselves into the picture, and right now that's not too hard to do.

But as the marketplace matures, stratification is likely. Just as traditional academics has two-year degrees, four-year degrees, and postgraduate levels, certifications are likely to break into basic, advanced, and exceptional designations, with plenty of special interest/continuing-education offerings on the side. And, as with academic degrees, there will likely be a significant correlation between certification level and salary level.

In January 1997 IBM, Lotus Development, Netscape, Sun Microsystems, and Novell formed a worldwide training and certification consortium to establish standards for Internet-related certification programs. These are not companies that jump first and worry about the landing area later. Their joint commitment strongly suggests that certification is here to stay, at least for the foreseeable future.

20. Can This Book Help Me Advance my Career through Certification?

Many computer people are increasing their earnings by getting certified. They are finding great personal satisfaction in measuring themselves against the latest and best technologies and receiving independent confirmation that they have what it takes. And they are using certification to bridge to a fresh specialty, add in-depth expertise, or bolster professional credentials.

But not everyone who completes a certification program walks away a satisfied customer. Sometimes precious time and money spent on training returns nothing but a sense of disappointment. When that happens, it's usually because either the program wasn't well matched to individual goals and aspirations, or because the person didn't know how to take advantage of the certification once they received it.

Neither shortcoming is surprising since most people are aware of a mere fraction of the certifications open to them. This book has been created to remedy that. It's designed as a one-stop guide packed with the information about the whats, whys, and hows of professional certifications in the computer field.

You'll find out what you need to know to differentiate between the 170-plus certification options, how to select and obtain one, which mistakes to avoid, and how to get the most out of a certification once you've earned it. So yes, this book really can help you advance your career through certification.

CHAPTER 2

Evolution of Computer Certification

Certification was a part of the computer industry even before ASCII (American Standard Code for Information Interchange) was invented to allow computers to exchange data. Today, the array of certification sponsors includes numerous computer organizations and a list of industry vendors that reads like a who's who of computing. But back when interest first began to stir, the only participant was a single professional society.

The First Certification

The year was 1962. Vacuum tube computers had given way to machines built with individual transistors, and the integrated circuit was new on the scene. The COBOL programming language, which seems to have been around forever, was entering its tender second year. Such was the state of the industry when, in New York, the first computer professional certification exam was conducted, and the certification marketplace was born.

That exam, called the Certificate in Data Processing, or CDP, was developed and administered by the National Machine Accountants Association (NMAA). Later that same year, the NMAA changed its name to the Data Processing Management Association (DPMA). It's recently undergone another name change and is currently called the Association of Information Technology Professionals (AITP).

For eight years, the CDP was the only certification for computer professionals. Then, in 1970, the DPMA added a second exam and professional designation: Registered Business Programmer (RBP).

The DPMA's experience with certification led them to believe that an organization other than their own was needed, an independent group focused solely on the definition of computing knowledge and skills. In 1973, the DPMA joined with seven other professional associations to establish the Institute for Certification of Computer Professionals (ICCP). The other founding organizations included such well-known groups as the Association for Computing Machinery (ACM) and the Canadian Information Processing Society (CIPS). According to plan, the ICCP took over administration of the CDP program in early 1974.

Following Other Footsteps

It might surprise you to learn that certification has been a part of the computer industry practically since its birth. But it's actually not that remarkable when you examine the evolutionary process most occupations seem to follow.

When a new occupation first appears, there will usually be a few scattered individuals with the skills and knowledge to perform it. In the course of adding to their expertise and mastering their profession, these individuals seek each other out. When enough of them come together, a professional association or society is born.

The professional society then works to further the field in a number of ways. Members collect and disseminate related knowledge and finance advances in the field, and they work to gain recognition and acceptance for the occupation.

During this process, a definition of just what an individual in that occupation needs to do and to know to be considered competent is developed. This definition may be formal or informal.

A profession can have more than one society, and each society may have a different definition of competence. The societies and their occupational definitions are often linked to subspecialties of the field. When developments in the field warrant it, members may revise the society's guidelines or even spin off a new society organized around new developments.

Sound familiar? It's an age-old process—the same one that the computer profession has participated in and still does.

From 1974 to 1989 the computer certification marketplace idled. Professional societies and organizations added a few certifications, but not much else happened until commercial powerhouse Novell Corporation jumped in with both feet.

Novell Dives In

Seizing upon certification as a business growth strategy, Novell launched its CNE (Certified Novell Engineer) program in January 1989 (Figure 2-1 shows the CNE Web page). At the time, local area networking was catching on like wildfire. Because of the early stage of the technology, Novell found itself with overloaded customer support lines and resellers with limited technical knowledge. The company, on its own, couldn't supply all the expertise needed to use its products. It was a condition that threatened to seriously hamper the company's potential for continued growth. The answer proved to be a variation of what we today call *outsourcing*.

Novell's initial intention was to train its resellers to handle many technical support issues on their own. So the CNE, at first, was aimed not at computer systems professionals but at computer salespeople. Novell provided the training through its own education centers.

The company's success soon began to get in its way again. Resellers weren't the only ones signing up for CNE training; staff who supported Novell networks within individual companies found the training valuable, too. And they signed up in droves. As with Novell's technical support people before them, the education centers were quickly overwhelmed. So they again off-loaded the burden to resources outside the company.

Figure 2-1
Novell's CNE
Web Page

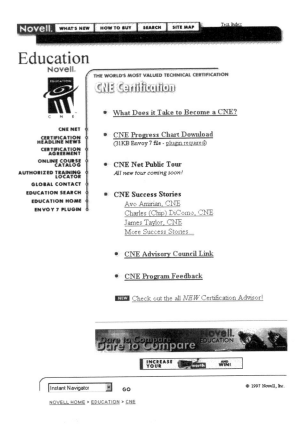

Figure 2-1
Novell's CNE
Web Page

Because certification worked so well, it must have made sense to use it again. That's just what the company did by creating an international network of authorized (certified) training centers. Before a training company could become a Novell Authorized Education Center (NAEC), it had to meet Novell's curriculum requirements, which set standards for equipment, facilities, and instruction. To ensure qualified instructors, Novell launched its second professional designation: the Certified Novell Instructor (CNI), which went live in April 1989.

There's little doubt that Novell's pioneering efforts in the certification marketplace were strictly devoted to its own commercial goals. The first training classes reflected that. But as the certifications evolved and criticisms were leveled, the focus of Novell certification training steadily shifted from sales aspects to technical support issues.

Today, the question of tainted certifications still lingers in the marketplace, especially when a certification is sponsored by an industry vendor. That's one reason why it's important to evaluate the quality and reputation of individual training programs before enrolling in them.

QUOTE

Novell's Early Certification Woes

I was an early Novell CNE. I found little direct benefit in having the certificate and even less value in the course content. My company made mention of the certificate in the fine print of various brochures, so it may have been beneficial in that regard.

I was very disappointed in the course I completed. I felt the course put too much emphasis on which Novell product to sell for a particular situation and too little emphasis on how to configure or correct configuration of the Novell product the customer already had implemented.

I understand the current CNE course does more than make good Novell salespeople—but that's my two cents....

—**Steve Sommers, Director of Applications Development, Shift4 Corporation**

The 90s: Certification Takes Off

Although the ICCP and other professional groups had been promoting certification-based designations for years, many in the business community had never heard of them. Awareness barely stretched beyond the individuals that belonged to the sponsoring societies. Employers presented with evidence of certification were likely to shrug their shoulders and say: "So?" Certification's minimal track record and poor recognition severely limited its value. All of this meant that although certification might have value and meaning to the individuals who went through the process, broad-based career and employment boosting power just wasn't there.

That began to change shortly after Novell joined in. Recognizing the tremendous potential of certification to boost the company's presence in the marketplace, Novell put its marketing might behind certification. Suddenly, everyone in the computer field had heard of the CNE program, and so had much of the business community. A Novell certification became a hot ticket for IT professionals.

But all was not rosy in CNE land. Although the designation was proving wildly successful for Novell and for companies operating Novell networks, its shortcomings became apparent. Not only was it product-specific, it was also version-specific. It promoted strictly Novell products and solutions, which rankled many potential candidates. And, to professionals and organizations operating a non-Novell environment, it was worthless.

Waiting in the wings were those other certifications, those platform-independent designations that had been slowly gathering strength since 1962. They began to emerge from the shadows. Novell's efforts to gain acceptance for its certifications were working, and not just for Novell. As the concept of certification for computer professionals became more widely known and accepted, other certification sponsors received a boost. They were perfectly positioned to market themselves as an alternative to the product-centric certifications from industry vendors. They could promote their features of product and platform independence, while still promising the other professional benefits of certification that Novell's programs offered.

Novell really did a great deal to advance professional certification in the computer industry. The company's development of a network of independent training centers opened up the certification marketplace to other industry vendors. When other computer companies considered emulating Novell's successes, the training delivery channel was already in place. Having witnessed the potential of certification programs to further product recognition and market share and to boost the bottom line with direct revenues, other industry vendors began rolling out their own certifications. From 3Com to IBM to Texas Instruments, new vendor-sponsored computer professional designations appeared at a great rate. However, vendors entered the certification marketplace to different degrees. Some offered a single basic certification with easily met requirements. Others launched an extensive array of certifications, covering virtually every possibility and combination in their product line. IBM leads the second group, offering a dizzying array of certifications covering everything from AIX to OS/2. Figure 2-2 shows IBM's master certification Web page.

The most common program configuration in the 90s, among both vendor-sponsored programs and vendor-independent programs, has been a tiered model. At the first level is the basic product certification. The requirements are relatively straightforward and can be accomplished in a short period of time, especially by individuals with related work experience. The second tier certification builds upon the first and often requires a candidate to hold the first certification and meet additional requirements.

Many certification programs stop with two tiers for each specialty or area of certification, but some go on to four or more. As a rule, vendor-independent certifications have fewer levels than their commercial counterparts. It's not unusual for independents to offer a single, one-level, "you're-an-expert-or-you're-not" professional designation.

Figure 2-2
IBM Certifications
on the Web

IBM.
© IBM Corporation

Certification

Professional Certification Program from IBM
Certification Roles

IBM offers a variety of certifications to help you make the most of your professional drive and expertise.

AIX

- IBM Certified AIX User
- IBM Certified Specialist - AIX V4.1 System Administration
- IBM Certified Specialist - AIX V4.1 Support
- IBM Certified Specialist - RS/6000 SP
- IBM Certified Advanced Technical Expert - RS/6000 AIX V4.2

AS/400

- IBM Certified AS/400 Integrator for NetWare
- IBM Certified AS/400 Professional Network Administrator - Network/Multiple Systems Environment
- IBM Certified AS/400 Associate System Operator
- IBM Certified AS/400 Professional System Operator
- IBM Certified AS/400 Associate System Administrator
- IBM Certified AS/400 Professional System Administrator

Database and Transaction Processing

- IBM Certified DB2 Database Administrator
- IBM Certified DB2 Application Developer
- IBM Certified Specialist - MQSeries
- IBM Certified Specialist - Transaction Server

eNetwork Software

- IBM Certified Specialist - eNetwork Software
- IBM Certified Network Communications Engineer

Internet

- IBM Certified Solutions Expert - net.Commerce
- IBM Certified Solutions Expert - SNG Firewall

Networking Hardware

- IBM Certified Specialist
- IBM Certified Networking Solutions Engineer - I
- IBM Certified Networking Solutions Engineer - II
- IBM Certified Networking Solutions Engineer - III
- IBM Certified Networking Solutions Instructor

Networking Software

- IBM Certified LAN Server Administrator
- IBM Certified LAN Server Engineer
- IBM Certified LAN Server Instructor

- IBM Certified OS/2 Warp Server Administrator
- IBM Certified OS/2 Warp Server Engineer
- IBM Certified OS/2 Warp Server Instructor

Object Technology

- IBM Certified Developer Associate - Object-Oriented VisualAge for C++
- IBM Certified Developer - Object-Oriented VisualAge for C++

- IBM Certified Developer Associate - Object-Oriented VisualAge for COBOL
- IBM Certified Developer - Object-Oriented VisualAge for COBOL

- IBM Certified Developer Associate - VisualAge for Smalltalk
- IBM Certified Developer - VisualAge for Smalltalk

- IBM Certified Developer Associate - VisualAge for Java
- IBM Certified Developer - VisualAge for Java

OS/2 Warp

- IBM Certified OS/2 Engineer for OS/2 Warp Version 3
- IBM Certified OS/2 Engineer for OS/2 Warp 4
- IBM Certified OS/2 Instructor
- IBM Certified OS/2 Warp Developer

PC Servers

- Professional Server Specialist
- Professional Server Expert - IBM LAN Server
- Professional Server Expert - Microsoft Windows NT Advanced Server
- Professional Server Expert - Novell NetWare

Storage Management

- IBM Certified Specialist - ADSM

No matter which avenue you choose, the Professional Certification Program from IBM will enable you to take your expertise in a new direction!

Professional Certification Program from IBM home page
IBM Certification and Testing Consulting Services
IBM home page
Order | Search | Contact IBM | Help | (C) | (TM)

Because product cycles can be as short as six months and vendor certifications are so product-specific, vendors face the challenge of continually updating their training courses to reflect the current product version. Novell again served as a trailblazer in this area when it created its CNI (Certified Novell Instructor) designation. Following this model, the vendor only has to disseminate the new information to the instructors, who then incorporate it into their classes. The certification trainer basically has to know everything about a product to be able to tutor candidates for all the certification levels and tracks within a particular program. Because of this, the instructor designation is considered the ultimate, top-of-the-heap accomplishment. In tiered programs, it's the highest level. Vendors that follow this model include:

- Adobe—Adobe Certified Instructor (ACI)
- Banyan—Certified Banyan Instructor (CBI)
- Borland—Certified Trainers for Delphi and C++ Builder
- Check Point—Check Point Certified Security Instructor (CCSI)
- Corel—Corel Certified Instructor
- Microsoft—Microsoft Certified Trainer (MCT)
- Novell—Certified Novell Instructor (CNI)

Probably because they are structured differently, vendor-independent certification programs don't include a trainer/instructor designation. Without the extensive network of training programs, vendor-independent programs have little need for a cadre of trainers. That doesn't mean they don't offer and require continuing education from their professionals; they just don't have the same product life cycle issues to deal with.

There is, however, a single vendor-independent trainer certification. The Certified Technical Trainer (CTT) designation was developed by Educational Testing Services (ETS) in conjunction with the Computer Education Management Association (CEdMA) and the Information Technology Training Association, Inc. (ITTA).

The CTT Program is geared to measure an individual's mastery of fundamental instructor knowledge and classroom performance as defined by the International Board of Standards for Training, Performance, and Instruction. Requirements for obtaining the CTT designation include both passing an exam and providing a videotape demonstrating the candidate's satisfactory performance as a trainer. Figure 2-3 shows the CTT Web page.

Figure 2-3
The CTT Web Page

Overall, the 90s have been a period of explosive growth in the computer training and certification marketplace. In 1990, there were a handful of vendor-independent certifications and a single vendor-specific certification. As the decade draws to a close, more than a dozen organizations sponsor vendor-independent certifications for computer professionals, and over thirty computer industry vendors sponsor certification programs.

The ICCP is now made up of representatives from more than 20 national and international computer societies, and the original professional certification it administers, the CDP, is now called the Certified Computing Professional (CCP). Over 50,000 professionals have obtained it. As of mid-1997 more than 200,000 professionals held Novell certifications and another 100,000 had obtained designations from the younger Microsoft Certified Professional program.

The two most notable features of the early and mid-nineties were:

1. The establishment of professional certification as a force in the computer industry.
2. The rapid growth in the quantity and variety of certifications.

Establishing the value of certification is well underway, but it's not by any means complete. Although employers and professionals are vastly more aware of the potential of certification than they were in the eighties and earlier, there are still questions to be answered and doubts to be addressed. Nonetheless, the foundations have been put in place and are ready to be built upon.

As for the second characteristic, indications are that the computer certification marketplace is moving from a period of rapid growth to a time of consolidation and refinement. When you consider that most of the major industry vendors and many of the minor ones have already launched programs, it becomes obvious why the rate of growth can't continue apace; most of the players are already in the game.

Recent Developments

The certification marketplace appears to have entered into a new stage. Additional factors are coming into play and shaping its future direction. They include:

- The widespread effects of the Internet
- The growing complexity of computer systems and businesses' dependence on them
- The expanding gap between traditional education and market needs
- The increasing maturity of the certification marketplace

There is little that the Internet hasn't affected. People who work with computers are being called upon to implement all of its wonders and promises and to overcome its barriers and bottlenecks. Despite the multiplicity of options and platforms, keeping a server up, connected to the Internet, and at the same time protected from the Internet, requires a significant amount of expertise. Yet, this is where businesses are or want to go.

The Internet is but one element of the deepening complexity of computer systems. The success of the open systems initiative has had a major impact as well. Now, instead of picking a proprietary system and sticking with it for all business purposes, companies can pick and choose from a smorgasbord of hardware and software alternatives. Equipment and applications from different vendors now interact in every environment. Although this has opened up options for users so far as what they can do and how much they will have to pay to do it, it also means that knowing one vendor's system isn't enough any more.

Now, there are likely to be numerous platforms operating in any given environment. Consider the organization that uses its mainframe for batch processing for years and also uses it as an in-house network and an Internet-based catalog order center. The components all feed into each other. Somebody (or more likely a bunch of somebodies) needs to be able to operate, fix, monitor, and configure the whole shebang, not to mention keep up with technologies that competitors are adding. On top of this complexity is the mission-critical nature of information systems today. If a business network goes down, work can come to a virtual standstill. And that can be very expensive.

This complex, heterogeneous nature of modern computing environments, coupled with the absolute dependence that businesses and organizations have on them, makes it critical to have qualified technical people who can keep them operational. But determining just who is qualified and who is not isn't a simple task.

At a time when information processing errors can have a devastating impact, certification offers several protections. First, it protects business by indicating which potential hires are likely to do a competent job of managing and developing systems. Certainly there are individuals who somehow manage to gain certification but are less than competent, but they are much fewer in number than their noncertified counterparts.

Second, certification is becoming a tool to define a path for professional development. In this role, it serves both employer and worker. Because the body of knowledge has been explored and defined by the certification sponsor, the professional can simply adhere to their recommendations and be reasonably assured of keeping current in the field.

Moving into Academe

The issue of keeping current is an important one. Although traditional institutions (such as colleges and universities) have been training people for careers in the computer field for some time, they are falling behind. The design of two- and four-year curriculums just isn't fluid enough in its present incarnations to keep pace with the latest developments in computer technology. That means the gap between what a college graduate has learned and which technologies are coming into vogue can be significant. Employers are looking for up-to-the-minute expertise. Certification by its very design is intended to qualify people in the latest technologies. Thus, it's increasingly being used as a template for continuing career development in place of university courses.

Meanwhile, colleges are waking up to this gap and realizing that they can't ignore it. Certification is beginning to move into the traditional classroom. Partnerships are forming between certification sponsors and educational institutions. Both vendor and nonvendor sponsors are taking part in this movement. The Network Professional Association (NPA) is working with vendors such as IBM and Microsoft to set up networking technology laboratories in colleges. This is a change from the previous structure where vendors donated equipment, piecemeal, on their own, replacing it with a coordinated effort guided by the NPA. These hands-on laboratories give college students a critical educational component they were missing: hands-on experience with the latest hardware and software. As this book was being written, NPA-sponsored laboratories were operating at:

- Arizona State University, Tempe, Arizona
- Brigham Young University, Provo, Utah
- Clark University, Boston, Massachusetts
- College of San Mateo, San Mateo, California
- CompuCollege, Halifax, Nova Scotia
- Florida Institute of Technology, Melbourne, Florida
- Normandale College, Minneapolis, Minnesota
- Oakton Community College, Oakton, Illinois
- Point Park College, Pittsburgh, Pennsylvania
- Regis University, Denver, Colorado
- University of Cincinnati, Cincinnati, Ohio
- University of South Carolina, Columbia, South Carolina

The Institute for Certification of Computing Professionals (ICCP) is working with educational institutions as well. Together with the computer science departments of a number of institutions, they are developing a process for using certification standards to assess and verify the competence of computer science graduates.

Meanwhile, Novell and Microsoft have both announced new programs that bring certification to university students. Through these programs students can follow the identical certification curriculum, using the same official materials that established computer professionals have access to, but for less cost and converted to fit the traditional academic format.

Novell's education partners, called Novell Education Academic Partners (NEAPs), can be found by visiting Novell's training locator Web site (**db.netpub.com/ nov_edu/x/naecloc**) or by calling Novell at 1-800-233-EDUC.

To locate schools participating in Microsoft's Authorized Academic Training Program (AATP), call Microsoft at 1-800-688-0496.

Blending and Blurring the Boundaries

With well over a hundred certifications, the certification marketplace has become a bit crowded. Redundancies and duplications of effort are apparent. Standardization is missing. This has become especially apparent as sponsors roll out versions of Internet-centered certifications. If each sponsor develops its own Internet certification program, there's a tremendous and expensive duplication of effort. There's also likely to be market confusion, which could detract from the value of such certifications.

These faults are not unusual, given the stage of development of the training and certification marketplace. Everyone's in there, and they're all doing their own thing. Sponsors have tailored their programs by following one of the two schools of thinking: vendor-specific or vendor-independent. Each has noted the other's shortcomings as well as its own, and now they're beginning to address them. The dichotomy that's marked computer professional certification is beginning to give way.

The vendor-independent and vendor-specific models are blending in two ways. First, training companies are getting into the picture. These companies are commercial entities, like vendors, so their main purpose is profit. But because their primary business is training rather than hardware or software sales, they have no allegiance to a single platform or vendor. Thus, when they develop a certification program, they can design it to fall squarely into the niche between the vendor certifications and the professional organization certifications. This type of program incorporates the knowledge aspects of an area of expertise and the ins and outs of its implementation using particular products. The products are chosen based on their popularity and market share rather than vendor affiliation.

At first glance, this certification seems perfectly suited to overcome the weaknesses of the original certification categories. However, its strength may also be its weakness. It remains to be seen whether these certifications will successfully combine the best aspects of the original vendor-independent and vendor-specific categories. Vendors know their products inside and out. Professional organizations know their industry inside and out. The question is whether training companies, without such in-depth, inside knowledge, can produce certifications that accurately measure and reflect the relevant expertise. The answer will likely become apparent within the next few years.

As strange as it sounds, the other way the traditional certification boundaries are being broken is by vendors incorporating each other's products into their certification curriculum. This has come about because of the heterogeneous nature of today's computing environment. It's not unusual to find both Novell Netware and Windows NT running at the same installation. By including a small amount of training on another vendor's product, a certification gains increased appeal.

It's reasonable to speculate that another goal of incorporating a competitor's technology is the hope of acquiring some of its customer base. Imagine that someone who manages a Novell network attends the Microsoft class "Integrating Microsoft Windows NT Server 3.51 With Netware Networks." It's possible that through that class, the professional will be impressed enough with Microsoft products to encourage migration in that direction back at the office.

Sometimes this incorporation is accomplished simply by giving credit for another vendor's training. This works in the same way as transferring college credits from one institution to another. (Figure 2-4 shows Microsoft's offer to waive exams for candidates already certified by another vendor.) It saves experienced professionals from expending time and money meeting requirements that are basically repeats of those they've already completed for another certification. You'll also find that many of these classes are organized around understanding the intricacies of getting a product to interface well with the products of another vendor.

Figure 2-4
Microsoft FAQ
Offers to
Waive Exams

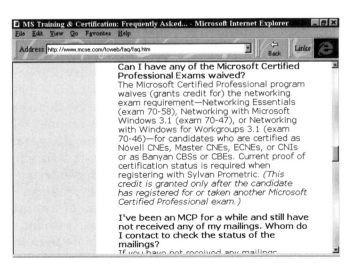

On a final note, probably in direct response to charges that vendor-specific certifications are too limited in scope, experience and general knowledge requirements are slowly beginning to appear as requirements by the larger vendor sponsors.

QUICK TIP

An Industrywide Training Consortium?

In January 1997, **Information Week** reported the formation of a worldwide training and certification consortium to develop standards for Internet-related educational programs. Plans are in the works for the development of professional certifications in five vendor-neutral Internet and intranet areas: electronic commerce, security, application development, connectivity, and enterprise messaging. The consortium was created to address both redundancy in existing vendor training programs and the need for Internet certifications. Students will be able to customize their training track to reflect the operating environment they use.

Members of the consortium include industry giants IBM, Lotus Development, Netscape Communications, Sun Microsystems, and Novell. Notably absent from the initial consortium membership list is Microsoft. It's unclear whether Microsoft declined to participate or simply wasn't asked.

The program began to appear in mid-1997, and details can be found on the Web at (**www.netboss.com**). Figure 2-5 shows the site's home page.

Figure 2-5
The Consortium
on the Web

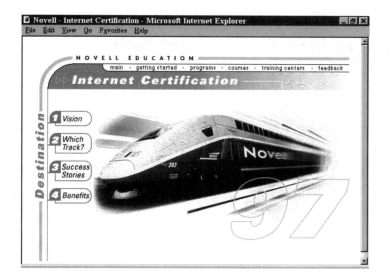

Remote Training

One of the most significant changes occurring in the training and certification marketplace is increased access to certification-related training. For a long time it's been classroom training or book learning on your own. The first typically entails a large expense, and the second requires a great deal of self-motivation and determination.

But now the Internet and World Wide Web are taking off as tools for delivering certification instruction. Training is going online in an incredible array of formats, from self-paced to virtual classes uniting students at remote sites (Chapter 9 discusses training alternatives, including use of the Internet, in greater detail). Utilization of the Internet in this way is making certification training more affordable and more convenient.

Besides facilitating training, the Internet is being utilized as an information conduit, ferrying pertinent details between computer professionals, the certification sponsor, and potential employers. This enables the sponsor to disseminate information quickly and provides an inexpensive way for sponsors to actually bring together certified people and employers who seek them.

When a person becomes certified today, they are granted access to this online world of job opportunities, software updates and patches, technical support, and the community of other certified individuals. All of this dramatically increases the practical value of certification.

Looking Into The Crystal Ball

Now that we've seen how the certification marketplace has evolved, it's time to take out the crystal ball and make some predictions about the future of certification. To begin with, boundaries will probably continue to blur between vendor-independent and vendor-specific certifications. Commercial certification sponsors will continue to lead the way at first, but professional societies will have to pay attention to the merits of the other side and participate in this trend. More training companies will join the picture with their own mixed certifications.

There is also likely to be a bit of a shakeout in the certification marketplace. Certifications of lower quality and less value will fall by the wayside, while a handful will gain increasing prominence. Sponsors will find that to benefit from certification they will have to invest significantly in their programs. Those that aren't willing to do so will drop out. Sponsors that seem to have solid foundation in place and are probably here to stay include Microsoft, Novell, Cisco Systems, the Network Professional Association (NPA), and the Institute for Certification of Computer Professionals (ICCP). During this period, it won't be surprising if some alliances form between vendor-specific sponsors and the professional groups.

As the certification training delivery system grows more robust, especially delivery of education on demand via the Internet, technical classes will become significantly more affordable and widely available. This easy access to low-cost alternatives, combined with an increasing number of certification instructors, is likely to pull down training center prices as well. Adding to the competition training centers face, many more colleges and universities will realize what they're missing out on and find a way to get into the act. They will probably begin to offer more condensed technical update curriculum options, not just for certification, but for technical training in general. Certification courses will serve as the prototype for these processes.

Above all, look for certification to gain increasing prominence in the computer industry. As awareness of the benefits of certification continues to expand, more professionals will become certified. Employers will begin to place greater reliance on certification as an answer to the education gap and increasingly use it as a measure when hiring and when providing an in-house career development path. Certification will move from its current status as a qualification that elevates one professional above another to one that is present on more resumes than not.

CHAPTER 3

Opportunities and Benefits

A major attraction of certification is its flexibility of purpose and application. If you want to move on to a new and better job, certification can help you. If it's a new specialty that's caught your eye, certification can simplify the transition. If you want to become more of an expert at what you already do, certification can serve that purpose as well.

That's not to say that professional certification is a career cure-all; it isn't. What it does do is offer a powerful set of tools that you can use to make significant, positive changes in your work life.

Imagine a vast hardware store in which row upon row of wondrous tools await use. That high-speed nail gun is tops for driving enough nails to build your deck, but if you bought it to polish your car, you'd be making a critical mistake.

The certification marketplace is like a career hardware store, full of gleaming possibilities. But before you spring for a particular one, you'll want to know just what it is that these tools *can* and *can't* do. Fortunately, many certifications are versatile, multipurpose wonders.

More Options, Better Pay

When you become certified, you open doors to new and different career options, increase your professional credibility, learn where your knowledge gaps are and how to plug them, and receive an objective measure of your technical accomplishments. Whether you stay where you are or move on to another employer, these benefits will give you a leg up the career ladder.

QUOTE

Been There, Done That, Will Again

The certification process has enabled me to make major advances in my career. I believe there are many who have the practical everyday operational skills, who have not yet undergone any formal certification process.

I had some practical skills, but I was advised by a manager long ago that we live in a credentialed society and if I wanted to advance I would need the credentials to "prove" or "demonstrate" that I knew what I was talking about.

After I dove into certifications, I've seen my income triple; I've changed jobs several times, leading to ever more interesting and challenging assignments. Now I am paid well for doing what I enjoy, and my spouse (a technical systems engineering type herself) now has the luxury of staying home and taking care of our children.

—**Eric Charbonneau, holder of MCSE, IBM Professional Server Expert, and other certifications**

Jobs, Jobs, Jobs

A recent search of a Web site that caters to job hunting computer professionals turned up close to four hundred positions that either require or desire applicants with one or more certifications (a job posting seeking a certified individual is shown in Figure 3-1). The site is an electronic repository of open positions posted by technical recruiters and is only one site among many that includes job opportunities for certified professionals. The certifications mentioned in this particular employment search were quite diverse and included:

- Banyan certifications
- Cisco Certified Internetwork Expert (CCIE)
- Windows NT certification
- Certified Lotus Professional (CLP)
- A+ Service Technician certification
- Oracle Master certification
- Certified PowerBuilder Developer (CPD)
- SAP certification
- Visual Basic certification
- Novell CNA/CNE
- Microsoft MCSE/MCSP
- and others

Why are so many employers beginning to seek people with certifications? Simply because they are recognizing the value of an objective measurement of applicant skills and expertise. Hiring the wrong person is an expensive mistake that employers strive to avoid. When you present yourself with a certification in a particular area, you're making it easier (and less risky) for the hiring manager to assess your technical qualifications.

Figure 3-1
An Internet Job Posting Seeking Certified Applicants

Training to Train

Besides improving your chances for the "standard" mix of technical jobs, you can take advantage of an interesting and potentially lucrative outgrowth of the certification explosion. People are needed to teach the necessary classes, write exam questions, and develop certificate curriculums.

Firms hiring technical trainers like to see people with related certifications and experience. Because training requires a high level of expertise in both the technology at hand *and* the ability to teach and communicate well, salaries can be impressive.

You really have to know what you're doing to be able to handle the questions and problems that arise during a training session, but it's often possible to land such a position without a trainer certification. Based on a review of advertised openings for trainers, it appears possible to break into this field based on non-training–related technical certifications coupled with other technical skills you hold. Once you're hired, you'll be put through trainer certification, *at the employer's expense*.

Employers who hire trainers this way pay less than those who want a certified trainer from the get-go, but it's still likely to be quite reasonable. And once you demonstrate your capabilities and go through the new certification, you're golden.

Writing exam questions is rarely available as a full-time job (an advertisement for Microsoft exam writers is shown in Figure 3-2). It's most often done on a contractual basis by people who've already taken the exam (or its predecessor) and earned the certification. This translates into an opportunity to develop exam questions on the side for the same organization you previously paid to certify you—an interesting turn of events. Besides adding to your income, exam writing serves as an impressive addition to your professional credentials and provides extra incentive to stay on top of evolving technologies. It's also likely to increase your pull with the organization, which could serve you well if you need to call upon them for technical assistance in the future.

Figure 3-2
Microsoft
Advertisement
for Exam Writers

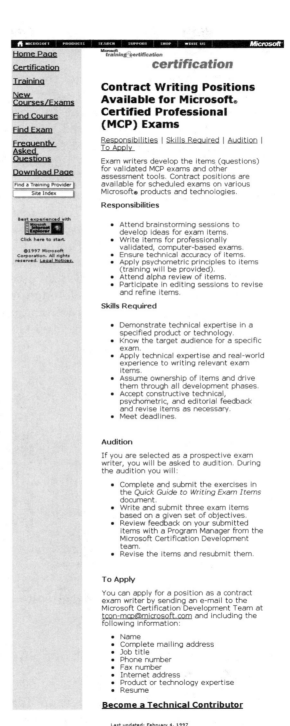

certification

Contract Writing Positions Available for Microsoft. Certified Professional (MCP) Exams

Responsibilities | Skills Required | Audition | To Apply

Exam writers develop the items (questions) for validated MCP exams and other assessment tools. Contract positions are available for scheduled exams on various Microsoft. products and technologies.

Responsibilities

- Attend brainstorming sessions to develop ideas for exam items.
- Write items for professionally validated, computer-based exams.
- Ensure technical accuracy of items.
- Apply psychometric principles to items (training will be provided).
- Attend alpha review of items.
- Participate in editing sessions to revise and refine items.

Skills Required

- Demonstrate technical expertise in a specified product or technology.
- Know the target audience for a specific exam.
- Apply technical expertise and real-world experience to writing relevant exam items.
- Assume ownership of items and drive them through all development phases.
- Accept constructive technical, psychometric, and editorial feedback and revise items as necessary.
- Meet deadlines.

Audition

If you are selected as a prospective exam writer, you will be asked to audition. During the audition you will:

- Complete and submit the exercises in the *Quick Guide to Writing Exam Items* document.
- Write and submit three exam items based on a given set of objectives.
- Review feedback on your submitted items with a Program Manager from the Microsoft Certification Development team.
- Revise the items and resubmit them.

To Apply

You can apply for a position as a contract exam writer by sending an e-mail to the Microsoft Certification Development Team at tcon-mcp@microsoft.com and including the following information:

- Name
- Complete mailing address
- Job title
- Phone number
- Fax number
- Internet address
- Product or technology expertise
- Resume

Become a Technical Contributor

Last updated: February 4, 1997

Adding to Your Bottom Line

If, like many people, one of the main reasons you're considering certification is because you want to increase your earnings, you'll be encouraged to hear what International Data Corporation (IDC) found when it investigated that question. The 1996 study revealed that, on average, certified employees earn 12% higher salaries than noncertified employees. That's probably directly related to another statistic from the same study. Seventy-eight percent of IS managers believe that certified employees are more productive.

In its second annual salary survey, published in the January/February 1997 issue, *Microsoft Certified Professional Magazine* included statistics detailing the financial consequences of obtaining one of their certifications (data from the survey is shown in Figure 3-3). The survey was sent to U.S. Microsoft Certified Professionals and to candidates who had completed at least one exam. Fifty-eight percent of respondents reported receiving a raise because they became certified. Forty-six percent credited their certification with triggering a job promotion in 1996.

Figure 3-3
Results from **MCP Magazine**'s "2nd Annual Salary Survey—Are You Making What You're Worth?"

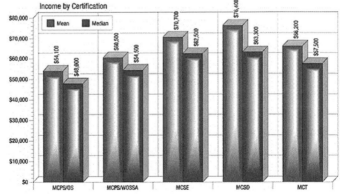

Chart 1. Income by Certification (Salaries, Bonuses, Benefits) We asked respondents for personal income before taxes, plus expected bonuses and benefits (such as profit-sharing and retirement). The mean is the average; the median is the mid-point and tends to be somewhat lower.

Large Demand Plus a Short Supply Equals a Higher Market Price

According to the Information Technology Association of America (ITAA), one hundred ninety thousand information technology jobs are *currently open* in mid- to large-sized companies in the United States. Employers need skilled workers, and, for many, certification rates a premium.

Articles in trade publications confirm the power of certification to boost income. In its July 1996 issue, *VARBusiness* reported that newly certified workers have been known to "bolt from their employer" to take advantage of their dramatically increased marketability (to get paid more). From the employer's viewpoint, that's a problem; from yours, it's evidence of the value of certification. The same article reports a survey of value-added resellers (VARs) finding that "in nearly every major market, there is a shortage of people with the 'right' certification." It's fundamental economics in action.

In an article titled "Everybody Wants One," in the October 1996 issue of *Chicago Computer Guide*, writer Scott L. Brown says, "A Ph.D. might get you tables at fine restaurants, but an MCSE certification could enable you to buy them." Hyperbole, perhaps, but it's also another clear indication of the desirability of certification.

Leading The Crowd

Although it hasn't reached that point yet, it's reasonable to predict that the increasing popularity of this type of credentialing will make it more universal. When and if that eventually happens, people who have ignored the trend will have to play catch-up. Certifying now or in the near future will place you near the leading edge of the trade, at least in the perception of potential employers. Wait too long and certification may become a requirement for basic success rather than a springboard for career advancement.

One Recruiter's Perspective

We're already beginning to see shifts [in the job market]. Because there are more people getting certifications, the competition is getting tighter. That's one of the reasons I would encourage someone to really think about certification and to work it into their schedule, even if it's just for their own satisfaction. You might as well have more ammunition than less.

—Monica Ortiz, marketing communications manager,
Computer Resources Group, San Francisco

Career Shifting

Are you feeling a bit bored and restless within your current computer specialty? Perhaps it's not as hot as it once was, and you like to work with technology that's more cutting edge? Maybe you've simply topped out where you are and would like to move on to something new. A certification program may be just what the career counselor ordered.

If you want to switch your career focus, then, by definition, you already have one big thing going for you: experience. It isn't in the specific area you want to move into, but at least it's there, and that's very valuable. Nevertheless, you still face a resume and training gap that stretches between where you are and where you want to be. A well-chosen certification can be your bridge.

In fact, one of the more prevalent uses of certification is as a springboard to a new job. That makes employers anxious about the subject. They like to hire certified people, but when their current workers get on a certification track, managers may lose a little sleep. They probably wonder if you're planning to leave for greener pastures or if another company will attempt to lure you away.

Now, although some people (but surely not you) might find the idea of stressing out their boss appealing, the point is that managers recognize the meaning of certification. People who get certified are pursuing something more than they already have—something better, something different.

The person who gives you your first job in your new postcertification area of specialty is likely to be a manager. Remember, managers like to hire people who are already certified, as you'll be. And by getting this training, you have demonstrated that you take initiative and are serious about this career move; it's not just a passing fancy. Perhaps, more importantly, you'll have gained knowledge and skills relevant to your new domain. *And* you've added a credential directly related to the position you are seeking. If you get asked technical questions during interviews, you'll be able to field them fairly competently.

This is not to say that obtaining a certification will automatically enable you to jump from one computer field to another at the same or higher level of pay and responsibility. But it's likely to significantly ease that leap, and to enable you to start in your new field at a higher level than you might otherwise. Who wants to go back to square one?

Power Perks

As an added incentive to professionals and employers contemplating certification, most sponsors bestow a range of perks on those who complete their programs (Bay Networks' perks list is shown in Figure 3-4). The value and utility of these items run the gamut from superior to ludicrous.

The best perks incorporate elements that help you to perform your job at a higher level. They address your reasons for pursuing the certification and add value to the program for you and for your clients/employer.

Figure 3-4
Bay Networks'
Certification
Perks Page

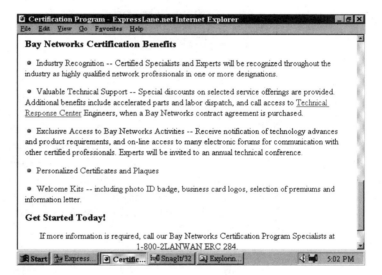

Off The Mark?

QUICK TIP

On the lower end of the benefits ladder are items that are downright hokey. Many if not most sponsors offer items bearing their logo, but they don't bill them as a particularly meaningful benefit. Some organizations handle things a bit differently.

Consider one group's "awards collection." As you work your way up through the certification ranks, you earn points. When you accumulate enough points you can redeem them for merchandise such as—are you ready for this?—a Swiss Army knife or a suede twill cap.

This type of incentive program is of questionable taste and value and borders on an insult. Do they really think that tantalizing you with gadgets and clothing will motivate you to work harder on their certifications? Not likely. An "award" system like this serves only to diminish the certification's image. Fortunately, such misguided merchandise programs are in the minority. In fact, the organization that created this one appears to be in the process of rectifying its mistake.

Priority Technical Support

Think about the last time you placed a call to a technical support line. Did you spend upward of half an hour listening to tinny music in a phone queue? Or perhaps you had to leave your phone on automatic redial all morning just to make it into the queue. Such delays are especially frustrating when your project is on hold until you get the answers you need from tech support. You don't feel good, and you certainly don't look good.

But once you're certified by a particular vendor, your success or failure is a direct reflection on them. To put it bluntly, if you look bad, they look bad, and vice versa. Therefore, your calls for technical support will be treated expeditiously. Most vendor-sponsored certifications come with a variation of this valuable perk. A few restrict the number of priority calls you can make or apply time limits. Other vendors offer a discount on the standard technical support rates. A few examples from sponsor promotional materials and/or program coordinators follow.

- **Adobe:** "Priority access to high level, free technical support of the product(s) for which you are certified."
- **Cisco:** "Cisco Certified Internetwork Experts may elect to have their cases queued immediately to second-level support engineers in Cisco's Technical Assistance Centers."
- **Compaq:** "ASEs are privileged to free, priority access to Compaq technical support reducing hold times to a minimum."
- **Microsoft:** "You gain access to support for any Microsoft product, 24 hours a day, 7 days a week."
- **Novell:** "50% off all technical support calls and on-line incidents."

What a relief not to spend forty-five minutes on hold when you run into a snag or obscurity in the documentation. Your redial finger might miss the workout, though.

Of course, this priority access only proves valuable if you have reason to contact your sponsor and not some other vendor. Nonvendor sponsors don't offer telephone technical support, because they're not set up for it.

Technical Databases

From Corel to Novell, certification sponsors work to add value to their programs. Again, since your success reflects back on the organization that certified you, they have every interest in giving you access to technical tools. And they provide gigabytes of programs, code, documentation, technical support databases, and virtually any resource that can be digitized and posted on a server or burned onto a CD-ROM. Only people with a password or PIN (Personal Identification Number) can get past the server's front door, only the certified can lay their hands on the CD at no charge (an IBM restricted technical support area is shown in Figure 3-5). When the technical information is on a CD-ROM, most sponsors will supply you with an updated version each time you complete your continuing education requirements. Web server databases are updated continuously.

Figure 3-5
For IBM ACPs Only

WELCOME TO THE TECH SITE FOR AIX CERTIFIED PROFESSIONALS

This site is exclusively for our AIX Certified Professionals (ACPs). We help you stay on top of the heap by providing technical tools and information designed to keep you one step ahead of the game.

As a member you have access to a set of private newsgroups, access to various knowledge databases and enhanced fix distribution services.

Registration

AIX Certified Professionals from around the globe are entitled to access this site. If you do not have a login account or have forgotten yours, please fill out the registration form. We will send your userid and password to your e-mail address after verifying your eligibility.

Enter

If you already have a login account then come on in!

Enter ACP Tech Site   Request a login ID

▶ HOME   ▶ ORDER   ▶ EMPLOYMENT   ▶ CONTACT IBM   ▶ LEGAL

No Riffraff Allowed

In some ways it seems counterproductive for a company to lock technical information (the keys to superior use of a product) behind a security wall. One can only speculate why they don't offer such access to any interested party who surfs by. After all, every person who manages to dig up the answer to their technical problem from a database will be one less aggravated customer trapped in a call queue.

Perhaps it's because exclusivity increases perception of value. Maybe companies want to offer professionals a place to dig in without the potential annoyance of amateurs. Or it could boil down to a security, profit, or resource issue. Then again, the idea might not have been as well considered as it could have.

Whatever the logic, the fact remains that on the other side of that password screen (or encoded on that CD-ROM) is the mother lode of information, information that has the potential to make your job easier and more successful. Become certified, and it's yours.

Exclusive Forums

Vendors and some nonvendor sponsors create forums designed around their certification. When you want to hash over an idea, glean some arcane advice, or discuss the pros and cons of a new release, these forums can serve as a valuable resource. Because only individuals with the same certification as yourself gain entry, there is a much higher signal-to-noise ratio than in unrestricted discussion forums. That means you won't have to wade through dozens of off-topic postings, like you would in a typical Usenet newsgroup. In addition, the sponsor usually maintains a presence in the forum, so you may even get your feedback straight from the horse's mouth.

Training and Conference Discounts

Once you're certified, you can't (and probably won't want to) rest on your laurels. Due to the same rapid pace of change that makes your certification valuable, you'll need to keep updating your skills. Many sponsors recognize this, and require that you complete continuing education each year to retain your designation. They will specify exactly what qualifies and what doesn't. Usually you'll be allowed to choose from a fairly broad menu of training options that include employer-sponsored seminars, third-party courses, and online classes.

When the sponsor is a vendor, they often will make it easier (and less expensive) for you to meet continuing training requirements by organizing conferences, seminars, and classes and inviting you to attend at a reduced cost, or for free. Bay Networks, for example, invites its Certified Experts to an annual technical conference.

Nonvendor sponsors often hold special events as well. The Building Industry Consulting Service International (BICSI), nonprofit sponsor of the Registered Communications Distribution Designer (RCDD) certification, holds educational conferences and technical seminars to help its members stay abreast of developments in the telecommunications industry.

Even when retaining your certification isn't the issue, you may want to take advantage of free and reduced cost training offered by your certification sponsor. It can be an inexpensive way to expand your technical skills and network with others in the computer industry.

Product Discounts and Beta Participation

If you're one of those people who can't wait to get your hands on the latest versions of software, there's another perk you're going to like. Once you're certified, you may start receiving new releases even sooner than you want them—at the beta stage. Many vendors use their product certified professionals as guinea pigs for the latest incarnations of their software. If you're so inclined, you can obtain new software, be up on all of its new features, have actual input into the final edition, and develop an attitude about its viability before the average IS staffer even sees it.

Should you prefer to wait until the worst of the bugs have been discovered and exterminated, there's another option: you may be able to purchase official release versions and other products directly from the vendor at a substantial discount or even get them free. Pass the savings on to your boss or client, and you *know* they'll appreciate it.

Free Subscriptions

Another perk of varying value is the free subscription. Both vendor and nonvendor sponsors may offer these. Contents range from program specific announcements, such as certification news and schedules of upcoming training events, to industry updates and detailed development information. A few examples are:

- *Banyan:* the *CBInsider* newsletter
- *Compaq:* *ASE Newsletter*
- *Corel:* monthly education newsletter
- *IBM:* subscriptions to technical newsletters and magazines
- *ICCP:* the *CCP Professional Development Chronicles* newsletter
- *Informix:* quarterly issues of *TechNotes* and *CS Times*
- *Microsoft:* subscription to *Microsoft Certified Professional Magazine*
- *Sybase:* subscription to *Sybase Magazine*

Use of Logos and Marketing Materials

Certification sponsors are interested in helping you promote your new status (and, along with it, their program). To that end, many have developed a useful product recognition tool—a logo (the Certified Internet WEBmaster logo is shown in Figure 3-6). When you obtain certification, you'll be granted permission, and even encouraged, to use the logo to advertise your status. You'll be able to place it on your business cards, stationary, Web site, and in other places. The sponsor's advertising experts expend time and money promoting logo recognition, and you reap the benefits.

Independents especially may appreciate the ability to include the logos on marketing materials. The sight of a professional logo increases customer confidence in your abilities. Suddenly you're not an unknown or a risky proposition anymore. You're A+ certified (or Microsoft, or ____,) after all.

If you work for an employer, you may have less use for these logos. On the other hand, your employer may wish to place the logos on company materials in association with your name, which can work out well for both of you.

You can expect to receive specific instructions on the proper use of the logo, and you may have to submit your plans/samples for approval before taking them public. Although this might seem a bit controlling at first, it's actually in your best interest. If the logo is misused, its value may be diminished.

In addition to logos, certification sponsors sometimes provide (or offer at a low price) glossy, professional marketing materials about their product or organization. Again, you gain the benefit of someone else assuming the design and production costs of high-quality marketing materials.

Figure 3-6
Certified Internet
WEBmaster Logo

Database Listing

The Internet continues to evolve as a tremendous tool for addressing an incredible array of business needs. Generating business and opportunities for you can be one of them. The majority of certification sponsors maintain online referral databases, which they call registries or resource locators (Centura's directory is shown in Figure 3-7). Businesses and individuals in search of someone with particular skills—say, Web site development—can conduct a database search and find your contact information. Some sponsors will also publish your name in a print directory, or give it to people who call them seeking a referral.

In conjunction with the databases of certified professionals, organizations often maintain a job database that you can search for contracts and positions that appeal to you (the CISSP job database is shown in Figure 3-8). Nonvendor sponsors seem to build these most frequently.

In some instances you can also submit your job requirements to be kept on file. When a position matching the specifics you defined gets added to the job database, an email message is automatically generated and sent to you. Even if you're perfectly satisfied with your current employment arrangement, you might want to enter the specs for that dream job you sometimes imagine (you know, the one where you get lots of money, flexible reduced hours, and an annual paid vacation to Hawaii). You might just find a fateful email message waiting in your mailbox someday.

Figure 3-7
Centura's Certified
Developer/DBA
Directory

Figure 3-8
CISSP Job
Openings Database

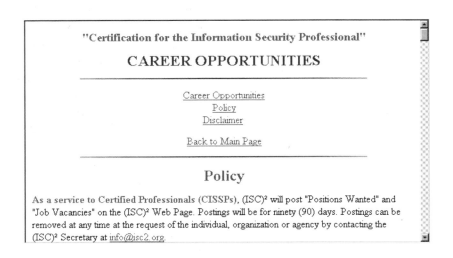

It would be negligent to conduct a discussion of certification benefits without mentioning lapel pins. A large percentage of sponsors supply one of these little gems, which bear the logo associated with the certification. Wear it as a discreet, yet visible, advertisement of your accomplishment.

Other Payoffs

The benefits and opportunities mentioned so far are largely concrete and directly related to income or career advancement. But as we all know by now, there are other less tangible aspects of career satisfaction that are equally important.

Study Dividends

If you get certified simply by taking a test, you won't expand your knowledge of the subject area. But, in most cases, you'll attend one or more classes, participate in a hands-on lab session, or at the minimum, work through a self-study guide. In doing so, you are virtually assured of gaining exposure to new areas in your field and to different ways of doing things.

You already know how to perform the duties required by your current position, but do you know the most efficient ways to do them? And how do you learn about what could be or should be done in the near future? Through the certification process, you'll achieve added exposure to the issues related to your area of expertise and answers to these questions. This has the potential to make your work life easier by:

- Augmenting your level of proficiency
- Increasing your personal productivity
- Decreasing downtime
- Familiarizing you with product and technology advances

Peace of Mind

Serenity is probably beyond what any of us can hope to achieve in the workplace and may not even be desirable. Freedom from various job-related fears and anxieties is another story. How can certification bring you increased peace of mind? As you have probably already have guessed, it does this in several ways.

Let's start with that most basic of workplace concerns: the possibility of getting downsized, rightsized, released, phased out, riffed (subjected to a reduction in force), or just plain laid off. Whatever your company calls it, it comes down to two little words: job security.

Certification has the potential to address job security in two key ways. It does this

1. By increasing your value to the company
2. By increasing your value to *other* companies

Let's take number one first. By keeping in tiptop technical shape through certification, you multiply your value to your employer, enabling you to keep your employer's customers satisfied. In fact, the more integral you are to smooth daily operations, the more painful it would be for your employer to let you go. Why would they want to discharge a valuable employee?

By demonstrating your desire to excel at your current duties, you simultaneously communicate your ability to take on new or different tasks (for increased compensation, you hope), should the need arise. Transfer within the company then becomes a distinct possibility when layoffs threaten.

In reality, you only have control over your own actions, not those of "the boss." That's what makes job security key number two so critical. Suppose that one day the dreaded pink slip does land in your mail slot. If you've chosen your certification wisely, it won't be as big a deal as it might otherwise. Yes, losing your job would still be stressful (unless you're lucky enough to receive a generous severance package). But by adding to your technical credentials, you'll have secured a competitive advantage over many other job seekers; you'll have greater marketability.

During a time in which companies are hungry for the latest technical expertise, recent training and certification is likely to translate into quicker and more lucrative job offers. If you're any good at all, you're not likely to be idle for long. And since changing jobs is one of the most effective ways to obtain a significant salary boost, you may actually find yourself thanking your employer for pushing you out the door.

Code of Ethics

One benefit that you won't find accompanying many vendor certifications, at least not so far, is a code of ethics and/or standard of conduct that's been carefully thought out and written down. Certifications that are sponsored by professional organizations often feature them (the CISSP code of ethics/conduct is shown in Figure 3-9).

Why might you want someone else determining how you should behave? If you're like most people, ethics isn't something you spend much time thinking about until you run into trouble. We often assume that as long as we do what we think is right, we are behaving properly. The big snag is that what one person thinks is okay can vary considerably from the opinions of someone else. That's where an ethics code comes in. Read it up front, and you'll be able to recognize ethical trouble while it's still on the horizon, rather than when something blows up in your face.

The code also serves as an extra item of credibility that you can hand over to clients in appropriate situations (or include in your marketing materials). It says: I am a professional; I have thought about ethics and pledge to be ethical; this is the code of conduct I subscribe to. And it gives you an easy out of dubious requests from your client or boss, as in, "I can't do that. It's against my professional code of ethics. Let me show you a copy."

Although many elements of a code of ethics will seem obvious, others aren't as instinctive. Consider the following from the ICCP code of ethics protection of privacy clause: "One shall have special regard for the potential effects of computing-based systems on the right of privacy of individuals, whether this is within one's own organization, among customers or suppliers, or in relation to the general public."

When an organization has a code of ethics, you'll usually be required to agree to it, in writing, before receiving certification. For that reason, it's a good idea to give it a thorough read before you invest yourself in a particular certification. Although it's not terribly likely, there may be sections of the code that you just don't agree with.

Figure 3-9
CISSP Code
of Ethics

"Certification for the Information Security Professional"

(ISC)² Code of Ethics
for the Certified Information Systems Security
Professional™

"All information systems security professionals who are certified by (ISC)² recognize that such certification is a privilege that must be both earned and maintained. In support of this principle, all Certified Information Systems Security Professionals (CISSPs) commit to fully support this Code of Ethics. CISSPs who intentionally or knowingly violate any provision of the Code will be subject to action by a peer review panel, which may result in the revocation of certification.

Individuals certified by (ISC)² agree to abide by the following:

- In the course of my professional activities, I shall conduct myself in accordance with the highest standards of moral, ethical and legal behavior.

- I shall not commit or be party to any unlawful or unethical act that may negatively affect my professional reputation or the reputation of my profession.

- I shall appropriately report any activity related to the profession that I believe to be unlawful, and I shall cooperate with any resulting investigation.

- I shall support efforts to promote the understanding and acceptance of prudent information security measures throughout the public, private and academic sectors of our global information society.

- I shall provide competent service to my employers and clients, and shall avoid any conflicts of interest; I shall execute my responsibilities in a manner consistent with the highest standards of my profession.

- I shall not misuse information to which I become party in the course of my duties, and I shall maintain the confidentiality of all information in my possession that is so identified."

Back to Main Page

© Copyright 1996 (ISC)², Inc. All Rights Reserved. May be reproduced with attribution.

Food for Your Ego

Last but not least is an extremely personal benefit of professional certification: self-satisfaction. Individuals often report a feeling of pleasure and accomplishment after achieving certification. It arises from the professional recognition conferred by your peers within the industry, from the knowledge that your skills and expertise have been assessed by someone (or some organization) other than yourself, and from the fact that you've successfully measured up to professional standards.

CHAPTER 4

Inside Perspectives

Three professionals who have ventured into the certification marketplace report: the view from inside appears rosy.

The Way In

No matter which program you choose to pursue, the process of achieving certification is straightforward. The basic steps are as follows:

1. Choose a certification.
2. Identify gaps between what you know and what you need to know.
3. Determine what you will do to fill those gaps.
4. Choose an exam and prepare for it.
5. Take the exam.
6. Repeat steps 4 and 5 until all requirements are met.
7. Put your certification to work for you.

Each of these seven steps can be further broken down (and will be later). But this is the basic process for obtaining the majority of certifications. Depending on your choice of certification and your current level of experience and skills, the commitment needed to go through this process will vary considerably. Significant time and expense may be involved, and self-motivation is an absolute must. Bottom line: you should know what you're getting into.

Reports from the Field

If you want to find out what skydiving is like, you might begin by asking someone you know who's seen parachutists in action. But that would only give you a partial picture—the pieces that a spectator can observe and convey. To fill in the details, you'd also want to ask a participant, perhaps a parachutist or the pilot of a jump plane.

In the same way, when it comes to getting a good sense of the roles certification can play in the careers of computer professionals, statistics, study, and trend observations can provide only part of the story. The most meaningful insights come from people who've been through the certification process and/or encounter it on a daily basis.

The interviews that follow offer the inside scoop on certification. Three computer professionals who've taken the plunge share their personal perspectives on certification and the process of obtaining it.

Michael J. Corby, CCP,CISSP

M. Corby & Associates, Inc.
Date of first certification—1982

 Which certifications do you currently hold, when did you get each of them, at what cost, and why?

- Certified Computer Professional—1982
- Certified Information Systems Security Professional—1992

I acquired [the CCP] certification because it gave me an opportunity to measure my application skills against the industry. I came from a technical background and was developing my design and management skills. The CCP gave me a comprehensive study outline to help channel my learning experiences. [It cost about $150.]

I acquired [the CISSP] certification by taking the CISSP Exam [for $250]. I founded the organization that sponsors the CISSP, the International Information Systems Security Certification Consortium Inc. (ISC²), because I saw that many people who had been "downsized" were deciding to become Computer Security Consultants. The CISSP was a means to differentiate between those who actually have the skills and those who simply select the title of Security Consultant. I see the CISSP certification as a precursor to a licensed security consultant who determines an organization's security effectiveness for insurance and stockholder comfort-like a CPA conducts a financial audit.

 What do you see as the major benefits and opportunities that come with certification?

1. Self-study direction and measurement.
2. Enhanced job opportunities.
3. Credentialing.
4. Comfort for those who employ certified professionals; evidence that they have acquired the services of an appropriately skilled person.

 What advice would you give to someone who is considering some sort of certification but hasn't decided which to pursue or even whether it makes sense to get one at all?

The certification should be as narrowly focused as possible to be effective. I believe it is worthwhile to become certified for two reasons: sense of professional accomplishment, and peer/employer recognition of skills. Certification by passing a test should not be sufficient, however. To be properly certified, an individual should also have a minimum of direct, practical experience.

 What do you think are the most important distinctions between vendor and nonvendor certifications, and why?

Vendor certifications are dangerous. There is a risk of the candidate "buying" certifications simply by taking the class or paying the fee. Many vendors offer competing certification programs, and, as such, they fall into a second tier of quality. I prefer to see and to hire individuals who have been certified by an independent test plus have practical work experience, not just vendor-supplied book learning.

Which of the different learning options—CBT, classroom, self-study guides, and others—have you found useful?

Study guides with a thorough bibliography are my favorites. CBT is okay but can be easily brushed over too quickly. Classroom is also okay, but it's hard to gauge actual knowledge versus time spent.

 What mistakes do you think people are prone to make when choosing and/or pursuing certification?

Biggest mistake: pay the money to get the certificate. Second biggest mistake: pursue certification that has no verified practical experience.

 What else do you have to add about certification?

When dealing with areas that are not easily measured or have a direct relationship to financial exposure, I will always seek and [always] prefer a certified employee or contractor over someone who isn't certified, even if the noncertified person looks slightly stronger. With the [certification designation] letters, I have an easier time defending the resulting actions.

We presently have about twenty people doing security work, some full-time employees, others contract personnel. Approximately 50 percent are certified, depending on the work being done and the level of supervision required. All work done in the security area has at least one certified person review task plans and conclusions.

Eric Charbonneau, MCSE, IBMPSE, and other Certifications

Date of first certification—1992

 Which certifications do you currently hold, when did you get each of them, at what cost, and why?

Microsoft Professional Certifications

- Microsoft Certified Systems Engineer—MCP #6006

Microsoft Product Certifications

- MS DOS and Microcomputer Hardware—August 1993
- Implementing and Supporting Microsoft Windows 95—October 1995
- Networking Basics —March 1996

- Implementing and Supporting Microsoft Windows NT 3.51 Workstation—April 1996
- Implementing and Supporting Microsoft Windows NT 3.51 Server—May 1996
- Microsoft Mail for PC Networks V3.2—Enterprise—June 1996
- Implementing and Supporting Microsoft Systems Management Server—July 1996
- Implementing and Supporting Microsoft Windows NT 4.0 Workstation—December 1996
- Implementing and Supporting Microsoft Windows NT 4.0 Server—March 1997

IBM Certifications

- Professional Server Expert—September 1996
- IBM Customer Engineer—Certified Hardware Engineer—1992
- Certified Instructor—Skill Dynamics, an IBM company—1994

I have attained most of my certifications at my employer's expense. Indeed, most were job requirements and/or conditions of continued employment. I have used my own funds, primarily for supplemental reading materials or software, and I have devoted a *lot* of hours of personal time in the pursuit of these certifications. Some of these certifications resulted following employer paid formal training, as in the case of the IBM certifications. Some of my Microsoft certifications followed an employer paid formal ATEC (Authorized Technical Education Center) course using the MOC (Microsoft Official Courseware).

Have you noticed any trends as far as who's getting certified, the types of certifications being offered, and so on?

Yes, let me get on my soapbox a bit. I've followed my gut instinct to go where I felt the most demand was and where I had personal technical interests. Currently, there are approximately one hundred thousand Novell Certified Netware Engineers (CNEs) worldwide, there are approximately fifteen thousand Microsoft Certified Systems Engineers (MCSEs) worldwide. The Novell program is older, many would say the first really successful certification program in the industry. Right now, Novell is going through some tough times; conversely, Microsoft is doing well and there is a groundswell of interest in Microsoft Windows NT and Microsoft Backoffice software. Having the MCSE certification makes me *much* more employable and at a higher salary (demand driven) than having the CNE certification.

Currently, I see much more certification interest by people seeking to retrain from their current occupations to the "Computing Support" industry, I see this largely as a response to demand, a shift to skills more sought after in the Information Age, and a desire to have portable skills that enable someone to find quality work at quality salary levels wherever they may choose to live.

It's my opinion that certifications are becoming a "ticket to admission" to job interviews for certain job categories. For example, most local computer stores that offer service require that prospective technicians hold some type of certification—often they use the A+ certification by the vendor-neutral CompTIA organization as a base-level requirement. Many IS staffers that support PCs, LANs, [and other platforms] are expected to hold Novell or Microsoft certifications if they want to be hired. The interesting thing is that most of the incumbents in these positions don't hold these same certifications. Many folks who do this type of work and have practical hands-on skills simply do not take the time (or are unwilling to make the requisite sacrifices) that go along with completing the requirements of the various certifications.

Many employers prefer to look for certified people when hiring but are somewhat reluctant to certify their current employees. This phenomenon has appeared because of the value of certified workers. Employers are reluctant to expend the expense and effort to certify current employees for fear of subsequently losing them to competitors. It's apparently fairly common for the newly credentialed to be poached by other companies or leave of their own accord for higher paid positions.

There are some areas where certification simply hasn't proven its value yet. Programming/Software Development is one of these. Despite Microsoft's work towards getting the Microsoft Certified Solution Developer (MCSD) program off the ground, there are very few of these folks out there (approximately three thousand), this despite Microsoft's repeated claims that there are 2 to 3 *million* Visual Basic developers alone in the world... kind of makes you wonder. The Internet, with all of its hype, has yet to see any Web developer certifications take hold, despite the efforts of several different organizations to create some sort of baseline credential.

Here's part of the problem. Certifications that result in tangible benefits to the holder are usually vendor-specific and vendor-developed. Independent vendor-neutral certifications simply haven't taken off. So you have to guess which train to be on and get on the train early enough to reap the maximum benefits of a specific certification. Because a certification that is meaningful will have stringent recertification requirements to ensure the holder is maintaining a current high level of professional skills, you'd better be certified in something you enjoy working at, because you'll need to invest a lot of time on an ongoing basis to keep it up.

What advice would you give to someone who is considering some sort of certification but hasn't decided which to pursue or even whether it makes sense to get one at all?

Hands-on experience is a key factor. Even if you achieve the desired certification status, you're unlikely to get hired without some practical, related work experience to show. Often, this means that you might have to do some grunt work. Staffing a help desk is a great entree because you get a feel for what problems end users experience with both hardware and software. Usually, these positions are not very well paid, so they are constantly looking for people.

Part of this on-the-job experience is to determine what certification you feel would enable you to fulfill the demand you see day-to-day. You're also simultaneously networking with people who can help you find the next job opportunity in the field.

Sometimes the employer will pay for training if it is job related. If you are really lucky, you'll find a skilled individual who will mentor you through your skill development.

You need to plan out your certification goals. I keep a running six-month view of the certifications I'm interested in and mileposts of when I want to take them (see sidebar for Eric's sample certification plan). This is a working document that I revise constantly as new certifications become available and as my interests change. Just having this document forces me to identify the steps, training, reading, and research I will have to do to acquire the information/skills I will need to pass the certification and, more importantly, to actually know the material at a professional level.

Sample Certification Plan

June 1997

- Compaq Systems Technologies Test ID # 10-046
  http://www.compaq.com/training/ 2060.html

- Implementing and Supporting Microsoft® Windows™NT®
  Server†4.0 in the Enterprise Exam 70-68
  **http://www.microsoft.com/Train_Cert/Mcp/exam/
  stat/SP70-068.htm**

July 1997

- Compaq Integration & Performance Test (NT) ID # 10-047
  http://www.compaq.com/training/2061.html

- CompTIA A+ Certification Core Module
  http://www.comptia.org/atestobj.html

- CompTIA A+ Certification DOS/Windows Module
  http://www.comptia.org/atestobj1.htm#dos

August 1997

- Compaq Systems Management Test ID # 10-048
  http://www.compaq.com/training/2063.html

- Internetworking with Microsoft TCP/IP on Microsoft
  Windows NT 4.0 Exam 70-59
  **http://www.microsoft.com/Train_Cert/Mcp/exam/
  stat/SP70-059.htm**

September 1997

- Implementing and Supporting Microsoft® Internet Information Server™3.0 and Microsoft Index Server™1.1
  Exam 70-77
  **http://www.microsoft.com/Train_Cert/Mcp/exam/stat/
  SP70-077.htm**

October 1997

 Networking Essentials Exam 70-58
**http://www.microsoft.com/Train_Cert/Mcp/exam/
stat/SP70-058.htm**

 Implementing and Supporting Microsoft Proxy Server
Exam 70-78
**http://www.microsoft.com/Train_Cert/Mcp/exam/
stat/SP70-078.htm**

 What do you think are the most important distinctions between vendor and nonvendor certifications, and why?

If your interest is primarily money, stick with the vendor certifications. An MCSE is probably more marketable right now than a masters in computer science with no work experience. Many corporations decide to implement a certain vendor's technologies. When they make that decision, they usually insure their investment by hiring or training staff with that vendor's certification program. They want people who can implement and deploy those technologies efficiently and effectively within their organization. That requires vendor-specific product focus.

I work for a computer systems manufacturer. To sell their products to corporate customers, I must have practical industry knowledge based on years of experience and vendor certifications that are meaningful to validate my (and my company's) technical credibility. Nonvendor certifications are nice to have but hard to market.

 What mistakes do you think people are prone to make when choosing and/or pursuing certification?

Some folks buy certification training packages. The problem with this approach is that you may just not have the knack, you may not test well, and you may not respond well to this type of training. Everyone learns differently. I recommend trying to use self-study to get through the initial test just to see if this is something you are going to pursue for the entire process. Don't spend a lot of your own money up front. It's cheaper to buy $100 worth of books and pay $100 for a test to see if you've got an affinity for this kind of thing than it is to spend $4,000 on a comprehensive soup-to-nuts training program that may not work for you.

Outline your certification roadmap so that you understand the requirements and the options, then figure out the best, logical flow for you. Find professionals with the certification you are seeking and ask them to review your plan. Talk to people about the test, and understand the process of the test.

Get all of the information about the testing process up front and get any questions about what will happen during the testing process out of the way before you even sit down to take it. Some folks have had excellent results by taking commercially available sample tests to see if they are ready for the actual tests and to augment their studying.

Have you found the perks that come with the certifications useful? In what ways?

Mostly no, with the exception of TechNet. The TechNet CD-ROM in the Microsoft arena is the "Holy Grail" (Figure 4-1 shows Microsoft's TechNet Web site). This lovely perk contains enough Microsoft technical information to become a primary product and certification study resource for Microsoft certifications exams all by itself.

Figure 4-1
Microsoft's TechNet
Web Site

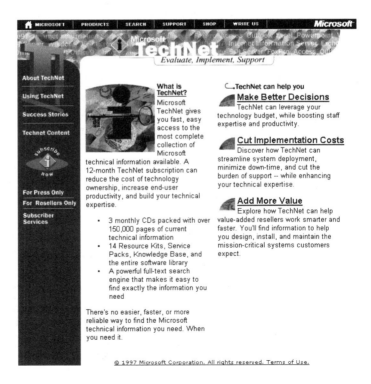

Wayne Lindimore, CNE, MCPS, IBM CLSE, 3COM 3Wizard

Date of first certification—1991

 Which certifications do you currently hold, when did you get each of them, at what cost, and why?

- Certified Novell Engineer—May 1991
- Certified Novell Administrator (NetWare 3)—August 1996
- Certified Novell Administrator (NetWare 4)—August 1996
- Microsoft Certified Product Specialist—March 1995
- IBM Certified LAN Server Engineer—March 1996
- 3COM-3Wizard Technologist—May 1997

All of my certifications were obtained through self-study. The average cost for self-study materials was about $250. I pursued and continue to pursue certifications for personal gratification and potential job advancement.

 What advice would you give to someone who is considering some sort of certification but hasn't decided which to pursue or even whether it makes sense to get one at all?

Pursue a certification in the fields you are interested in. I enjoy the challenge of networking, and so my certifications are networking related.

I've found that certifications are good for separating you from the crowd and getting you an interview. I always advise people to pursue certifications; it's hard to imagine a situation where they would count against you.

 What mistakes do you think people are prone to make when choosing and/or pursuing certification?

They choose a field because the pay is good or a company needs this type of person. You should choose a field because you enjoy (or think you would) working in it.

Some people try to get a certification by just memorizing information—no hands-on [experience], no classroom. If you get a certification with no hands-on, you're unlikely to do well, and so won't get the job satisfaction and raises you feel you deserve as a certified professional. It's the classic "paper" problem.

Have you found the perks (priority tech support, special forums, logo use, and the like) that come with many certifications useful? In what ways?

The perks that supply free services are good. Free tech support calls, free TechNet, and the rest save money and enhance your technical resources and so your abilities. The logos are nice for self-advertisement, both on consultant business cards and on employee resumes. I find the special forums to be of more limited value.

What has getting certified done for you?

Being certified has gained me respect at work (although simply doing a good and correct job gains you more). I got my current job, at least in part, because I had a CNE and the department was implementing Novell for the first time. I have joined the Network Professional Association (NPA) by being certified. I feel more confident about future employability, which is important.

What else do you have to add about certification?

Certification does not get you jobs. It does, however, enhance your ability to get interviews. It really gets the headhunters excited. It seems that many companies use the CNE as a technical breakpoint, even when not using Novell software. Many people have one certification, fewer have multiple. Multiple certifications show cross-platform expertise, a valuable commodity.

Putting the Pieces Together

As you can see, these professionals agree that certification is a valuable career tool. Two aspects of their comments probably jump out at you:

1. Disagreement on the relative values of vendor and nonvendor certifications.
2. Consensus that certification really swings open the door to client/hiring manager offices, but your skills and experience are still critical to landing a particular job.

Number one, the merits of vendor versus nonvendor certifications is an area that generates considerable difference of opinion. The good news is that this is an issue with no right or wrong side; it's one of those situations where both positions have merit. You'll have to analyze the arguments and decide which type of certification will best serve your career and professional beliefs. To help you do that, Chapter 6 will lay out the pros and cons of both vendor and nonvendor certifications in detail.

Number two, that certification will open doors for you but then it's up to you to keep them open, is a good sign of effective and reasonable use of credentialing in any industry. Those extra letters on your business card or resume signify that you have (or once had) particular expertise. Although that will get you a quicker and closer look, you'll still be required to provide evidence of your accomplishments in additional ways. That's as it should be, and if you've pursued certification in the proper spirit, backing up your credentials should be no problem.

Certification processes provide a method and motivation for keeping up on the latest products and technologies, a key to career success in the computer field. Although a few computer professionals have been disappointed by their efforts in the certification marketplace, many more report that obtaining professional designations is personally and professionally satisfying.

How to Get (Happily) Certified

CHAPTER 5

Dollars and Sense: Financial Answers Before You Begin

Depending upon the program and training methods you choose, obtaining a professional certification can entail a substantial investment. Because there are numerous routes to a single certification, it can be difficult to make an accurate assessment of what your actual cost will be. However, it's worthwhile to work up an estimate in advance so you won't be blindsided by unexpected expenses.

A detailed expense estimate can also help convince your employer to pay for part or all of your certification costs. When you itemize the figures on paper, you demonstrate that this is not just a whim; you have carefully considered the path to your goal, its costs, and its consequences.

Once you've developed your estimate, you'll also be able to create alternate scenarios. This will enable you to compare the costs of various approaches. With that information, you'll be able to decide, for example, whether the classroom training classes are worth **X** dollars more to you than the self-guided CBT course covering the same material. You'll also be able to identify potential savings points, which can prove very useful if your funds are in short supply.

Throughout the process of estimating your expenditure, it's important to remember that while you may be laying out a substantial chunk of change today, you're doing so in the expectation of an even larger payback in the future. That payback comes in the form of increased income, a better job, and increased personal and professional satisfaction.

Total Expenditure

Standard certification expenses include study materials, training costs, testing fees, and application fees. Depending upon the program, you may also find yourself paying for travel to a training site or lab test, purchasing equipment or software, or incurring other charges.

Another expense you'll encounter is opportunity cost. Opportunity cost addresses the value of what, besides money, you'll be giving up in order to pursue certification. If you'll be studying during your usual work hours, then you won't be producing the income you would otherwise. If that will be the case, then your opportunity cost is measurable in dollars.

Some might argue that another opportunity cost is time out from other career advancement or networking activities. But focusing on certification is really a shift in method rather than a replacement for such activities; the time is still being dedicated to the same purpose but in a different way. In fact, you'll most likely be spending more time (or at least more effective time) on career enhancement activities than you would otherwise.

If you plan to do the majority of your studying outside your usual business hours, then you won't be trading income for study time, but you'll still be taking time from somewhere else, such as family time or other areas of personal life, and dedicating it to your professional goals. That's an opportunity cost that's more difficult to quantify but still important to keep in mind.

Table 5-1 lists both the monetary and opportunity costs of certification.

Table 5-1
Certification Costs

Out-of-Pocket Expenses	Opportunity Costs
Training tuition	Foregone earnings
Study materials	Reduced personal/family time
Test/lab fees	
Application fee	
Travel to testing/training facilities	

Creating A Worksheet

In estimating your total expenditure, it's helpful to use a spreadsheet like the one in Figure 5-1, or you can develop your own. You can make it the old-fashioned way—with paper and pencil—but a spreadsheet generated using Excel, Quattro Pro, or other programs will be quicker and more versatile. An electronic version of the spreadsheet in Figure 5-1 can be found on this book's companion Web site.

Figure 5-1
Expenditure Worksheet

Estimate Your Certification Expenditure

Certification Name

Your Hourly Rate (enter 0 to exclude opportunity cost)

Individual Requirement Costs

Requirement Description	Tuition for Related Training	Cost of Study Materials	Test Fees	Related Travel/ Lodging Costs	Work Hours Spent on Req. (opportunity cost)	Opportunity Cost	Total for Req.
					0.0	$0.00	$ -
						$ -	$ -
						$ -	$ -
						$ -	$ -
						$ -	$ -
						$ -	$ -

Total Requirement Costs: $ -

Miscellaneous Fees
Application Fee
Other Fees

Total Misc: $ -

Estimated Total Expenditure $ -

To calculate your total expenditure using the worksheet in Figure 5-1, first enter the certification name at the top of the sheet. If you prepare multiple worksheets (to compare various certifications), the name will make it easy to identify which worksheet goes to which certification program.

Next, enter your hourly pay rate. Your hourly rate is needed to calculate your opportunity cost. If you don't wish to include opportunity cost in your estimate, simply enter 0 (zero) for hourly rate.

The next section contains the meat of the worksheet. Beginning with the first requirement needed to obtain the certification, enter a brief description of the requirement. Then go across the row, filling in estimated tuition, cost of study materials you'll need to meet the requirement, any test fee related to the requirement, associated travel costs if you'll need to attend training elsewhere, and, last, the number of hours you'll take from work and apply to meeting this requirement. If you're using the electronic spreadsheet from the companion Website the opportunity cost and total cost for meeting the requirement will calculate and fill in automatically. If not, you'll need to perform the calculations and fill in the blanks by hand.

To manually determine the opportunity cost, multiply your hourly rate by the number in the **Work Hours Spent On Req.** column. The total cost of the requirement is calculated by summing all numbers in the requirement row *except* the entry in the **Work Hours Spent On Req.** column.

For each requirement you need to meet, fill in another row. Don't be afraid to make an educated guess at figures you don't know. You can dig up the actual numbers by calling vendors, surfing the Internet for course listings, or asking friends.

The last step is to add in the application fee, if there is one, and any other fees or expenses you've identified. The estimate of your total certification expenditure will appear at the bottom of the spreadsheet. If you're completing the worksheet manually, add the total requirement expenses and the total miscellaneous expenses to obtain the same number.

Save the completed worksheet, or print it out. Then you can go back and play with the numbers to create "what if" scenarios. If you complete the necessary training through CBT self study instead of instructor-led training, how will the total expenditure be affected? If you work on certification strictly outside your regular business hours, how much will you save in opportunity cost? To go back to your beginning worksheet, you can simply reload the version you originally saved. Additional scenarios you want to keep should be stored under other file names or printed out.

How to Cut Your Costs

You can significantly cut your certification expenditures in a number of ways. Most of them will come with one or more trade-offs that you'll have to measure against your savings. As we all know, cheaper isn't always better and sometimes may not even be adequate. Which cuts make sense in a particular situation is a highly personal decision that involves factors such as your available free time, your individual learning strengths and weaknesses, your financial situation, the extent of your employer's support, time pressures, and so on. With that in mind, the basic ways you can make certification more affordable are:

- Convince an employer to shoulder part or all of the cost
- Cut your training costs
- Spread out your expenses over time
- Take any related tax deductions you qualify for

Getting Subsidized

As part of its second annual salary survey of professionals who have obtained or are in the process of obtaining one of the Microsoft Certified Professional (MCP) designations, *MCP Magazine* asked respondents who paid for the last certification/training program they attended. Nearly three-quarters of respondents reported receiving financial support for their training from their employer. Of those, more than half (61%) of respondents said that their employers footed the entire bill, while 11% shared the expense with an employer. 26% of respondents paid for their own training. Clearly, the odds are good that you'll be able to convince an employer to subsidize your training, at least to some extent. First, you have to know where the available money is.

Tapping the Company Budget

At least two areas of the company budget are potential contributors of certification funding, especially at larger organizations: the departmental training budget and the company-wide tuition reimbursement program. Your employer's department training budget is likely to cover a broader variety of training options than the tuition reimbursement plan. Still, it may have been created largely with manager-selected and in-house training in mind, so you'll have to approach your manager (or the appropriate human resources person) and convince him or her that certification training and/or testing is an appropriate use of the funds. Be prepared to explain how your certification training would provide value to the company and why the company should fund it. Think of this as a business presentation, and prepare for it by collecting the necessary facts and practicing beforehand in private.

When taking your case for certification to your boss, it often helps to present independent verification of the value of certification. Two potential sources are:

- The IDC (International Data Corp.) white paper *Benefits and Productivity Gains Realized Through IT Certification* (**www.software.ibm.com/os/warp/pspinfo/proidc.htm**). Figure 5-2 shows the online version.
- Microsoft Corporation's *Microsoft Certified Professional Program Corporate Backgrounder* (**www.mcse.com/tcweb/cert/bkground.htm**).

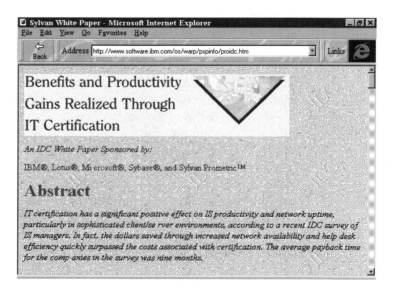

Figure 5-2
Benefits of
Certification
White Paper

A tuition reimbursement plan is typically more narrowly defined than a training budget; it's often limited to courses that qualify toward a traditional degree. But that doesn't mean it can't fund certification training. If you are working toward a degree of some kind, many certification courses and programs are accepted by colleges as transfer credits and applied toward your degree. If you can demonstrate to your company that the programs will count toward your degree and the company has a tuition reimbursement policy, there's a good chance you'll be able to get certification training coverage.

If you hope to receive funding from your employer, it's important to investigate both the tuition reimbursement and training budget possibilities before you begin your program. There may be steps you'll have to take to qualify for the funds, and you'll want to find out just how much of which kinds of training will be covered.

Questions to Ask the Budget Minders

At a large corporation, there's usually a human resources department, and within it, an individual who is in charge of employee benefits. That person is the one to bring your questions to. In smaller companies, start with your manager or supervisor. If she can't answer your reimbursement questions, she'll be able to direct you to someone who can. Here are the important questions to ask:

- If you take certification courses that are recommended for college credit, will the company cover the tuition?
- If the certification and/or training will benefit your job, will the company cover your costs?
- Besides tuition itself, will the company reimburse you for related expenses such as books and travel? If so, which expenses are covered?
- What evidence will you need to provide in order to obtain reimbursement?
- Are there limits on the total reimbursement you can receive?

In addition to the above questions, take care to clarify any reimbursement-related concerns you have. It's a good idea to present your queries in the form of a memo, and to request the answers in writing, signed by the person who provided them. Then, if a difference of opinion arises later over just what was promised, you'll have indisputable evidence to support your side.

The Payback Plan

When you can't obtain funding as part of an existing budget category, consider working out an arrangement with your employer. One reason that employers may be reluctant to finance certification is the fear that the newly qualified employee will jump ship. You can understand how, from the employer's perspective, spending money on an employee to enable that person to leave (taking their expensive training with them) for another job would be counterproductive. So you may have to offer some reassurance.

One of the more common methods of overcoming this impediment is to form an agreement with your employer that insures the company against your departure. Basically, you agree in writing that if you leave the company within a certain period of time after receiving company-financed certification training, you will reimburse the company for its expense. If you decide to move on after the end of the specified period, you won't owe the company anything.

An arrangement like this often allows for prorating the amount of refund you would owe the company, based on how long you remain with your employer after training. Recruiting companies may also agree to an arrangement like this in return for your promise to continue to use them as your placement agency.

Look ahead. If you're very dissatisfied with your current position (or recruiting company) and expect to leave in the near future, this probably isn't a good way to pay for certification.

QUOTE

The Ties that Bind

Something I'm seeing that's brand new is that contracting companies are starting to pay for training costs as a way to keep their contractors from leaving and going to another contracting company. Generally, the contract is going to be prorated. For example, the company will say, "The training and your salary while you were at training costs us $5,000. If you leave tomorrow, you owe us $5,000. If you leave after one year, you owe us nothing. If you leave after half a year, you owe us $2,500." The amount prorates over whatever that agreed to period is. If the company continues to provide training to you during that year, the end date keeps pushing out a little bit further.

It sounds like indentured servitude, but it's really not a bad setup. It may appear as if you're stuck, but you're not because, generally, you can bill more, the more that you learn. If you're like many contractors, you really don't care which placement firm is taking a chunk of your paycheck, so it might as well be this present company as long as they're finding you contracts. And, of course, it gets easier for them to find you contracts because of the training.

—Joe Upshaw, consultant for Winter, Wyman Contract Services

Hitting The Road

Your current employer isn't the only potential source of certification funds. Another route used by computer professionals is to begin training on their own and then look for a new position. Some employers consider an individual who has already embarked on the road to certification to be a superior job candidate. As an incentive for you to switch jobs, a new employer may well agree to pay for the rest of your certification program as part of your new employment contract.

To follow this route, go ahead and complete your first requirement and test. Then begin searching online databases and elsewhere for job opportunities that appeal to you. Your resume should note that you're in the process of obtaining certification. When you reach the negotiating table, work to include funding for continuing training as part of your employment contract.

A New Wave

As certification penetrates the computer industry, companies are busy developing new ways to take advantage of it. When Wave Technologies, a leading industry training company, found their phones ringing several times a day with employers requesting the names of individuals graduating from the company's classes, the company found itself in a bind. It couldn't service those callers because the vast majority of the professionals passing through the Wave classrooms were doing so at their employer's expense.

Imagine for a minute that you were the employer, and a staff member you sent through Wave Technologies' courses was recruited by a competitor while attending classes. Would you send any more of your employees to Wave? Not if you had an ounce of business survival instinct.

There were other calls coming into the switchboard, too. In this second batch, as many as 3 out of 10 calls came from computer professionals who had job experience but lacked the funds to get certified. Again, Wave couldn't help. Or could it?

Faced with a demand it couldn't meet through current offerings, Wave did what any basic marketing course recommends: it created a product to meet an identified need. In this case there were two needs that dovetailed:

- Experienced computer professionals seeking affordable certification
- Employers seeking experienced and certified computer professionals

Wave Technologies has used its training expertise to build a profitable bridge between the two. In July 1996, Wave's specially created division, called WaveSource, rolled out its new program (Figure 5-3 shows the WaveSource Web site). Individuals with a strong technical background can apply for free training. Wave will train and certify accepted candidates, usually at no charge other than for the test fees. Graduates of the program, now MCSEs, CNEs, or A+ Technicians, are then placed in jobs by affiliated recruiters. Wave makes its profit by receiving a chunk of the placement fee that hiring companies pay to the recruiters. This new service benefits all parties: computer professionals obtain the certification they want, employers get the certified employees they crave, and Wave Technologies adds to its bottom line.

Figure 5-3
The WaveSource
Web Site

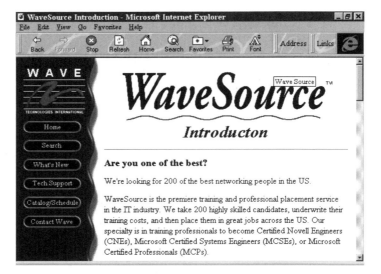

Understandably, the company is a bit picky about who it chooses to receive free training. Application details can be found on the WaveSource Web page (**www.wavetech.com/careeropt.html**).

Individuals who don't qualify for the WaveSource program may want to investigate other options the company offers.

Training on the Cheap

One of the most effective ways to cut your certification expenditure is also perhaps one of the simplest: be budget conscious when selecting and purchasing training for your certification. Because of the popularity of certification, there are many vendors and an extensive array of training options to choose from. A few rules of thumb to keep in mind are:

- Self-study is less expensive than instructor-led training.
- A training package is often cheaper than purchasing the components separately.
- Special discounts are frequently available, if you ask for them.
- Training time span affects costs.
- Prices vary significantly among training vendors.

Training Methods and Costs

Self-study is radically cheaper than instructor-led training. Although a typical three-day Learning Tree International course comes with a standard tuition of $1,995, including related exams, you can purchase a self-study kit covering similar material for less than half that amount. Depending on your learning style, abilities, existing knowledge, and access to other resources, you may be able to get by with a study guide or even just studying the manuals that accompany hardware and software related to your topic.

You'll also find "study kits" and CBT software on the market. The kits incorporate several training media, such as videotaped presentations, text material, and self tests, into one package. Each package is dedicated to a specific certification designation or requirement. The price and quality of these products vary widely, so don't commit to any of them without a solid preview. This book's companion Web site contains demo versions of a variety of CBT programs and training materials, but you'll find even more by searching the Internet and reading trade magazine advertisements.

Professionals who've taken the self-study track often recommend study materials that include practice tests, so that may be an important feature to look for. You'll also find that some companies actually guarantee that if you use their materials (or take their classes) you will pass the associated test, but don't be misled; the best guarantee in the world isn't as meaningful as your personal determination—you're in this to get certified, not to get your money back.

If you don't feel confident that self-study will work for you, the next level up is facilitated training online. Courses offered via the Internet are cheaper than their classroom cousins and offer some of the same benefits. You'll have access to an instructor and interaction with other students, but you won't have to travel to a training center or follow as rigid a schedule.

Step up to another price level and you'll encounter another option that may prove just the ticket if time isn't in short supply: college classes. Increasingly, the same exact certification classes offered by authorized training companies are available as college courses. The major difference is the time span; instead of blasting through requirements with several intense, sequential days of training, you'll complete them at a more leisurely pace. For some people, the pace is a bit too leisurely. The selection of supported certifications is also quite limited, with courses for Microsoft, Novell, and the A+ certifications being the most widely available. But when instructor-led training appears to be what you need, colleges will save you money over commercial training centers.

The top tier of certification preparation, in cost, is the authorized training center class. For some people and for some requirements, it can be irreplaceable. You'll have the equipment, trained and certified instructors, and other resources at hand. But you will pay for it. This type of class may be the way to go for requirements you find especially daunting, but in other cases, lower-cost options will do the job handily. Table 5-2 illustrates the comparative costs of the various options. The table provides a general expense assessment based upon typical market prices, but individual products may sometimes fall outside their category.

Of course, price isn't the only consideration in choosing a training method, or necessarily the most important. Additional pros, cons, and characteristics of available training options, including resources that are free, are discussed in detail in Chapter 9.

Method	Standard Price Level
Self-study book/manual	$
Single CBT program	$$
Online class	$$$
Self-study kit	$$$
College course	$$$$
Unauthorized training vendor	$$$$$
Authorized training vendor	$$$$$$

Table 5-2 Comparing Training Costs

Package Deals

Just as stocking up in a supermarket can pay off, bulk purchasing training can, too. If you're preparing for one of the more complex certifications, there will be multiple requirements and corresponding exams. Training vendors want to keep your business, and one way to do that is to hook you in for an extended period. In exchange for customer loyalty, they offer substantial savings.

Consider Learning Tree International's Alumni Gold Tuition Discount. Everyone who attends a Learning Tree course receives the discount card, which entitles the holder to a 20% discount off additional courses you take in the following 12 months.

Another type of package deal is one that your employer can enter into, especially if yours is a medium- to large-sized company. Your employer agrees to use the vendor as the company's trainer of choice, and employees receive discounted tuition in return.

Maxwell Training Centers, an authorized trainer for Symantec, Microsoft, and Lotus, promises via their Web site "a variety of group pricing plans with savings as much as 40% off standard rates." With a little research on the Web you'll be able to turn up more. Many training providers offer similar bulk purchase discounts.

Make any bulk certification training purchase with extra care. It's a good idea to try a single course first to make sure the training style and materials are a good fit with your needs. Ask for the names of satisfied customers, and talk to them about what they liked and didn't like in their dealings with the company. Signing up for a package training deal only to discover afterwards you don't like that certification, training company, or learning method can be a costly error.

You may come across deals, especially with the newer "online universities," where you pay one fee in return for all the classes you can or care to complete within a given period of time. These sound like a great deal, and for some people, they may be. If this is an option you're considering, carefully assess:

- The quality of the classes
- The selection of classes offered
- How many you will realistically complete within the stated time period

You may find a great deal or, instead, discover that although the offer sounds like a bargain, the quality of the courses or your ability to utilize them makes it much less so.

Special Discounts

Make sure you ask about any available discounts. You may find that government employees or other specific groups to which you may belong are eligible for reduced rates with a particular vendor.

Shop Around for the Best Deals

In contrast to purchasing the entire shebang from a single vendor, you can also purchase a piece here and a course there. This method requires a greater investment of your time and legwork (or keyboardwork), but will allow you to purchase each training item at the lowest price you can uncover.

To locate training vendors in your area, you can contact the sponsor of the certification you're pursuing. But that's only a starting point because the listing is likely to be limited to authorized trainers. Internet search engines are a powerful tool for uncovering training vendors. A few places to start your search are:

- **www.yahoo.com/Business_and_Economy/Companies/ Computers/Software/Training/**—Yahoo's indexed compilation of software training companies.
- **www.nerdworld.com/nw190.html**—Nerd World Media's list of computer training companies. Each entry contains a brief summary and link to a related Web page.
- **www.1800training.com/traintest.html**—part of the 1-800 Training site created by Sylvan Prometric. From here, you can enter your zip code to retrieve a list of certification training centers near you.

Part of effective price shopping is to ask others who've pursued the same credentials where they obtained training and materials, how much they paid, and how they rate their vendor. In this way, you can gather tips that will spare you both search time and quality problems.

Make Your Funds Do Double Duty

If you can't trim your training costs appreciably, you may be able to get double mileage for your money. A certification training course may qualify for college credits toward a degree program, so be sure to check with your academic institution beforehand to see if and how you can get your training applied toward your degree.

Condense Training

Getting back to opportunity cost, one of the simplest ways to cut your expenses is to reduce the amount of time you spend earning certification. When work time is being devoted to certification, it isn't being used to generate income. That's the age-old time-equals-money equation.

Correspondingly, less time equals less money. That is, reducing the amount of time away from work can drastically reduce total certification costs. For example, if your income works out to a rate of $35 per hour and you cut 20 hours off your certification training time, you've trimmed $700 from your certification bill (or conversely, returned that 20 hours to the income side of your budget, resulting in an additional $700 to your bank account).

Another way to compress certification time is to take intense, condensed courses or sequences of courses. Because the vendor doesn't have to repeatedly set up the training environment, coordinate staff and facilities, or lay out other one-time costs, the vendor's cost is lower than offering the same material over a more extended period of time. The savings are often passed on to the student.

Stretch It Out

If financing certification will just put too much of a squeeze on your budget, you may be able to manage it more easily by meeting the requirements over time. Your overall cost may well be higher than if you didn't follow this route, but it will be spread out into more manageable outlays. You may even find that once your certification is underway, you'll be able to boost your billing rate, and financing your education will no longer be a problem.

It's important to remember that, other than death and taxes, nothing in life is guaranteed, including an income boost from certification. So if you're considering relying on your credit cards (with their high interest rates) to pay for certification, look for another way. Perhaps a loan at a more reasonable rate from a bank or family member will tide you over. Otherwise, seriously consider putting off certification until your financial picture improves.

Join the Exchange

Certification training materials, especially "authorized" materials, don't come cheap. A price tag of $75 to $100 or more isn't unusual. After the exam, they become like last semester's college textbooks; an expensive reminder of courses gone by. College students cope with the issue by selling used textbooks to each other, and, now, certified professionals have begun doing the same thing. Cyber Pass Inc., creators of the CNEQUIZR certification preparation software, have created a free online book exchange center (Figure 5-4 shows the Bookswap site). Here you can buy, sell, or swap authorized Novell and Microsoft course materials. The company does this strictly as a public service, at no charge to participants. If enough people make the request, perhaps they'll open their database to authorized materials for all computer certifications.

Figure 5-4
The Bookswap Site

Taking Advantage of Tax Breaks

Although taxes may be an inevitable price of life in the United States, that doesn't mean you have to pay more than your fair share. Luckily for people pursuing professional training, Uncle Sam smiles on citizens who work to improve themselves and their economic position. A strong worker makes for a strong economy and all that. So employees who pay out of pocket for certain types of education get to deduct their expenses from their federal tax return. The available deductions apply whether you're self-employed or on the payroll of a national conglomerate. If you're not self-employed, you'll need to itemize your deductions in order to claim these, too, and the amount will be subject to the 2% limitation.

This section details federal tax deductions in force *at the time this book was written*. Tax consequences vary depending on individual situations and circumstances, and although I'm not qualified to, nor do I intend to advise you on, your personal tax position, this book can provide a good overview of some potential deductions. Because of the ever-shifting nature of the tax landscape, it's a good idea to consult a tax professional or study up, using publications from the IRS for the latest details and tax laws.

Do You Qualify?

To calculate your deduction(s), the first thing you'll have to determine is whether your courses are considered "qualifying education" according to the IRS definition. Specifically, the education must either:

1. Be required by your employer or the law to keep your present salary, status, or job (and serve a business purpose of your employer).
2. Maintain or improve skills needed in your present work.

That sounds pretty straightforward, and as long as you already work in the computer field, your certification training is likely to fall squarely under Number 2, which, according to the IRS, includes refresher courses, courses on current development, and academic or vocational courses.

But, the tax code being what it is, there are complicating exceptions—namely, education is not "qualifying" if it:

1. Is needed to meet the minimum educational requirements of your present trade or business, or
2. Is part of a program of study that can qualify you for a new trade or business, even if you have no plans to enter that trade or business.

Again, assuming that you are already a computer professional, neither of these is likely to invalidate your certification expenses as qualifying education. If this seems confusing, check out Figure 5-5, which contains a reproduction of a handy decision flowchart included in IRS Publication 17 (1996) to clarify the definition of qualifying education.

Figure 5-5
IRS flowchart: Are Your Educational Expenses Deductible?

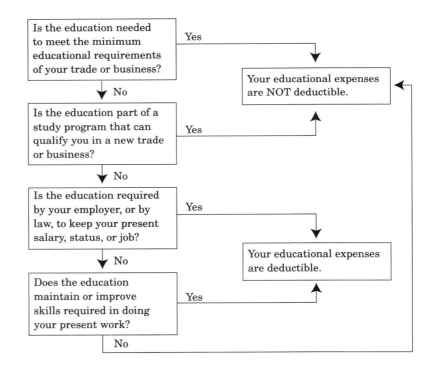

What You Can Deduct

Once you've determined that your training qualifies, you'll need to know which expenses are deductible. They are:

✐ Tuition, books, supplies, lab fees, and similar items

✐ Certain transportation and travel costs

✐ Other educational expenses, such as costs of research and typing when writing a paper as part of an educational program

You can't deduct personal or capital expenses (which include opportunity expense).

The IRS further defines "certain transportation and travel costs." Basically, you can deduct your transportation from work to school and then school to home, as long as you're attending school on a temporary basis (defined as a matter of days or weeks). If you go to school from home, again, on a temporary basis, you can probably deduct your transportation both ways. Longer term educational engagements may only be eligible for mileage from work to school.

Cab, subway, and bus fares, car expenses, and parking fees and tolls are all transportation costs. Car expenses can be either your actual expenses or at the standard mileage rate (31.5 cents/mile in 1997).

If your training takes you away from home overnight, then you've moved into the realm of travel expenses. As far as education-related travel expenses, the IRS says that you can deduct expenses for travel, up to 50% of the cost of your meals and lodging, if you travel overnight to obtain qualified education and the main purpose of the trip is a work-related course or seminar.

Claiming Your Deductions

If you're self-employed, your qualifying education expenses should be deducted on your Schedule C Profit or Loss from Business or Schedule C-EZ Net Profit from Business. When using Schedule C (see Figure 5-6) your tuition, lab fees, books, and similar items will fall under Part V Other Expenses. Other amounts should go under their matching headings elsewhere on the form.

If you're an employee, the form you're after will be 2106 Unreimbursed Employee Business Expenses (or its shorter cousin 2106-EZ). Form 2106 is shown in Figure 5-7. Note the word *Unreimbursed* in the form title; if an employer already refunded your expenses, you're not allowed to double-dip.

Figure 5-6
Schedule C Profit or Loss From Business

SCHEDULE C (Form 1040)
Department of the Treasury Internal Revenue Service (99)

Profit or Loss From Business
(Sole Proprietorship)
▶ Partnerships, joint ventures, etc., must file Form 1065.
▶ Attach to Form 1040 or Form 1041. ▶ See Instructions for Schedule C (Form 1040).

OMB No. 1545-0074
1996
Attachment Sequence No. 09

Name of proprietor | Social security number (SSN)

A Principal business or profession, including product or service (see page C-1)
B Enter principal business code (see page C-6) ▶
C Business name. If no separate business name, leave blank.
D Employer ID number (EIN), if any
E Business address (including suite or room no.) ▶
City, town or post office, state, and ZIP code
F Accounting method: (1) ☐ Cash (2) ☐ Accrual (3) ☐ Other (specify) ▶
G Did you "materially participate" in the operation of this business during 1996? If "No," see page C-2 for limit on losses. ☐ Yes ☐ No
H If you started or acquired this business during 1996, check here ▶ ☐

Part I Income

1 Gross receipts or sales. **Caution:** *If this income was reported to you on Form W-2 and the "Statutory employee" box on that form was checked, see page C-2 and check here* ▶ ☐ | 1
2 Returns and allowances | 2
3 Subtract line 2 from line 1 | 3
4 Cost of goods sold (from line 42 on page 2) | 4
5 **Gross profit.** Subtract line 4 from line 3 | 5
6 Other income, including Federal and state gasoline or fuel tax credit or refund (see page C-2) | 6
7 **Gross income.** Add lines 5 and 6 ▶ | 7

Part II Expenses. Enter expenses for business use of your home **only** on line 30.

8 Advertising | 8
9 Bad debts from sales or services (see page C-3) | 9
10 Car and truck expenses (see page C-3) | 10
11 Commissions and fees | 11
12 Depletion | 12
13 Depreciation and section 179 expense deduction (not included in Part III) (see page C-3) | 13
14 Employee benefit programs (other than on line 19) | 14
15 Insurance (other than health) | 15
16 Interest:
a Mortgage (paid to banks, etc.) | 16a
b Other | 16b
17 Legal and professional services | 17
18 Office expense | 18
19 Pension and profit-sharing plans | 19
20 Rent or lease (see page C-4):
a Vehicles, machinery, and equipment | 20a
b Other business property | 20b
21 Repairs and maintenance | 21
22 Supplies (not included in Part III) | 22
23 Taxes and licenses | 23
24 Travel, meals, and entertainment:
a Travel | 24a
b Meals and entertainment
c Enter 50% of line 24b subject to limitations (see page C-4)
d Subtract line 24c from line 24b | 24d
25 Utilities | 25
26 Wages (less employment credits) | 26
27 Other expenses (from line 48 on page 2) | 27
28 **Total expenses** before expenses for business use of home. Add lines 8 through 27 in columns ▶ | 28
29 Tentative profit (loss). Subtract line 28 from line 7 | 29
30 Expenses for business use of your home. Attach **Form 8829** | 30
31 **Net profit or (loss).** Subtract line 30 from line 29.
• If a profit, enter on **Form 1040, line 12,** and ALSO on **Schedule SE, line 2** (statutory employees, see page C-5). Estates and trusts, enter on Form 1041, line 3.
• If a loss, you MUST go on to line 32. | 31
32 If you have a loss, check the box that describes your investment in this activity (see page C-5).
• If you checked 32a, enter the loss on **Form 1040, line 12,** and ALSO on **Schedule SE, line 2** (statutory employees, see page C-5). Estates and trusts, enter on Form 1041, line 3.
• If you checked 32b, you MUST attach **Form 6198.**
32a ☐ All investment is at risk.
32b ☐ Some investment is not at risk.

For Paperwork Reduction Act Notice, see Form 1040 instructions. Cat. No. 11334P **Schedule C (Form 1040) 1996**

Schedule C (Form 1040) 1996 Page **2**

Part III Cost of Goods Sold (see page C-5)

33 Method(s) used to value closing inventory: a ☐ Cost b ☐ Lower of cost or market c ☐ Other (attach explanation)
34 Was there any change in determining quantities, costs, or valuations between opening and closing inventory? If "Yes," attach explanation ☐ Yes ☐ No
35 Inventory at beginning of year. If different from last year's closing inventory, attach explanation | 35
36 Purchases less cost of items withdrawn for personal use | 36
37 Cost of labor. Do not include salary paid to yourself | 37
38 Materials and supplies | 38
39 Other costs | 39
40 Add lines 35 through 39 | 40
41 Inventory at end of year | 41
42 **Cost of goods sold.** Subtract line 41 from line 40. Enter the result here and on page 1, line 4 | 42

Part IV Information on Your Vehicle. Complete this part **ONLY** if you are claiming car or truck expenses on line 10 and are not required to file Form 4562 for this business. See the instructions for line 13 on page C-3 to find out if you must file.

43 When did you place your vehicle in service for business purposes? (month, day, year) ▶ ....../....../......
44 Of the total number of miles you drove your vehicle during 1996, enter the number of miles you used your vehicle for:
a Business .... b Commuting .... c Other ....
45 Do you (or your spouse) have another vehicle available for personal use? ☐ Yes ☐ No
46 Was your vehicle available for use during off-duty hours? ☐ Yes ☐ No
47a Do you have evidence to support your deduction? ☐ Yes ☐ No
b If "Yes," is the evidence written? ☐ Yes ☐ No

Part V Other Expenses. List below business expenses not included on lines 8–26 or line 30.

48 **Total other expenses.** Enter here and on page 1, line 27 | 48

Figure 5-7
Form 2106 Employee
Business Expenses

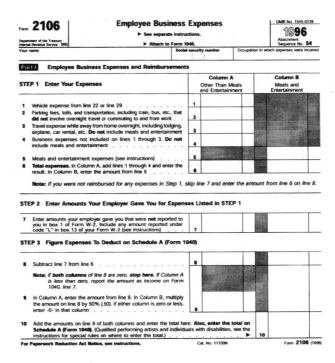

As always, when dealing with tax matters, document, document, document. Collect and keep all receipts related to your education expenses, whether they're for $2,000 worth of tuition or a $1.20 highway toll, and keep an expense log that includes mileage records. Store the documents with your personal copy of your return. You'll probably never have to look at them again; but should the need arise, they'll be there.

Education Provisions of The 1997 Tax Act

The Tax Act of 1997 contained several provisions that will change how much and in what ways you can claim tax breaks for education expenses. The provision most relevant to computer professionals obtaining certification is the one called the lifetime learning tax credit, and it will be available for education expenses paid after June 30, 1998.

Unlike a deduction, which reduces the amount of income you pay taxes on, a credit is a dollar for dollar reduction of your tax bill. The lifetime learning credit equals 20% of the first $5,000 of your qualifying education expenses (a $1,000 maximum). That amount will increase to 20 percent of the first $10,000 in expenses (or a $2,000 maximum), after the year 2002. The amount of the credit is reduced for filers with higher incomes.

There may be other additional provisions of the 1997 act that you qualify for, so be sure to check with your tax advisor before filing your return for any year in which you spent money on professional education. It may be your duty as an American citizen to pay taxes, but there's no reason to pay more than you're legally obligated to.

Related IRS Forms Publications

The following forms and publications pertain to various aspects of deducting education expenses. If you don't care to wade through them all, start with the bible of individual tax returns, Publication 17 (fondly referred to by tax professionals as Pub 17). It may adequately answer your questions.

You can retrieve the most recent versions of any of these items (and a vast quantity more) from the IRS Web site at **www.irs.ustreas.gov/prod/cover.html**. Or call 1-800-TAX-FORM and ask for them to be mailed to you.

- Publication 17 Your Federal Income Tax
- Publication 334 Tax Guide For Small Business (C or C-EZ filers)
- Publication 508 Educational Expenses
- Publication 529 Miscellaneous Expenses
- Publication 535 Business Expenses
- Publication 552 Recordkeeping For Individuals
- Form 1040 U.S. Individual Income Tax Return
- Schedule A Itemized Deductions
- Schedule C Profit or Loss from Business
- Schedule C-EZ Net Profit from Business
- Form 2106 Employee Business Expenses
- Form 2106-EZ Unreimbursed Employee Business Expenses

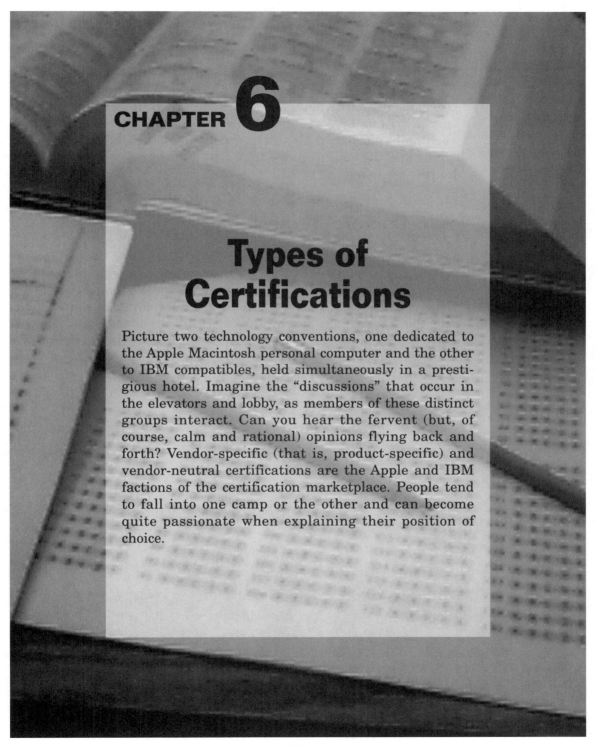

CHAPTER 6

Types of Certifications

Picture two technology conventions, one dedicated to the Apple Macintosh personal computer and the other to IBM compatibles, held simultaneously in a prestigious hotel. Imagine the "discussions" that occur in the elevators and lobby, as members of these distinct groups interact. Can you hear the fervent (but, of course, calm and rational) opinions flying back and forth? Vendor-specific (that is, product-specific) and vendor-neutral certifications are the Apple and IBM factions of the certification marketplace. People tend to fall into one camp or the other and can become quite passionate when explaining their position of choice.

Recently, training companies have begun to bridge the gap between vendor-specific and vendor-neutral certifications. Their hybrid creations attempt to combine the best features of the other two categories. The ability to clearly differentiate between certification programs by sorting them into a few distinct categories may eventually disappear. Meanwhile, it helps to understand these segments and the subcategories they contain before selecting a particular certification.

Vendor-Specific Certifications

Computer hardware and software merchants offer vendor-specific certifications because they recognize expertise related to the vendor's own product line. Table 6-1 lists some of the companies that offer these certifications. In some cases, the vendor develops and administers the certification program from within its education or support department. However, it's not uncommon for the management of a certification program, and especially the testing component, to be handled by another company.

Table 6-1
Companies that Sponsor Vendor Certifications

Company Names		
3COM	Corel	Novell
Adobe	DEC	Oracle
Baan	Folio	ParcPlace-Digitalk
Banyan	Hewlett-Packard	Powersoft
Bay Networks	IBM	Softdesk
Borland	Informix	SAP
Centura Software	Lotus	Sun
Cisco Systems	Microsoft	Sybase
Cognos	Motorola	Symantec
Compaq	Network General	

The rationale behind vendor-specific certifications is pretty straightforward: companies don't run "a network;" they run a Microsoft NT network, a Cisco network, or a Novell network, each of which has its own features, quirks, and specialties. Similarly, databases aren't developed in a generic format using standard tools; they're created using Oracle, Informix, or some other specific development environment. Although these products may share concepts and even standards, they are indisputably individual; what optimizes one product may trigger errors in another.

Because, theoretically anyway, no one can know a product as well as the people who developed it, the vendor is in a unique position to teach the ins and outs of its own product line and to declare exactly who qualifies as an expert it its implementation. Not coincidentally, the vendor also has access to the intricate, technical details from development and testing phases of the product. This intimate knowledge translates into the power to make the product perform to its full potential. Peak performance is good for the vendor, the business using the product, and the people in charge of making it work.

As competition in the training and certification marketplace heats up, vendors are searching for ways to increase the value of their certification programs and to distinguish them from the crowd. One way this is being accomplished is by acknowledging that the nature of today's technology environment makes it likely that most companies will be running more than one platform. Vendors have begun offering training courses and information that focus on how to integrate their product with those of other popular vendors and how to migrate from another environment to theirs. Mastery of these aspects of a product is increasing as a requirement for the higher levels of certification.

Multiplatform Computing

A common scenario, especially in larger firms, is the existence of a three-tiered environment. The bottom tier is a mainframe system running legacy systems; the middle layer is some sort of networking environment; and the upper tier contains the most recent technologies, including client/server and Internet connections. This happens because even if it was technically possible for organizations to keep up with the latest technologies, it isn't financially possible or necessarily practical.

Switching between technologies is complex, time-consuming, and expensive, especially when it involves porting hundreds of thousands of lines of code. For some applications, it simply doesn't make sense to make the transfer. The result is a heterogeneous

> computing environment that encompasses several different platforms. Getting them to work together provides special challenges.

This cross-platform support also begins to narrow the dividing line between vendor-sponsored certifications and vendor-neutral certifications, bringing them a half step closer together.

Marketing departments being what they are, this development is also being used to lure professionals whose area of expertise is with a competitor's product line into the fold of a different vendor, or alternatively, to discourage customers from defecting to a different environment. Banyan, for example, added a Windows NT track to its Certified Banyan Specialist program in 1997. Certification in this track requires that candidates pass one of Microsoft's Certified Product Specialist NT tests, as well as complete Banyan courses related to using Street Talk with Windows NT.

Qualifying for a Vendor-Sponsored Certification

To obtain one of the vendor-sponsored certifications, you'll have to pass a series of tests. Some certifications are granted after successful completion of a single exam. Keep in mind, however, that not all certifications are equally valuable. A designation that requires a broader demonstration of skills and expertise is going to signify more than a designation that shows you are an expert in a single application. If the single application is one you use at work, then the simpler certification can certainly prove valuable to you. The important thing is to realize exactly what it is you're attempting to have certified, so that you can compare apples to apples.

For example, to obtain an Adobe Certified Expert (ACE) certification, you'd have to take and pass a one-to-two-hour product-proficiency exam. To become a Cisco Certified Internetwork Expert (CCIE), on the other hand, requires passing an exam that covers items ranging from data encapsulation to switching algorithms, as well as completion of a two-day laboratory that includes implementing a complex internetwork and then fixing it after an instructor inserts faults. Although each of these is in a sense a single certification, one is clearly much more involved and extensive than the other. That will be reflected in the required investment of time, money, and effort, as well as in the value you can reasonably expect to receive in return.

QUOTE

The Big Picture

I'm a Novell CNE (1991) and currently going through Microsoft MCSE certification. When I'm done, it will have cost me $6,000 to $8,000, not to mention the lost billable hours while I'm in training, so obviously I believe in the value of certification. I've found it to be a good marketing advantage when seeking opportunities with larger organizations. In my experience, it's not as useful with smaller companies.

The important fact to understand is that you [also] need real-world experience (and bruises). The certifications can help you get in the door or give you a notch above the other person, but you need on-the-job experience to go along with them.

—Dan Cronin, Independent Consultant

Certification programs are sometimes broken into subprograms called *tracks*. Tracks give you a choice of placing emphasis in a particular area over another. Requirements will vary between tracks, with some overlap.

Within each track, you're likely to encounter a list of courses and a corresponding list of exams. It's important to note that very often the courses are suggested, *not* required. If you can obtain the necessary knowledge and pass the associated exam without taking (and paying for) the recommended course, that's perfectly acceptable.

One course or exam will often build, at least to some extent, upon the prior requirement. When this is the case, you'll probably find it easiest to complete the requirements in order. In other instances, the order won't matter, and you can choose any sequence that proves convenient to you.

Be sure to check for time limits governing how long you have to complete the requirements. The time frames generally are very reasonable and just intended to keep you from dragging it out forever. You certainly don't need to use the entire allotted time period, and you probably won't want to.

Exams for vendor-sponsored certifications commonly take one of two forms. The first form involves a computer-based multiple-choice test. When you feel ready to take a particular exam, you'll register for it at a testing center near your home. On the appointed day, you'll walk into the center, take the test sitting at the computer, and walk out with your score.

QUICK TIP

Sylvan Prometric

The development and implementation of a certification program is a complex process. One of the significant logistic problems is the question of how to test individuals who are dispersed across the country and even around the world.

If obtaining and completing an examination is an onerous procedure, candidates are less likely to do so. On the other hand, testing is necessary to provide a quantitative measurement of skills. There's also a potential appearance of bias if the testing organization is the same one that designed the curriculum, trains individuals, and grants certification. Add that development and administration of meaningful tests is a science in and of itself, and the need to schedule individual times, provide testing facilities, and shuffle all the related paperwork, and it becomes apparent that the testing component of any certification program is logistically challenging.

Enter Sylvan Prometric (Figure 6-1 shows the Sylvan Prometric home page). A division of Sylvan Learning Systems, Sylvan Prometric (formerly Drake Prometric) boasts more than 1500 testing centers in over 80 countries. Through these centers, the company administers tests ranging from graduate school admission classics like the GRE to scores of professional certification exams. As you explore the certification process, you'll find the company name popping up again and again, usually in a sentence such as: "To schedule an exam at a testing center near you, contact Sylvan Prometric at 1-800-961-EXAM."

That's because Sylvan Prometric has contracts and strategic alliances with many companies in the IT industry, including Microsoft and The Chauncey Group (part of Educational Testing Services or ETS). In 1989, Sylvan Prometric (then called Drake Prometric) administered a single company's certification program—Novell's. As of October 1996, that number exceeded 40. The exams are typically multiple-choice, closed book, and administered via a personal computer. You'll be asked for two forms of ID, one of which must be a photo ID (so don't even think of having that guru down the hall take the test for you). The company maintains an online testing center locator, which you can access from its web site at **www.sylvanprometric.com**.

Product-specific certifications may also include a lab test in which the computer equipment and software that are needed to perform actual tasks within the certification's focus are set up for the candidate's use. This type of exam allows you to demonstrate your abilities by performing tasks using the actual hardware and software rather than by responding to written questions. In some cases, this type of measurement is especially important because it provides a more accurate measure of your ability to perform in the environment in question. During a lab test, you may be required to implement a particular LAN environment or configure security software, for example. This type of test seems most prevalent among vendor-specific certifications.

Because specific equipment and facilities are required, you'll find that hands on tests (also called *practicums*) are significantly more expensive than other exams. These types of tests are more likely to be proctored by the product vendor's staff, instead of by an outside testing service. They are less readily available, so you're more likely to have to travel to the testing site, and you'll have fewer scheduling options.

Figure 6-1
Sylvan Prometric's
Web Site

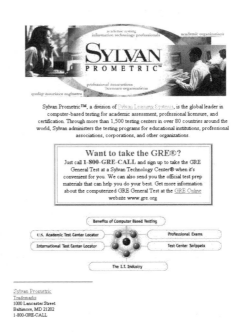

Passing Scores

The definition of what constitutes a minimum passing score on product-specific exams varies from vendor to vendor and even between tests by the same vendor. A few examples include:

- Bay Networks Hub Specialist: 65 points out of 100 (65%)
- Microsoft certification test 70-026—SQL 6.5 Server Administration: 730 points out of 1000 (73%)
- Microsoft certification test 70-068—NT Server 4.0 Enterprise: 784 points out of 1000 (78.4%)

    ✐ Novell Test 656—Web Server Management: 662 points out of 800 (82.8%)

    ✐ Novell Test 605—TCP/IP: 541 points out of 800 (67.6%)

Very few vendor-sponsored certifications include an experience requirement. Some require continuing education to maintain certification; most do not. When a new product version is released, an exam and/or class that will allow you to upgrade your certification will often accompany it. The upgrade test is usually not required to maintain your certification.

Vendor-Neutral Certifications

Vendor-neutral certifications are primarily offered by professional associations and industry organizations, with a few sponsored by computer-related companies that aren't associated with specific hardware or software products. Table 6-2 lists some of the sources of this type of certification. These programs are structured to certify individuals in a particular technology arena rather than in specific products. The sponsoring organization is usually directly affiliated with the sector in question. Areas covered by these certifications include document imaging, computer repair, technical training, disaster recovery, business computing, Internet skills, intranet skills, systems security, and the like.

Proponents of vendor-independent certifications point out that technologies last much longer than individual products. The software package that's king today may be history two years from now, even as the related technology sector (LANs, for example) continues with a robust expansion. This leads to a concern that computer professionals who train on the ins and outs of a particular product may know just how to get that package or platform to perform but may lack a solid foundation on the principles and theories behind it.

Professionals with skills that are technology-focused rather than product-specific are able to analyze and address business problems and come up with the best solution for the given circumstances. These neutral certifications imply a professional freedom from dependence on Microsoft (or Novell, Cisco, or other vendor-specific) products.

Vendor-neutral certifications also address more universally the nature of computing environments as multivendor melting pots of technological tools. In such an environment, broad knowledge and experience are more valuable than expertise in a single hardware or software product. Although vendor-certification sponsors are just beginning to acknowledge this, vendor-neutral certifications have been built around this concept from the beginning.

Table 6-2
Organizations that Sponsor Product Independent Certifications

Organization Names
Building Industry Consulting Service International (BICSI)
Computing Technology and Industry Association (CompTIA)
Disaster Recover Institute International (DRI)
Educational Testing Service (ETS)
Inacom
Information Systems Audit and Control Association (ISACA)
Institute for Certification of Computer Professionals (ICCP)
International Information Systems Security Certification Consortium (ISC^2)
International Programmers Guild (IPG)
International Society of Internet Professionals (ISIP)
Network Professional Association
Software Publishers Association

The Institute for Certification of Computing Professionals (ICCP) is a founder of this breed of certifications (which predate vendor-specific designations). Figure 6-2 shows the ICCP home page. Among many other subjects, the ICCP Certified Computing Professional (CCP) examinations cover such topics as systems development, data resource management, systems security, procedural programming, and communications theory. Since its founding in 1973, more than 50,000 professionals have completed ICCP certification.

Figure 6-2
ICCP on the Web

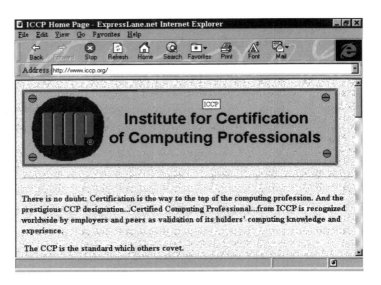

QUOTE

Certifications With Staying Power

The secret to certification is not that it teaches you anything; you either know the subject matter or not. It evidences some skill level, but, to be truthful, even that is subject to much question. In any profession there are people who studied for a short time, took the test, passed it, but still didn't know what to do in the real-world situations.

I don't respect certifications, like CNE, CNA, MSCE, [and others]. They purport to attest to your technical competence, but these are the very areas that test well but are not enough to make you good in the real world. Plus, they are very narrow in scope. I hear it all the time on the online forums. "Wow, I want to be a CNE. **That** will make me marketable!" "Are you a network person?" "No, I'm a software developer, but this just has to look good on a resume!" The point is that their applicability is limited in scope (only people doing **that** job, with **that** vendor's product, benefit). They are also limited in time. What if you were a certified Lotus 1-2-3 guru? Or a dBase wizard? Or a Commodore 64 certified genius? Where would you be now? As the market changes, it invalidates many of these things.

The CCP tests the general concepts and a general level of professionalism. Applicants take a core curriculum in information management principles, computer fundamentals, database design, analysis, and other long-term valuable knowledge. The applicant then specializes and goes for a particular discipline (a programming language, database design, networks, Internet, [or so on]). This produces a well-rounded test of the whole person, not just a single discipline.

I hold the CCP (Certified Computing Professional) designation and have for fifteen years. I've found it very useful, and it has great staying power (when I got it in 1985, **most** of the technology we use today didn't exist).The proof's in how it works: clients seem to value my CCP, and it leaves the right impression: that of a broadly competent information professional.

—Steven Thomas, CCP

Qualifying for a Vendor-Neutral Certification

Like the certifications themselves, the requirements for vendor-neutral designations cover more territory. To receive one, you'll have to pass a series of hurdles designed to assess your competency in a particular area of technology. As usual, there are minimum test scores involved. Sometimes you'll be required to attend specific training courses prior to sitting for the exams.

You'll also be required to submit proof of experience in the applicable technology sector for many of these designations. This is in sharp contrast with vendor-specific certifications, which rarely incorporate an experience requirement. Figure 6-3 illustrates the components of Network Professional Association's (NPA's) Certified Network Professional (CNP) requirements. In some cases, a college degree or other educational achievement such as certification in a different area will be accepted in lieu of actual work history, or at least serve to satisfy part of the experience requirement.

A condition for obtaining the designation may be your promise to adhere to a code of ethics, especially when a certification is sponsored by a professional organization. The code of ethics will spell out what constitutes acceptable conduct in your field and what is considered morally responsible behavior. These documents range from a few paragraphs to multiple pages.

Vendor-neutral certifications often come with continuing education requirements. These encourage you to keep up with industry developments and can be satisfied through a variety of methods. Activities that qualify for credit include formal education such as college and vocational technical courses, self-study, and training seminars.

Certifications sponsored by professional associations are more likely than vendor designations to carry an annual "maintenance fee" as a requirement of continued certification. ICCP, for example, charges $50 per year.

Figure 6-3
Composition of CNP
Requirements

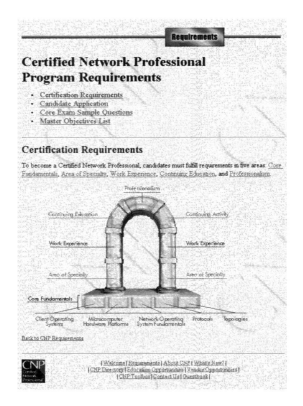

Passing Scores

The definition of what constitutes a minimum passing score on vendor-independent exams varies between sponsors.

- A+ core exam: 72 points out of 100 (72%)
- ICCP Certified Computing Professional (CCP) core exam: 70%
- Certified Network Professional (CNP) core exam: 70%

Hybrid Certifications

Recently a third breed of certifications—hybrids—has appeared on the scene. These are the fence-straddlers of the certification marketplace, and are designed to fill the formerly barren middle ground between vendor-specific and vendor-neutral certifications. They do this by blending the technology concepts and background requirements of a vendor-neutral certification with the specific hardware and software product know-how.

Instead of focusing on a single vendor, the hardware and software products covered by these certification programs are usually grouped by function. The USWeb Internet- and intranet-related certifications, for example, encompass background knowledge and skills particular to Web development *and* its implementation using a cross-section of specific tools and platforms.

Because these are relatively new on the scene, there aren't too many of them around. Training companies are behind most of these programs. Current sponsors include Learning Tree International, Net Guru Technologies, and USWeb (Figure 6-4 shows the USWeb home page).

Figure 6-4
The USWeb
Home Page

Novell has recently ventured into this market segment as well by creating the Novell Certified Internet Professional (CIP) designation. Professionals can choose from five tracks, including Internet business strategist, Web designer, Web developer, intranet manager, and Internet architect. Figure 6-5 shows Novell's CIP track selection page. Although several of these tracks incorporate training on Novell products, others don't even mention the *N* word. Expect more of these middle-of-the-road certifications to appear in the near future.

Once you complete certification requirements, you can expect to receive a "welcome kit." It will include the information you need to access restricted forums, receive technical subscriptions, and otherwise utilize the perks that come with your certification. It will also include the logo in several formats and a logo-use agreement that specifies when and how you are permitted to use the certification logo. You'll probably be required to sign the logo use document and possibly another "terms of certification" agreement and/or ethics statement. The welcome kit may also include a certificate, plaque, lapel pin bearing the logo, and other goodies of varying value and use.

Figure 6-5
Certified Internet
Professional Track
Selection Page

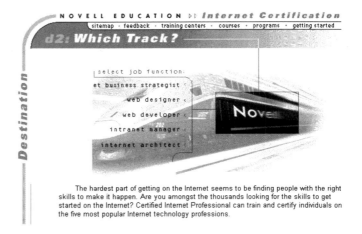

The hardest part of getting on the Internet seems to be finding people with the right skills to make it happen. Are you amongst the thousands looking for the skills to get started on the Internet? Certified Internet Professional can train and certify individuals on the five most popular Internet technology professions.

None of these certification categories is universally superior to another. However, depending upon your personal experience and future goals, a particular category may indeed prove superior *for your purposes*. You should also remember that you don't have to stick with a single designation; you can obtain more than one. For example, you might want to cover several bases by going after a vendor-independent certification related to your technology interests, and add a product-specific certification from the vendor that manufactures the most widely used application in your field. Another common approach is to obtain more than one vendor-specific certification. Understanding the distinctions between available professional designations will enable you to better choose programs that will, alone or in partnership, work for you the way that you want them to.

CHAPTER **7**

Certification Mistakes You Don't Have to Make

The time, money, and effort you put into achieving certification will depend upon the certification you choose and how much it's a natural extension of your current skill level. It's a calculated financial and psychological investment in your future, one that you can expect to provide dividends for years to come. Like any investor, you need to choose your investment options wisely and learn from the mistakes of others. As the saying goes: "If you can't afford to do it over, you'd better do it right the first time."

Fortunately, computer professionals who have been embracing certification since its earliest beginnings have blazed a path for you. By understanding where earlier certification candidates went astray, you can avoid making the same mistakes. What follows is an exploration of the most common certification errors and suggestions on how to steer clear of them.

The errors are grouped into three categories:

- Choosing the wrong certification
- Mistakes made while working toward a chosen certification
- Mistakes made after achieving certification

Each of these areas contributes to your overall success and satisfaction. Although a small misjudgment here or there isn't going to cancel out all of your hard work, you might as well benefit from other people's hindsight. After all, that's one type of vision that's always 20/20.

Choosing the Wrong Certification

Choosing the wrong program is one of the more common mistakes people make when pursuing certification. What makes a certain certification a bad choice? Either it's chosen for the wrong reasons or it's lacking in some way that easily could have been detected (but hasn't been) with a little research. This type of mistake is easier to make than you might suspect. Here's why it happens:

Choosing a Certification Because it's "Hot"

OUCH!

When Novell first came out with the CNE certification, no one knew what it was. But that quickly flipped around and now you'd be hard-pressed to find anyone in the computer field who hasn't heard of it. Because it was the first vendor-specific certification (and for a while the only vendor-sponsored certification), it was the one everyone wanted. Forums and lunchrooms echoed (and still do, to a lesser extent) with conversations that went something like this:

"I want to get a CNE because *that* will make me marketable."

"Oh yeah, I've heard of that. Are you a software developer?"

"No."

"You administer a LAN then?"

"Well, no."

"Then what do you want a CNE for?"

"Because it's *hot*! People with CNEs get more money, more respect, and better jobs!"

At this point, a strident logic alarm should start sounding: Error! Error! Error! There's a leap in logic here that this CNE wannabe and others like her keep missing. Yes, a CNE was a hot ticket (and still can be), but not in and of itself. The value comes when the CNE caps existing professional experience *in the same area*. If a certification is totally unrelated to the job you already do or the nature of the experience you have, it's not going to do a whole lot for you.

Choosing a certification strictly because you hear it's a ticket to a bigger paycheck is a huge mistake. Even if you somehow manage to obtain that top guru designation that you've heard lets you write your own ticket, the certification alone doesn't guarantee that you'll get the job to go with it. Employers look at the total picture, and certification is just one (potentially very important) part of it.

Certifications currently enjoying "hot ticket" status include Certified Cisco Internetwork Expert (CCIE) and Microsoft Certified Systems Engineer (MCSE) with Windows NT. The Novell fire has cooled, for the moment, although it certainly hasn't gone out. Plenty of other certifications vie for runner-up spots in this status competition.

That said, you should certainly investigate any certification that catches your eye. Maybe a CCIE or MCSE is a good choice for you, but in making that decision, don't depend solely on where the certification ranks in the marketplace. Also consider what you already have in your career arsenal to combine it with.

Today, computer professionals have a broader array of certifications to choose from than they did just five to ten years ago. That means there's probably a close match to what you want to accomplish; all you have to do is uncover it. And because this is a marketplace and not a horse race, there can be more than one winner.

Choosing a Certification Because it's Easy to Get

OUCH!

Did you know that you can get certified by attending a seminar? Yes, it's true. Some companies are angling for a free ride on the certification bandwagon, and they're hooking up with computer professionals hoping for the same thing. What do these certifications mean? Nothing substantial. Who do they fool? Nobody, except perhaps the people who are lured in by the promise of certification rather than by the material covered. Maybe you'll add a line to the continuing education section of your resume, but think about how you'll answer when an interviewer's finger lands on that line and he says, "Tell me about this certification."

But putting aside certifications that are more hot air than substance, the fact is, some certifications are dramatically more involved, expensive, and difficult to obtain than others. Acquiring

Learning Tree International's client/server systems certification requires four core courses and one elective course, along with their associated examinations. The total tab will run between $6,000 and $10,000, depending on choice of savings plan and time frame. (Figure 7-1 shows Learning Tree's client/server systems certification Web page.) To become a Certified Software Manager (CSM), on the other hand, requires passing one test for which you'll need to study a manual ($195) or attend a seminar ($395). Figure 7-2 shows the CSM certification site.

Although the extent of the requirements should be a consideration when choosing a certification, the most important aspect is how the certification will serve your career goals. If you're looking for a quick career fix and choose the program you can complete most quickly, you're going to be disappointed.

Does this mean that if a certification program doesn't involve a half dozen tests, hands-on laboratory sessions, and a slew of instructor-led cources that it's not worth your time? Absolutely not. You don't have to spend a fortune or devote a huge chunk of your time on certification to benefit from it; what you must do is choose wisely.

QUICK TIP

Certifications for Sale

The growing presence and value of specialized credentials has lead to a familiar phenomenon: certifications not worth the paper they're printed on. It's something that's long plagued academics, and it's a concern with computer certifications too.

A still large, but ever-shrinking portion of certification sponsors, promise that you can earn certification solely on the basis of passing exams, and those exams aren't all that difficult.

Almost anyone can obtain one of these by paying to take the test (and maybe cramming just a bit). The future employer then receives an ugly surprise: the skills they hired you for aren't really there. This leads hiring managers to be understandably wary, concerned that a certification may only prove you're good at taking tests.

To protect yourself, always assess the substance of any certification program before undertaking it. If you suspect it's an empty credential, look elsewhere. These types of programs give certification a bad name, and if you list one on your resume, it may well do the same to you.

Figure 7-1
Learning Tree's
Client/Server
Systems Certification
Web Page

Professional Certification

1-800-THE TREE   http://www.learningtree.com

Client/Server Systems
Certified Professional

PROGRAM DESCRIPTION

Client/server systems offer the benefits of reduced hardware and software costs, rapid application development, ease of use and open, flexible computing solutions. To fully realize these benefits, organizations need highly trained Client/Server Systems Professionals who can apply today's architectures, methodologies and tools.

Figure 7-2
Software Publisher's
Association CSM
Web Site

Manage Your Organization's Legal Use of Software

The Certified Software Manager (CSM) Seminar is offered in a six-hour training seminar format throughout the United States and Canada. The seminar fee ($395) includes the cost of instruction, the student manual and lunch. Those interested in obtaining the professional designation, CSM, must pass an exam. CSMs are entitled to up-to-the-minute news on software management issues, inclusion in the CSM networking directory and access to further educational events related to software asset management. The student manual is necessary to adequately prepare for the CSM certification exam, and the seminar is recommended.

Failing to Ascertain a Certification's Practical Applications

OUCH!

A key part of selecting a certification is to research its practical value. Without doing this homework, you won't know the real-world value of the program. What the certification sponsor says may indicate that you've found the perfect match between your goals and a certification program, but that's only one part of the picture. And it's an understandably biased part.

On paper, the certification may appear to provide the perfect entree to that new technology you've been coveting. The curriculum looks sound, and your experience might even get an exam or two waived. But what do people who've been through it report? Has it helped them achieve what they intended? Did it fall short of what was promised? How do potential employers react to the certification? Do employers shrug their shoulders and say "So what?" or nod approvingly?

The only way to answer these questions is to contact people who know something about the program and ask them. Potential sources include professionals who have earned the certification, career counselors, recruiters, and coworkers you trust. Seek them out online, through the certification sponsor, and/or through professional organizations you belong to. If your intention is to boost your position at your current place of employment, ask your boss what she thinks about it. Before committing to any certification program, gather as much independent information about it as you can. And continue until you're certain that the certification has practical value that is relevant to your expectations.

Unrealistic Expectations

OUCH!

Speaking of expectations, what are yours? Do you anticipate that a significant career boost will result from gaining the certification of your choice? Are you planning on earning more money? Incrementing your level of expertise? Moving into a new specialty? Switching to a different (and better) job? If so, you've got lots of company. Figure 7-3 shows the reasons candidates give for pursuing certification.

Figure 7-3
Why Candidates
Seek Certification

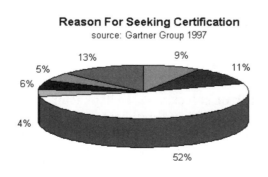

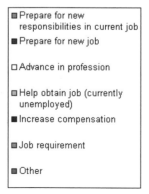

All of these goals are, indeed, possible outcomes of certification. However, it's important to remember that certification isn't a guaranteed cure-all for what ails your career. If your boss is a jerk, getting certified won't change him. It may, however, enable you to find employment elsewhere with a boss who has more positive attributes. Or it might serve as an impetus to go independent and become your own boss. (Of course, if the boss is still a jerk, than what are you going to do?)

Similarly, the skills you add in the course of earning a network management certification will improve your ability to keep a large network up and running, but won't transform it into a stress-free job. And that network management certification won't do a thing for your Visual Basic programming bill rate or get you a date. So to avoid unnecessary disappointment, identify and assess your expectations *first*. Then line them up against what a particular certification has to offer.

QUOTE

It's What You Know

I think some computer professionals believe that these certifications alone will guarantee employment and command a high salary, overlooking the fact that the individual lacks significant work experience. This may be because of the salary surveys that say a person with zero to two years experience with an MCSE, for example, can make $50,000. This is very attractive because that's without a four-year college degree. The Certified Novell Engineer certifications of past years showed that many people became certified engineers but lacked the basics of computer background and architecture, mainly hardware, and were unable to perform such basic tasks as component-level troubleshooting and repair. This has been a scar for computer certifications ever since.

Unfortunately, if you're sorely underqualified even though you're certified, that will probably come out in a painful interview with another engineer, or even worse, revealed on the job when you can't perform to expectations.

—Cameron Brandon, MCSE, CNE, CNA, A+ Certified, MCPS/Internet Systems

Underestimating Cost

OUCH!

There are so many variables to consider when estimating how much certification will cost that it's not surprising that the calculation is often done wrong. Sometimes, it isn't done at all.

Why is underestimating the cost of certification such a big deal? Consider these potential scenarios:

- You run out of funds before you're done. If you end up taking an extended break from your certification program, some of your qualifications may expire and you'll have to meet them again. At best, you'll have to spend time reviewing to get back up to speed once your budget gets back on track. At worst, you'll never pick it up again and your efforts will have been largely wasted.
- Based on ballpark figures you described, your employer agrees to pay for certification training and testing. You then submit a bill that's double what you initially suggested. How will that go over?
- You decide that a particular certification will more than pay for itself. But as the bills mount up, you realize you've grossly miscalculated the figure in question. What will you do if the certification isn't worth the cost at the "new" price, yet you've already committed significant time and resources?

As you can see, miscalculating the cost or failing to calculate it at all can be a big mistake. It's a mistake that happens because naming a figure isn't always a simple process. Part of the confusion arises because there are usually several different routes to achieving any particular certification. The largest variance comes under the heading of training expenses. Whether you self-study from manuals or attend instructor-led, sponsor-approved training can make thousands of dollars of difference in your total tab.

Then there's the somewhat nebulous question of opportunity cost. To some people, an estimate that doesn't include it is meaningless. Others consider adding opportunity cost an inaccurate inflation of price. Either way, coming up with a reasonable figure for it requires a little math.

Given the potential consequences of underestimating the price tag of a certification program, it's worthwhile to work out a few figures. The worksheet in Chapter 5 will walk you through the steps, and you can even plug the numbers into the Microsoft Excel spreadsheet included on this book's companion Web site and let your personal computer do the calculating for you. When in doubt, guess a little high. Having extra money left over is a problem you can live with.

Mistakes While Working Toward Certification

When you're undertaking something new and exciting like professional certification, it can be tempting to rush ahead at full speed. After all, you want to see results as soon as possible, don't you? But haste has its costs. People in a hurry tend to make assumptions to save time. Although these assumptions may seem reasonable at the time, they sometimes turn out to be wrong and end up disrupting your plans.

The following mistakes often result from eagerness and the desire to get on with the task as much as anything else. Although these errors have less dire consequences than choosing the wrong certification, they can still cost you time, money, and frustration. Happily, forewarned is forearmed. Once you read about the pitfalls that other professionals have encountered, you can easily dodge them.

Purchasing a Complete Certification Package Right Away

OUCH!

When you're offered a significant discount to purchase a package deal, it's tempting to leap at it. You'll get all your arrangements taken care of with one vendor and grab a discount besides. But—and this is a big but—it's a good idea to hold off making such a major investment until after you pass your first exam, at the earliest. Only then can you be fairly confident that the certification you've chosen is one you can work with. There's always a chance that you'll discover you've bitten off more than you care to chew or have a sudden change of heart over the direction you want to pursue.

If you buy a package up front, there's another risk: if this is your first foray into certification, how can you know which learning alternatives will become your favorites? What if you invest in a series of computer-based, self-preparation programs only to discover that you can't bear to sit down and face your PC each evening after doing the same all day at work? If it's instructor-led training that you've purchased in bulk and you discover that you don't need such a degree of support and instruction, you'll be faced with thousands of dollars of training you don't need but have already contracted for—a truly costly mistake.

It's fairly simple to protect yourself from this particular pitfall. Start with one test and one preparation package. In fact, it's not a bad idea to see how you feel working strictly from free study guides and product manuals. Then if you want to escalate to third-party preparation materials, such as workbooks, computer-based training,

Web-based instruction, or a classroom staffed by a living, breathing technical trainer, you can easily do so. And if you discover that the resources that are free will serve your purposes adequately, you won't have expended a single extra penny.

Assuming Your Employer Will Pay for Your Training

OUCH!

This is a big oops and a totally avoidable one. It happens when people recall that educational incentives were mentioned somewhere in the slew of paperwork they received as part of new employee orientation, but don't spend the time to pin down the details. Perhaps you don't just think so, you *know* that the company pays for continuing education, making it unnecessary to research further.

The problem is, even if your employer does, as a rule, pay for continuing education, the definition of just what this encompasses may be limited. Some companies only reimburse for courses completed as part of a degree program. Others further require that the degree be related to your job functions.

It also occurs when a coworker mentions, in passing, that the company paid for his certification training. But perhaps he neglected to mention that it was through a special arrangement or that a dollar limit was imposed. Or maybe he really meant that the company paid his certification test fees, but you missed that clarification.

The bottom line is that what another employee got isn't necessarily something that you will receive, too, and vice versa. It's important to check into employer funding/reimbursement before you begin. If the purse strings do open, which they often will, you'll still need to be aware of which paperwork needs to be submitted when, time limits, restrictions, and so on. Before you can comply with any guidelines, you need to know about them. To know about them, all you need to do is ask.

Assuming Your Employer Won't Pay for Your Training

OUCH!

Just because it isn't in the employee handbook doesn't mean your employer can't be persuaded to share the expense of your continuing education with you. Chapter 5 offers advice on how to bring this about. Why spend your own money on professional training if someone else is perfectly willing to foot the bill for you?

Failing to Shop Around

Don't you hate it when you buy something at what you think is a good price only to see it advertised a week later somewhere else for a third less? It happens all the time with consumer purchases, and it can happen with training purchases, too.

You might not be willing to expend much effort to save three dollars on a pair of shoes, but when it comes to training packages, your potential savings are much higher. For a time investment of an hour or less, you may save $50, $100, or even $1,000. In addition to financial dividends, when you give yourself more training options to choose from, it's more likely you'll find one that closely matches your learning preferences and style.

Why, then, do so many people neglect to shop for certification training? Often because they:

- Aren't aware that drastic price differences exist
- Don't know where to look
- Are unsure of how to compare vendors and products

Because each of these items is addressed in this book, you can easily overcome these obstacles. Chapter 9 explores the wide selection of learning alternatives from which you can choose. Chapter 10 explains how to find certification preparation training and tools through the Internet, telephone book, and certification sponsors. It also describes what to look for in a training center and how to assess the quality of an instructor.

If you were in the market for a new television or lawn mower, you wouldn't purchase the first one you came across. Give your selection of certification training at least as much attention and, preferably, more. Pay attention to the features each option has to offer, and weigh benefits against cost. Because prices vary widely between vendors, your dollar savings alone will make it worth your while. Unless, of course, money is no object.

Ignoring or Missing Time Constraints

Both vendor-sponsored and vendor-neutral certifications often limit how long you have to complete their requirements. Miss one and you'll have to repeat it, which may well include retaking an exam (and paying for it again). You might also end up paying a second registration/application fee.

There are two types of limits you're likely to encounter. The first specifies how long you have to complete all requirements for the certification and begins when you enroll in the program. The second common limit applies to certifications that include a laboratory exam. The lab is usually the final requirement you'll complete. The limit specifies how long you have, after finishing the other requirements, to attend the lab session. It's more likely that you'll have to travel for a lab exam than for a written exam, which is one reason it's easy to put off.

Although time allowances are typically generous, it's important to keep an eye on them so you don't inadvertently slip behind. When you begin your program, inquire up front if there are any time limits specifying how long you have to complete the entire program or any element of it.

Failing to Get Certified After Your Employer Agrees to Pay

OUCH!

Once you've announced your intentions, failure to deliver isn't going to reflect well on you. This is especially true if you've approached your supervisor or boss and secured a promise of financial reimbursement. Fortunately, changing one's mind after starting a certification program is a rare occurrence.

Your goal in pursuing certification is to use it as a tool to further your career. It would be ironic if you ended up damaging your image instead. If you find yourself faced with completing a certification that you've changed your mind about—one that your employer already approved—consider completing it anyway to avoid risking a reputation as someone who doesn't follow through. Alternatively, you may be able to transfer some or all of your completed efforts toward another program. If so, be prepared to explain how the new one is even better.

The best course of action for this potential mistake is prevention. Develop a solid feel for the program before you enter it, including how much time you'll have to put in and what benefits you hope to achieve. If you've done your homework in advance, it's unlikely that you'll find yourself participating in a program you don't like and highly probable you'll land yourself in one that you do.

Neglecting Your Job to Study for Certification

OUCH!

Even if your employer has agreed to let you study during regular working hours, it's important not to allow your normal duties to go unattended. This can be a difficult balancing act, especially if you have a demanding schedule. But it can be done.

Keep in mind that there's nothing like hands-on, on-the-job training for learning how to perform specific tasks. Try to apply the technology you're getting certified on to your duties at work. If you don't have access to the technologies in question but a coworker does, take him to lunch and explain your situation. Ask if you can shadow him during your lunch hour or at other times. Once you've learned how a particular task is done, try to get a chance to do it yourself.

When taking this approach, it's important to recognize that the person you're learning from may feel threatened. If you're after his job, this plan is a bad idea. But more likely you're not, in which case it's a good idea to clearly explain what you are after to reassure him. Try offering something in return, perhaps sharing skills you have with him.

But even if you get plenty of hands-on practice, you're going to have to hit the books to pass exams. Even in the busiest schedule there's room for study time. You just have to find it. The time management guidelines in Chapter 11 can help you with that. Another trick to keep study time from encroaching on work time is to study less. Learning efficient and effective study habits will drastically reduce the amount of time you'll need to prepare. Chapter 11 can help you on that front, as well.

The key to keeping your certification plans from interfering with your current job duties is to pay attention. In your eagerness to get certified, you may devote more time to preparation than you realize. Setting up a schedule will help you keep study and work hours in the proportion you want them. With the world being the unpredictable place that it is, you can expect to find your schedule disrupted at one time or another. When it happens simply get back on track as soon as you can.

Throughout the process, keep your goals in sharp focus. The purpose of certification is to enhance your career. If you irritate your employer in the process, getting ahead is going to be that much harder. But if you manage to juggle work and study effectively, you'll create the impression of a capable professional who takes initiative and follows through.

Assuming You Don't Need to Study

OUCH!

Obtaining certification requires two forms of competency: knowing what to do and being able to prove that you do. These are really two separate skills. The first concerns the extent of your experience and understanding. The second reflects your ability to perform well on a test. A shortfall in either area will hinder your success.

People who make the mistake of assuming they don't need to study are likely to be individuals who are masterful in handling the technology in question, as demonstrated by their performance at their current job. Consider a LAN administrator pursuing a network certification. As the person who manages a company LAN day in and day out, this individual probably has an excellent grasp of the skills required to keep the LAN operating smoothly.

But what would happen if this administrator arrived at work one morning to find a LAN with twice as many nodes, a modem pool, a dedicated link to the Internet, and running an application that led to twice as much traffic load as she was used to? She probably would feel a lot less expert.

Although this LAN administrator's network would not change as dramatically overnight, she could easily face this scenario on a certification exam. And she wouldn't be familiar with it. Don't assume that a certification test you'll be taking will be limited to the environment you're an expert on. In fact, expect it *not* to be.

The second component of successful certification is the ability to recall information in a test setting. You'll need to respond in theory instead of in practice. A situation that you may handle easily when you've got your LAN at your fingertips can suddenly seem foreign when it's presented as words on an exam. Spend time studying, and the written version will become second nature, too.

Assuming You Know the Best Way to Study

OUCH!

Chances are, it's been a while since you were in school. And it's also likely you've received little instruction about how to study. Studying doesn't consist of simply opening a book or manual and reading it through, perhaps several times. It's a lot more than that and it's a lot less.

Effective study techniques enable you to learn new information and recall it as needed. Certainly, reading skills are critically important. You already know how to read, but do you know how to read to learn? A skilled learner knows the tricks that make it possible to read faster and remember more. And test preparation doesn't have to be a torture session if you approach it in an organized fashion.

Even if you do know how to study effectively, you'd probably benefit from brushing up on your skills. Doing so is as easy as reading Chapter 11.

Failure to Set Deadlines for Yourself

OUCH!

You've no doubt heard the saying, "the squeaky wheel gets the grease." If you have multiple priorities competing for your time, you may well find yourself playing the role of grease monkey and running from project to project, applying the lubrication that will keep things going. Meanwhile, projects that aren't in crisis go untended until they begin to squeak, too, or are completely forgotten. Certification preparation is rarely one of the squeaky wheels. Because of that, it often falls low on the scale of daily priorities. Unless you take action to keep this from happening, your certification plans will languish and your goals will go unmet.

The best way to avoid the pitfall of inaction is to create deadlines for yourself. This should occur as part of the process of creating your personal certification plan. Each requirement should have a deadline date. If the requirement is that you pass a test, go ahead and schedule the test. As each deadline approaches, the urgency of finding time to train and prepare will grow until, like the proverbial squeaky wheel, it demands your attention. Tending to these artificially induced squeaks will keep your "certification wheel" turning.

A second challenge to your progress is the big P: *procrastination*. If you're a person who doesn't get things done until the last minute, deadlines will generate time pressure to keep you on track.

Mistakes After Certification is Achieved

Once you've completed all of the requirements for a certification, it may be tempting to sit back and enjoy your accomplishment. But if you do that, you won't be taking full advantage of your new status. That would be like buying a new sports car and leaving it in the garage most of the time. To get the most benefit from certification, you need to use it at every opportunity and maintain it in tip-top condition. Correspondingly, the mistakes that occur after certification is achieved are largely due to inaction or inattention. Consider the following:

Forgetting About Continuing Requirements

OUCH!

Many certification programs specify that to retain certification over time, you'll have to submit evidence of continued professional development. This is to encourage you to keep up with technological changes, and it's to your advantage to do so. Certification programs with this requirement tend to have greater staying power than those without it.

Don't count on the sponsor to remind you when updates are due. It's up to you to track how often professional development activities are required and to fill those requirements. The definition of what type of training qualifies will be spelled out by the vendor. Generally, you'll have a broad selection of options to choose from, although a few programs may have very specific requirements. Record professional development deadlines on your calendar, allowing plenty of time to complete them. Once you've attended a qualifying class or seminar, immediately collect and submit the necessary information to your certification sponsor. Figure 7-4 shows ICCP's professional development submission form.

Even though you may pay an "administrative fee" as part of obtaining certification, the only person responsible for keeping your status current is you. Failure to do so may cause your certification to expire, and that would be a needless mistake.

Failing to Take Advantage of Perks and Privileges

OUCH!

Some of the benefits of certification will accrue to you even if you do nothing else once you have your certification in hand. Free subscriptions and early product news, for example, will arrive in your mailbox whether or not you request them. But other perks and privileges are provided to you on an as-needed basis. To benefit from them, you have to access them. What if someone offered you free valuable services such as:

- Priority technical support
- Early product updates
- Software discounts
- Access to special forums
- Marketing tools and assistance, including customer referral programs

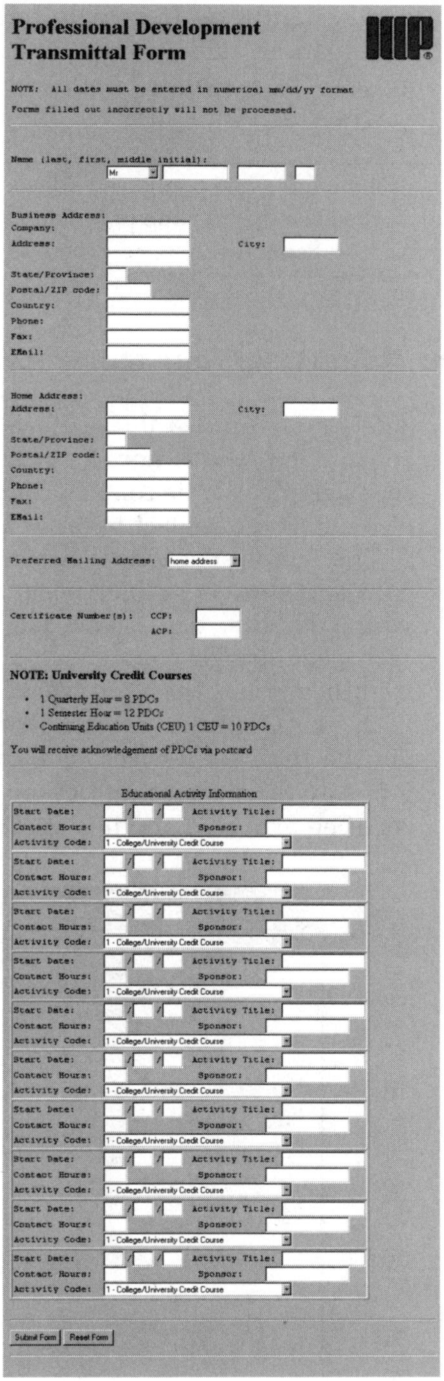

Figure 7-4
ICCP's Online
Professional
Development
Submission Form

Professional Development Transmittal Form

NOTE: All dates must be entered in numerical mm/dd/yy format

Forms filled out incorrectly will not be processed.

Name (last, first, middle initial):

Business Address:
Company:
Address: City:
State/Province:
Postal/ZIP code:
Country:
Phone:
Fax:
EMail:

Home Address:
Address: City:
State/Province:
Postal/ZIP code:
Country:
Phone:
Fax:
EMail:

Preferred Mailing Address: home address

Certificate Number(s):   CCP:
                         ACP:

NOTE: University Credit Courses

- 1 Quarterly Hour = 8 PDCs
- 1 Semester Hour = 12 PDCs
- Continuing Education Units (CEU) 1 CEU = 10 PDCs

You will receive acknowledgement of PDCs via postcard

Educational Activity Information

Start Date: / /	Activity Title:
Contact Hours:	Sponsor:
Activity Code: 1 - College/University Credit Course	
Start Date: / /	Activity Title:
Contact Hours:	Sponsor:
Activity Code: 1 - College/University Credit Course	
Start Date: / /	Activity Title:
Contact Hours:	Sponsor:
Activity Code: 1 - College/University Credit Course	
Start Date: / /	Activity Title:
Contact Hours:	Sponsor:
Activity Code: 1 - College/University Credit Course	
Start Date: / /	Activity Title:
Contact Hours:	Sponsor:
Activity Code: 1 - College/University Credit Course	
Start Date: / /	Activity Title:
Contact Hours:	Sponsor:
Activity Code: 1 - College/University Credit Course	
Start Date: / /	Activity Title:
Contact Hours:	Sponsor:
Activity Code: 1 - College/University Credit Course	
Start Date: / /	Activity Title:
Contact Hours:	Sponsor:
Activity Code: 1 - College/University Credit Course	
Start Date: / /	Activity Title:
Contact Hours:	Sponsor:
Activity Code: 1 - College/University Credit Course	
Start Date: / /	Activity Title:
Contact Hours:	Sponsor:
Activity Code: 1 - College/University Credit Course	

Submit Form   Reset Form

Wouldn't it be an incredible waste to ignore them? But that's exactly the mistake some people make. Perks such as these are regularly granted to successful certification candidates. These tools can help you increase your success. Use them.

Over time, the benefits and continuing education requirements associated with a certification may change. To keep up on the latest developments, make regular visits to your certification sponsor's Web site.

Failing to Advertise Your New Status

The first thing to do with your certification is to add it to your resume, but that's not the only way you can promote your new status. Certification is a marketing tool that can be applied in a variety of ways. Don't neglect to put it to work for you.

The simplest methods are as basic as redesigning your business card and stationery, incorporating the certification logo. Include it on your Web site, too. If you don't have a Web site, create one. Basic Web page design tools are available for all levels of site developers, from beginners through expert, and at affordable prices, too. Some, such as AOLpress (**www.aolpress.com/press/**) can be downloaded via the Internet for free. The AOLpress Web site is shown in Figure 7-5. Advice on these and other methods for marketing yourself as a certified expert is provided in Chapter 12.

Figure 7-5
AOLpress Web Site

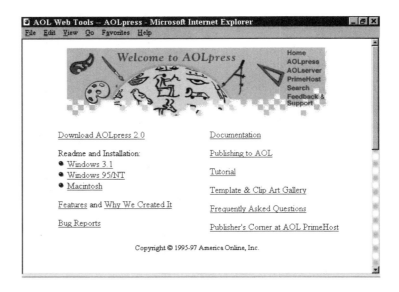

Completing the requirements for certification is 90% of the job, but the remaining 10% is important, too. With a little effort, you can use certification as a launching pad to develop a reputation as an expert on the related technology or simply to add to your credibility. You can bet that your competitors will be doing just that.

QUOTE

It's the Process

The biggest mistake (in my opinion) is to think of the certification process as just one of gaining enough knowledge that you can pass one or more tests. The value of the certification process is in the process itself—that is, in the studying you do, the exploration of new concepts, the experimentation.

The next biggest mistake is to think you can stop learning once you get the certification. I've always viewed the completion of my certification requirements as a beginning rather than an end of the learning process, somewhat as one might view graduation from college.

Finally, your pay is going to depend on what you bring to the table apart from just the specific technical knowledge that enabled you to get a vendor's certification. Technical degrees, advanced degrees, and years of solid experience all make you more desirable as an employee. A well-groomed appearance, good writing skills, and presentation/communication skills are necessary for the highest-paying jobs.

—Pamela Forsyth, CCSI, ECNE, MCSE, and other certifications

Plan, Perform, and Follow Through

If there's one key to successful use of certification as a career booster, it's attention. You control each stage, starting with how carefully you develop your personal certification plan, continuing through how closely you follow it, and culminating in application of certification as a marketing tool.

Certainly there are mistakes that can occur along the way, but most are minor. If you make one, back up, recover, and get back on track as soon as you can. Better yet, learn from the mistakes others have made so you can avoid them yourself.

CHAPTER 8

Which Certification is Best for You?

When determining which certification will do the most for you, you could choose the most widely known, one that's related to the hottest skill on the market, or the program you received promotional materials for in yesterday's mail. But all of these are risky methods that may leave you less than satisfied with the results. That's because certification achieves its greatest value when linked with individual experience and career goals.

No certification is going to boost your career to new heights if it doesn't fit with what you've already done and what you hope to accomplish. It doesn't matter if the person in the next cubicle can't stop talking about a particular certification she just obtained—that same program may be a dismal disappointment for you. Or it could prove to be the perfect choice.

You could just go for it and hope for the best, but if you like to gamble, you might be better off purchasing lottery tickets. You could buy a whole lot of them with the amount of money certification will cost you. However, the certification marketplace is nothing like the lottery. You can analyze the lottery for days and be no closer to picking the jackpot numbers, but if you put that same analysis into choosing a certification, you're almost guaranteed to come out a winner.

The following six steps will help guide you through the process of selecting a certification that will serve you well. You may want to come back to this section again if at some point in the future you decide to add more credentials to your collection. The steps are:

1. Identify your employment goals.
2. Assess your current employment situation.
3. Consider the amount of resources you're willing and able to expend on certification.
4. Make a preliminary list and contact the certification sponsors for details.
5. Research the real-world potential of the certification.
6. Evaluate the results of your research and select your certification.

Let's explore each of these steps in detail. A series of three worksheets will assist you along the way; to help illuminate the possibilities, we'll follow a fictional software engineer named Bob as he works through this process.

Identify Your Employment Goals

The first step is to carefully consider what kind of work life you would like to have. This goal identification section assumes that the computer profession is where you want to be. If you suspect this isn't the case, consider a visit to a career counselor, who can help you through a more extensive career evaluation.

Assuming you've decided that, at least for now, computers are your thing, let's continue. It's important to note that the question to ask yourself first *isn't*: "What do I want to get out of certification?" That question will come up shortly, but before you're ready to address it, you need to look at the bigger picture. The first question to ask yourself is: "Where do I want to go in my career?"

Don't be intimidated by the potential scope of the question. Coming up with a reasonable assessment isn't going to be as hard as you think. Besides, this is something that you should do whether or not certification is on your mind. Successful careers rarely just happen. They're planned.

It may help to think of career development planning the way you would structured software development, because the method is basically the same: input, process, output. It's amazing how many aspects of the world this same procedure can be applied to. Shuffling this paradigm around to more accurately reflect the software developer's perspective results in a different ordering: output, input, process. This is the approach used here.

We already know what your desired output is: the answer to the question "Where do I want to go in my career?" With that taken care of, we can move right on to your input. For our purposes, your input is the database of dreams, ambitions, personal preferences, lifestyle preferences, and so on that you carry inside yourself.

Now, for the process of turning these inputs into that output. This, of course, is the tricky part. Fortunately, this program is already written and all you have to do is execute the instructions. It's important to remember along the way that:

- You're not a computer. Don't expect to be able to answer every issue with a clear yes or no.
- The plan you're developing won't be set in stone. You aren't required to adhere to it for life. You can change it (and likely will) at some point down the line.

With these considerations in mind, you're ready to begin the process of defining your goals. First, study Table 8-1. It includes ten key areas that play a role in career satisfaction, along with a brief explanation of each. The factors are listed in alphabetical order.

Next, complete Worksheet 1 (Figure 8-1) to get a feel for how important each factor is to you. Read each statement and mark an X under the column heading that completes the sentence in the way that most accurately reflects your definition of optimum employment. Take your time, be completely honest, and put as much thought as necessary into your answers. You might even want to discuss some of the items with someone you trust. Figure 8-2 shows how Bob, our fictional software engineer, filled in his Worksheet 1.

Factor	Description
Compensation	The amount of salary and benefits you find satisfactory
Effect on personal life	How much your work comes home with you
Growth	The chance to learn new skills and advance within an organization or profession
Nature of tasks	Whether tasks are cutting edge, routine, repetitive, or full of variety
Recognition	How important it is for you to obtain visibility and recognition
Responsibility	How much control, authority, and accountability you like
Security	How much you can depend on keeping the same job
Status	Admiration of your skill level, profession, and accomplishments
Travel	Trips away from the office
Work hours	Quantity and flexibility of time spent working

Once you've worked through the items in your worksheet, you should have a better sense of which elements of job satisfaction matter most to you. Your ideal work would contain all of the highest ranking features and would avoid those you've identified as undesirable. In Bob's case, that means that his ideal work would include a high level of responsibility and come with company benefits. It would exclude overtime, extensive business travel, and on-call duties. He doesn't feel strongly about occasional travel, working with the latest technologies, performing consistent tasks, being in a visible position, having a well-regarded title or credentials, or working a full forty hours a week. The other characteristics, including earning a high salary and job security, are somewhat important to him.

Take a few moments now to review your own answers. Pay greatest attention to the first and last rating columns (the ones labeled **Undesirable** and **Very Important**). They indicate which elements you feel most strongly about.

Figure 8-1
Deciding What's
Important

Career Self-assessment Worksheet 1
What Matters To Me

Instructions: For each item, place an X under the column heading that best completes the sentence.

	Undesirable	Not Important	Somewhat Important	Very Important
1. COMPENSATION				
Earning a high salary is:				
2. EFFECT ON PERSONAL LIFE				
Bringing work home on a regular basis is:				
Being on call is:				
Being able to take time off for personal/family needs is:				
Business travel is:				
Company supplied benefits are:				
3. GROWTH OPPORTUNITIES				
Adding new skills is:				
Advancing within the organizational structure is:				
4. NATURE OF TASKS				
Working with the latest technologies is:				
Variety of tasks is:				
Consistency of tasks is:				
5. RECOGNITION				
Visibility of my work is:				
Acknowledgment of my work is:				
6. RESPONSIBILITY				
Mentoring others is:				
Having a leadership role is:				
Being accountable for important functions is:				
7. SECURITY				
Keeping the same position for a long time is:				
8. STATUS				
Having a highly regarded title/credentials is:				
9. TRAVEL				
Frequent business trips are:				
Extended business travel is:				
10. WORK HOURS				
Maintaining a consistent schedule is:				
Flexibility of daily work hours is:				
Working more than 40 hours a week is:				
Working less than 40 hours a week is:				

Figure 8-2
Bob's Self-
Assessment

Career Self-assessment Worksheet 1
What Matters To Me

Instructions: For each item, place an X under the column heading that best completes the sentence.

	Undesirable	Not Important	Somewhat Important	Very Important
1. COMPENSATION				
Earning a high salary is:			X	
2. EFFECT ON PERSONAL LIFE				
Bringing work home on a regular basis is:	X			
Being on call is:	X			
Being able to take time off for personal/family needs is:			X	
Business travel is:		X		
Company supplied benefits are:				X
3. GROWTH OPPORTUNITIES				
Adding new skills is:			X	
Advancing within the organizational structure is:			X	
4. NATURE OF TASKS				
Working with the latest technologies is:		X		
Variety of tasks is:			X	
Consistency of tasks is:		X		
5. RECOGNITION				
Visibility of my work is:		X		
Acknowledgment of my work is:			X	
6. RESPONSIBILITY				
Mentoring others is:			X	
Having a leadership role is:			X	
Being accountable for important functions is:				X
7. SECURITY				
Keeping the same position for a long time is:			X	
8. STATUS				
Having a highly regarded title/credentials is:		X		
9. TRAVEL				
Frequent business trips are:		X		
Extended business travel is:	X			
10. WORK HOURS				
Maintaining a consistent schedule is:			X	
Flexibility of daily work hours is:			X	
Working more than 40 hours a week is:	X			
Working less than 40 hours a week is:		X		

Your completed Worksheet 1 is a blueprint describing the characteristics of the work you'd like to do. Just as planned you've put your input (opinions and aspirations) through a process (ranking individual career satisfaction characteristics) and produced your output; a spec sheet describing your ideal employment. Your goal is to obtain that ideal, or, barring that, to come as close as possible.

Assess Your Current Employment Situation

Once you've developed an understanding of the characteristics of your ideal work, the next step is to examine your current job situation using the same criteria. Once you've done so, you'll be able to pinpoint differences between aspects of your current position and the position you'd like to have. These two steps are embodied in two additional worksheets.

Worksheet 2 (Figure 8-3) is provided to help you assess the employment satisfaction factors of your current work. To complete it, read each sentence and decide whether it describes your current position. Indicate your answer by marking an X under the appropriate column heading. Choose *Yes* if the statement is definitely true or *No* if it's untrue. If the statement is somewhat true or occasionally true, but you feel you can't answer with an unqualified *Yes* or *No*, then place your X in the *Sometimes* column. When you're finished, your worksheet will serve as a summary of the characteristics of your current job. You may be pleasantly surprised by how many positive things it has going for it. Bob's completed Worksheet 2 is displayed in Figure 8-4.

To finish assessing your current employment situation, you'll combine the results you came up with in Worksheets 1 and 2. By doing this, you'll pinpoint gaps between your current employment situation and your goal situation. Worksheet 3 (Figure 8-5) will facilitate this process.

To begin, place Worksheets 1 and 3 side by side. On Worksheet 1, run your finger down the column titled **Very Important** until you encounter the first X. Follow the row across and note which statement the X corresponds with. Write the entire statement, along with your answer, onto a line of Worksheet 3. Repeat this for each X in the **Very Important** column. Then do the same thing for each X recorded in the column titled **Undesirable**.

Figure 8-3
Current Employment
Satisfaction
Worksheet

Career·Self-assessment·Worksheet·2
Current·Employment·Satisfaction

Instructions:·Read·each·sentence·and·place·an·X·in·under·the·column·
heading·that·best·describes·your·current·employment·situation.

	Yes	No	Some-times
1.·COMPENSATION			
I·earn·a·high·salary.			
2.·EFFECT·ON·PERSONAL·LIFE			
I·bring·work·home·on·a·regular·basis.			
I·have·on·call·duties.			
I'm·able·to·take·time·off·for·personal/family·needs.			
I·take·business·trips.			
I·receive·company·supplied·benefits.			
3.·GROWTH·OPPORTUNITIES			
I·regularly·learn·new·skills.			
I·have·opportunities·to·advance.			
4.·NATURE·OF·TASKS			
I·work·with·the·latest·technologies.			
I·have·enough·variety.			
I·have·consistent·tasks·to·perform.			
5.·RECOGNITION			
My·work·is·visible.			
My·accomplishments·are·acknowledged.			
6.·RESPONSIBILITY			
I·mentor·others.			
I·have·a·leadership·role.			
I'm·accountable·for·important·functions.			
7.·SECURITY			
I'll·be·able·to·keep·my·job·as·long·as·I·want·it.			
8.·STATUS			
I·have·highly·regarded·titles/credentials.			
9.·TRAVEL			
I·take·frequent·business·trips.			
I·take·extended·business·trips.			
10.·WORK·HOURS			
I·maintain·a·consistent·schedule.			
My·work·hours·are·flexible.			
I·work·more·than·40·hours·a·week.			
I·work·less·than·40·hours·a·week.			

The **Very Important** and **Undesirable** columns are considered first because they include the items you've indicated matter most to you. In the unlikely event that you have only a few career satisfaction factors that fall under these two headings, you can also transfer the Worksheet 1 items that you rated as **Somewhat Important**.

When you're finished transferring the statements, put Worksheet 1 aside and put Worksheet 2 in its place. For each statement that you recorded on Worksheet 3, locate the corresponding statement on Worksheet 2 (the statements are in the same order). Compare the two. If they both reflect the same sentiment, circle the thumbs-up icon beside the statement on Worksheet 3. If they conflict, circle the thumbs-down icon. Your completed Worksheet 3 will list your most important job satisfaction characteristics and identify the ones that are targets for improvement.

Figure 8-4
Bob's Satisfaction
Worksheet

Career·Self-assessment·Worksheet·2
Current·Employment·Satisfaction

Instructions:·Read·each·sentence·and·place·an·X·in·under·the·column·
heading·that·best·describes·your·current·employment·situation.

	Yes	No	Some-times
1.·COMPENSATION			
I·earn·a·high·salary.		X	
2.·EFFECT·ON·PERSONAL·LIFE			
I·bring·work·home·on·a·regular·basis.			X
I·have·on·call·duties.		X	
I'm·able·to·take·time·off·for·personal/family·needs.	X		
I·take·business·trips.	X		
I·receive·company·supplied·benefits.	X		
3.·GROWTH·OPPORTUNITIES			
I·regularly·learn·new·skills.			X
I·have·opportunities·to·advance.	X		
4.·NATURE·OF·TASKS			
I·work·with·the·latest·technologies.		X	
I·have·enough·variety.	X		
I·have·consistent·tasks·to·perform.	X		
5.·RECOGNITION			
My·work·is·visible.			X
My·accomplishments·are·acknowledged.			X
6.·RESPONSIBILITY			
I·mentor·others.		X	
I·have·a·leadership·role.		X	
I'm·accountable·for·important·functions.		X	
7.·SECURITY			
I'll·be·able·to·keep·my·job·as·long·as·I·want·it.	X		
8.·STATUS			
I·have·highly·regarded·titles/credentials.		X	
9.·TRAVEL			
I·take·frequent·business·trips.		X	
I·take·extended·business·trips.		X	·
10.·WORK·HOURS			
I·maintain·a·consistent·schedule.	X		
My·work·hours·are·flexible.			X
I·work·more·than·40·hours·a·week.			X
I·work·less·than·40·hours·a·week.		X	

Figure 8-6 shows Bob's completed Worksheet 3. A review of it reveals six statements that were transferred from Worksheet 1 because they ranked as either **Very Important** or **Undesirable**. Only three of them aren't met by his current job. If the number was any fewer, Bob might want to add the factors he identified as **Somewhat Important** to his Worksheet 3 to give himself a bigger selection of goals to aim for.

Once you've identified your prime areas for improvement, it's time to look at them to determine which ones certification can help you achieve. Although certification is not a panacea for career shortcomings, it can serve as a powerful tool for change. As you've learned it can help you increase your level of expertise, add to your professional qualifications, and serve as a path into a new area of specialty.

Certification can perform many additional functions that are more subtle and less direct. They result from how you apply your certification rather than from the professional designation itself. Although it won't directly affect your company benefits or convince your boss that overtime is no longer necessary, it *can* do so indirectly. If you choose, you can use the power of a respected certification to open the door to new job opportunities or to positions with more reasonable hours or better benefits. If you're working long hours because of how much needs to be done rather than because of company expectations, then pursuing the right certification may lead you to the skills that will enable you to work more efficiently at your current job, thereby requiring fewer hours to complete your tasks.

Figure 8-5
Worksheet 3

Career·Self-assessment·Worksheet·3
Determining·What's·Missing

Instructions: For each row of Worksheet 1 that contains an X in its Very Important or Undesirable column, copy the entire statement, along with your answer, onto a line below. Then compare each statement listed with its corresponding statement on Worksheet 2. If they both reflect the same sentiment, circle the adjacent thumbs up icon. If they conflict, circle the thumbs down icon.

Figure 8-6
How Bob Completed
Worksheet 3

Career Self-assessment Worksheet 3
Determining What's Missing

Instructions: For each row of Worksheet 1 that contains an X in its Very Important or Undesirable column, copy the entire statement, along with your answer, onto a line below. Then compare each statement listed with its corresponding statement on Worksheet 2. If they both reflect the same sentiment, circle the adjacent thumbs-up icon. If they conflict, circle the thumbs-down icon.

Company-supplied benefits are very important.

Being accountable for important functions is very important.

Bringing home work on a regular basis is undesirable.

Being on call is undesirable.

Extended business travel is undesirable.

Working more than 40 hours a week is undesirable.

With this versatility in mind, it's time to review the list of target areas you identified on Worksheet 3. Study each thumbs-down item on the worksheet. Ask yourself the following questions:

- Would increasing my skills and qualifications in one or more of the technologies I currently use have a positive impact on this item?
- Would expanding my knowledge to encompass a new area of technical expertise help me gain ground on this issue?
- Is this something I think is possible to improve at my current work?
- Would it require obtaining a new job, possibly even in a new specialty, to improve this, and if so, am I willing to do that?

Answering *yes* to any of the above questions means that professional certification is a reasonable approach for addressing the factor under consideration.

When Bob, our fictional software engineer, analyzes his target areas, he sees several ways certification can work for him. His current position features some of the factors that are important to him, and he feels that further improvement is possible without changing employment. Noting his desire to be accountable for important functions, he theorizes that it can reasonably be addressed by working his way up the organizational hierarchy. Bob decides that increasing his skill level above that of his coworkers will boost him in the right direction.

Next, Bob realizes that his other two target statements are related. Basically, they show that his work is overflowing the work week. If he can learn to do his job more efficiently, he can perhaps reduce the total hours he puts in.

Determine Your Available Resources

After you've identified the goals you want to achieve using certification and before you set your heart on a particular designation, it's a good idea to determine what you're willing to commit to in order to obtain certification. The three resources to consider are time, money, and effort. How much of each you're willing to invest will have a big impact on your choice of certifications. If you have a plentiful supply of all three resources, then you can skip this section. Otherwise, it pays to give the issue some thought. Some programs require substantial amounts of all three resources; others can be obtained with significantly less commitment.

Time

Achieving certification takes time: time to study, time to sit for exams, and time to attend classes. Think about how much of this increasingly precious resource you have available. Will you be able to study on your lunch hour? Is your boss likely to give you time off to sit for exams or will you have to schedule them on evenings and weekends? How much are you willing to cut back on your social/personal life while you focus on professional advancement? Remember to consider the needs of your family members as well.

Money

Certification costs run from a few hundred dollars to well into five figures. How much money do you have available, and how much of it are you willing to part with? Your total cost will depend on the certification and the training methods employed. You might want to review Chapter 5, which explains how to calculate the price tag of a particular certification and explores the costs of various training methods.

When considering the amount of money you're willing and able to spend on certification, don't make the mistake of looking at cash outlay alone. Certification is an investment in your career. The price of an investment only becomes meaningful when you look at it *in relation to expected benefits*. Consider a cost of $10,000; that's a lot of money. But what if it enables you to earn an extra $50,000 over the next five years, changes your work from draining to fulfilling, or pays off in other ways important to you? It may suddenly become a much more reasonable figure.

Effort

Think of effort as directed energy. How much of your energy are you willing and able to focus on obtaining certification? Are you the type of person who easily immerses himself for extended periods? Do you enjoy the processes of learning and studying, or are they low on your list of preferred activities? Drawing on your past experiences and personality, try to determine if pursuing certification is likely be a pleasure or a task. If it will be a task, how are you at buckling down and sticking with such things? Do you think you'll be willing to keep at it for six months? A year? Or only a week?

In Bob's case, he decided that time is his biggest issue, especially while work keeps overflowing the forty hours he'd like to limit it to, because he has a wife and young children with whom he likes to spend time. Because Bob's salary is already pretty respectable, money won't be much of a problem. As for effort, although Bob doesn't think of educational pursuits as especially enjoyable, he's never had much trouble following through once he's made a commitment.

Make a Preliminary List

If you've followed along this far, you're more than halfway to selecting a certification that will work for you. You've identified your goals, determined which ones certification can help you obtain, and considered the quantity and types of resources you're willing to commit.

The time you've already invested will pay off as it enables you to make a wise choice from among the many available certifications. Just which certifications should you consider? No doubt a number of possibilities have started circulating through your mind. Now it's time to take everything you've learned up to this point and use it to create a list of certifications that make the first cut.

To create your list, you're going to browse through the certifications detailed in Resource A (and also included on the companion Web site) of this book. Scan every entry at least briefly so you don't miss any possibilities. First, read over the descriptive information to understand the nature of the certification to see if it relates to your goals. If it looks like it might, check over the requirements more carefully to see what would be involved in obtaining it.

- If you're aiming to improve your work status at your current job, you should be looking at certifications that are related to the work you already do or, at least, that your company does. These would include product-specific and vendor-independent certifications.
- If you intend to use certification to move into a new specialty, focus on certifications related to that specialty.
- Choose only certifications with requirements that can be met within the time, money, and effort restrictions you've identified.
- Pay attention to how long the certification has been offered and how many people have earned it in that time. A program that's been in existence for some time but has few takers may not be a good choice.

Keep in mind the goals you've defined and the resources you're ready to commit. Remember, this is a preliminary list, so don't be too discerning. Add any certifications that appear to have potential to your list. Figure 8-7 shows our software engineer/guinea pig Bob's list.

When your list is complete, contact the sponsor for each certification and request that current information be sent to you. Phone numbers and mailing addresses for the sponsors are included with each certification listing in the Resource section.

While you're waiting for the materials to arrive, you can visit the sponsor's Internet site. It will often contain all the information that's in the printed brochures and more. This book's companion Web site includes direct links to Internet sites for certifications discussed in these pages.

Figure 8-7
Bob's Preliminary
Certification List

Bob

Certified C++ client/server developer (Borland)

Certified Computing Professional (Institute for Certification of Computer Professionals)

Software Development Certified Professional (Learning Tree)

Microsoft Certified Solution Developer

Microsoft Certified Systems Engineer

Project Management Professional (The Project Management Institute)

Figure 8-7
Bob's Preliminary
Certification List

Research the Certification's "Real-World" Potential

The materials you receive from any certification sponsor will paint a decidedly biased picture of the value of the program. That's because the materials are designed to sell you on a particular program's merits. Nonetheless, you will probably be able to use them to trim down your preliminary list to a few finalists.

As you study the materials, you may develop gut feelings about certain certifications. If a particular program just doesn't seem substantial to you, cross it off your list. If it involves a lot more hoops than you're willing to jump through, exclude it. Keep an eye out for curriculum changes that make a program more attractive than you originally thought.

The wise certification shopper only uses marketing materials as a starting point. Check out what other professionals think of the certification. If the sponsor has a database of certified professionals as part of a Web site, browse through it and contact some of the people listed within. Ask them what benefits they've gained from the certification, and ask if it's lived up to their expectations. You can also call the sponsor and ask them to provide you with a few references. Be aware, though, that if you let the sponsor choose the references, you risk being directed only to especially satisfied individuals.

Another good place to check is a site called TechWeb (**www.techweb.com**). Figure 8-8 shows the TechWeb advanced search page. This is a central index of computer articles published by CMP Media, which puts out *WINDOWS Magazine*, *Computer Reseller News*, *InformationWeek*, *InternetWeek*, and other industry publications. From here, you can search for any mention of certifications you are interested in. If you're lucky, you'll turn up an article or two that will provide you with some extra information.

Figure 8-8
The TechWeb
Search Page

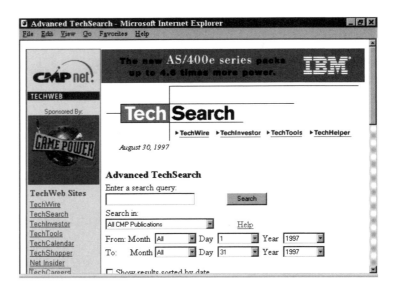

Other places to check include certification-related Web pages created by individuals. The content of these ranges from a single page to in-depth multipart sites that include discussion boards and forums. They're a good place to connect with other professionals who are interested in certification and have some experience with it. A number of these sites are identified throughout this book and are included on the set of HTML pages on the companion Web site. You can also uncover them by using one of the search engines, such as Infoseek or Yahoo!, using the name of the certification as your search criteria.

Finally, consider contacting a few recruiters to ask them what they think of the certification's value. Do they have employers asking for it by name? A yes is a big plus, but don't write a certification off just because a recruiter doesn't know anything about it. The certification marketplace is still developing, and many of the programs are fairly young. Employers and recruiters don't know about all of the designations currently available.

And the Winner Is...

By the time you've finished researching your certification list, both on and off the Web, you should have developed a pretty good picture of each program. Before making a final decision, review your work-sheets to refresh your memory regarding your career self-assessment. Keep in mind that up isn't the only direction a career can move. A lateral change can be equally valuable. Don't be swayed by other enthusiastic professionals. Remember that what works best for you may well be different than what they found successful.

If you're having trouble choosing, you may find it helpful to put your thoughts in writing. Write the title of each of the certifications you're finding it difficult to choose between on a piece of paper. Then write down the pros and cons of earning each certification beneath its title. Read and compare the pages, keeping in mind that there is no one "best" certification, only a certification that is best for you.

CHAPTER 9

Learning Alternatives

Although many certification programs will grant accreditation solely on the basis of exam scores, few people can walk in, take the tests cold, and walk out certified. If you feel confident about your skills in your chosen area, you can consider taking the exam with only your existing experience to draw upon, but it's unlikely that you'll be successful. This can be a mistake that costs you money and time; you won't get your money back if you fail, and there's often a waiting period before you can try again.

It's difficult to pass a certification exam without studying because an individual's knowledge is usually limited by job function. Imagine for a moment that your current job is to keep your company's intranet in tip-top shape. You may be quite the wizard when it comes to managing that intranet, but if you were suddenly placed in charge of an intranet at Company B instead, you'd likely find yourself stumbling around a bit, at least at first. That's because every organization's computing environment is unique. Hardware and software are combined in different ways and configured to serve specific purposes. Company B's intranet architecture is completely different from the one you're used to working with.

In the above scenario, you'd probably pick up what you needed to know by turning to documentation and technical coworkers, but certification tests don't offer the same opportunities. They aren't open book exams, and you can't bounce ideas off of the person at the next desk. Questions won't be limited to one company's computing environment either.

This doesn't automatically mean that you need to sign up for thousands of dollars in intensive training before you can pass certification exams, but you do need to prepare in one way or another. Fortunately, you have many options to choose from.

Thanks in large part to the computer industry, the classroom and textbook are no longer the only, or even the primary, education venues. Current alternatives include:

- Computer Based Training (CBT) prepared by the certification sponsor
- CBT and training programs offered by independent vendors
- Online classes
- Courses at authorized training centers
- Self-paced workbooks and study guides
- College courses
- Video tapes

Each has attributes that may make it attractive to you, and each has drawbacks. To select training that will serve your purposes, it helps to distinguish between two types of learning you'll need to undertake:

1. Adding to your body of knowledge.
2. Learning new practical skills.

Think of the first item as the *what* and *why* of your subject area. Returning to the internetworking example, extending your knowledge would include understanding the functions and differences of bridges and routers, and knowing which one you'd need under what circumstances. This kind of learning revolves around concepts, theory, and case studies. You can reasonably expect to master the material through absorption methods: reading, listening, and watching presentations of the material. And yes, repetition and regurgitation of what you've just learned help lock it into your memory.

Learning new practical skills is equivalent to the *how* of your subject area. It involves applying the knowledge you've gained; you perform instead of observe. You'll install and configure a bridge and a router; you'll deploy a firewall. The ideal way to accomplish this is to have the applicable hardware and software at hand, along with someone who can answer any questions and help if you get stuck. But that's not the only way. You may be astonished by what can be accomplished via simulation these days.

Both types of learning are valuable and important. How much you need of each kind will depend on the gap between your current knowledge and experience, and what you'll require for the certification you've decided to pursue. Self-study will carry you a long way. For some people and some certifications, it's all that's needed. Other certified professionals swear that formal training classes are the way to go. A combination of the two may best meet your personal training needs.

In the next chapter, you'll find out how to develop a personal, explicit training plan. But first, let's explore the education options that you're likely to encounter.

Workbooks and Study Guides

Text materials, including study guides, workbooks, instructional texts, and product manuals, are very attractive to certification candidates (Figure 9-1 shows a page from the online version of the CNX preparation manual). A big factor working in their favor is cost. You can frequently obtain workable study guides and exam preparation outlines directly from the certification sponsor via mail, or as downloads from the certification Web site. Texts that must be purchased are relatively inexpensive when compared to other routes for learning similar material.

If you aren't strongly motivated, learning by reading about a topic may not be the best alternative for you. But then, if motivation is really a problem, perhaps you should rethink your career goals with that in mind.

People may also bypass basic reading as a route to learning because they find it a slow and tedious way to learn. Whipping through the latest Dick Francis mystery may be pure pleasure, but page after page of dry technical exposition can seem like torture in comparison. Fortunately, you can drastically increase your reading speed and comprehension level by investing $6 and a bit of effort (see Speed Learning sidebar).

Figure 9-1
Sample Page of the
CNX Preparation
Manual

Depth of Questioning in the Token Ring Certification Examination

To help you understand the depth of questioning which is to be expected in the CNX exam, consider the following questions and their associated answers. To answer the questions completely you will need both academic background and field experience. *(Note: There are NO essay questions on the test. The test is multiple choice only.)*

1. During station insertion you see four unfulfilled requests for initialization sent to the Ring Parameter Server. What do you know about this ring relative to Source Route Bridging?

   Answer:
   Source Route Bridging may not operate properly on this ring. The RPS downloads the ring number into each participating station at the time of initialization.

2. A station receives a Beacon Frame with the beacon type subvector equal to Signal Loss. The receiving station observes that the reported NAUN address in the beacon frame is its own address. What action is taken by the receiving station?

   Answer:
   The station removes itself from the ring and performs the Beacon Removal Self Test after which it attempts to reinsert into the ring.

3. A station receives a frame and observes that the destination address in the frame is its own address. At the same time, the receiving station notices that the Address Recognized and Frame Copied indicator flags are set. What action does the station perform and what caused this situation?

   Answer:
   The station starts the Soft Error Report timer (which has a default value of 2 seconds) and logs an AC error. After 2 seconds the station sends the Soft Error Report. The AC error indicates that another station on the ring is using the same address as the receiving station. This would result if two rings were connected together with conflicting locally administered addresses.

4. What is the result of mixing ETR and non-ETR stations on the same ring?

   Answer:
   Transmissions by the non-ETR stations cost 1 ring rotation time worth of delay. There is no implied incompatibility with mixed stations. The only effect is that each time a non-ETR station sends a frame the ring must wait for the release of the token for the extra time required to circulate and strip the transmitted frame.

5. During ring poll a station receives a Standby Monitor Present frame with the Address Recognized and Frame Copied indicators set to ZERO. What action does the station take and what happens if user data is presented for transmission during that action?

   Answer:
   Upon receipt of either an Active or Standby Monitor Present frame with AR/FC set to ZERO a station will compare the source address in the received frame to its Stored Upstream Address register. If the address is different then the station will update its SUA register and queue an SUA Change Report for transmission. In addition, the station will queue a Standby Monitor Present frame for transmission as part of the Neighbor Notification process. If user data is presented for transmission it will preempt the transmission of the MAC frames for up to 20 milliseconds.

6. Can a bridge separate a group of interconnected devices into two or more separate NETWORKS?

   Answer:
   No. Bridges, which operate at the OSI data link layer, segregate traffic within a single network. They do not separate one network from another. [Note how this query is worded. This is typical of test question wording. You are required to understand the technical implication of the word 'network' and base your answer on that understanding].

7. Can a router divide a SINGLE NETWORK into two or more sections?

   Answer:
   No. When a router is inserted between two groups of communicating stations it divides the communicators into separate networks, each having its own network designation. Hence, when a router is placed into a single network it becomes two or more separate networks. [Note how this query is worded. This is typical of test question wording. You are required to understand the technical implication of the word 'network' and base your answer on that understanding.]

8. The DEC LAT (Local Area Transport) protocol does not have a network layer. What frame switching function is unavailable to LAT as a result of this aspect?

   Answer:
   The routing function is unavailable making this a non-routable protocol. Any protocol without a network layer does not have the information which would be used by a router to make a forwarding decision. Whether DEC LAT or some other protocol is being used as an example is not important.

9. Internet Protocol (the 'IP' of TCP/IP) contains the logical address of the initial source device which originated the frame and the logical address of the ultimate destination for the frame. This address is used by what type of device, and at what OSI layer, to make a forwarding decision on a TCP/IP frame?

   Answer:
   A router uses the logical device address at the network layer to make a switching decision. A bridge examines the physical device address at the data link layer, the router examines the network layer information which identifies the initial source and ultimate destination for a frame. Whether the TCP/IP stack or some other stack is being used as an example is not important.

10. When a device sets up a Type II LLC connection, what is the expected sequence of commands prior to the exchange of the first numbered information frame?

    Answer:
    The first command is the 'Set Asynchronous Balanced Mode Extended' (SABME) which is followed by an 'Unnumbered Acknowledgment' (UA). Next the two communicators should notify each other that their receivers are ready ('RR') and that they are expecting frame number ZERO next. In some implementations you may see an exchange of ID information (XID) preceding the SABME.

11. A host or server is providing file service to the user community. Do you consider it acceptable to have a 31% CPU utilization and a 84% rate of cache hits? Which of these two statistics is more critical and how would you improve this situation?

    Answer:
    31% CPU utilization is fine. Until a device begins to report somewhere in the neighborhood of 65% CPU utilization you probably don't have much to worry about. In fact, until CPU utilization goes over 100% you still have MIPS to spare. 84% cache hits is somewhat low. This could be due to a user community with widely differing needs. You may be able to increase the amount of cache memory in the device or load balance the user applications across different servers. The cache hit issue, while not a critical problem at this point, is more serious than the 31% CPU utilization.

Go Back to the Previous section
Go Forward to the next section
Go Back to the Table of Contents

Speed Learning

If you've made it this far in this book, you can obviously read at a decent level. But what exactly does that mean? The average reader proceeds at a rate of about 250 words per minute. Especially "fast" readers race along at 400 to 600 words per minute. But the limits of human reading speed are vastly higher: 1,200 to 3,000 words per minute can be achieved through training. And that same training will improve your comprehension and recall. You'll not only read faster, you'll understand and be able to recall more of what you read.

What kind of practical difference would this make in your certification training? If you have a 200-page manual to plow through (about 100,000 words), and your reading speed is above average at 300 words a minute, you'll need nearly six hours of reading to get through the manual. Up your speed to 900 words a minute, and you'll be able to read that same manual in under two hours.

But how can you accomplish such a vast increase in your learning rate? By purchasing a slim paperback book for $5.99 and following the advice within. The book is titled *The Evelyn Wood 7-Day Speed Reading & Learning Program*, by Stanley D. Frank, Ed.D. (Avon Books, 1992). Even if you just read and follow the steps in the first two chapters (about 40 pages), you'll dramatically increase your reading speed. But going through a lot of pages in a little time is only one aspect of leveraging your reading abilities. Along with step-by-step instruction on how to accelerate your reading, you'll find study tips and advice on how to increase your comprehension and recall and on how to prepare for exams.

When it comes to squeezing learning into a crowded schedule, this is one method that can really pay off. You can pick up this book (or a similar one) at most major book stores, or call Avon Books at 1-800-238-0658. You can also order this book online from Amazon Books (**www.amazon.com books**).

For some purposes, reading is no substitute for doing, but it's been a solid way to gain new knowledge or to expand upon what you already know. Table 9-1 lists learning characteristics of books. And a book is the ultimate portable classroom. You can use it beneath the florescent lights of the company cafeteria, inside a clattering subway car, or deep in the shade of an ancient oak in your favorite park—and the battery never runs out.

Table 9-1
Learning
Characteristics of
Workbooks and
Study Guides

Advantages	Disadvantages
Very portable	Not interactive, therefore less engaging
Can serve as a reference	May not be completely current
Relatively low cost	No external motivation, easy to get off track
Proceed at your own pace	Predetermined linear format

Computer-Based Training (CBT)

The term *computer-based training* refers to educational software developed and delivered via computer technology. It's also referred to by many other names, including *computer-aided instruction* (CAI), *computer-based instruction* (CBI), and courseware.

Good CBT programs are interactive. By requiring you to answer questions, step through tasks, and perform other actions, CBT *involves* you. By responding to the program, you become an active learner. Most people find that participating in this way increases their enjoyment of the process.

Another way CBT eases learning is by adding a "wow" factor. CBT software increasingly blends multimedia wizardry with voice tracks, video clips, animation sequences, and a big bag of tricks for transforming mundane information into fun.

CBT software also provides freedom from the predefined, linear style, of many other educational formats. You can largely elect to work with the topics in the order you choose, and at the pace you prefer. If you've already got a particular area down cold, you can skip right over it. If a lesson misses the mark, you can return to it as many times as you like.

On the down side, the software is limited as to what its instructions include. There's no trainer to answer free-form questions or to urge you onward, and you have to be sitting at a computer (usually equipped with a CD-ROM and loads of memory) to use it.

Current CBT software seems to be developed in one of two styles:

- Task-oriented
- Knowledge-focused

Task-oriented programs lead you step-by-step through the procedures native to the software, hardware, or environment you're studying. If the topic of the CBT is Novell LAN configuration, a single lesson might cover how to add a new user. In a textbook, you would read about it. In a traditional classroom, you would hear about it and possibly observe a demonstration by the instructor. With CBT, the applicable software is simulated on your computer screen. You'll be instructed, often by text, but sometimes via voice clips, on the proper sequence of steps to perform. And you'll follow the instructions as if you were actually adding a new user, clicking on the appropriate menu items, filling in variables, and coding switches. You can concentrate fully on what you're doing with no worry that you'll inadvertently bring the entire LAN crashing down, because there is no LAN, only an accurately reproduced interface with nothing on the other side.

But don't get too used to all that hand-holding, because it will diminish as you advance through the course. Procedures that were spelled out in detail the first time won't be later on. You'll have to "setup and configure the new LAN server." Step nine might be to add the users. Since you already learned that procedure, you won't be walked through it this time around. This building block, hands-on, simulation-type of learning can prove very successful when your goal is to acquire a specific, concrete set of skills.

Knowledge-focused CBT takes a completely different approach. Instead of facing the simulation of a particular program's GUI (graphical user interface) and being given the goal of completing a specific task, you'll find yourself in more of an open-ended, exploratory environment.

Learning Tree International (**www.learningtree.com**) is one company that makes excellent use of this style for some of its CBT courses. When you fire up the "Client/Server Computing" course, you are greeted by Ken, leader of the AcmeTech development team you've just joined. You're introduced to other team members, each with a particular perspective and area of expertise. You'll probably call on them later. Or they may have questions for you. Your job? To help develop and implement a client/server environment at a prestigious university. Get to work. (Table 9-2 pinpoints learning characteristics of CBT and Figure 9-2 shows a Learning Tree CBT program).

Not all CBT software is created equal. Some programs place block after block of text on the screen, which will quickly fatigue your eyes. Others fail to utilize multimedia capabilities in an interesting and beneficial way. These and other shortcomings can limit the value of

CBT software. Investigate your CBT options, preferably by test-driving a demo, before purchasing a CBT program.

Table 9-2
Learning
Characteristics of
Computer-Based
Training

Advantages	Disadvantages
Somewhat portable	Less practical as a reference
Interactive	Requires fairly powerful personal computer to use
Moderate cost	No external motivation, easy to get off track
Proceed at your own pace	Often available in PC compatible only, not Macintosh
Multimedia format is engaging	
Can review as desired	

Figure 9-2
Learning Tree CBT
Software

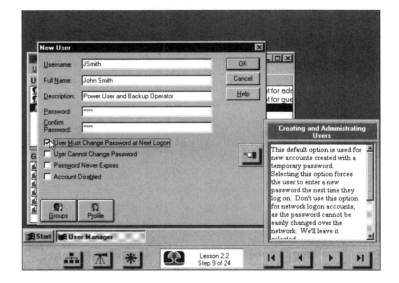

Online Classes

One of the more recent developments in technical training is the use of the Internet as a delivery medium. Although online classes might appear to fall under the umbrella of CBT, they're distinct enough to deserve a category of their own.

Just what is an online class? Think of it as a virtual classroom, equipped with an instructor and populated by fellow students. It enables you to attend instructor-led courses via the Internet without leaving your desk. The classroom is usually open twenty-four hours a day, seven days a week.

The way it works is this: to begin, you'll connect to the Internet and use your Web browser (Microsoft Internet Explorer or Netscape) to connect to the "classroom." There you'll find a weekly lecture and assignment posted by the instructor, message boards you can use to interact with other students in the course, and lists of additional resources relevant to the course subject. The instructor will participate in the message boards, respond to your questions, and review your assignments. Most online courses also offer office/chat hours, when students can directly interact with the instructor in real-time.

Online courses may be offered by commercial education centers, colleges, consulting groups, and private individuals. The format and content details of a particular online course vary considerably from vendor to vendor. Prices run all over the spectrum, as does degree of instructor support, class quality, qualification for continuing education credits, and just about every other aspect you can imagine.

Ziff-Davis University

Ziff-Davis Corporation, publisher of numerous industry magazines, has jumped into the online training market with both feet. They've created a virtual university and named it ZD Net University (ZDU). You'll find it at **www.zdu.com**.

ZDU structures itself this way: individuals pay a monthly fee (currently $4.95) to become members. While you're a member, you can register for and attend as many classes as you like. For each class, you log on at least once a week (at a time of your choosing) to read the instructor-posted assignment and submit questions that are posted on the class message board. According to ZDU, the message board is managed by "the instructor, teaching assistants, moderators, and other students." Classes generally last four to eight weeks, and additional materials, including books or downloadable files, may be required. Instructors stage live chat "office hours."

For a processing fee (currently $15), ZDU will submit your information along with the course name and *recommended* number of continuing education units (CEUs), to the National Registry of Training

Programs (NRTP) of the American Council on Education (ACE). If the CEUs are granted, you'll receive a notice from ACE via mail.

Microsoft Online Institute

As you would expect, the Microsoft Online Institute (MOLI) was created to assist individuals who are pursuing one of Microsoft's certifications. Each course incorporates "one-on-one interaction with a professional instructor," called a *Learning Advisor*, and self-study materials. The self-study materials might be CBT software, workbooks, or videos. You can begin your course at any day and time, and proceed at your own pace (within a specified time frame). As with ZDU, you will log on to a virtual classroom where you will find assignments, resources, and messages posted by other students. Your Learning Advisor will correspond with you via email about your assignments, questions, and additional comments.

It's interesting to note that the courses aren't taught by Microsoft employees but, rather, by approved outside professional training organizations. A survey of the catalog revealed a wide range of pricing. The "NT 4.0 Upgrade" class will set you back just $99, but the "Supporting Microsoft NT" course lists at $795 plus shipping. Many courses were listed in the $250 to $500 range. To explore MOLI, visit **moli.microsoft.com** (Figure 9-3 shows the MOLI Web site).

Figure 9-3
The Microsoft Online Institute Web Site

DigitalThink

Another variation of an Internet education center has been created by a company named DigitalThink (Figure 9-4 shows a DigitalThink course interface). This implementation is, in some ways, more like traditional CBT learning. Instead of an instructor posting periodic assignments, the modules that make up a course are always available. You load a course syllabus to jump to the lesson, quiz, or exercise of your choice, and complete it at your own pace.

While logged on to DigitalThink, you participate in a course-specific message board or classroom, check out your scores, send messages to other students currently online and in your class, or send e-mail to your tutor. There's also a button to click for course-specific help, and the standard resource collection of bookstore, shareware, software, and links.

Figure 9-4
The DigitalThink
Interface

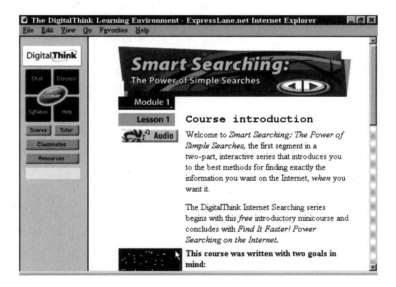

The DigitalThink course catalog isn't limited to information systems courses, but also covers topics such as personal finance. The course "Java Certification For Developers" is listed with an introductory price of $125 and an estimated length of 10 hours. Access to a Java SDK is required, and the textbook is *Java Certification Exam Guide for Programmers and Developers* by Barry Boone.

The DigitalThink site (**www.digitalthink.com**) also boasts a money-back guarantee. If you decide that online classes aren't for you (within a specified time period), you can withdraw, and your course fee will be refunded.

There are many more online instruction vendors besides those described here. Their course roster may be limited to just a few classes or fill an extensive catalog. Their nature will vary considerably, too. Because this is an evolving business arena with exciting possibilities, you're likely to encounter an extensive variety of vendors, including colleges, individual entrepreneurs, technology businesses, and education companies.

As this book was under development, two technology training companies, National Education Training Group (NETg) and Interactive Learning International Corp. (ILINC) announced an alliance created in order to deliver a new level of instructor-led training via the Internet. Together they promise to deliver "the world's first live, virtual corporate classroom, which simulates an actual live classroom experience with synchronized viewing of multimedia content, real-time audio, text chat and shared whiteboard." (Table 9-3 outlines learning characteristics of online classes.) Their goal is to get students interacting with classmates and the instructor as they do in a traditional classroom. Students will even be able to "raise their hands." What they don't mention is whether the teacher will call on you even if you don't.

Table 9-3
Learning Characteristics of Online Classes

Advantages	Disadvantages
Self-paced (within time limits)	No future value as a reference
Access to expert instructor	Requires computer and Internet connection
Interaction with other students	Price, format, and quality vary widely

Authorized Training Centers

Novell calls them *Novell Authorized Education Centers* (NAECs). Microsoft prefers the term *Authorized Technical Education Center* (ATEC). But whatever you call them, some veterans of certification report that when it comes to in-depth, hands-on training, they're irreplaceable.

These training centers are entitled to use the label "authorized" because they've obtained a seal of approval from the certification sponsor. Some deliver a predetermined curriculum provided by the sponsor; others create a program of their own that meets the sponsor's requirements.

Because they've worked directly with the certification's sponsor, training center staff have the inside scoop on what it takes to pass particular tests, and what sort of practice is likely to pay off. You can get this same information elsewhere, but here it will be delivered to you practically on a silver platter. Your instructors will be professional technical trainers, extremely well-versed in the issues at hand. If you run into a stumbling block, you won't be stuck for long.

Another big plus these centers offer is an appropriate computing environment. Instead of simulating an NT server on your own PC, you'll get your hands on the real thing. And it will be free from the restrictions or potential for disaster that your employer's live network is likely to have.

The big downsides are cost and inconvenience. Intense authorized training can run up quite a tab. Complete MCSE training obtained this way, for example, can run $10,000. Of course, if your employer is willing to pay for it, cost won't be as big an issue.

Unlike other training you can pursue at your own pace, you'll have to learn at a rate set by the rest of the class and the instructor. That rate may be slower or faster than you'd like. You'll have to adjust your work and leisure time to meet the training center's schedule, and if you miss a session, it may be difficult to catch up to the rest of the class.

To find a training center that supports the certification you've chosen, you can either call the certification sponsor or visit their Web site (Figure 9-5 shows the search page for Novell NAECs). For the more popular certifications, you may be able to locate a nearby center through checking the yellow pages of your phone book under the computer training and education heading.

Shop around and compare price, course format, instructor experience, lab equipment, and convenience factors. You may find considerable variation among training centers. Table 9-4 details learning characteristics of training center courses.

Figure 9-5
Novell's Online
NAEC Search Page

Figure 9-5
Novell's Online
NAEC Search Page

Novell. *Everything's Connected.* Education — Global Training Locator

Welcome to the Authorized Training Locator. If you need help using the locator, please view our instructions.

Select Country: United States

Select Training Partner Type:
○ Novell Authorized Education Center (NAEC)
○ Novell Education Academic Partner (NEAP)
○ Both

and any combination of the following search fields:

Telephone Area/City Code: (optional)   and   and   and

Don't forget to include toll-free prefixes applicable to your region.

State or Province (optional)   Press to Select

City (optional)

NAEC/NEAP Name (optional)   (partial spelling allowed)

Authorized Course/Service: Press to Select

Search   Clear Form

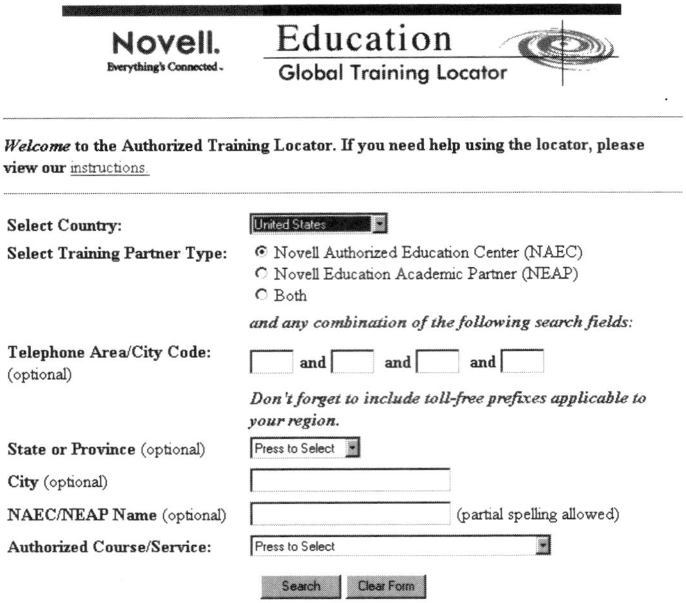

Table 9-4
Learning
Characteristics of
Training Center
Courses

Advantages	Disadvantages
Interactive	No future value as a reference
Access to expert instructor	Most costly
Access to expensive technology	Often require time in large blocks
Interaction with other students	Not self-paced
Easy to locate through sponsor	Compressed nature may reduce skill retention
Lots of training in a short time	

College Courses

Another way to fill in your knowledge gaps is to take one or more courses at a nearby college. The classes will be less condensed, because they take place over the course of a semester, and generally less expensive (especially if you utilize a community college). Because they extend over a full semester, you'll have more time to learn, study, and absorb information.

The institution you choose may or may not have a direct connection to your certification sponsor. If it does, you can often obtain the exact same training curriculum you'd get at an authorized training center but at a lower price and spread out over a longer period of time. Even colleges with no official link to your certification program may offer classes that teach the material you need to know.

To address the need for more routes to certification, sponsors have begun to actively seek out alliances with traditional academic institutions. Microsoft, for example, has created the *Authorized Academic Training Program* (AATP). To participate in this program, educational institutions must be accredited and meet hardware and classroom requirements specified by Microsoft. They must deliver the same curriculum that Microsoft ATECs do, but do so in the manner of the typical college course. Instead of condensed training given on three to five consecutive days, AATPs are limited to a maximum of 16 hours per week per course. AATPs are also more likely to offer evening and weekend class times, which may be a better fit with your lifestyle. AATP instructors aren't required to hold Microsoft's Certified Trainer designation but must, at a minimum, be a Microsoft Certified Product Specialist (MCPS).

Novell operates a similar program but uses the term *Novell Education Academic Partner* (NEAP) instead of AATP. At an increasing number of community colleges, you can take the same exact Certified Novell Engineer (CNE) curriculum offered by a Novell training center at a fraction of the cost. A series of intensive training center CNE courses over consecutive days may run you $6,000 to $8,000. The same material covered at a community college during one semester can cost less than half as much (Figure 9-6 shows Howard Community College's price comparison page).

It's reasonable to expect that an increasing amount of certification training will begin to appear in college catalogs. Professional organizations and vendors, including the Network Professional Association (NPA), IBM, Microsoft, and Novell have clearly begun working to bring top-level computer technology training capabilities to traditional educational institutions. This is a wise move by an industry faced with a shortage of adequately trained workers. It adds another effective alternative for you to obtain any certification training you need, and simultaneously helps the computer industry gain the qualified workers it's thirsting for. Table 9-5 features the learning characteristics of community college courses.

Tuition and Fees

Novell (Includes Student Kits)
(Add $23.70 per course Consolidated Fee)

Course	In-County	Out-of-County	Out-of-State	Compare to Private Ed. Center Prices	Percent of Private Ed. Center Contact Hours
NT200	$562	$727	$979	$895	
NT508	$667	$832	$1084	$1,195	
NT518	$752	$917	$1,169	$1,390	
NT520	$712	$877	$1,129	$1,995	
NT525	$762	$927	$1,179	$1,990	
NT526	$762	$927	$1,179	$2,390	
NT532	$692	$857	$1,109	$995	
NT605	$667	$832	$1084	$795	
NT801	$842	$1,007	$1,269	$1,995	

Microsoft (Includes Student Kits)
(Add $23.70 per course Consolidated Fee)

Course(Old)	In-County	Out-of-County	Out-of-State	Compare to Private Ed. Center Prices	Percent of Private Ed. Center Contact Hours
MS351	$612	$777	$1,029	$1,195	
MS377	$612	$777	$1,029	$1,195	
MS688(472)	$962	$1,127	$1,379	$2,125	
MS505	$962	$1,127	$1,379	$2,125	
MS798(540)	$912	$1,077	$1,329	$1,875	
MS659	$962	$1,127	$1,379	$2,125	
MS771(632)	$962	$1,127	$1,379	$2,125	
MS922(687)	$962	$1,127	$1,379	$2,125	
MS689	$962	$1,127	$1,379	$2,125	
MS867(756)	$962	$1,127	$1,379	$2,125	
MS803	$787	$952	$1,204	$1,295	

A+ Certification (does not include books)
(Add $23.70 per course Consolidated Fee)

Course	In-County	Out-of-County	Out-of-State
CS105	$337	$502	$754
CS106	$337	$502	$754
CS219	$267	$432	$684

For further information about Novell or Microsoft courses, email Tracey Artuso at *mailto: tartuso@ccm.howardcc.edu.*

For further information about A+ courses, email Vinitha Nithianandam at *mailto: vnithian@ccm.howardcc.edu.*

Return to Certification Programs Home Page

HCC Home Page

	Advantages	Disadvantages
Table 9-5 Learning Characteristics of Community College Courses	Interactive	No future value as a reference
	Access to experienced instructor	Trainer may be less qualified than at a training center
	Interaction with other students	Not self-paced
	Less costly than training center	Takes longer to complete course
	Gentler learning pace	
	Access to necessary equipment	
	Often eligible for college credits	

Online Resources

An excellent way to augment any of these learning methods is to seek out additional information on the Internet. You can search for certification-specific resources or sites that contain the details of a particular technology that you're studying.

To locate sites with information of either type, connect to one of the search engines such as Yahoo! (**www.yahoo.com**), Infoseek (**www.infoseek.com**), Excite (**www.excite.com**), or OpenText (**index.opentext.net**). Make your search as specific as possible. For example, to find Web pages relevant to Smalltalk certification you might enter "**Smalltalk certification**." Placing both words inside a set of quotes makes the search engine treat them as a phrase rather than as separate keywords. This will return a list of links to pages that contain the exact phrase. To find documents relating to a Microsoft Windows NT test, you could use the keywords **"Windows NT" AND certification AND exam**. You'll get a list of pages containing all three of the keys, but they're allowed to be separated by other words not on your list. The more specific you make your search words and phrases, the less trash you'll have to wade through to find the bits of treasure.

If you find that you're having little success, try a different search engine. Each search engine collects, indexes, and retrieves information in its own way. By executing an identical search on three different search engines, you'll come up with three different (although overlapping) sets of results.

What types of resources can you expect to uncover with these searches? Both commercial and noncommercial sites will turn up. Some will be hosted by businesses who want to sell you their related services, others by individuals with special interest in your search topic. The bounty you'll uncover is likely to include some of the following resources:

- Certification resource centers created by interested individuals (one such site is shown in Figure 9-7)
- Resource sites about a particular technology
- Exam-specific learning aids such as quiz programs, books, and testing tips
- Unofficial (that is, not officially authorized) training programs and books
- Sponsor-authorized training venues
- Related discussion forums
- Home pages of individuals who hold a particular certification
- Sponsor Web sites and pages
- Articles and papers about the technology or certification
- Online versions of software and hardware manuals
- Related newsgroups and mailing lists you can join
- Study groups organized around your certification

Figure 9-7
Wayne's
Comprehensive
Computer
Professional Certifi-
cation Resource

You'll probably have to spend some time sorting the wheat from the chaff before you find the online resources that will prove most valuable to you. But one of the great things about online resources is that when you find one good page, it often contains direct links to other sites of similar quality and content. Table 9-6 provides learning characteristics of online resources.

Remember to take what you find on the Internet with a grain of salt. Excellent, accurate, and in-depth resources are out there, along with slapped together, error-ridden pages. Most Web pages contain a link you can click on to contact the page's author. Don't hesitate to use it if only to get a feel for the person behind the information. You may well run across a kindred soul who is willing and able to serve as a fountain of knowledge about your certification program.

Table 9-6
Learning
Characteristics of
Online Resources

Advantages	Disadvantages
Free	No guarantee of expertise
Usually contain many useful links	Information may be out of date, inaccurate, or incomplete
Tips and advice from certification veterans	May have to dig for the gold
Place to connect with other candidates	

Unofficial Training Programs

It's a consumer truism that generic goods are generally less expensive than the name brand version of the same item. That holds true for certification training, too. Entrepreneurs and others, who for one reason or another haven't obtained official sponsor approval, have established themselves in the training business (Figure 9-8 shows the home page of one of these companies). The lack of a certification sponsor's seal of approval doesn't automatically indicate poor quality or anything shady about the operation. It may simply be a business choice not to go the authorized route, and plenty of trainers have made that decision, for one reason or another.

These "unauthorized" vendors offer seminars, workshops, CBT software, software-based study aids, video tapes, textbooks, and study guides—virtually the same mix of resources you can obtain through official channels. But as independent operators, they are free to develop their own curriculum and course format.

The good news is that unofficial vendors usually charge lower fees than their sponsor-authorized counterparts. Many are operated by skilled, knowledgeable professionals who know just what they're doing and how to best help you achieve certification. The bad news is that you can't count on the presence of either attribute. Table 9-7 enumerates learning characteristics of unofficial training vendors.

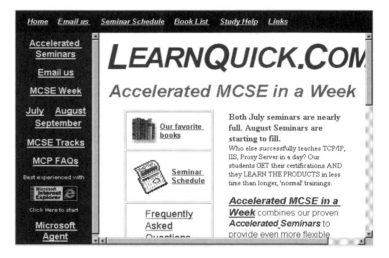

Figure 9-8
Home Page of WWW.LearnQuick.com

Before purchasing goods or services from any unfamiliar vendor, check them out as thoroughly as you can. Find out how long they've been in business, and if certification training is their product, inquire as to the exam success rate of their graduates. Request the names and contact information of some past customers, then contact those people to find out the details of their experience with the vendor. Spend some time nosing around forums and Web sites for any bad press about the particular vendor. When people feel ripped off, they generally aren't shy about sharing the details via an online site.

If a substantial amount of money is involved, it's worth it to call or write the better business bureau in the vendor's home state and ask if there are any complaints on record against the company, and, if so, whether or not they have been satisfactorily resolved. Chances are that the vendor you're considering is running a quality operation, but it pays to be sure.

Table 9-7	Advantages	Disadvantages
Learning Characteristics of Unofficial Training Vendors	Usually less expensive than authorized	No guarantee of expertise
	Not restricted to preapproved curriculum	Greater risk of inferior services and products
	May get more candid view of product	

Training Videos

If you prefer learning from an instructor but the classroom setting doesn't suit you for one reason or another, videos are an alternative that you may find appealing. While you won't be able to interact with the instructor, you will be able to observe demonstrations of particular procedures. Voice, music, and visual stimulation will involve you; in many cases, animation, close-up shots, and virtual field trips will help to clarify concepts. Some videos apply a lead/follow approach. The video instructor demonstrates how to operate a particular piece of software, then you recreate the process using your own equipment. But many are passive affairs where you just sit and watch.

Training videos often come with a support package that includes printed materials, review questions, and self-quizzes. They're significantly less expensive than other forms of instructor-led training. In some cases, you may even be able to rent instead of purchase them, but then you won't have them on hand for future reference. Table 9-8 highlights learning characteristics of videotapes.

Table 9-8	Advantages	Disadvantages
Learning Characteristics of Video Tapes	Relatively low cost	Not interactive
	Self-paced	May contain excessive "talking heads" sections
	Can review as needed	Requires access to VCR equipment
	Opportunity to see techniques in action	

QUOTE

Does Training Method Really Matter?

I don't believe in a single method of getting certified over any other. I believe that people should take advantage of all methods that are appropriate for them. I don't believe people should say that they learn best one way, I think that they should just learn—kicking screaming, clawing—any way they can learn, they should learn. If they get a chance to go to school and they want to go to school then they should go to school. If they don't, they should find books and go to the library. If they have to, borrow books. If you want to get ahead in this business, there's still plenty of room for those people willing to learn. Do it any way you can get it.

—Herb Martin, MCSD, MCT, MCSEx2, one of the first in the world to hold all four of the major certifications from Microsoft and founder of LearnQuick.Com, a training company that focuses on helping people earn Microsoft certifications fast

It's important to remember that although a particular training option may seem ideal to you, it may not be available for your certification program, in your area, or in your price range, or it may not be available for some other reason. If you can't obtain your first choice in training, there are probably several other options that will serve you nearly as well. There's also a lot of variation within categories, so be sure to shop around to get a clear understanding of what various training outlets have to offer.

Keep in mind that different certification requirements may be best met by different training alternatives. To learn how to dissect an Apple Macintosh, for example, you might prefer a hands-on workshop with tools, equipment, and an experienced technician on hand. But to understand the evolution of Apple personal computers, a videotape, audio cassette, or book may do the job as well or better.

In the next chapter, as part of developing your personal certification road map, you'll find out how to analyze your learning style and how to take that into consideration when choosing a training alternative. You'll also determine just how much training you'll need and how to evaluate individual training outlets.

CHAPTER 10

Your Personal Training and Certification Road Map

Once you've decided which certification to pursue, you're ready to lay out your plan for obtaining it. Is a detailed plan really necessary? Only if you want to save time, money, and frustration.

A certification plan is often referred to as a road map, and with good reason. The process of obtaining certification is very similar to the process of traveling from your home to a distant location. In both cases, there are many possible routes between your starting point and intended destination. Which route is best depends upon individual preferences. Is speed of the essence or do you prefer to see more along the way? Will you be camping out to save money or lodging at five-star hotels? Do you have the endurance and tenacity to undertake marathon drives, or are shorter hops more to your liking?

The same issues apply to certification. Do you want to finish ASAP or delve more deeply into the elements? Are you aiming for minimal financial outlay or maximum comfort? Do you have the time and energy to immerse yourself for intense and extended training events, or are shorter study and training sessions more to your liking?

Although it might be tempting to hop on the certification road as soon as possible and figure out each turn as it approaches, such impatience has a price. You're likely to spend more time and money than you have to and risk taking wrong turns along the way. By taking the time to understand your learning style and plot out which exams and courses you will take, in what order, and when, you'll be assured of meeting all the requirements and deadlines for your certification. You'll also be able to move smoothly from one requirement to the next, without needing to constantly interrupt your progress to stop and figure out what to do next.

Your completed certification road map lists the requirements you need to meet, in the order you need to accomplish them. It also identifies the methods you intend to use to prepare for each exam and includes a timeline to keep you on target.

Some sponsors provide road map software specific to their certification. You can download the programs from the sponsor's Web site. These programs will step you through the process. Figure 10-1 shows the Novell CNE Advisor that you can download on the Web at **education.novell.com/whatshot/cneadvis.htm**.

Figure 10-1
Novell CNE Advisor

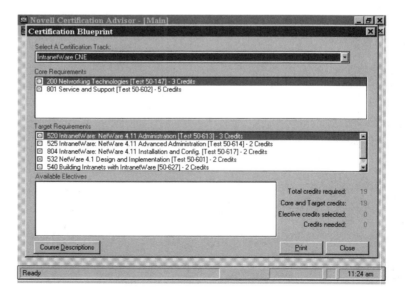

Creating your personal certification road map involves the following steps:

1. Select a track.
2. Record the requirements on your Personal Certification Plan.
3. Eliminate any requirements you can.
4. Decide how you'll meet the remaining requirements.
5. Set deadlines.

Your plan will be an evolving document. Expect to adjust and fine-tune it as you progress toward certification.

A Word on Tracks

Many certifications allow some amount of customization so you can closely match them with your needs. It's like the electives component of college degree programs where you get to choose what to minor in. Correspondingly, you can act as some college freshman do and choose the courses that are easiest to pass, or you can take advantage of this flexibility to follow a certification path that's tailored to your career goals.

These alternate paths are called tracks. They typically are organized in one of two ways:

- Around specific platforms and operating environments
- By job function

The best way to choose your track is to read over the descriptions provided by the sponsor. You'll find them included in the sponsor's literature and usually on the certification's Web site, if there is one. Select the option that most closely matches the goals you intend to achieve through certification. For example, if you're planning to leverage your career at your current position, choose the track that most closely matches the operating environment you work in or that best describes the functions related to your job. If you're using certification to move into a new area, look for the track that best bridges what you already know and what you'd like to know. Or if your goal is simply to advance your skills, select the track that best represents the skills you want to add or augment.

It's a good idea to discuss your options with other people who are familiar with the certification process and/or your goals. They can help you decide if a particular track or elective is "hot" or going out of style.

Once you've settled on a track, begin filling in the Personal Certification Plan in Figure 10-2 by listing the requirements you'll need to meet, in the order that you intend to complete them. Be as detailed as possible. At this point, you should be able to list specific exams, experience requirements, applications to submit, fees you'll need to pay, and anything else that will be needed to obtain your certification. Write only in the requirements column for now. This is the "what" of your certification plan. The other columns, which will address "how" and "when," will follow shortly.

Figure 10-2
Personal
Certification Plan

Personal·Certification·Plan

Certification:_____
Target·Completion·Date:_____

X	Requirement	Target· Date	Training/Study· Method(s)	Notes

Getting Credit for What You Know

Once you've determined your track and recorded the requirements on your Personal Certification Plan, it's time to figure out which of the requirements, if any, you can get out of. No, this isn't cheating;

this is getting credit for what you've already accomplished. Generally, there are two ways to do it: meeting experience requirements and getting exams waived.

You might think that meeting an experience requirement is pretty straightforward; you either already have the requisite time in or you don't. Not so. It's sometimes possible to satisfy experience requirements through substitution. Consider the Institute for Certification of Computing Professionals (ICCP) Certified Computing Professional (CCP) designation. Eligibility requirements state that candidates must have at least four years of "professional computing experience" before sitting for the core examination. At first, this sounds like you have to have four years of computer-related employment under your belt. But that's not necessarily the case. Upon closer study of the sponsor materials, you'll find that either educational achievement or holding the entry-level Associate Computing Professional (ACP) designation can account for two of those years. If you're short on work history but you have a computer science degree, you're set. Otherwise, it would be worth your while to look into obtaining the ACP designation to shorten your path to the CCP designation.

IBM's instructor certification allows a shortcut, too. Candidates who already hold a Certified Technical Trainer, Certified Banyan Instructor, Certified Novell Instructor, or Microsoft Certified Trainer designation are excused from submitting evidence of a college degree in education or listing all training classes they've taught within the last 12 months.

If you fall on the short side of an experience requirement, contact the certification sponsor and ask if they will accept alternative accomplishments. If the answer is no, don't be afraid to push (politely) a little; spell out the extent of your education and training and how you think it qualifies as experience. Although this tactic won't work every time, you won't lose anything by trying, and you stand to gain quite a bit.

While finessing experience requirements will save you time, getting one or more exams waived will save you both time and money (the exam fee). The opportunity to get an exam waived is typically extended to candidates who can demonstrate that they passed an equivalent exam through another sponsor. For example, Microsoft certification candidates who already hold certain Novell or Banyan certifications can get the networking exam requirement waived. Participants in Learning Tree International certification programs can apply for "transfer credit" of up to two courses if they have extensive on-the-job experience or have attended similar training elsewhere.

These certification sponsors aren't alone in allowing leeway in meeting experience requirements. Information on exam waivers and experience alternatives are often found on the sponsor's Web site or in certification literature, but don't count on it. You should make a phone call and ask.

If you determine that you can bypass any of the requirements on your Personal Certification Plan, draw a nice, fat line right through them. Now you have that much less to do.

Deciding How to Prepare

Now that you've spelled out and pared down your requirements, it's time to determine how you will approach each of them. Depending upon your background and skills, some requirements will entail more preparation than others. That's why the next step of developing your Personal Certification Plan is to review each requirement and choose the study/training methods you will apply to achieve it.

Certification candidates have a rich array of learning alternatives to choose from—Chapter 9 explores them in detail. Deciding which method to apply toward a particular requirement is a highly individual process, and to make effective choices you first need to understand your personal learning style.

How Do You Learn?

People differ in how they perceive, understand, retain, and recall information. We all know individuals who can find their way anywhere providing they have a map to refer to, and others who are virtually guaranteed to get lost unless they're given oral directions. Give the map reader oral directions or the directions person a map and both will eventually reach their destinations, but their journeys will probably be longer and more stressful. Just like these travelers, learners have preferred methods of receiving and using information.

QUICK TIP

For an excellent (if extensive) discussion of many aspects of adult learning styles, read the Wave Technologies International white paper, **Learning: The Critical Technology**, which you can find at **www.wavetech.com/whtpaper/ abttmwp.html**.

The people who study the science behind learning have identified and mapped these preferences in a number of different ways. By identifying and understanding your personal learning styles, you'll be able to select the training methods and tools that work best for you. To help you do that, an exploration of two of the more widely accepted models follows. As you work to understand your learning preferences, keep two important things in mind:

- There is no "best" learning style.
- Sometimes, options that cater to your learning preferences are unavailable or impractical. Although other learning styles may not be as ideal, they will still work.

One of the more common (and understandable) learning frameworks is organized around how we take in information. This theory identifies three basic learning styles based on human senses: visual (by sight), auditory (by sound), and tactile/kinesthetic (by touch and motion). Although most people can learn using any of these senses, most favor one over the others.

Visual learners take in information most easily by seeing it. If you prefer to look at pictures and images rather than listen to explanations, you may be a visual learner. The map reader mentioned above is a visual learner.

Readers are not necessarily visual learners. Many people "hear" the words in their head as they read them. For that reason, readers are considered auditory learners. Auditory learners understand ideas more quickly when they hear them spoken. If you learn more from a lecturer than from watching demonstrations on the same subject, then you may be an auditory learner. A tendency to "think out loud," is another indication that you learn through listening. In the earlier example of following directions, the person who prefers oral directions over a map is an auditory learner.

Tactile/kinesthetic learners prefer to touch and manipulate things. If you're one of those people who abhors reading directions and are happier diving right into whatever it is and figuring it out as you go along, you're likely to be a tactile/kinesthetic learner. A tactile/kinesthetic traveler typically has a good sense of direction and location and is less likely than the map reader or auditory traveler to get seriously lost.

The most effective instruction incorporates more than one learning style. The better teachers have been aware of this for some time and deliberately appeal to different learning styles. Kindergarten teachers, for example, often apply all of these perception styles when teaching the alphabet. When introducing a new letter, they show what the letter looks like (visual), say the letter out loud and have the students repeat it (auditory), and direct children to trace the shape of the letter with a finger or crayon (tactile/kinesthetic).

QUICK TIP

To help determine whether you're more of a visual, auditory, or tactile/kinesthetic learner, complete the Wave Technologies self-assessment in Figure 10-3, or take the online learning styles inventory at **www.howtolearn.com/personal.html**.

Figure 10-3
Wave Technologies'
Learning Style
Self-Assessment

Learning Styles Assessment

Read the word(s) in the left column and circle the description that best expresses how you usually handle each situation. The column with the most choices circled represents your primary processing style. The column with second most is your auxiliary style.

When you	Visual	Auditory	Kinesthetic and Tactile
Spell	Do you try to see the word?	Sound out the word, or use a phonetic approach?	Write the word down to find if it feels right?
Talk	Talk sparingly, but dislike listening for too long? Do you favor words such as *see*, *picture*, and *imagine*	Enjoy listening, but are impatient to talk? Use words such as *hear*, *tune*, and *think*?	Gesture and use expressive movements? Use words such as *feel*, *touch*, and *hold*?
Visualize	Do you see vivid, detailed pictures?	Think in sounds?	Have few images, all involving movement?
Concentrate	Do you become distracted by untidiness or movement?	Become distracted by sounds or noises?	Become distracted by activity around you?
Meet someone again	Do you forget names, but remember faces? Remember where you met?	Forget faces, but remember names? Remember what you talked about?	Remember best what you did together?
Contact people on business	Do you prefer direct, face-to-face, personal meetings?	Prefer the telephone?	Talk with them while walking or participating in an activity?
Relax	Do you prefer to watch TV, a play, or movie?	Prefer to listen to the radio, music, or read?	Prefer to play games or work with your hands?
Try to interpret someone's mood	Do you primarily look at facial expressions?	Listen to tone of voice?	Watch body movement?
Read	Do you like descriptive scenes? Pause to imagine the action?	Enjoy dialogue and conversation, or hear the characters talk?	Prefer action stories or are not a keen reader?
Do something new at work	Do you like to see demonstrations, diagrams, slides or posters?	Prefer verbal instructions or talking about it with someone else?	Prefer to jump right in and try it?
Put something together	Do you look at the directions and the picture?	Like to talk with someone or find yourself talking out loud as you work?	Ignore the directions and figure it out as you go along?
Need help with a computer application	Do you seek out pictures or diagrams?	Call the help desk, ask a neighbor, or growl at the computer?	Keep trying to do it or try it on another computer?
Teach someone	Do you prefer to show them?	Prefer to tell them?	Do it for them and let them see how it's done or ask them to try it?

Courtesy: Wave Technologies International

Peter Honey and Alan Mumford, building on the work of David Kolb, developed a second, widely referenced model. This framework is organized around how we think about things rather than around perceptive preferences. It identifies four types of learners: the activist, the pragmatist, the reflector, and the theorist. Once again, these categories aren't mutually exclusive. It's likely that you have traits linked to more than one of these learning styles, but you'll find one that describes you more accurately and completely than the others.

Individuals who fall under the first category—activists—are eager to dive right in and try out novel things. Do you enjoy new projects and frequently find yourself looking for the next project to tackle? Do you approach new ideas in an open-minded and enthusiastic fashion? Are you always primed and ready for the next new experience? If so, then your learning style is probably activist.

Pragmatists are most interested in the application of what they learn. Do you return from a seminar filled with fresh ideas that you want to try out? Do you think of yourself as a practical person and like solving problems? Are you impatient with meetings that don't seem to be accomplishing a specific purpose? These are all signs of a pragmatist learner.

Reflectors are happiest when they can collect all the relevant information and study it carefully before reaching a conclusion. Do you prefer to make decisions at the last minute so that you can have as long as possible to consider potential ramifications? Do you enjoy collecting and analyzing data? Would you (or others close to you) describe yourself as a cautious person? If so, then you're probably a reflector.

Theorists like to understand how things fit together and what they mean. Do you prefer to analyze problems in an objective, step-by-step fashion? Do you look for the logic behind the ideas? Are uncertainty and ambiguity difficult for you to endure? These are all characteristics of a theorist learning style.

Once you have a good sense of your learning strengths, it's time to fill in some of the blanks in your Personal Certification Plan. For each requirement you have listed, fill in the training/study method(s) you want to use. Keep in mind which learning alternatives are best matched to the learning styles you've identified as your favorites. If you've determined that you're a tactile/kinesthetic person, for example, you'll find hands-on options more effective. If that's the case, consider interactive computer-based training (CBT) or instructor-led training (ILT) that includes lab work as your first choice. An auditory learner should turn to books and audio and videotapes, while a visual learner should seek out alternatives that include videotapes, print materials that include extensive illustrations, and instructor-led training.

A reflector may be happiest pouring over the details found in product documentation, while a theorist will prefer a study guide that pays more attention to the why of things. An activist may be best served by getting his or her hands on the technology in question before worrying about the details of how it works. A pragmatist should look for methods that begin by explaining what something is good for. Printed materials and instructor-led training are likely options for a pragmatist.

You can expect to find a lot of variety among products within a single category. Though some CBT programs involve lots of interaction, others depend more heavily on reading from the screen. Some "talk to you" quite a bit. Others just settle for a beep and chirp now and again. Study guides can contain block after block of dense text or include diagrams, photos, and self-tests.

How Certification Candidates Study

As part of a 1997 Gartner Group study sponsored by Sylvan Prometric, IBM, Microsoft, Novell, and Sybase, more than 7,000 certification candidates were asked about their training methods. The results show which study methods candidates used most and which proved most useful.

Self-study was the primary method used by the majority (44%) of those surveyed. 35% of respondents reported using instructor-led training (ILT) as their predominant preparation tool. Vendor-approved methods were more widely utilized than independent training and products, especially for ILT, where vendor-approved training was used nearly five times as often as training from unofficial sources. Figure 10-4 shows the breakdown of primary study methods reported.

Interestingly, the choice of a primary study method doesn't always correlate with the method that candidates identified as most useful. This is most apparent in on-the-job-training (OJT), which only 14% of candidates identified as their primary learning method, but 43% pegged as one of the most useful. Self-study methods were overwhelmingly designated useful (72%), and instructor-led training got the nod from just (41%). Percentages total more than 100% because multiple selections were permitted. Figure 10-5 shows the study methods certification candidates found most useful.

Figure 10-4
Primary Study
Method

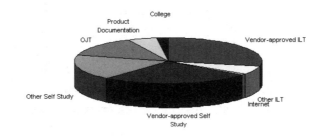

Primary Certification Study Method
source: Gartner Group 1997

Figure 10-5
Most Useful Study
Method

Most Useful Study Method
source: Gartner Group 1997

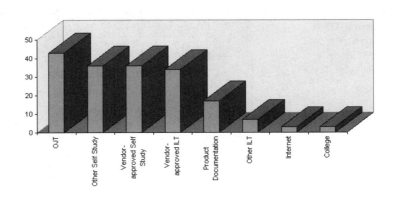

Finding Preparation Tools

Although there are many preparation tools available, you'll need to conduct a bit of a search to uncover a good selection:

✐ Ask the certification sponsor for suggestions and check the sponsor's Web site. It may contain a database of authorized training providers.

✎ Sample the trial versions of preparation software included on this book's companion web site.

✎ Contact vendors listed in the resource section and ask if they have materials related to your certification.

✎ Use Internet search engines, such as Yahoo! and Infoseek, to uncover sites that include the name of your certification along with the word "preparation."

✎ Visit Web sites and forums that you uncovered while researching your certification, and post a message asking for suggestions.

✎ Consider using generic (non-certification specific) self-quiz programs that let you create your own practice tests. You can find them in shareware catalogs and on the Internet.

✎ Call your local community colleges and inquire about computer technology offerings.

✎ Visit a nearby bookstore or one of the bookstores on the Web, such as Amazon Books (**www.amazon.com books**), and search for titles related to your certification and/or study topic. Figure 10-6 shows the results of an Amazon Books search for Sybase materials.

✎ Look in the business pages of your local phone book under computers—training.

Figure 10-6
Sybase Search
Results from
Amazon Books

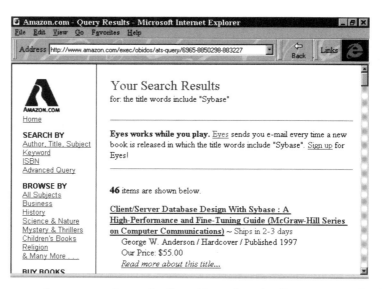

There are also a number of education clearinghouses on the Web. They include information on training companies and products and are searchable by geographic area and topic. Sites to visit include:

⬢ The Computer Training Network (**www.crctraining.com/train-ing/default.htm**) offers a searchable database of trainers and training companies. You can search by product, geographic area, or software category.

⬢ Virtual University Enterprises' training locator (**www.vue.com/training-locator/**) links students with authorized training. Figure 10-7 shows the locator.

⬢ Nerd World Media's computer training list (**www.nerdworld.com/nw190.html**) is quite extensive.

Figure 10-7
VUE Training Locator

Once you've added preparation methods for the requirements listed on your Personal Certification Plan, pull out your calendar and fill in a deadline for each requirement. Setting these target dates will help you keep on track and give you a picture of the time frame. When setting deadlines, remember to allow for vacations, holidays, business trips, and the like. Give yourself a little more time than the bare minimum you think is necessary. Then if something unexpected comes up and you fall a day or two behind what you expected, your schedule won't be thrown completely out of kilter. Finally, as mentioned before, remember that your plan isn't written in stone. You can change and adapt it to meet your needs along the way. But try to stick to the deadlines if you possibly can. Doing so will assure you make continued progress toward your goal of certification.

How to Evaluate a Training Center

There are two categories of training centers that you'll encounter: authorized and "other." Authorized training centers have an agreement with a certification sponsor that specifies the details of its operations. The agreement typically covers curriculum, facilities, equipment, and instructor qualifications. The theory behind authorized training centers is that you can obtain the same quality and level of training no matter which one you attend. However, the real world doesn't always conform neatly to a plan. Instructors are individuals with varying classroom presence and skills. Equipment upkeep may be more meticulous at one center than another.

The "other" category encompasses all training firms and programs that lack the official seal of approval. This may be because they don't (or can't) meet sponsor requirements or because they simply want freedom from the complications of oversight and sponsor regulations.

Whichever type of facility interests you, it's important to evaluate how good of a job it's likely to do providing the services you want. The two most important aspects to investigate are the instructor and the classroom.

To assess the skill of the instructor, ask the training facility for the name of the instructor who will be teaching your class. Request a copy of the trainer's resume and copies of past course evaluations from classes that trainer led. Find out if the training facility is willing to direct you to students who've taken classes from the trainer in the past. Opinions from people who've taken past classes with an instructor are an excellent resource.

You may find the training center unwilling to provide such information. That may simply mean that they don't know who will be teaching the class; contract instructors are often brought in to teach courses. If that's the case, find out if the facility uses the same contractors again and again. If so, you can ask for information on each of the trainers who may teach your class. If the training company uses different trainers each time, they're taking a gamble with an unknown, and so are you. If that's the case, you may want to look elsewhere.

The best way to assess a training facility's physical setup is to visit the classroom in which your course will be held. If it's too far away, you'll have to do your best to find out the relevant information via telephone. Ask what kind of computers will be used in class. Is the hardware up to date? How much RAM does each computer have? What speed are the CPUs? Is there a computer for each student, or will you be expected to share? Are the relevant hookups, such as network and Internet connections, present?

Don't overlook the layout of the classroom itself. Is there room to spread out your materials and move around or are desks crammed tightly together? What presentation devices, such as overhead projectors or whiteboards, will be used to display information to the entire class? Are they clearly visible from all seats? Are the chairs comfortable enough to spend hours in, or are they ergonomic nightmares?

Inquire about lunch arrangements, satisfaction guarantees, and whether you can come in before or after class to practice on your own. Think about your past training experiences and what you liked and disliked about them. If specifics come to mind, find out if they will occur at the facility you're now considering.

If you feel uncomfortable poking and prodding like this, remember that you are considering spending a significant amount of time and money at the facility, and you have every right to know just what you'll be getting in return. Politely make your inquiries and jot down notes about what you discover. If the training facility has been in business for any time at all, they'll be used to it. And the time you spend checking out the center will be paid back tenfold if it saves you from enrolling somewhere that doesn't measure up.

Following Your Plan

As you step through the requirements in your Personal Certification Plan, it helps to take a methodical approach. Your process should go something like this:

1. Read objectives for that exam.

2. Read any exam study guide provided by the sponsor.

3. Complete any study/training classes and materials.

4. Get hands-on experience.

5. Review/practice.

6. Register for the exam.

7. Take the exam.

Don't hesitate to modify these steps to suit your personality and needs. Some people prefer to schedule their exam first and use the exam date as motivation to keep on track. You'll also find that, for some requirements, your existing knowledge and experience will make it possible for you to skip steps and still perform just fine on the exam.

Once you've completed the preparation of your plan, store it somewhere close at hand so that you can refer to it at will. Whenever you complete a requirement, mark an X in the column provided for that purpose. Those Xs will accumulate into a tower of accomplishment, and before you know it, you'll reach your goal and become a certified computer professional.

CHAPTER 11

Study Secrets

Is it possible to graduate from high school, college, or even graduate school without mastering effective study skills? In a word, yes. Learning how to learn rarely receives the attention it should in our system of education. It sometimes seems to be assumed that learning is something everyone knows instinctively, like putting your hands out to catch yourself when you stumble.

But in fact, extending your arms to cushion a fall isn't instinctual, it just feels that way because you've been doing it for so long that it's become second nature. If you observe young children who've just begun to walk, you'll notice that they stumble a lot. And when they stumble, they fall, usually face first. It's only after repeatedly banging their forehead or nose that they begin to catch themselves with their hands.

At first glance, studying might also seem like an inherent skill that you either have or you don't. But like putting your hands out when you trip, it's a learned behavior. And, similarly, once you've mastered effective techniques, you'll be able to apply them again and again throughout your life. At first it will require deliberate effort, but with time and practice, it, too, can become second nature.

You already know how to study, you say? If you're really fortunate, then you do. More likely, you know just enough to get by. When study skills are lacking, an increase in effort can sometimes compensate for lack of ability. But studying doesn't have to be a mind-numbing feat of endurance, and exams don't have to tie your stomach in knots. Nor should you feel embarrassed if your study skills are weak; it's not that difficult to fix them. Once you do, you'll find the act of learning can become downright pleasurable.

As an adult learner, your educational circumstances are significantly different than they were when you were in high school or college. It's likely that you have more demands competing for your time, including a full-time job and possibly a family. But you have an advantage over your counterparts in a very important way—motivation. You're studying because you've identified a goal you want to obtain (certification). You have a concrete vision of how achieving your goal will benefit you. You're placing at least some of your own money on the line. Getting down to business will be easier this time around.

Learning to study effectively means gaining control and understanding in three main areas: environment, methods, and motivation. The skills you already have in these areas can be strengthened and augmented with new techniques. First, let's look at a few myths about studying.

You Might Have Heard That...

Smart people don't have to study. This is one of the most widely held misconceptions about studying. Everyone knows an individual who appears to glide through academics with little effort. They always get excellent scores on exams yet never seem to crack a book. How can this be?

It simply isn't true. Some people do need less study time than others, but that often can be linked to efficient and effective techniques rather than to a high I.Q. score. Consider reading speed. One student may read at a rate of 250 words a minute and will take about six hours to read a 90,000-word book. A faster reader, cruising along at 500 words per minute, will finish that same book in only three hours. Is the slower reader as smart? Of course. He's just not as skilled a reader.

The other contributing factor to the myth that smart people don't have to study has to do with where they study. Rather than trying to concentrate in the midst of a crowded cafeteria, for example, they hit the books in a private (and quieter) environment. Only those that live with them see them studying. And if word starts to circulate that they're so smart that they don't have to study, why deny it?

Cramming is a good way to remember things. No, cramming is the way to forget things! Think back to a time when you applied this technique yourself, probably out of desperation over an exam looming the next day. You may have achieved a decent score the next day, but what do you remember of the material now? Or even just a week after the test? If you're like most people, the facts quickly evaporated from your mind.

The human brain strengthens the connections between bits of information through repetition. Although cramming may stuff enough facts into short-term memory to pass an exam, short-term memory is just that; here today and gone tomorrow. Storing information in long-term memory requires repetition and sustained effort. Certainly, last-minute studying does have its place as a review tool. But its true effectiveness is as a supplement to a more sustained kind of learning that will place information at your service today, next week, and next year.

The more you study, the more you learn. Longer study periods covering greater quantities of material may, in fact, be detrimental to your ability to recall the information. Your attention span isn't unlimited. Everyone reaches a saturation point where information seems to flow into one brain cell and then proceed directly out of another. It's as if your brain is saying "give me a break!" In fact, that may be just what is happening. Recent research suggests that the human brain requires time for new information or skills to become "hard wired," and that introducing a second skill or batch of information right on the heels of the first interferes with that process. Essentially, the brain needs time to process what it has just received.

Think about learning two phone numbers. If you work on both simultaneously, you'll probably exchange digits between them and take more time to be able to correctly recall either one. However, if you take them one at a time, and get the first down cold before taking on the next, such confusion is unlikely to occur. More studying is not automatically better.

Background noise can help you concentrate. Studying with the television running may feel like less work, but it's also working less. When part of your mind is occupied filtering and interpreting background noise, it's not available to focus on the information you're studying. Background music also interferes with your ability to concentrate, although music without lyrics is significantly less distracting than music with them. For best results, focus your full attention on your task. You'll finish sooner and can then fully enjoy your music or television show.

Studying requires substantial, uninterrupted blocks of time. Ideally, you should have at least some interrupted periods. But not having them doesn't preclude study opportunities. Squeezing "study snacks" into the margins of your daily life can be very beneficial. Consider the times you find yourself waiting: for the bus, for an elevator, for the next available bank teller, or for a take-out lunch. If you carry notes in some form in your pocket, you can whip them out at these times and grab a few minutes of power studying. Over the course of a week, these "study snacks" can add up to a significant meal of information.

When to Study

You don't have to be a time management expert to recognize that most people cram an incredible array of activities into the course of a week. If you're one of them, you may be wondering how you're going to squeeze study time into an already crowded schedule. Although small amounts of study time can prove quite valuable, longer, uninterrupted blocks are necessary. Finding them can be a challenge. Fortunately, it's one that you can conquer.

Every week contains 168 hours. That's more than 10,000 minutes. A basic eight-to-five job, with no overtime and a half hour commute each way, cuts fifty hours off the top. Allocate another 45 minutes to shower, dress, and eat breakfast before leaving the house, and that's another three and three-quarters hours gone. What about sleep? At eight hours a night you're snoozing away 56 hours each week. Take another half hour a day to microwave and eat dinner and the total reaches 113 hours. That's 6,795 of your precious allotment of minutes expended on basic living, without even getting to sleep in on Saturday morning.

That's the bad news. The good news is that the above bare-bones regimen still leaves another fifty-five hours or so (specifically, 3,285 minutes) in your time bank. It's up to you to spend it wisely.

Granted, much, if not all, of that time is already spoken for. Some of it is devoted to activities you won't want to give up. But if you examine your use of time closely, chances are you'll be able to massage your schedule and slide study time into your life fairly painlessly.

If the time slots open to studying aren't obvious, a time usage chart will reveal them. To make one, mark fifteen minute time increments along the left side of a piece of paper. Create seven columns across the top, one for each day of the week. During the next week, record what you do throughout the day by listing the activity and blocking off the amount of time used. Figure 11-1 shows a partially completed time usage chart.

Figure 11-1
Sample Time
Usage Chart

	Monday	Tuesday	Wednesday	Thursday	Friday	Saturday	Sunday
7:00	Rise &						
7:15	Bkfst						
7:30	Commute						
7:45	to work						
8:00	Work						
8:15							
8:30							
8:45							
9:00							
9:15							
9:30							
9:45							
10:00	Break						
10:15	Work						
10:30							
10:45							
11:00							
11:15							
11:30							
11:45							
12:00	Find keys						
12:15	Lunch						

At the end of the week, add the total amount of time you spent on each activity. Analyze your chart to determine:

✐ Which activities do you spend the most time on? Is the amount of time you devote to them reasonable? If not, think about how you can cut back.

✐ Which are the biggest time wasters? Does your time chart show hours of television watching, excessive phone calls, or frequent nights out? Looking for misplaced items is a frequent time waster that probably won't even make it onto your chart.

✐ What can you cut back or eliminate to make room for studying? The time wasters are prime candidates for the ax. You can let the answering machine take phone calls, become more organized so you don't spend as much time finding things, and/or turn off your television. You also might identify commitments, such as volunteer work or league sports, that you can reduce while you're working toward certification.

This isn't to say that you should completely cut out your social life and leisure activities. In fact, those are things you should be careful to include in your schedule. To succeed as a learner, you also need time away from the books so you can relax and maintain your health.

When choosing study times, keep the following principles in mind:

✐ Schedule study time during those times of day that you feel best. If you're a morning person, consider getting up early so you can get in a half hour before work. Are you a night person? Then skip the evening news and work on your certification program instead. You'll absorb material quickly and more easily when you are fully alert.

✐ Learn to say no. During this time, try to avoid taking on extra work. Some people find it hard to refuse any request, especially those that come from coworkers or charities. But a simple reply like: "I'd love to be able to do that for you, but right now my schedule is booked solid. Maybe another time?" will protect your study time without hurting feelings. If you're someone who finds it difficult to say no, practice in front a mirror until the words just flow from your lips.

✐ Build a cushion into your time estimates. Avoid the temptation to schedule things to the minute. Inevitably, something unexpected will occur. If you haven't allowed time for it, you'll end up chasing your schedule for days afterward.

✐ Study the worst first. If you are dreading a particular study unit or practice material, take it on first. Chances are you'll discover it isn't nearly as onerous as you expected, and with the hardest part out of the way, the remaining materials will be a cake walk.

Where to Study

Where you choose to study affects how successful you will be at learning and remembering the information you cover. While it's possible to study on the subway, a park bench, or at the kitchen table, your best study space is likely to be elsewhere. What makes a study area ideal? The perfect study environment is one where you can work in distraction-free comfort. It's physically and psychologically conducive to the work at hand, without being so comfortable it puts you to sleep.

Selecting a regular study place has another advantage: mental conditioning. Think of Pavlov's famous dogs. Each time the animals were to be fed, Pavlov rang a bell. Soon, the dogs began to salivate at the sound of the bell alone. They developed a physical response to the expectation of food. They were conditioned to respond to the bell.

Similarly, you can condition yourself to study. If you use the same study spot again and again, you will begin to associate it with studying. Over time, your mind and body will become conditioned to learn whenever you enter your study area. Sitting down and getting to work will become more automatic.

Your chosen space should have adequate lighting, bright, but not glaring. It should provide a chair and desk or table. The chair should be a standard desk chair, or one you might find in a conference room or classroom. Don't study in a cushy arm chair. You'll end up slouching and holding your study materials at an awkward angle, both of which can interfere with your ability to concentrate and cause muscle soreness. If you're laying back in a soft chair, especially in a warm room, you may doze off.

The work surface can be a desk or table. Whichever it is, there should be plenty of space to spread out your study materials. It should be at a comfortable height so you can study for extended periods without strain. The surrounding environment should be quiet and free from distractions and interruptions. That means the television and radio should be off, and, if you're at home, let the answering machine answer the phone. Don't park yourself in front of a picture window either; a blank wall will be less distracting. Instruct family members and coworkers not to interrupt you. Have all your study materials—notebook, extra pens, and so on—at hand, so you won't have to get up to fetch something.

Schedule regular study times. It will help you get into the habit of studying and will aid the conditioning process mentioned above. Choose a time of day when you usually feel alert. Consider eating a high-protein snack beforehand so you don't get hungry.

Study sessions don't have to be marathon events. If you need a break, take one. Get up, stretch, and wander down the hall for a few minutes. Try to limit breaks to ten minutes or less. Four one-hour study sessions will prove more beneficial than one four-hour session.

Common study locations include a library, an empty conference room, or a kitchen table. Lack of the perfect study area shouldn't keep you from the task at hand. Though a comfortable, well-lit, and distraction-free environment is best, reality may dictate other circumstances. Do your best to schedule study periods following these ideal conditions. But when it comes down to it, if life interferes, study where and when you can.

How to Study

Once you've nailed down the when and where of your study plan, it's time to focus on study techniques. By making effective use of your study time, you can cut down the amount of time needed while simultaneously increasing your comprehension, recall, test scores, and self-confidence.

Study skills are best organized by task. Thanks to the perennial fountain of students and teachers, methods have been developed for getting the most out of a textbook, taking effective notes, tricks to improve your memory, test preparation, and more. Although there are also tips and tricks for writing papers, you're not likely to need to do that in the course of certification training, so it isn't covered in this book.

The key to all of these methods is your involvement. To be an effective learner, you need to be an active learner. The information that comes your way via self-study and classroom activities won't stick with you just because it passes by your eyes or ears. But if you operate with the intention of making it stick by using methods that have been proven to work, you will learn and remember.

How to Read a Textbook

One of the most effective and most widely taught textbook study methods has been around since the 1940s, when it was first developed by Dr. Francis Robinson. It's called SQ3R. The acronym is derived from the five steps of the system: *Survey, Question, Read, Recite,* and *Review.* Following them will greatly increase your comprehension and recall of textbook material. They can be applied to an entire book, to a single chapter, or to any reading assignment. Let's go over the steps in order.

Survey

The first step is to survey the reading material. Just like a construction surveyor determines the lay of the land, your goal is to determine the overall shape of the book. Read the title, preface, introduction, and table of contents. Then flip through the rest of the book (or chapter), reading only the boldface headings and subheadings. Scan any illustrations to see what they are about. Surveying an entire book should take less than a half hour. When you're finished, you'll have a good feel for what the book is about and how it's organized.

Question

The next step, signified by the *Q* in SQ3R, is to question. This very important step transforms you from a passive reader to an active one. Instead of expecting the book to feed you information, you'll be able to work to extract it by focusing on learning the answers to questions you develop in advance. To develop your questions, scan back through the reading material, again focusing on the headings and subheadings. This time, rephrase them as questions. Table 11-1 shows headings from a book chapter about Visual Basic, along with questions that could be derived from them.

Table 11-1
Headings and Questions from a Visual Basic Text

Section Heading	Question
Specifying Visual Basic Data Types	What data types are available in Visual Basic?
Creating Variables and Constants	How are variables and constants created?
Creating User-Defined Types	What is a user-defined type, and how do I create one?
Determining Scope	What determines the scope of a variable or constant?

Read

The third step (the first *R*) is to read each section, keeping in mind the questions you formulated in the previous step. Pay especially close attention to the first and last sentences of each paragraph. The first sentence, called the *topic sentence*, will reveal the main idea of the paragraph. The last sentence typically brings discussion of that particular idea to a conclusion.

 The first time through new material, leave your highlighter pens on the desk. Otherwise you will tend to underline too much and the wrong things. Save highlighting for a later read-through, when you'll be better able to identify key points.

Recite

The second of the three *R*s in SQ3R stands for recite. After you read each section, *without consulting your notes or the text*, do your best to recite the questions you developed and their answers. You can do this silently or out loud. Out loud is better because it applies an additional sense (your hearing) to enhance your learning. If you can't answer the questions from memory, look back through the text and try again. When you can answer the questions from memory, go on to the next section.

Review

The final *R* stands for review. This is where you begin seriously building your memory of the information. Go back over all the questions you created for all of the sections you read. Try to answer them again. To add kinesthetic (touch/movement) learning, write out the questions and their answers. If you jot them down on index cards, you can them review the information pretty much anywhere, any time you have a few spare minutes. Repetition will help solidify the information in your mind.

That's all there is to it. Next time you open a textbook remember the acronym SQ3R. Then do it. After you (S)urvey, (Q)uestion, (R)ead, (R)ecite, and (R)eview, you'll know a lot more than if you had simply read the book.

How to Get the Most from a Class

Just as you can get more from a textbook by becoming an active reader, you can boost your classroom comprehension by becoming an active listener. To become an active listener in a classroom setting, you'll need to prepare, pay attention, participate, and take notes.

Before Class

What you do before class dramatically affects how much you learn during class. If you prepare properly, the actual class time will be almost a review, reinforcing information you've already learned. You won't be struggling to keep up because you will have developed a good idea of what's coming and familiarized yourself with the concepts and language that are likely to arise.

- *Preview the material to be covered.* Before the first meeting of a new course, obtain a course outline from the professor, along with a set of objectives. Read over it to find out what will be covered. Determine exactly what you will be expected to know when the class is complete. If a textbook accompanies the course, scan through it ahead of time, using the survey method described above.
- *Prior to each class session, check over the course outline to see what material is due to be covered.* If you have a textbook with corresponding chapters, read it using the SQ3R method *before* class.
- *Arrive early.* The first few minutes of class time are often very important. During this time the instructor is likely to introduce the topic at hand and sketch the shape of the material to come. If you're busy opening your notebook and greeting your neighbor, you won't be paying attention and you'll miss out on this important information, and you'll be a step behind for the remainder of the class session. It's much wiser to arrive ten or fifteen minutes beforehand to get yourself organized and mentally in gear.

During Class

- *Pay attention.* You can't remember what you haven't learned in the first place.
- *Take notes.* Research has shown that students who take notes during class remember more than those who don't, even if they never look at those notes again. The process of taking notes forces you to pay attention and to organize your thoughts.
- *Participate in discussions.* Again, this forces you to be an active listener. Besides that, you'll also have the opportunity to clarify any points you find confusing. By speaking, you'll also reinforce your learning by verbalizing some of what you've read and heard.

After Class

> ✐ *Stay late.* At least a few minutes late. It can be tough to pay attention when others around you are packing up their books, but those last few minutes of class are as important (if not more) than the first few. Your instructor may use them to summarize what was covered, or, if she has run short on time, may cram fifteen minutes of material into the last five. The end of class is also when you're likely to find out what will be covered next session and what you should do to prepare.

> ✐ *Review your notes immediately after class and fill in any gaps.* This will take just five or ten minutes and could save you hours later on. That's because while you'll remember most of the lecture/material for a short time, by the next day, much of what you heard will slip away unless you've reinforced it mentally.

> ✐ *In conjunction with reviewing your notes (or in lieu of, if time doesn't permit you to sit down with them immediately after class), conduct a mental review of the class session.* You can do this in the car on your way home or in the cafeteria. Recall what the main points of the session were and why they are important.

Note Taking 101

Taking good notes isn't a hit-or-miss proposition, it's a learned skill. Effective note taking will help you focus on what is being said, understand it, and recall the material later on. You can gain all of this without requiring a minute more than you'll spend sitting in class anyway.

Although taking notes isn't as simple as pulling out a piece of paper and recording what the instructor says, it's not much more difficult either. To begin, start each class with a fresh piece of paper and record the date and lecture title (if there is one) at the top. Then draw a vertical line about two inches from the left edge of the page, dividing it into two columns. Most of your notes will go into the second, wider column. The first column is for comments, words, and other marks that will enable you to quickly identify key sections of your notes. Little or nothing will go there until you review your notes later.

When class begins, start writing your notes. Don't try to record every word the instructor utters. Instead, aim to capture key points and subtopics, using a structure similar to outlining. Distinguish between major and minor points by indenting or underlining. Write in your own words, not the instructor's. By rephrasing what is said, you'll deepen your understanding of it. The exception to this guideline is if the material is a definition, formula, or rule. In those cases, it's best to record exactly what the instructor says, to ensure accuracy.

For expediency in note recording and review, use descriptive words and phrases instead of whole sentences. You can save additional time by developing your own shorthand. To do so, substitute symbols and abbreviations for words or parts of words that appear frequently (see sidebar for shorthand suggestions). Add new short-cuts gradually, so you don't find yourself with a page of jumbled shortcuts that you can't decode easily. Remember, your personal shorthand is intended to save you time, not add confusion. Let it develop over time.

Shorthand Substitutions

- Replace *ing* with *g*: *configurg* instead of "configuring"
- *w /* for with: *w / program loaded* instead of "with program loaded"
- *w / o* for *without*: *w / o reformat* instead of "without reformat"
- *R* for are, *U* for you: *U R here* instead of "you are here"
- + for and: *compile + bind first* instead of "compile and bind first"
- Use digits for numbers: *4 principles* instead of "four principles"
- < for less than or lower: *< cost* instead of "lower cost"
- > for greater than or more: *> flexibility* instead of "greater flexibility"
- = for is the same as: *time = money* instead of "time is money"
- leave out vowels that aren't critical: *prgrm* for "program"

Deciding what to include or exclude can be challenging at first, but once you develop your skills and grow familiar with your instructor's style, it will become second nature. Try to capture the main ideas and their subtopics. Listen for key phrases that indicate important information will follow, such as:

- "The four principles are…"
- "Most importantly…"

   ✎ "The most frequent mistake is..."
   ✎ "Always remember..."
   ✎ "In conclusion..."
   ✎ and of course, "will be on the test."

Through voice and body language, the instructor may give cues that key points are imminent. Watch for increased animation or a change in the pitch of the speaker's voice, which should alert you that important points are forthcoming. Pay close attention to anything that is emphasized through use of the chalkboard. If you miss something, leave a blank space in your notes so that you can fill it in later.

Review your notes as soon as possible after class. This is the time to use that left-hand column. Use it to highlight especially key points and to serve as a quick index to your notes. For example, you might mark ! next to an important point and ? next to something you need to clarify. Identify sections of your notes with key words describing the topic, so that you can locate them easily. Figure 11-2 shows a sample page of notes from a class about systems implementation strategies.

Make sure you record your name and phone number on the inside of the front cover of your notebook. Then, if you accidentally leave it somewhere, you may get it back; otherwise a moment of inattention may cost you all of your notes.

Figure 11-2
Sample
Lecture Notes

9/20/97
Implementation Strategies: Changeover

	chngeovr = how 2 swtch 2 new sys
	3 mthds: parallel, immediate, phased
parallel	**parallel**
	old + new run @ same time
	< risk; can go bck 2 old if probs
	> time 2 run 2 sys
	can b expnsv 2 op 2 sys simul
	can slow adopt by persnl
plunge	immediate (=plunge)
!	>risk

How to Remember

Do you have a good memory or a bad memory? While the ability to recall information does vary between individuals, it's another study skill (and life skill) that you can significantly improve.

In *Learn to Be a Master Student*, authors Robert Rooney and Anthony Lipuma identify three basic functions of memory: labeling information as you learn it, storing it in your brain, and recalling it. You can improve two of these functions. The third, storing, doesn't need enhancement. Your brain already has more storage capacity than you can possibly use in your lifetime, no matter how much information you stuff in there. Don't you wish your computer's hard drive was like that?

The labeling part of the memory process involves deliberately identifying information as you learn it. This can be accomplished through linking new information with other things you already know or by organizing it in a way that makes it easier to remember. There are several tricks you can use to improve your labeling skills, including mnemonics and memory mapping. Both will be described shortly.

Your ability to recall information improves with practice. Every time you remember a particular piece of data, your brain becomes better at retrieving it. The brain path to where it is stored becomes more clearly delineated and more deeply entrenched. The process can be compared to finding your way to a new place of employment for the first time versus finding your way there for the twenty-first time. That initial trip requires considerable attention and maybe a wrong turn or two. By the time you've worked there three weeks, you can practically drive there in your sleep (and some mornings it probably feels like you do).

You can also create more than one pathway to a particular piece of information. Doing so enables you to do what you would have to if you encountered a road closure on the way to work—take an alternate route. The more routes you have to work (and the more pathways you create to the information stored in your brain), the less likely it becomes that you'll get stranded without reaching your destination.

GRASP

The word *grasp* means to lay hold of with the mind. Here's how to GRASP what you want to learn.

✍ (G)et it the first time. If you're not paying attention, you won't learn, and you can't remember what you haven't learned.

✍ (R)emember to remember. Learn with the intention of remembering information for a long time (not just until the next exam).

✍ (A)ssociate new information with something you already know, or arrange it in a pattern that's easy to remember.

✍ (S)tudy the same information different ways to create more than one path to retrieving it.

✍ (P)ractice remembering. The more you recall a piece of information, the easier it will become.

Mnemonics

Remember SQ3R? That's right, it stands for Study, Question, Read, Recite, Review. Because you have linked the acronym to the process of reading a textbook, you can more easily remember the individual steps. SQ3R and GRASP are examples of mnemonic devices—memory cues that help you label and recall information. Other mnemonics you've probably encountered include: Every Good Boy Does Fine, which helps you remember the notes (EGBDF) associated with the lines of the treble clef; and ROY G. BIV for the colors of the rainbow (red, orange, yellow, green, blue, indigo, violet). Remember the verse "Thirty days hath September?" That's a mnemonic, too.

Mnemonics are powerful tools that make memorization easier, more interesting, and even fun. They also enable you to remember longer. How many years has it been since you first met good old ROY G. BIV?

You can create your own mnemonics. Acronyms are a form of mnemonics that the computer world is awash in already. Consider LAN (Local Area Network), RAM (Random Access Memory), SDLC (Systems Development Life Cycle), PROM (Programmable Read Only Memory), and WORM drive (Write Once Read Many), just to name a few.

To create your own acronyms, consider the items you need to memorize. Can you rearrange them so that the first letters form an acronym you can remember? What if you needed to memorize the stages of the systems development process, in order? They are:

1. Requirements Stage
2. Evaluation Stage
3. Design Stage
4. Implementation Stage

How handy that the first letters form the acronym REDI! Just remember that to develop a new system, you have to get REDI first. In this example, the items needed to be recalled in order. But when they don't, feel free to play with them, rearranging them to see what you can come up with.

Another powerful type of mnemonic is rhyme. Putting information into rhyme format or to the tune of a familiar song creates a fun association that makes it easier to recall. Suppose you want to remember the names of Visual Basic data types, along with how much storage space each requires. You could memorize Table 11-2.

Table 11-2
Visual Basic
Data Types

Data Type	Storage Required
Integer	2 bytes
Long	4 bytes
String	1 byte per character
Currency	8 bytes
Single	4 bytes
Double	8 bytes
Variant	Depends on value stored

Or you could put the information to the tune of a familiar song, as in Figure 11-3. Aural learners may find this method especially useful, but you probably won't want to practice in the company cafeteria.

Another helpful memory trick is to count. For example, if you know that there are four principles of forms design, you'll know to keep trying if only three come to mind at first.

The Power of Pictures

Consider using pictures to help you remember, especially if you are a visual learner (Chapter 10 explained how to determine your learning style). Visualize or actually draw a picture that illustrates a concept you want to remember. You can put yourself in the picture or not. If you can conjure up a humorous scenario, so much the better.

For example, if you study communication, you'll discover that communication requires a sender, a receiver, a message, a channel to convey the message, and feedback that informs the sender if or how the message was received. The sender transmits the message over the channel to the receiver. Anything that disrupts the smooth operation of any of the elements is called noise.

The·Seven·Visual·Basic·Data·Types·
(Sing·To·the·tune·of·The·Twelve·Days·of·Christmas)

The·first·VB·data·type·is·the·variant,·its·size·depends·upon·value.

The·second·VB·data·type·is·the·double,·eight·bytes·to·store.
And·a·variant's·size·depends·upon·value.

The·third·VB·data·type·is·the·single;·four·bytes·to·store.
A·double·takes·eight.
And·a·variant·depends·upon·value.

The·fourth·VB·data·type·is·currency;·eight·bytes·to·store.
A·single·takes·four.
A·double·takes·eight.
And·a·variant·depends·upon·value.

The·fifth·VB·data·type·is·the·string;·one·byte·per·character.
Currency·takes·eight.
A·single·takes·four.
A·double·takes·eight.
And·a·variant·depends·upon·value.

The·sixth·VB·data·type·is·the·long,·four·bytes·to·store.
One·byte·a·character·for·strings.
Currency·takes·eight.
A·single·takes·four.
A·double·takes·eight.
And·a·variant·depends·upon·value.

The·seventh·VB·data·type·is·the·integer;·two·bytes·to·store.
A·long·takes·four.
One·byte·a·character·for·strings.
Currency·takes·eight.
A·single·takes·four.
A·double·takes·eight.
And·a·variant·depends·upon·value.

How might you turn this information into a memorable image? Here's just one of the infinite possibilities: picture your boss and her boss talking via two tin cans connected by a string. At various points between the sender (your boss) and the receiver (her boss) the string (the channel) bulges with words (the message). Now picture yourself standing midway between the two, hoisting a chainsaw over the delicate string. Can you guess which element you represent? The noise, of course. The feedback, in this case, might be your boss's boss hurling his tin can in frustration.

Another way you can capitalize on the power of pictures is through a technique called *memory mapping*. Don't worry, it doesn't require a class in cartography or any artistic ability. If you can draw basic shapes and lines, you can create a memory map.

Memory maps are similar to other tools you may be familiar with—data flow diagrams and structure charts. All of these tools provide a way to organize information in a logical fashion by arranging it as parts of a diagram. The act of creating them helps you organize your thoughts and forces you to identify how the pieces of whatever you're mapping fit together.

To create a memory map, begin by drawing a shape of your choice, such as a circle, square, diamond, or star, in the center of a blank page. Inside the shape, write a word describing what you're mapping. For each main idea associated with the topic, draw a line extending outward from the shape. Add additional lines branching off of the main ones for associated ideas and topics. Figure 11-4 shows a memory map for the GRASP system.

Figure 11-4
GRASP
Memory Map

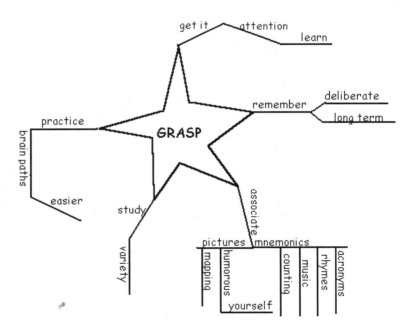

No two memory maps will look alike. Each is unique to the topic and to the person who created it. Illustrating and organizing information this way utilizes both motion and sight (visualization) to help you remember it later on.

Study Groups

Contrary to popular assumption, a study group isn't a place to learn new information; it's a place to practice and reinforce what you've already learned. Depending on other group members to provide you with an introduction to something you haven't studied yet is risky—it may be presented inaccurately, and once you learn something the wrong way, learning it correctly is more difficult. It's wiser to get the facts down first, then use a study group setting to reinforce them.

Study groups are good for increasing your understanding of a topic. Since no two people see things exactly the same way, another participant may be crystal clear on a concept that you're struggling with and can guide you through it. You can return the favor for a different concept. You can also compare interpretations. The process of discussing subject matter will clarify material and solidify it in your mind.

Study group members can also drill each other with flash cards or exchange essay questions. This sort of interaction is very valuable when preparing for tests.

You may be able to join an existing study group, but, more likely, you'll have to form your own. Look for two or three individuals working on the same material (or certification) as yourself. You may find them online or through a class you're participating in.

Set regular meeting times—once a week is a common interval—and choose a site conducive to your purpose. A library may not be a good option unless there's a room you can use so your discussions won't disrupt others. An empty classroom or someone's dining room table are also possibilities. Limit meetings to about an hour per session; any longer and the extra time is likely to be spent on socializing rather than studying.

If you're preparing for certification through self-study, your best bet for forming a study group is likely to be via the Internet. Prowl forums and newsgroups devoted to the topic(s) you're interested in, and consider posting a message seeking individuals interested in forming a virtual study group. You can also use the Web search engines to seek out such groups. Use the name of your certification and the phrase "study group" as search keys.

Self-Quizzing

One of the simplest ways to practice recalling information is via the self-quiz. Talk about versatility and convenience—you can self-quiz almost anywhere. You can do it with spiffy software, audio tape, or cheap 3 x 5 index cards. You can time yourself, or not. And how often do you get the chance to make up your own questions for a test?

Depending upon your choice of certification and how deep your pockets are, you can purchase quizzes that other people have made specifically for your certification. Figure 11-5 shows a screen from Self Test Software's preparation package for Lotus.

Figure 11-5
Self Test Software's
Certification
Preparation
Program for Lotus

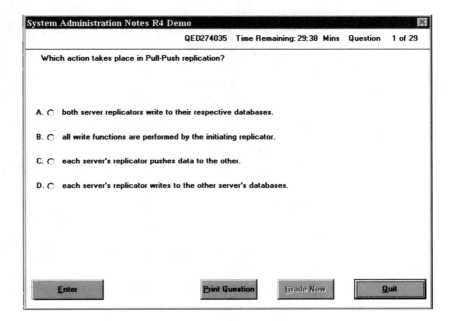

Many of these prepackaged quizzes are available in software format. Others come in workbooks. This book's resource section includes contact information for the most widely known vendors of certification preparation software. Their product lines are always evolving, so visit their Web sites or telephone their offices for information on current offerings. Trial versions of various self-tests are included on this book's companion Web site and are often available from the vendors.

Besides certification-specific software, there are a number of shareware programs that allow you to create quizzes on any topic of your choice. These can be especially useful if commercial programs are too expensive or unavailable for the material you wish to practice. Figure 11-6 shows WinFlash, by Open Window (**www.openwindow.com**). You can also sample the trial version that's included on this book's companion Web site.

Figure 11-6
WinFlash
Self-Quizzing
Software

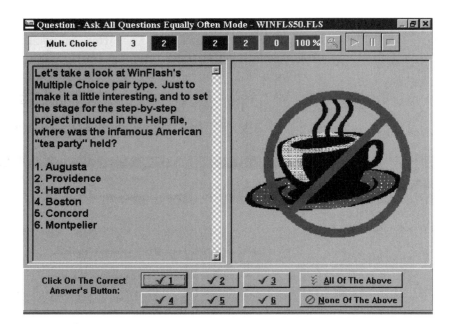

Figure 11-6
WinFlash
Self-Quizzing
Software

If you prefer to go low tech, you can create a set of flash cards using 3 x 5 index cards. Write the question on the front of the card and the correct answer on the back. If you keep a deck of these cards on hand, you can sneak in practice whenever it's convenient to do so. When you think you have one set of cards down cold, put them aside and start another. Come back to the first set later, and see how much you remember.

Books on tape are becoming popular with people on the go. You can create a quiz on tape to listen to during your daily commute or during exercise workouts. To do so, prepare a list of questions and answers. Then insert a fresh tape into your tape recorder and press **record**. Read a question aloud, let the tape roll for a few seconds (however long you want to allow yourself to answer the question you must read), then read the answer aloud. Repeat the procedure for each question on your list. When you play back the quiz later, try to answer the questions before the recorded answer plays. Before you record an entire quiz, run a test batch of a few questions to verify that the tape recorder is set up and operating properly.

Taking Tests

If you asked learners to choose the aspect of the educational process that causes them the most anxiety, the overwhelming majority would cite tests. Why? Because a test presents an opportunity for failure, and nobody likes to fail. In fact, fear of failure sometimes leads people who know the material cold to blank out on test day, and just what they feared most would happen, does.

But wait a minute. Consider what will happen to you if you do fail a test. Will your coworkers burst into laughter when you return to the office? Will your spouse or lover leave you? Will you lose your job and, as a result, be unable to pay your mortgage, which will then cause you to lose your house and end up dying penniless, in a gutter and alone some cold night? Of course not.

So, putting first things first, don't blow this test thing out of proportion. If you don't pass the test, you'll probably have to take it again. Big deal. It might not be your idea of a good time, but it's hardly life-shattering. And the fact is, if you prepare effectively, you're infinitely more likely to succeed than fail.

QUOTE

How-to Advice from an Exam Veteran

To prepare, find the Web page that describes the objectives of the test and study to those objectives. Find a discussion group on the Net, certification-related Web pages, or a local study group, and talk to people who are taking or have taken the same test. You're not after any specific answers; the tests almost always vary. What you're trying to do is identify the areas covered. If the folks you talk to indicate that there's a lot of emphasis on a certain topic, review and study that topic until you can answer any question about it.

Most tests are computer-based nowadays; mark and skip any question that you don't have a ready answer for, run through the entire test answering the questions you know, then go back and reason through the marked questions (determine beforehand if there is any penalty for guessing or providing a wrong answer). Often one or more of the answer options can be eliminated. Once you've got an answer for every question, review if you have time.

Get plenty of sleep before the test because it's counterproductive to take the test when you are exhausted, and relax as much as possible. Even if you don't pass the test, you can usually retake the test later without a penalty, although you'll have to pay an additional testing fee.

—Eric Charbonneau, veteran of MCSE, IBM Professional Server Expert,
and numerous other certification exams

Before the Test

What constitutes effective preparation? Most importantly, it doesn't begin the night before the exam. As discussed earlier in this chapter, cramming is an ineffective learning tool and only marginally successful as a last-minute act of desperation. Pull an all-nighter and your mind may be stuffed with facts, but they will be shrouded in a fatigue-induced fog. When the fog dissipates, the facts are likely to go with it.

If, on the other hand, you've been studying throughout a course, you're already halfway prepared for the final exam. That's because you've GRASPed the majority of the information and only have to review and practice recalling it the way the test will ask you to.

The first step is to find out as much as possible about the format and content of the exam. Questions to answer include:

- What will you be expected to know?
- Which question format will be utilized—multiple choice, essay questions, or true-false? Currently, most computer certification tests are multiple choice.
- How long will you have to complete the test?
- Will you be able to return to questions later if you skip over them?
- Will points be subtracted for wrong answers?

You should be able to obtain the answers to these questions from your certification sponsor, instructor, and/or testing center. Once you've identified the characteristics of the particular test, you can tailor your review methods accordingly.

Adaptive Testing

The tests that most people are familiar with are linear. Every person who takes the test receives the same questions in the same order. But as you pursue certification, you may find yourself taking a different kind of test, called an *adaptive test*. You're especially likely to encounter one if you pursuing a certification sponsored by Novell.

In adaptive testing, the number and order of questions varies each time the test is given. Exactly how these vary is decided by an algorithm in the testing program that is intended to dynamically assess the test subject's competency level.

Adaptive tests are given via computer. The first question given to any certification candidate is one that is judged to be of average difficulty. The computer program chooses which question to give next based on the candidate's response to the first question. If the question is answered correctly, then the next question is more difficult. If the answer to the first question is incorrect, an easier question is offered next.

This process continues throughout the test, with the computer algorithm analyzing the accuracy of previous answers to determine which question to ask next. The purpose is to pinpoint a candidate's competency level without subjecting him or her to questions that are obviously above or below the person's capabilities (per the program's algorithm). In this way the test is tailored (that is, adapted) to each test taker.

According to Novell, a pioneer of adaptive testing, the exam ends when "a) your ability is estimated with sufficient accuracy, b) the program is at least 95% confident that your ability score lies somewhere above the passing score, or c) the maximum number of questions is given." The maximum number of questions for Novell's adaptive tests is 25, and the minimum is 15.

Adaptive tests are shorter than their nonadaptive counterparts, and untimed. The sequence of questions is unique to each candidate. Because candidates see a small portion of the available question pool, security of test questions is easier to maintain.

When taking adaptive tests, candidates have no control over the order in which they answer questions. Once a question is presented, it's a now or never situation; you can't pass on a question and come back to it later.

Proponents of adaptive testing, which has been around in one form or another for about fifteen years, cite efficiency as the number one benefit. A test that typically takes an hour in the standard linear format can be administered in less than half that time through adaptive technology. But from the candidate's perspective, the process can feel arbitrary and even unfair. Can a computer really calculate a person's ability level on the fly? What if you have the bad luck to get a question on the one area you don't have down cold? Perhaps these concerns address why adaptive testing hasn't really caught on.

Review the material that you've identified as likely to be on the test. Try to guess what questions will appear on the test, then practice answering them. You can practice by reciting aloud, creating written or recorded self-tests, or using commercially available self-testing software and certification preparation guides. If you belong to a study group, quiz each other and discuss your answers.

Pay special attention to vocabulary and terminology words. Make certain you know exactly what they mean. If you don't understand a question, you won't be able to answer it.

Develop an overall test strategy, depending on the type of exam. The following advice focuses on multiple-choice exams, the most common format of current certification tests. Most, but not all of these exams, count an unanswered question the same way as an incorrect answer. If you won't be penalized for wrong answers (as opposed to skipping the question entirely) then it pays to guess when you don't know the correct answer.

If the exam will be time limited, and you can go back and revisit questions (not always the case), plan to answer the questions you're certain of first, and then return to those that give you more trouble. This strategy enables you to answer a larger percentage of the questions and to answer the easiest ones right away.

The night before, do a brief review and remind yourself that you've prepared and are as ready as you're going to be. Don't stress yourself out pouring over your notes again and again. Instead, spend the evening in some pleasant, relaxing way, then get a good night's sleep so you'll be rested and ready to excel.

The Day of the Test

On the day of the test, allow yourself plenty of time to arrive at the test site. Would you rather arrive at the last minute, adrenaline pumping from the stress of too many red lights, or ten or fifteen minutes early, time you can easily fill with a final review of your note cards or trip to the restroom?

Make certain to bring a plentiful supply of the materials you'll need. That might include pens and pencils, scrap paper, and a calculator. If you'll be going to a testing center, bring several forms of identification including a photo ID, and, of course, payment.

If you feel tense or anxious, apply a few relaxation techniques. One of the most basic is breathing. Take a deep breath, filling not just your chest, but every nook and cranny of your insides all the way down to your abdomen. Inhale from your navel, like a baby does. Exhale slowly, and feel your muscles relaxing as you your breath carries the tension out of your body. Repeat the breathing several times.

When the test begins, follow your preplanned strategy.

- If the test format is suitable, remember to go through and answer the easy questions first.
- Pay close attention to instructions. Are you supposed to select just one answer or all answers that apply?
- Read each question carefully, and twice. It's easy to misread a question and end up with the wrong answer as a result. It's also a waste and something you can avoid.
- Be alert for modifiers like *always*, *never*, *not*, and *except* that can radically affect the meaning of the question.
- Mentally answer the question before reading the answer choices. Then look for the choice that most accurately reflects your answer. This can spare you unnecessary confusion created by the test itself.
- If you don't know the answer, make an educated guess (see sidebar).
- If you finish before the time limit, go back over the test and verify your answers. But *don't* change an answer unless you have good reason to believe it's wrong. Research indicates that when in doubt, our first guess is usually our best.

If other people are taking the exam at the same time, don't pay any attention to when they finish. Just because others are done before you doesn't mean that they will end up with a better score. Correspondingly, if you finish first, it doesn't mean you must have missed something. Take your time, keeping an eye on the exam clock if there's a time limit, and concentrate on regurgitating what you've learned. If you've prepared using effective techniques, such as the ones detailed in this chapter, you have nothing to worry about.

Making an Educated Guess

If you find yourself facing a question you just don't know the answer to, consider guessing. If there are four possible choices, you automatically have a 25% chance of randomly selecting the correct answer. Apply some guessing techniques, and the odds shoot upward in your favor.

Successful guessing relies heavily on the process of elimination. For that reason, the first step is to eliminate any choices that are clearly wrong. If you have four answers to choose from and you can discard two of them as incorrect, you've gone from a one in four chance of picking the right answer to a one in two chance.

Unless your exam format allows more than one answer choice for each question (which is unusual), "all of the above" is basically equivalent to "more than one of the above." If "all of the above" is an option, and you can see at least two correct answers, then choose it.

Sometimes you'll find that, in the course of presenting the question and answers, one test item will provide hints that can help you answer another. Be alert for these and use them when you find them.

Many test-taking experts advise that if you have no idea which choice is correct, and "all of the above" is an option, you should choose "all of the above." By the same token, if you can't decide between two similar answers, choose the one that gives the most complete information.

A Half Dozen Ways to Beat Procrastination—Today

Effective study techniques are powerful productivity boosters—if you use them. But if the procrastinator's mantra—"I'll do it tomorrow"—starts playing in your head, it can wreak havoc on your certification plans. Procrastination often masquerades as some other, ostensibly legitimate, demand for your time. Only on close examination is the disguise pierced. The following are examples of what you can do to the keep the procrastination beast on a leash.

Study 15 Minutes a Day

For some unfathomable reason, when it's time to study, the laundry in the corner suddenly becomes more urgent than the new material. So does mowing the lawn. Anything that delays the dreaded moment of sitting down and beginning becomes more attractive than work.

But getting started doesn't have to be so difficult. Simply set yourself a daily deadline by which you must sit down and commence 15 minutes of studying. That's right, a mere 15 minutes.

When that deadline arrives, force yourself into your study space and work until the time is up. The method's magic is that once you get going, you won't want to stop! You're virtually guaranteed to continue long beyond 15 minutes and accomplish plenty.

Put Procrastination to Work for You

Make procrastination your slave instead of your master. When you're reluctant to begin a particular project, consider other study tasks you could be doing instead. Is your Personal Certification Plan current? Have you reviewed your vocabulary list lately? Why not go back and draw a memory map for that concept you covered last week? Even if you don't get to the project you really ought to be doing today, other valuable tasks will be completed: there really is nothing like procrastination for getting things done. And once you begin, you just might find yourself picking up the work you're avoiding and completing that as well.

Quell Household Distractions

People who study at home know what it's like: the nearby refrigerator seems to call your name. Friends and family telephone to chat just as you settle in to study. You're wearing your last pair of underwear and really should run the laundry through.

While it's certainly the prerogative (and even pleasure) of someone who studies at home to tend to a chore during a break, don't let this *can* become a *should*. As in *I should do this chore* or *I ought to do that one because I'm right here and it needs to be done*.

During study hours, you are not at home—you are at work. If the refrigerator is a problem, weaken its pull by stocking it with lettuce and fruit instead of high fat treats. When callers disrupt your concentration, let the answering machine pick up or simply offer to return calls later. If tasks, such as piled up dishes, beg attention, imagine how you would respond if your study space was uptown at the library instead of upstairs. Would you drive home and suds up or leave them for later? Save your chores and errands for after study time. They won't go anywhere.

Respect What You're Doing

Frequently, adult learners give their educational efforts a back seat to everything else and consequently get little done. The logic goes something like this: it isn't that important, after all, I do it out of choice, and I already have a job.

The person who lets this thought pattern continue is placing serious limits on his or her success. Your certification goals are meaningful and valuable. You are just fortunate (and clever) enough to be in charge of your own future. Education and professional advancement are something you've decided to go after. Don't let insecurity stop you!

It may help to review your accomplishments. Go over your Personal Certification Plan, and review what you've already achieved. Revisit your reasons for pursuing certification in the first place. Count your successes, and see how you can build on them.

When you interact with others, don't be afraid to talk about your educational accomplishments and struggles or that troublesome exam. To become a confident and successful student, you must act and feel like one.

Get Regular

While a flexible schedule is overtly a plus, a regular routine will ensure productivity. Identify certain hours to study every week. You can pick how many and which ones, but decide on a core set of hours, with others you can add or omit as needed. Instruct members of your household not to interrupt you during those times unless there is blood or fire involved.

Have a designated study space and go there during your study time; your equipment and supplies will be at hand and you'll become conditioned to work when you're in that space. If you have children, arrange child care during your scheduled hours or plan to study when they're in bed or at school. Alternatively, study at work, the library, or another site away from home.

Entering The Zone

Imagine an ideal performance state, a "zone of productivity" where your learning flows unimpeded as if from a greased mechanism. It's a lofty aspiration, but you can certainly make strides in that direction, starting today. After all, it will only take 15 minutes.

Putting it All Together

Keep in mind that there are many study methods available. The methods you've read about here are solid, specific approaches to common learning tasks. Nonetheless, they are by no means the only solutions available. If you want to learn additional study methods, check out your local bookstore and library for books about studying. A selection of suggested titles is included in the Resource section.

Thanks to the many colleges and universities connected to the Internet, you can also access study tips via the Web. Educational institutions around the world have put study advice online for your free, 24-hour perusal. Virginia Polytechnic Institute (**www.ucc.vt.edu/ stdysk/stdyhlp.html**); University of California, Berkeley (**128.32.89.153/CalRENHP.html**); the University of Texas (**www.utexas.edu/student/lsc/handouts/stutips.html**); and Dartmouth (**www.dartmouth.edu/admin/acskills/index.html#study**) are good places to start. Figure 11-7 shows Virginia Polytechnic's Web-based study skills resource center.

At first it may feel like the effort that it takes to be an active learner requires more time and energy than it's worth. But once you get into the swing of it, you'll find that the time you put into learning how to learn will be paid back ten times over; you'll be able to remember more and maybe even study less.

Figure 11-7
Virginia Polytechnic
Offers Study Advice
via the Web

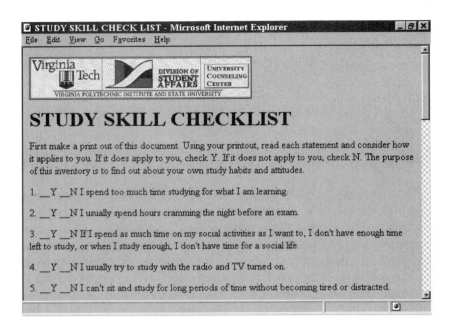

Utilize Your Certification to the Max

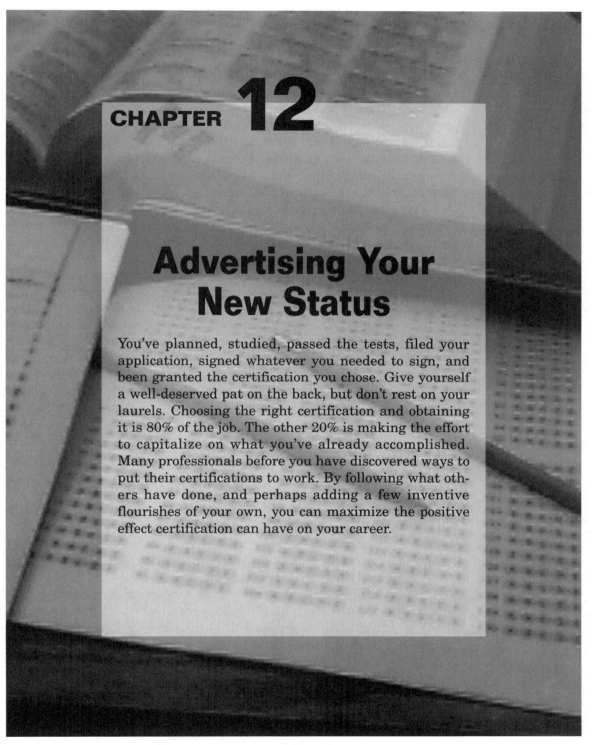

CHAPTER **12**

Advertising Your New Status

You've planned, studied, passed the tests, filed your application, signed whatever you needed to sign, and been granted the certification you chose. Give yourself a well-deserved pat on the back, but don't rest on your laurels. Choosing the right certification and obtaining it is 80% of the job. The other 20% is making the effort to capitalize on what you've already accomplished. Many professionals before you have discovered ways to put their certifications to work. By following what others have done, and perhaps adding a few inventive flourishes of your own, you can maximize the positive effect certification can have on your career.

Looking Good in Print

Most certification sponsors have created a logo that uniquely identifies professionals who have completed their program. These logos are professionally designed, and they're often heavily marketed by the certification sponsor to promote understanding of the logo's significance to your potential customers, to employers, and to others throughout the computer industry. This creates brand recognition, something marketing organizations across industries work to achieve. By utilizing these logos to promote yourself, you get to benefit from the effort and financing that have gone into the sponsor's logo program. Doing so is one of the easiest ways to advertise your status as a certified professional.

Certification logos can be used on your business cards, resume, marketing materials, Web site, and almost anywhere else you can think of. To prevent misuse and abuse of these logos, the certification sponsor usually provides guidelines for proper usage. In some cases, you'll have to submit your plans for advance approval. Although such restrictions may feel annoying, they're really for your benefit as much as for the sponsor's. By assuring that these logos are used in a professional and consistent manner, the certification sponsor is protecting and building their value.

Logos are generally provided in several formats. This makes it easier for you to utilize them for various purposes, and you end up with a more professional result. It's possible to convert files between graphical file formats using special utility file conversion programs, but some resolution may be lost, which is one reason sponsors are willing to offer logos in various formats. Electronic formats, such as GIF, JPG, EPS, and TIF, can be imported into word processing, desktop publishing, graphics (such as Web design), and other computer programs. Typically, the menu command to use will be some variation of **Insert | Picture** or **Import | Image**.

Camera-ready logos, another format for logo distribution, are, as the name implies, suitable for photographing, with good results. They're provided in a high-resolution, sharply printed format and can be pasted directly onto originals before reproduction.

Commercial printers sometimes prefer to receive graphics in a particular format—the one that works best with their system. If you're having the logo included on your business card or on other commercially printed materials, ask the printing company which format will produce the best results.

Besides incorporating a certification logo on your personal materials, consider the marketing potential they offer your employer. If you're the first person at your company to obtain the certification, you've added value to the company's service offerings. The company may well want to advertise your new status for its own benefit.

Consider a company specializing in expanding existing networks that can claim "Cisco Certified Internetwork Expert (CCIE) on staff," or "Enterprise CNE on staff." Such announcements would, of course, be accompanied by reproductions of the relevant logo. This type of employer marketing of your certification is a win-win situation. The employer wins through gaining increased credibility, which may well lead to added revenue, and you gain by boosting your value to your employer and earning a reputation for yourself as an expert.

QUOTE

Lending Your Employer Extra Credibility

I definitely used my certifications to market myself when I was looking for another job in the field I became certified in. The engineering certifications (especially Microsoft) are in such great demand that the sheer fact that you're certified gets you noticed. Many companies won't hire you if you're not certified, and many advertise that they're looking for certified professionals.

The company that I work for now will use my numerous certifications as a marketing tool for them to get more business. They've lost a few accounts based on the fact that they didn't have any certified engineers on staff. Once they advertise that they're a Microsoft Solution Provider and use my certifications when bidding for contracts, they have the potential to make thousands of additional dollars.

—Cameron Brandon, MCSE, CNE, CNA, A+, MCPS/Internet Systems

Marketing Magic via the Internet

More than a few publications rave about the potential of the Internet and World Wide Web as marketing tools, and most of the claims are true. The Web is a versatile medium. It's affordable, accessible, and, for most computer professionals, a do-it-yourself opportunity. This is especially true for computer-related services and products, such as your services as a computer professional. It provides access to an incredible number of interested potential customers/employers, and recruiters and employers use it as a tool to uncover talent and fill positions. You can use it to market yourself as a computer professional, to establish a professional reputation, and to display your talent to those who might be interested in compensating you handsomely for it.

The potential of the Web as a marketing medium to advertise your certified status is limited only by the extent of your creativity. To begin with, you can use it to:

- Communicate with your customers via electronic mailings
- Draw interested clients and employers to you by creating a Web site
- Make professional networking a pleasure
- Establish name recognition and expert status for yourself

Information on posting your resume online is included in Chapter 14, which covers how to use certification to land a new job.

You can do all of this with minimum financial outlay and a bit of your time. Best of all, the Web is an enjoyable medium to work with, and even though you'll be using it for professional purposes, the process can be as much (or more) fun as it is work.

A Quick Guide to Getting Connected

You don't need an ISDN connection, high-powered server, or any other high-end equipment to turn the Internet into your personal marketing tool. As a computer professional, you may already be Internet savvy and able to find your way onto the information superhighway with your eyes closed. But for those who aren't already logged in, here's a quick overview on getting connected.

The computer you use to access the Internet doesn't need to be especially powerful or cutting edge. Your current personal computer will probably do the job nicely. If you don't have a computer at home, it may well be time to buy one. A PC with a 486 or higher processor, 8MB of RAM at the bare minimum (16MB or more is better), and loads (preferably a gigabyte or more) of disk storage will do the job. Don't skimp on disk space. Between the needs of your Web browser software and the bounty of interesting files you'll want to download, you'll need plenty of storage at your disposal.

The modem should be capable of 28.8Kbps (Kilobits per second) or higher. Although it's possible to travel the Web using a modem as slow as 2400 baud, doing so may test the limits of your sanity. Imagine watching a full-length feature movie at less than a tenth of its normal playing speed, and you'll have a good understanding of why modem speed is so important.

The modem can be internal or external to your computer. Which one you choose is largely a matter of personal preference. Internal modems don't take any extra desk space and are slightly lower in price. However, you'll have to open your computer's system unit to install it, and some people experience hardware conflicts that can be difficult to track down and resolve. External modems give you the benefit of pretty flashing lights to reassure you that your connection hasn't crashed, which can be comforting during a long download. They're also easier to install. You just connect them to the serial port in the back of your computer; there's no need to open the system unit.

The telephone line can be the same one you use for everyday household conversations. You'll connect your modem to the wall jack in the same way you would a telephone, using the same type of phone cord. People who spend a lot of time connected to the Net (which isn't hard to do with all that interesting stuff out there!) often add a separate phone line so their home phone number isn't tied up for hours on end.

The final thing you'll need to get connected is access to the Internet. You get this by purchasing a subscription from a company that provides this service. When you dial the company, your call is answered by one of their computers, and linked to the Internet via a high-speed connection. The going rate runs about $20 a month, although you'll find rates that run slightly higher or lower. The fee usually includes email and space on the company's computer for your personal Web page.

These companies that connect you to the Internet come in two varieties: online services and Internet service providers (ISPs). Online services are company-run "virtual communities" that only subscribers can fully access. They provide topical discussion forums; software repositories; news, weather, and business feeds; and a host of other electronic services, including Internet access. The Internet access is sometimes called an Internet gateway. The two online services with the most subscribers are America Online (AOL) and CompuServe. ISPs, on the other hand, provide Internet access only. MCI and AT&T are two popular providers.

Each of the two subscriptions has its pros and cons. Online services provide an oasis of relative calm within the chaos of the Internet. Within the service, information is organized by topic, and some degree of control over content is exercised (which means that rude, nasty individuals are usually shown the door). They also have extensive technical support available for people who need it.

ISPs, on the other hand, do one thing and one thing only—provide Internet access. You'll usually find an Internet connection via an ISP to be significantly faster than one through an online service's gateway. And once you're connected, you're usually pretty much on your own. For many people, that's exactly as they prefer it.

As with most other products and services, quality varies between vendors. Some vendors don't have an adequate setup, which can lead to lost connections, busy signals, and other impediments. Logjams at peak times of Internet usage (evenings) are also common. You may decide to switch vendors if your connection is consistently unsatisfactory, so don't lock yourself in to a year's service in exchange for a price break until you're positive that you'll receive good service in return. It's always a good idea to ask friends and colleagues which Internet access vendors they recommend and which they don't. If you live in a large metropolitan area, you'll have many companies to choose from; in some other locations, the options will be more limited.

It shouldn't take long to get your computer, modem, telephone line, and Internet access lined up, and once you do, you'll have access to the marketing wonder of the Information Age.

Internet Connection Resources

This list includes some of the Internet access providers available to you. Online services will often send you free software and a free trial period. ISPs rarely provide the free trial.

Popular Online Services

- America Online (AOL); 800-827-6364; **www.aol.com**
- CompuServe (CSi); 800-336-6823; **www.compuserve.com**
- Microsoft Network (MSN); 800-228-7007; **www.msn.com**

continued

> ## Internet Service Providers (ISPs)
>
> To find an ISP with a local phone number can be a challenge. It's a good idea to inquire at a local computer store or ask friends which provider they use. ISPs that serve every state in the USA include:
>
> - aaaa.net; 888-732-1266; **www.aaaa.net**
> - Camelot Internet Access Services; 972-713-2630; **www.cias.net**
> - City Online; 888-4-CITYOL; **www.citycom.com**
> - EarthLink Network; 800-395-8425; **www.earthlink.com**
> - Epoch Internet; 888-77-EPOCH; **www.eni.net**
> - FNet; 805-373-8688; **www.ftel.net**
> - GTE; 800-927-3000; **www.gte.net**
> - MCI; 800-348-8011; **www.mci2000.com**
>
> If you can access the Internet, search for a new provider by area code, using The List, at **thelist.internet.com**. It contains over 3,000 ISPs, along with service and pricing information.

Direct Email

Whichever Internet access you have, chances are it comes with unlimited email access. This means that you have free access to one of the more effective forms of advertising: direct mail marketing. The trick with email, even more so than the earthbound variety, is to target your recipients carefully. In cyberspace, junk mail is very poorly received. If you are perceived as a junk emailer (also called a *spammer*), you will do your image more harm than good. Word travels fast on the Internet, whether or not the message is positive.

So how can you make appropriate use of email to advertise your status as a certified professional? One method is to send an FYI update to your past and present clients (and/or your employer's), reminding them of your skills, availability, and, of course, certified status. Keep such messages short and to the point. For example:

> ABC company is pleased to announce the we now have a Certified Network Wizard on staff. This certification, granted only by the International Network Excellence Foundation, signifies the attainment of the highest standards in design, installation, and management of complex network environments.

This would be followed by another paragraph or two about the services ABC company currently offers and a call to action, such as: "To boost your Network performance, call ABC," along with contact information.

If any companies or recruiters have your resume on file, you would then send them a variation of the above message, along with an updated version of your resume.

Your Cyber Billboard

Whether you obtain Internet access through an online service or ISP, your account will usually include space on the provider's server for your personal Web pages. You are paying for this as part of your basic subscription fee, so don't let it go to waste. ISPs, in particular, may charge extra for Web page storage, but usually the fee for a basic personal site will be nominal. Some Web sites will even host your home page for free, without your having to be a subscriber to a particular service. Yahoo! maintains an index of such sites at **www.yahoo.com/Business_and_Economy/Companies/ Internet_Services/Web_Services/Free_Web_Pages/**.

Creating a Web site that will showcase your talents doesn't require a degree in graphics design. The site can be a straightforward, one-page affair, or a multi-part masterpiece, depending on your goals, aspirations, and how much time you're willing to devote to the project. Thanks to the plentiful supply of Web design software packages available today, you don't even have to learn HTML (hypertext markup language), which is used to hard-code Web pages. Instead, you can point, click, and highlight, inserting pictures, text, and links where you'd like them. As you paint the screen with images and text, the design program translates the results into HTML for you. Figure 12-1 shows one such program.

You can find these Web design tools (sometimes called HTML editors) at your local software outlet or download them from Web sites on the Internet. The AOLPress program, for example, can be found at **www.aolpress.com**. You can jump to reviews of various HTML software programs and find out how to obtain them from Yahoo!'s index of HTML editors at **www.yahoo.com/Computers_and_ Internet/Software/Internet/World_Wide_Web/HTML_Editors**.

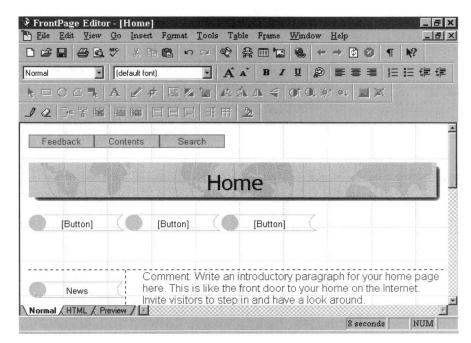

Figure 12-1
Using Microsoft's
FrontPage 98 to
Design a Web Site

An endless supply of available HTML tutorials will provide you with step-by-step advice on the creation of your Web site. You can find Web design books in the computer section of your local bookstore or order them from one of the online bookstores, such as Amazon Books (**www.amazon.com books**). You can also find plenty of free advice, much of it pretty good, on various Web sites. For starters, check out:

- The NCSA (National Center for Supercomputing Applications) Beginner's Guide to HTML (**www.ncsa.uiuc.edu/General/ Internet/WWW/HTMLPrimer.html**) is an excellent place to get the basics on what HTML is, its various components, and how to put it to work for you. You can also download this file to print out or read using Adobe Acrobat Reader, which can be obtained for free at **www.adobe.com**.

- If you already have HTML basics down cold, you might want to learn the ins and outs of more advanced techniques, including floating frames, marquees, meta tags, and more. You can read about all of these at **www.geocities.com/SiliconValley/ Park/7476/advancedhtml.htm**, Neil Johan's advanced HTML site.

What to Put on Your Pages

Give some thought to what you want to include on your Web pages. It's good to develop an overall plan before beginning, so your site will have a cohesive feel. Don't feel like you have to create the whole thing all at once. Start with a main page (this will be your home page), and add to it over time. Strive to make your site interesting by providing a variety of content.

 Check out what other computer professionals are doing with their Web pages to see what works and what doesn't. You can jump to many of them from Yahoo!'s high-tech resumes index at **www.yahoo.com/Computers_and_Internet/Employment/Resumes/Individual_Resumes/**.

Think of your main page as a table of contents for your site. Your contact information should be there, along with a brief introduction so visitors know what they are looking at and who created the site. You'll also need links to other pages in your site, accompanied by descriptions so visitors can choose whether or not to view them.

Web Site Design Tips

✐ **Go easy on the graphics.** Pictures take longer to download than text, and visitors may jump to another site rather than wait for a page full of graphics, no matter how amazing, to download.

✐ **Make navigation between pages simple.** Visitors should be able to return to the main page with a single mouse click.

✐ **Don't get too fancy.** Web pages with purple lettering on black backgrounds, or other jarring combinations, prove nearly impossible to read. When in doubt, it's best to be conservative with the use of color. For similar reasons, stick to one or two fonts in various sizes.

✐ **Don't incorporate large blocks of text that span the width of a monitor.** Narrow columns with wide margins will be easier on the eyes.

✐ **If you use a background texture or image, make sure it doesn't obscure the clarity of the text that overlies it.**

continued

> ✐ **If you include links to other sites, check them periodically to ensure that they still work.**
> ✐ **Include an email link to your electronic mailbox and display the address as well.** Sometimes people may not have the mail portion of their Web browser working properly, and they'll want to know your email address to respond using another mail program.
> ✐ **Don't put personal information you don't want the whole world to know on your Web site.** This may include pictures of your children or your home phone number.
> ✐ **Verify that your page appears properly to individuals viewing it with different Web browsers.**

Possible pages include: your resume; links and/or reviews of Web resources that are linked to your area of professional expertise; reviews of products you work with; links to the Web sites of clients who maintain an online presence; examples of your work; testimonials from satisfied customers (get their permission first); or a tutorial on something you're qualified to teach about. Make it a goal to create a page that will prove useful to people who stop by.

Ideally, you should make your Web site a resource that visitors come back to again and again. To accomplish this, it's important to add new material periodically. Michael Corby, CISSP, of Michael Corby & Associates, has done this by creating a newsletter containing articles about his area of specialty—computer security. The table of contents page of a recent newsletter from Corby's site is shown in Figure 12-2.

QUICK TIP

Few interesting Web sites begin with the author's resume, so create a separate page for yours, and link to it from the main page.

You'll also want to build what are called "keywords" into your site, especially on the main page. *Keywords* are words and phrases individuals searching through the Net are likely to use. The trick is to figure out which words the users you want to draw to your site are likely to be using. Think about words that are common to your field of expertise and to your goals. Include both the acronyms and the spelled-out words. For example, you might work in the words enterprise resource planning (ERP) and independent consultant.

Figure 12-2
Michael Corby's
Newsletter

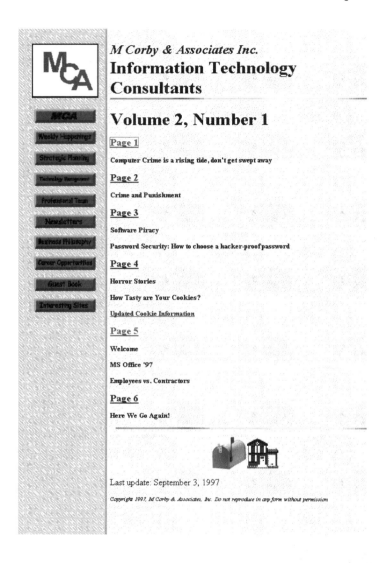

It's possible to imbed hidden keywords within a Web page by rendering the keyword in the same color as the background, thus making it invisible to the human eye, but readily available to computer search engines. Unscrupulous individuals have been known to incorporate the word **sex** in this way, to draw unsuspecting visitors to their Web site. When the visitor arrives, they, of course find no sexual content and have no clue why they ended up at your page. This kind of trickery is not likely to enhance the professional image you'd like to present and is best avoided.

QUICK TIP

When you're ready to present your Web site to the world, you'll need to upload it to your access provider's computer. Typically, this is accomplished using a special file transfer program, and your provider should supply you with instructions on how to do so.

If You Build It, Will They Come?

Creating a Web site and launching it into cyberspace doesn't automatically generate a readership. A few people will stumble across it, for sure, but your goal is to achieve much more than that. One measure of a Web site's success is the number of visitors (called *traffic* or *hits*) it receives. To build up traffic to your Web site, you'll need to spend a little time promoting it, but doing so won't take long.

To advertise your Web site, add the URL to your print materials, including your business card and marketing brochures. It should become a standard part of your contact information and be included in your email messages as well.

A second, arguably more powerful way to promote it, is via the Internet. You need to get your site included by the search engines (Yahoo!, Infoseek, AltaVista, and so on). To do this, you can visit the site of each search engine and follow the individual instructions. Or you can use one of the free tools, such as Submit It! (**www.submit-it.com**), that lets you submit your URL(s) to multiple search engines without having to independently visit each one. The Submit It! site is shown in Figure 12-3.

If your time is in short supply, consider signing up with a submission service. For a fee, these services will submit your Web site information to a specified number of search engines. To locate one, visit Yahoo!'s index of Web site announcement services, at **www.yahoo.com/Computers_and_Internet/Internet/World_Wide_Web/Announcement_Services/**.

As the number of certified computer professionals increases, so does the number of Web sites related to them. In particular, sites have begun to appear that serve as directories to certified professionals. These are in addition to those offered by specific certification sponsors. Such sites will happily link to your Web page(s), often including a summary of your credentials or what's to be found on your site. Figure 12-4 shows one such site.

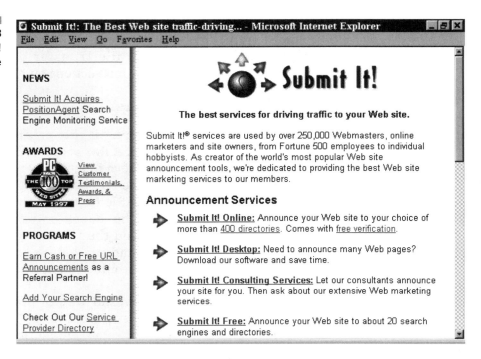

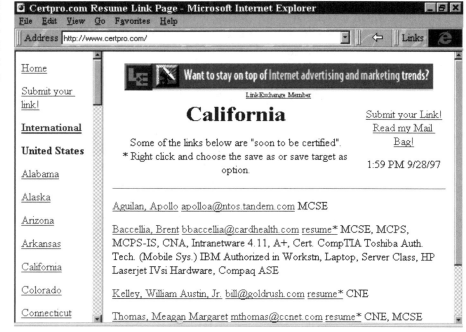

By getting yourself included in these directories, you'll add another no-cost route to promoting your professional status. Usually all it takes to get listed is an email to the site's creator. Before you send one, check through the site to make sure it's a place you'd like to be listed. If the pages are overly amateurish, include lots of broken links, or incorporate material you find objectionable, give that particular site a pass.

For the interested Web site promoter, many additional methods for increasing traffic to your site exist. Read about them in some of the excellent articles that have been written on the subject. You'll find plenty of them at the following sites:

- The Website Promoters Resource Center (**www.wprc.com**) is an excellent and robust site that contains tools and advice related to Web site promotion via targeted email, banner advertising, URL submissions, and press releases. If you want a consultant to assist you with your promotion efforts, you can find him or her here, too.
- Who's Marketing Online (**www.wmo.com**), an online newsletter from Sayers Publishing, contains loads of tips, resources, and articles related to online marketing. You can also elect to receive a free electronic subscription to the newsletter.
- Promotion World (**www.islandnet.com/~jreimer**) explains how to promote your Web site and build up traffic, all for free. You can also subscribe to The Promotion World Informer, a weekly electronic newsletter packed full of tips and tricks for promoting your Web site.

Clearly the Internet is not only a natural ally for the computer professional, it's also an easy-to-learn, low-cost marketing tool. Your potential employers and clients are out there trolling for experts like yourself. Why not make it easy for them to find you?

One Man's Web Site Plan

I had a three-pronged strategy for content with my Web page:

1. Place information that would promote my professional endeavors, which included my resume, bio, schedule, certifications, etc.
2. Place computer-related links that would benefit the computer professional audience. Examples: vendor certification, software companies, magazines, and news.
3. Place general interest best-of-breed links that simply encouraged people to stop by. Examples: sports, airlines, travel, and weather.

My URL has largely been distributed by word-of-mouth, included with my marketing materials, and listed by some Internet search engines. As my URL gets "discovered" by other people, they sometimes include a link to my page as a kind gesture or because they feel it has good content.

I've also added several additional resources. One is an MCP Resource Page dedicated to recognizing individuals who have attained the Microsoft Certified Professional credential. I believe it's the only one of its kind so far. I've also developed a Certified Instructors Resource Page that recognizes vendor-authorized instructors such as MCTs and CNIs. Listings are free.

My Web pages have evolved as needs change and my Web development skills improve. Traffic to my pages (while small by most standards) has exceeded my personal expectations and my customers have become regular visitors. It's been very beneficial to me. (Figure 12-5 shows Chan's Web site.)

—**Matthew Chan, MCT, MCSE, MCNE, CNI, IBM Lan Server Engineer,**
IBM Lan Server Instructor, and A+ Certified

Figure 12-5
Matthew Chan's
Home Page

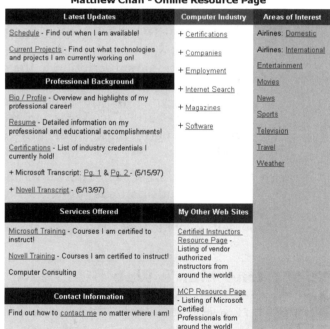

Networking and Lurking

In the career sense, networking means getting the word out about who you are and what you do. It means getting to know the people who may prove beneficial to your career at some point in the future. Perhaps they'll introduce you to the hiring manager of a company you want to work for, or maybe end up needing your professional services themselves. How do you know which people those are? You don't. It's impossible to predict who'll remember your name and pass it on when a need arises. Fortunately, the Internet provides an efficient networking medium, and you won't even have to endure any boring speeches or attend distant professional dinners to connect with clients and peers. You can do it all from your personal computer.

One of the strengths of the Internet is its power to bring people together. Individuals whose paths would never cross in a different environment can meet online and exchange information that will benefit one another. And part of the nature of the Internet community is that people are interested in helping each other out. Perhaps it's related to the age-old urge to offer advice, or maybe it's just a special cyber brand of good will. Either way, professionals online typically expect to receive help and advice and to offer it. By jumping into this community give and take, you can tap into the power of networking without leaving your desk. And you can use this environment to promote your professional abilities.

The primary places in which such networking occurs are forums and newsgroups. The two have much in common, and the terms are sometimes used interchangeably, but they are actually quite different. Both are repositories of discussion and information related to a particular topic. However, a forum is part of the World Wide Web, and as such, can be accessed using a Web browser. It will bear a name such as "The Client/Server Forum." Newsgroups, on the other hand, are a part of the Internet called *Usenet*. They are accessed using a program called a newsreader. Newsgroup names follow a standard format that indicates the subject matter at hand. Abbreviations or word fractions, separated by dots, are strung together to identify the topic. A newsgroup titled **comp.jobs.offered**, for example, is clearly identified as a place for messages about computer job openings. Table 12-1 lists common newsgroup abbreviations and their meanings.

Table 12-1
Newsgroup
Abbreviations

Abbreviation	Meaning	Example
alt	Alternative	alt.books.technical
biz	Business	biz.marketplace.services.computers
comp	Computer	comp.jobs
misc	Miscellaneous	misc.jobs.wanted
rec	Recreational	rec.games.computer.quake.playing
sci	Science	sci.physics.research
soc	Society	soc.activism
sys	Systems	comp.sys.att
os	Operating System	comp.os.linux.network
lang	Language	comp.lang.c

A forum is associated with a particular Web site or online service. Forums generally serve a smaller readership than newsgroups. They may be sponsored by a company with related products and services or by an interested individual. When you post a message to a forum, you often have the option to hide it from everyone but the person to whom you are replying. Although this is sometimes a good option to use, many times a reply will be of potential interest to others who follow the messages, so you won't want to conceal it. A forum is more likely (although not guaranteed) to be moderated, which means less off-topic ranting and raving.

Messages posted to a newsgroup are visible to all; anybody who wishes to read and respond to them can do so. They are more likely to include a high number of junk postings—off topic, often off-the-wall rantings. They also boast a greater number of readers and messages. In both forums and newsgroups, you can read messages, respond to them, and post questions of your own. However, neither is a place to post advertisements for yourself or your services, and doing so will get you an email box full of angry complaints (called *flames*).

Using newsgroups and forums to network and promote yourself is really very simple: all you have to do is share your expertise. The self-promotion is incidental to the advice you are offering and, thus, is acceptable according to the rules of Internet good conduct (sometimes called *netiquette*). It's also a powerful way to put your name and affiliations in front of many people, as well as demonstrate your expertise. To make this work, you'll need to do two things:

⬿ Create a signature
⬿ Identify appropriate newsgroups and forums

Your Signature

A *signature* is the closing section that will end each email and posting you create. Think of it as your electronic letterhead. Your signature should include your name, business title, email address, phone number, phrases conveying additional information about you, and sometimes a personal slogan. Depending on the nature of your message and where you post it, you may choose to include your physical address, too, or exclude your phone number.

The promotional parts of the signature are your business title and slogan. The business title conveys what kind of professional you are. The slogan can be a quote you feel is representative of yourself or you think is funny and can be included or excluded as you prefer. Any slogan should always be succinct—preferably one line. Figure 12-6 shows a signature that a certified professional might use.

Figure 12-6
Example of a
Personal Signature

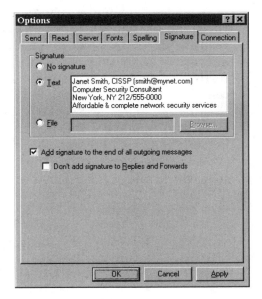

Prowling the Net

Once you've created your signature, it's time to identify target newsgroups and forums. There are thousands of them out there. Obviously, it's impossible to peruse them all. Instead, pick a few you'll want to visit regularly. How many depends on how much time you're willing to devote. Two is a manageable number to start with.

You're going to have to do a bit of exploring to uncover outlets that match your professional interests. A good place to begin your detective work is at the Reference.Com Web site at **www.reference.com** (shown in Figure 12-7). From here, you can search for newsgroups and forums that match your specialties. Don't limit yourself to computer-specific sites; if you're interested in a particular industry or technology, seek out forums and newsgroups related to it as well.

The first thing to do when you discover a promising newsgroup or forum is lurk. In Internet lingo, *lurkers* are individuals who are present but don't participate. In your case, that means read and pay attention, but don't post anything. This will enable you to get a solid feel for what material is discussed in the forum and what doesn't belong. It will also protect you from inadvertently posting something inappropriate that will generate ill will and start you off on the wrong foot. After several visits as a lurker, you'll be able to decide if the outlet is one in which you'd like to participate.

When you've found a forum or newsgroup that appeals to you and you've lurked enough to be certain of the content and format, you're ready to contribute. Watch for a question that you can answer with authority. When one appears, create a thoughtful, grammatically correct, spell-checked posting that addresses the issue at hand and concludes with the signature you've developed. Every time you do this, you're advertising your professional expertise, and, if you've done your signature file right, your credentials. Over time you'll become known to the people in the forum as a thoughtful, experienced professional. When they need just such a person, or know someone who does, your name will come to mind.

Figure 12-7
The
Reference.Com
Web Site

CHAPTER 13

Moving Up

Career advancement can follow many paths, and enhancing your professional credentials through earning a certification opens more of them to you. Now you're faced with the enviable (if somewhat daunting) task of deciding which route to pursue; you've come to an intersection on your career path, and you get to choose in which direction to proceed.

Straight ahead lies the path of least resistance: continuing as you are in the same job with the same responsibilities. You might choose to keep on going straight ahead if you're very content with your current position and/or have too much going on in other non-work areas of your life to devote mental energy to choosing one of the turns. Taking one of the turns, on the other hand, will require a bit of energy and effort, as they both involve upward movement. Turn one way to move up within your current organization, or the other to advance by moving on to a different employer (possibly even yourself). This career intersection is fast approaching, and you've earned yourself a green light through certification. It's time to step on the gas.

Up or Out?

Before you press the career accelerator too hard, you'll need to decide which way you're going to turn at this intersection. Since you've already made the choice to undertake certification, you're probably not completely satisfied with the status quo. That eliminates proceeding straight ahead, and leaves you with deciding whether you'd like to advance within your current company, or look elsewhere. Fortunately you've done most of work on this decision back in Chapter 8, as part of deciding which certification to pursue. As part of that process you completed three worksheets to help identify which career elements are important to you and whether or not they exist at your current workplace. You might want to go back and revisit your completed worksheets to refresh your memory.

If your review reminds you that your current workplace isn't meeting many or all of the needs you defined as important—and isn't likely to—then moving on may be your best option. Chapter 14 includes advice and hints on choosing that direction. If, on the other hand, your current employment has a lot going for it and has the potential to meet most or all of the needs you defined as important, then moving up within your current organization is your logical choice; this chapter will help speed you on your way.

There are two basic moves you can make to advance your career at your current place of employment: up or over. Moving up means increasing your responsibilities and place within the hierarchy of the organization without straying far from your current areas of expertise and/or department. Moving up makes you a more senior member of the organization. It should always come with a raise. Moving up can also mean staying where you are but going after a raise to reflect your increased value now that you've become certified.

A lateral move, on the other hand, may bring no raise or even a reduction in pay, but will provide you with something else of value instead. That something else may be a bridge into a new part of the company that offers potential for greater advancement in the long run. Or, it may be sliding into a new technical specialty that has attracted your interest.

Laying the Groundwork

Whether you're after a promotion or a raise, careful planning will maximize your likelihood of success. Before actually reaching the moment where you utter the words describing what you want, you need to do a little advance work to solidify your position. The goal of this work is to remind your employer just how fantastic of an asset to the organization you are, and how valuable. This isn't something you can do in a single day, at least not without hampering your chances of success. What you want to do instead is parade your value in front of the decision maker(s) in subtle and not so subtle ways over a period of time. What you don't want to do is come across as pushy. That's more likely to work against you than for you. Instead, your goal should be to strike a balance: going far enough to keep your accomplishments visible without becoming annoying.

Understand Your Manager

When planning your advancement campaign, it's important to distinguish between what you feel is important and what your boss does. You can't give yourself a raise or promotion; the boss can. If you don't already know his or her opinions of what makes an employee outstanding, do a little detective work. Does she value technical skills highly? Independent work? Fast work? Teamwork? Skillful interaction with customers? Does he notice whether you arrive at 7:50 or 8:01? Everyone has opinions and pet peeves; do your best to scope out those of your boss. If you've received employee evaluations in the past, go back over them for clues. Once you've identified what matters to those in control of granting your raise or promotion, you can describe your accomplishments in ways that cater to them.

Share the Good News

By now you've notified your manager that you've successfully obtained certification, but have you explained just what that means to the company? One way to do this is to pass on the results of research studies that have investigated the issue. Several studies have been conducted, some by certifying organizations and others by independent research organizations. The results quantify the value of certification to employers. You can obtain some of these studies free, via the Internet, and pass them on to your boss with a note that says something to the effect of "thought you might find this interesting." Because the data comes from someone other than you, it will seem less like tooting your own horn. Resources you can view and download from the net include the following:

- *www.software.ibm.com/os/warp/pspinfo/proidc.htm* is an IDC study titled Benefits And Productivity Gains Realized Through IT Certification. This study was sponsored by IBM, Lotus, Microsoft, Sybase, and Sylvan Prometric. It begins: "IT certification has a significant positive effect on IS productivity and network uptime," and continues with graphs and data that back up and expand up on that claim.

- *www.mcse.com/tcweb/cert/bkground.htm* is the Web site for Microsoft's Certification Backgrounder. It explains why Microsoft Certified Professionals are more productive than their non-certified counterparts, and how certification benefits employers. You'll have to download this one before you can read it.

- *education.novell.com/general/stratinv.htm* is an executive briefing for employers that touts the benefits of hiring a CNE. It includes positive study data such as "92% of the companies surveyed realize financial benefits with certified employees on staff." Figure 13-1 shows this site.

- *education.novell.com/whatshot/cneadvis.htm* contains Novell's CNEAdvisor program, which demonstrates the financial payback certification brings to employers.

- *www.itaa.org/* Visit this site for details on how to obtain the Information Technology Association of America (ITAA) IT Workforce Study, which identifies a severe future shortage of IT workers in the US. It wouldn't hurt for your boss to be aware of some of these statistics, like the one that states "68% of IT companies cite a lack of skilled/trained workers as a barrier to their companies' future ability to grow."

Be a (Visible) Problem Solver

Whether you're after a raise or promotion, you can help your position considerably if you create a reputation for yourself as a problem solver. This is a step that requires extra time, since you'll need to do this without compromising your current responsibilities. However, companies love problem solvers, and if you can manage to become one, advancement within the organization will come more easily.

Figure 13-1
Novell's
Executive Briefing

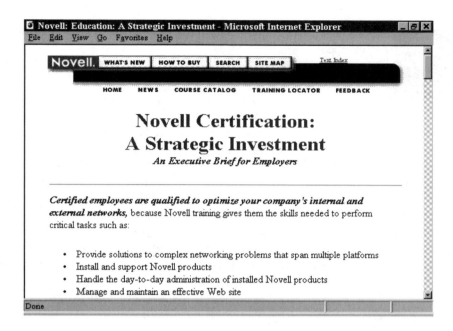

In order to solve problems, you first have to identify them. It's easiest to start with your personal area of authority. Examine quantifiable aspects of your daily activities, such as the number of support incidents handled, system down time, turnaround time for various tasks, or the incidence of software bugs. For each topic you examine, ask yourself:

1. Is this number the best it can be?
2. If not, why not?
3. What can realistically be done to change this?
4. How much will it cost to change this?
5. What will changing this accomplish for my organization?
6. Considering the answers to 4 and 5, is this a worthwhile change to implement?

You are looking for items that will improve the company's bottom line in a quantifiable way. Likely areas include heightening customer satisfaction (and thus retention), cutting costs, speeding production, or increasing quality. You may run across numbers that could be improved, but with methods that aren't cost-effective. Those are worth a second look—seek a creative approach that *would* be cost-effective.

QUICK TIP

Look for problems that are widely visible, so that your solutions will have an impact that's widely apparent too.

If you're fortunate and talented enough to already have your own bailiwick operating like a well-greased machine, then expand your problem search outside it. What do your coworkers complain about? Your customers? Or, best of all, your boss? The next time you hear them complain, probe a bit for details and make a mental note to brainstorm potential solutions.

You may think that you'll have trouble identifying problems and coming up with ways to solve them, but any company has processes that can be improved. Most employees are quite busy coping with the day-to-day tasks that make up their job responsibilities, and thus expend little if any time and energy on analyzing and problem solving. You'll find that once you develop a problem-solving mindset, potential areas for improvement will practically jump out at you. The difficulty won't be in picking them out, but in deciding which ones you have the time, energy, and interest to pursue.

Becoming a company problem solver has additional benefits. Coworkers will appreciate you (though maybe with a tad of envy attached) because you make their jobs easier by solving their problems. In addition, witnessing your personal efforts having a positive impact on the day-to-day operations of the organization can be quite satisfying. And, of course, it will enhance your image with the company execs.

If you're not already keeping a log of your accomplishments, you should be. Remembering everything you've done over the course of a year without one is practically impossible. Your log doesn't have to be anything fancy; a simple notebook or computer file will do. When you get or finish an assignment, record the date and a brief summary (a sentence or two should do) describing the task and possibly its consequences. If your boss praises you for something, jot that down too. Your entries don't need to go into intricate detail, but serve instead to jog your memory. If you make To Do lists, you can hold on to those as well (or instead) as evidence of what you've accomplished.

Asking for a Raise

If a coworker walked up to you in the lunch room and asked what your paycheck was last week, you'd probably be speechless for a moment or two. For better or worse, it's just not a question you go around asking—individual compensation details are very personal, and often cloaked in secrecy. Talking about them is practically taboo, and asking for a raise can feel quite intimidating.

This environment of secrecy benefits employers, because it provides them with an edge when it comes to negotiating compensation; they know what every other person in the office pulls down, you can usually only guess and estimate. But if negotiating a raise is rather a game of wits, employers don't hold all the cards. There are plenty of steps you can take to load the deck in your favor. Assuming you've already begun laying the groundwork as described above, here's a step by step guide to going after that raise:

1. Figure out what you're worth.
2. Study the organizational pay structure.
3. Bone up on the organization's performance data.
4. Prepare your case detailing why you're worth more.
5. Choose your moment.
6. Ask for the raise.

What are You Worth?

To receive a raise, you'll need to prove that your value to the organization justifies one. You can do this by:

- proving you're being paid at below market rate, or
- proving that you're worth more because of the contributions you make to the company's bottom line.

In either case you'll need figures to support your position. Developing them isn't very difficult, although it does involve a bit of homework.

Salary Surveys

Salary surveys are a good place to find out the going rate for your type of position. Fortunately, surveys covering computer professions are plentiful and easy to obtain. The fastest way to get them is via the Internet. Use one of the major search engines such as Infoseek (**www.infoseek.com**) or Yahoo! (**www.yahoo.com**) to ferret them out. Search using the phrases "salary survey" *and* "computer." Pay attention to the date and source of the information, to make sure that it is both current and credible. Figure 13-2 shows an online Salary Survey.

Figure 13-2
Computerworld
Salary Report

You can also get salary surveys from professional organizations and societies. Trade publications such as *Information Week* and *Computerworld* carry them periodically. Research and consulting companies in the computer field often publish salary surveys too. Source Services Corporation, for example, prints an annual survey that's free to anyone who requests a copy.

When using a salary survey to determine the going rate for your position, you need to match your job responsibilities and organization type as closely as possible. Don't go by the job title alone, as the same job can go by different names. Instead, focus on the description of duties. Some surveys break down pay rates by employer size, which will enable you to narrow your research even further.

Depending on the area of the country (or world) you're in, pay rates will vary. A programmer in New York City, for example, will typically receive a higher salary than one in Lima, Ohio. Of course, they'll have higher living expenses too. Look for a salary survey that provides regional information so you can determine the relevant pay rates for your geographical area. You can also check with recruiting and employment agencies in your area. They may have job listings similar to yours, and will have a good sense of going rates.

Internet Sources of Salary Surveys

- **www.experienceondemand.com/features/edpstats.html** is Source Services' online national salary snapshot. From here or by calling 1-888-ONDEMAND you can also request that a full survey, which contains figures specific to your geographic area, be mailed to you at no charge.
- **www.datamasters.com/survey.html** contains US regional salary information from DataMasters.
- **www.teleport.com/~gpost/djobs/salary.html** contains an ongoing survey of pay rates for full time and contract positions in the US and internationally. Visitors to this site add their own information to the database.
- **cwlive.cw.com:8080/home/online9697.nsf/All/970901survey** is Computerworld's 1997 Salary Survey.
- **www.jdresources.com/salaryf.html** is the Web site for J & D Resources' IT salary survey, and provides national rate ranges.
- **techweb.cmp.com/crn/sections/ssurvey/735ssindex.htm** is the place to look if you want to find out about IT executive compensation.
- **www.mcpmag.com/members/97janfeb/fea1main.htm** is *MCP Magazine*'s second annual salary survey of Microsoft certified professionals.
- **www.networkmagazine.com/9706/9706sal.htm** contains *Network Magazine*'s survey of networking professional salaries.

How Does Your Employer Pay?

The next thing to investigate is the compensation structure used by your employer. It's important to understand that you are much more likely to obtain a raise by working within the organization's pay structure than by ignoring or trying to circumvent it.

Many companies will provide job descriptions and pay ranges if you ask. You may also be able to find out the amount of the maximum raise given.

It's also important to ask how your performance is evaluated, and how raises are determined. There may be a formula in place that you should know about. For example, if you're already at the top of the pay scale allowed for your current position, then your efforts would be better spent on pursuing a promotion than a raise.

Find out if raises are given at a particular time (often following an annual performance review), but don't assume that such guidelines are carved in stone. If you can provide evidence that you deserve an increase even though it hasn't been a year since your last one, go for it.

How Has Your Organization Been Performing Lately?

You may have a sense of how your organization has done the last few years, in terms of growth and profits. Boning up on the details will enable you to bargain from a position of knowledge. If your boss says "we can't give you a raise—the company has been running in the red for the last two years," you won't be taken by surprise. On the other hand, if your employer's profits have been climbing, you can incorporate that fact into your case for a salary increase.

By the way, poor organizational earnings are not a bona fide, iron-clad reason to turn down your request for a raise. It's a factor to take into consideration when making your request, and definitely something you should be aware of, but it doesn't mean you should cancel your plans for advancement.

To find out your company's financial standing, read the annual reports for the past few years. You may also be able to look up the information online, through a business database resource such as Hoover's (**www.hoovers.com**).

Preparing Your Case

When you've completed the first three steps, you're halfway there. Now you'll use the information you gathered to make your case for why you should be given a raise. First compare your current compensation to the figures you obtained through your salary research. If yours is at or off the low end of the scale, you're in a good position to argue that you're not being paid market value for your work. Don't forget to point out that you're actually worth more than the market average, since you've continued your professional development and obtained certification.

If you're going to use the market rate approach, be prepared to identify the functions you perform, and provide the survey data that will support your claims of below-average compensation. Multiple survey sources will be greeted with more credibility than a single source; make your position very strong.

If you discover that your compensation ranks in the upper portion of the range for your area, skills, and responsibilities, then the going rate argument won't do you much good. The good news is that if you're at the top of the scale, you can feel reassured that the organization values you and your work; the bad news is, you may have to work harder to make your case for a raise. But it certainly can be done.

To justify a raise when your compensation is already at or above the ranges uncovered by your research, you'll need to show why you are especially valuable to the company, and therefore worth compensating at a higher rate than average. The best way to do that is to translate your activities into dollars. If you've followed the advice about becoming a problem solver, you can start there. How much money have you added to the company's bottom line through your efforts? Did you train coworkers in a technology? Find out what the going rates are for such training if it had been obtained from an outside source. Have you become more efficient at performing particular tasks? If you can complete a job that took you 50 hours last year in only 40 hours this year (perhaps due to your certification-related training), that's a 25% increase in productivity. If you do the math for other activities where your efficiency has increased, you'll be able to translate those into quantifiable savings for the company too.

If you want to carry your calculations a step further, figure out your hourly pay rate (don't forget to include the dollar value of your benefits) and multiply it by the number of hours of work you've saved the organization. The result will be a dollar savings you've provided your employer. Using the above example, you've saved the organization 10 hours of your time (which you were able to devote to other tasks thanks to your new efficiency). If you determine that your hourly rate is $25, then you've save your employer $250 each time you complete the task. If you do it once a quarter, that's $1000 per year in savings that you've personally generated. When you analyze your other improvements in a similar way, the dollar amounts may quickly add up.

Once you've got your approach figured out, practice your pitch in private or in front of someone you trust, like a spouse. You can also use a tape recorder or video camera to record your practice session, and review it until you are satisfied with your performance. Your presentation will come out much more smoothly if you've run through it a few times in advance. You'll also be able to relax a bit more once you know you can state your case effectively.

Timing

When your boss has just returned from a meeting where she got a chewing out, it's the wrong time to ask for your raise. When she returns from an annual meeting that included announcements of the organization's staggering gain in market share, led by a product produced by your division—that's a great time. Chances are that your range of timing opportunities will fall somewhere between these two extremes. Pay attention to the atmosphere in your workplace, and choose a time that seems favorable.

Raise Day

When your homework is complete and the time seems ripe, broach the subject of your raise. Something simple like "I'd like to speak to you about a raise. Can we schedule a time to talk?" will do nicely. Although it's unlikely that you'll be offered a meeting on the spot, be prepared just in case. If you get put off for a week or more, do your best to be patient, and use the delay as an excuse to get in a few more practice sessions and to further prove your worthiness.

When your meeting time arrives, follow these dos and don'ts:

- Do dress and groom yourself to business perfection the day of the meeting. Not only will it improve the image you present, but it will relieve you of any worry about your physical appearance.
- Don't say that you *need* a raise. Need isn't the issue here. What you *deserve* isn't exactly relevant either. What matters is that you can prove that your increased value justifies the raise.
- Do provide documentation that details your accomplishments. Your boss won't be able to remember everything and she'll be able to use your documentation to make her own case to higher-ups, if necessary.
- Do provide figures and be prepared to produce evidence that backs them up on the spot.
- Don't be confrontational. This is more like a sales meeting than a boxing match, and hostility won't sell anyone anything. Make eye contact.

Above all, relax. You know you've prepared your case as best as can be done. You've practiced and know what you will say. You're as prepared as a person can be. And whether or not you get the raise stand up, shake hands, and thank your boss for taking the time to meet with you. Remember, post-certification isn't the only time you can ask for a raise, it's just an especially good one.

Securing a Promotion

Shortly after you've earned certification can be a good time to make a play for a career move upwards, through a promotion. This is especially true if you chose your certification with an eye toward bridging into a new specialty.

Begin by laying the groundwork for career advancement, as described above. Pay special attention to increasing your visibility within the organization. Once that's underway, follow these steps to go after your promotion:

1. Identify a target position.
2. Research the position.
3. Get an interview with the right person.
4. Prepare for the interview.
5. Interview for the position.
6. Follow up.

Promotion to What?

To gain a promotion, you'll first need to identify a target position. Tell your boss you're interested in getting a promotion. Ask what the next step up is and what the requirements are. If the position one up from yours isn't likely to be open any time soon or doesn't interest you, look around for other options. Many organizations have an in-house job posting system, either on a bulletin board somewhere or accessible via the company network. Some organizations collect such postings in a notebook in the human resources department, and you'll have to go there and leaf through them.

When examining your alternatives, pay special attention to transition positions that will open the door to further advancement. For example, if many of the organizations managers came from a particular department or a particular position, you should focus on jobs in those areas first. To find this out, you can ask your boss or other higher-ups how they came to hold their current position within the company. Most will be flattered that you're interested, and happy to share with you the story of their advancement.

It's not necessary, or even desirable, to go for positions that seem easily within reach. Don't be afraid to stretch a little, and pursue jobs that you only have some of the qualifications for. You might just land one of them.

Honing in on Your Target

Once you've identified a target position, find out everything you can about it. Is it a newly created position or a recently vacated one? If the job isn't new, why did the person who previously held it leave? If the person is still at the company, or somewhere nearby, consider inviting him to lunch and asking about the details of the job and reasons he left it. You might find out that his boss is difficult to work for, which could lead you to reconsider your choice. At the very least, you'll gain an understanding of what duties and responsibilities the position really entails. Be sure to ask what the person liked most and least about working in that position.

If the individual who previously held the position is inaccessible to you, you'll have to dig up details in other ways. Study up on the functions of the department the job falls under. Take someone from that area to lunch and pump them (nicely, of course) for information. It's fine to explain to them why you're asking. In fact, you might even gain an edge if they happen to like you.

One way to learn more about a particular position is to volunteer to take on some of the tasks it includes. This will involve extra work, since you'll still have to complete your own job functions, but is an approach that has several things going for it. First of all, you'll gain first-hand experience by test driving part of the job. Second, you'll be demonstrating your ability to perform the functions, and to do them well. Third, you'll show your initiative and willingness to go the extra mile by extending yourself in this way.

Get on the Schedule

After you've chosen a position to pursue, find out who will be conducting interviews for the position, and who will be making the hiring decision. These may not be the same person. Approach the appropriate contact and state that you are interested in pursuing the position, and would like to schedule a meeting to discuss your candidacy. When choosing a date, allow yourself time to adequately prepare, but not so long into the future that your anxiety builds over the delay.

Preparing for the Interview

Unlike asking for a raise, for which you get to create and present a case that proves your position, an interview for a promotion to a new position will be structured and directed by the person doing the interviewing. Learn everything you can about that person. How did they advance to the position they now hold? Do they have particular peeves and preferences you should be aware of? If you can turn up someone else who's been interviewed by the same person, ask them what it was like, what questions were asked, and how the interview went.

Once you've researched the position and the interviewer, begin planning your approach. How will you demonstrate that you hold the skills and qualifications needed for the position? Create a list that records each requirement and how you fulfill it. Don't forget to mention your ongoing technical training, but don't limit yourself to technical qualifications. Pay attention to human relations, leadership skills, and personal work habits too, which can be very important as you advance within the organization. This process will help solidify your qualifications in your own mind, so that they flow smoothly from your lips during your interview.

Prepare a few questions to ask the interviewer. They might be about some of the technical details of the position or cover other issues. If you can phrase the questions in a way that demonstrates the knowledge you've gained through researching the position, so much the better. For example, you could say, "I know the department runs a token ring LAN with 52 workstations, is the number of workstations expected to change significantly over the next year?" The point is to show that you are interested, informed, and thoughtful. You may not get to use all of your questions, but prepare several to have in mind.

Consider reading a "how to interview" book to refresh your memory on successful answers and body language. You'll find many of these in the career center of your local library.

The Interview

Knowing that you are fully prepared will enable you to complete the interview process in a confident, relaxed manner. You may well feel stress from the pressure of the interview, but stress can be good as well as bad—it keeps you on your toes. Keep the following tips in mind:

- As always, dress for success. Choose attire that corresponds to the dress code of the position you are applying for.
- Be on time and pay attention to your body language. The interviewer will be taking cues from how you act as well as what you say.
- Maintain friendly eye contact and speak with sincerity.
- Do your best to avoid fidgeting. If you're a fidgeter by nature, direct your restlessness to a covert site: you can always jiggle your toes inside your shoes and the interviewer will never know.
- Bring extra copies of your resume in case they're needed.

As the interview gets underway, work to be an active rather than passive part of the process. Ask questions to clarify just what the interviewer would like to know. When answering, draw from your prepared material. Work in information that shows how you are suited to fill the position. Don't forget to ask some of the questions you prepared earlier.

At the conclusion of the interview, shake the interviewer's hand and thank him or her for their time. Restate that you want the position, and are looking forward to hearing from him or her.

Follow Up

Interview follow up is an often neglected part of the process. By making sure you don't overlook this step, you'll put yourself ahead of many of your competitors. As soon as possible after the interview, write a letter thanking the interviewer for his or her time. Summarize the nature of your meeting and reiterate your qualifications for the position. If you met with several individuals in the course of the interview, remember to thank them as well. Include a fresh copy of your resume.

If you don't hear within a few days, it's okay to call and ask when a decision will be made about the position. Just don't make a pest of yourself with numerous calls or messages.

If you don't get the job, don't take it too personally. There are often many candidates competing for a position, and you may have to repeat this process several times before you obtain a promotion. Ask the interviewer why you weren't chosen. It might be easier for both of you if you phrase the question in a way that explores why the other candidate was better suited to the position instead of asking for a list of your shortcomings. Consider whether you can augment your qualifications to strengthen your candidacy next time around.

Increasing Consulting Rates

If you're an independent consultant, you can't really seek a promotion, but you can boost your rates to reflect your increased value as a certified professional. At the same time, you need to be careful not to price yourself out of the market.

The best way to determine the rates you can reasonably charge is to find out what other consultants who provide the same services bill. There are several places you can turn for this information. One is the placement firms who connect professionals like yourself with potential employers. A firm in your area should be able to give you an idea of the local rates.

Contracting opportunities posted on the Internet are another source of rate information. You can search computer job boards for contracts that utilize skills like your own, and look for postings that contain rate information. A good place to look is DICE (Data processing Independent Consultant's Exchange) at **www.dice.com**. Another excellent Internet source is author Janet Ruhl's real rates survey (**www.realrates.com**), which collects rate information from consultants who visit the site and makes it available to anyone who's interested. The Real Rates site is shown in Figure 13-3.

Use your rate research to determine a range for your services and skills. Remember to take into account your experience level and any special qualifications, such as professional certification. If previous clients question your new rates, explain that you have simply revised them to reflect current market rates for services like your own.

Figure 13-3
Janet Ruhl's Real
Rates Survey

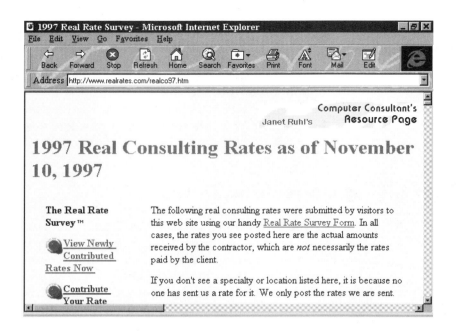

What to Do If Your Efforts Don't Work

Taking a planned, organized approach to career advancement will usually bring prompt results. This is especially true in the current IT industry environment, where demand for skilled technical people continues to outpace supply. However, your first or second attempts may still be unsuccessful. Persistence is an important factor in career advancement in any profession. If your first efforts at moving up don't come to fruition, analyze the reasons why, take aim at a new goal, and try again. Whether or not your efforts result in immediate advancement, keep a professional attitude. Things to keep in mind include:

- *Have a graceful fallback plan.* If the boss says no to your raise or promotion, or your clients balk at your rate increase, what will you do? Have your response planned in advance so that it can roll off your tongue, despite your disappointment. Remember, you can always try again.

- *Don't burn bridges* is a trite saying but wise advice. You never know if the person you aggravate today will be your boss or coworker at some time in the future. Make every effort to be considerate and professional. Don't let anger or hostility cloud your judgment (and potentially your future advancement).

✐ *Don't make a pest of yourself.* Persistence is important, but not to the point of becoming an annoyance. Constantly reminding your boss that you want a raise or a promotion will make you an irritation and work against you. Work to demonstrate your value and monitor yourself to prevent this problem.

Finding Career Advancement Advice on the Web

Although most Internet career sites focus on finding a job rather than moving up within your current organization, there are several useful resources you might want to visit.

✐ **careerbuilder.com/frames/frame_career.html** is the CareerBuilder career advancement site. It features articles, salary information, and a forum where you pose your questions to experts.

✐ **www.hardatwork.com/Escalator/career1.html** is the Web site of the Hard@Work Career Escalator. It contains an ongoing discussion of career advancment topics, articles on promotions, raises, and career breakpoints, and interview help.

By preparing carefully, you'll boost yourself to the front of the queue for raises and promotions. You'll also be able to move upward more swiftly than coworkers who wait for advancement to come to them instead of going after it. Throughout your career, you should work to keep your skills current with workplace needs. That requires constant reassessment and planning for where you want to go next. Although career advancement requires strategizing and effort to succeed, the payoff is well worth it.

CHAPTER 14

Moving On

Because earning a certification gives your marketability a sudden boost, it's often used as a springboard to a new position. In fact, many professionals pursue certification with the primary intention of using it to land a new job. A 1997 survey of certification candidates revealed that 15% of them expect certification to be a deciding factor in helping them secure a new job, 36% feel it will help a lot, and 21% expect it to help at least a little. Altogether, nearly three-quarters of those surveyed say certification will give (or already has given) them an edge in the job market.

28% of respondents felt certification would make no difference in helping them obtain a new job. That's nearly twice the number that gave the same response in a survey three years earlier. According to Richard Woodruff, Director of Product Marketing at Sylvan Prometric (a company that cosponsored the study), this can be partially attributed to the increasing prevalence of certification in the computer field. In some jobs, especially service technician positions, only candidates with a certification are even considered. Because all applicants for these positions hold certifications, it has become a basic requirement and no longer acts as a distinguishing qualification that elevates one candidate above another.

Although certification can also help you move up through the ranks at your current place of employment, for one reason or another, many professionals prefer to move on to an entirely new job situation. If you're ready to move on, or simply want to explore the possibilities, you first need to develop a profile of the type of job you'd like to obtain. Next, you'll need to dust off your resume and update it to reflect your certified status. Then, dive into the job market and begin exploring your options. There are loads of jobs out there, and one of them is bound to be just right for you.

Before You Start Your Search

Back in Chapter 8, you completed a self-assessment to help you choose a certification path. In doing so, you evaluated the characteristics of your current position and identified the features that would comprise your ideal job situation. Before tossing your hat into the job market, go back and review those worksheets. Refresh your memory on just what it is that you want to be different at your next job.

QUOTE

Entering a New Specialty

I got my first certification because I'd identified it as a way to help me break into a line of work that interested me—computer networking. At the time, that meant becoming a CNE. I began preparing for the CNE tests by reading Novell's CompuServe support forums, known as **NetWire**, and I responded to a classified advertisement I saw online there for an entry-level CNE wannabe. I got the job. The first day they told me to install a server. I did it, and I liked it. It didn't take me long to get my CNE after that.

However, as I'd gotten more involved with computer networks, I'd also started hearing about "Paper CNEs," and I didn't want to be one. I decided that I was going to excel at computer networking, and I wanted a certification that would set me off from the crowd, so I proceeded to become an Enterprise CNE. My following certifications were really just a continuation of this theme—using tests to prove that I am good at some aspect of networking. The harder the test, the more I liked it.

—David Yarashus, CCIE, MCSE, CNX, ECNE, and several other certifications

As you prepare to enter the job market, remember that it can be a stressful place. You're going to encounter rejection, especially if you go for positions at the upper range of your qualifications. Don't take it personally. Rejection isn't an indication of your personal worth. Rather, it signifies that there wasn't a match between yourself, the position, and the hiring manager. If you don't collect a few (or even many) of those "we regret to inform you" letters, then you're probably not aiming high enough.

Another stress factor to consider is the wait. It's unlikely your first resume will hit the optimum target. Patience is necessary, as is persistence. Don't expect immediate success or you'll almost certainly be disappointed. You may have to dig into vacation time to attend interviews and devote some of your leisure hours to researching positions and companies and performing other marketing tasks.

On the up side, remember why you started the certification process in the first place—to advance your career. Whether you're after higher pay, a position with greater responsibilities, entrance into a new area of expertise, or any other positive career move, changing jobs is a powerful way to put your certification to work for you.

QUOTE

Pay-Off Time

I believe my certifications have earned me higher pay than I would have had otherwise, but it's difficult to quantify that precisely. I know that my pay increases have averaged almost 20% each time I've changed jobs over the last three years (five times). I think the certifications have played an important role. Of course, I've sought out employers who have reason to value the certifications most highly.

—Pamela Forsyth, CCSI, ECNE, MCSE, and other certifications

A Resume Tune-Up

Once you've clarified the type of position you're after and reminded yourself of the nature of job searches, it's time to sharpen your resume. Later on you may create unique versions, tailored to a particular job opening, but first, you'll need a starting resume, one that's as strong as you can make it.

Resumes can be as individual as the person who creates them and may be classified into a half dozen formats. For a comprehensive discussion of resume formats and wording, visit your local bookstore or library for a resume writing guide. You can also try one of these handy online resume aids:

- ✍ **www.studentcenter.com/brief/resume/coxford.htm** is a basic resume writing guide excerpted from the book *Resume Writing Made Easy* by Lola M. Coxford. It gives you an overview of the anatomy of a resume, one section at a time.
- ✍ **www.his.com/~rockport/resumes.htm** *How to Write An Exceptional Resume* is an excellent, in-depth presentation on resume writing goals and practices. Figure 14-1 shows this Web site.

Figure 14-1
Exceptional Resume
Advice Web Site

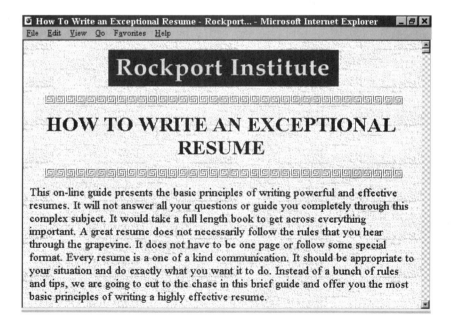

- ✍ **www.bio.com/hr/search/ResumeRocket.html** This article, *Resume Rocket Science*, puts resume writing in perspective and will help you make yours the best it can be.

Meanwhile, here's a resume refresher, which may be all you need. The two most widely used resume styles are chronological and functional. Any format you choose should lead off with your name, address, telephone number, and email address. An employment objective often follows, such as:

Professional Objective: A position managing a medium to large network in a corporate environment.

Because specific technical skills are of critical importance when hiring computer professionals, they are listed prominently. Depending on the diversity of your experience, you may decide to lump them under a single heading, such as "Technical Skills," or break them out by category. This is one possible place to list your certifications.

Software/OS: C/C++, COBOL, Oracle, Pascal, RPGII, SQL, Visual Basic, MS-DOS, Windows/ NT

Hardware: HP/3000, IBM compatible microcomputers, NCR Tower

Certifications: CNE, MCSE in progress

Work history or education follows next, depending on which you think is strongest. The work history section is where the chronological and functional styles diverge. Chronological resumes organize work history by employer, starting with the most recent (usually current) and working backwards. They work well to emphasize continuous growth in a single profession. Each entry includes dates, employer, location, and job title, followed by a succinct description of duties and accomplishments. For example:

1990 – Present   Associate Systems Analyst, ABC Corporation, Hartford, CT

Developed PC applications in C. Developed customer support system using ObjectVision. Performed technical support activities for relational database products. Responsible for software and hardware installation and maintenance of peer-to-peer LAN. Prepared and presented training seminars and materials at the data center and the customer site. Chairperson of the C standards committee.

Resumes organized in the functional style highlight work experience by job function rather than by date and employer. This format is especially useful when changing professions or if you want to emphasize the scope of your experience over the continuity. For example:

Project Leadership: Directed development of in-house customer support workstation from design phase through implementation. Supervised and coordinated team of four programmer-analysts. Delivered projects on time and under budget.

In the "Education" section, achievements should be listed from most recent to least recent. That means your certifications should be first. If you have a college degree, don't bother to list your high school diploma.

Your resume should also list professional affiliations, honors and awards, publications, and any additional qualifications you hold. *Don't* include personal information such as family/marital status, age, race, religion, health information, or a physical description of yourself. Such information is irrelevant to your qualifications for employment.

No matter how perfect your resume, it's not going to get you the job; you'll have to do that in person through one or more interviews. What your resume will do is get you that interview in the first place. For that reason, it's important to make it as perfect as you can and to emphasize your strengths. One certified professional came up with an impressive cover page (shown in Figure 14-2) that creates a strong, positive first impression.

You may be able to create a powerful resume on your own, especially if you have an existing resume to work from, but take advantage of one or more of the how-to books available to guide you through the process. If you don't feel satisfied with the result, consider utilizing a resume preparation service. You can also obtain resume help from the career resource office of a school you have attended.

Books to Help

- *Knock 'Em Dead 1997: The Ultimate Job Seeker's Handbook* by Martin John Yate (Adams Media Corp.)
- *Jobsearch: The Complete Manual For Job Seekers* by H. Lee Rush (Amacom)
- *How to Get Your Dream Job Using The Internet* by Shannon Bounds and Arthur Karl (The Coriolis Group)
- *Resume Writing: A Comprehensive How-To-Do-It Guide* by Burdette E. Bostwick (John Wiley & Sons)

Figure 14-2
Page 1 of Brandon
Cameron's Resume

Cameron Brandon-Roethle

860 Meadow Way   555-1212
Anywhere, OR 97000   cbran@direct-source.com

Objective

To acquire a position as a Network Engineer/Technician in a Novell/NT environment where my education, motivation, and determination to succeed will benefit a company.

Certifications

Microsoft Windows NT Server 4

Microsoft Windows NT Server in the Enterprise

Microsoft Windows 95

Internetworking TCP/IP on Windows NT 4

Microsoft Networking Essentials

Microsoft Windows NT Workstation 4

Microsoft Internet Information Server

Novell Networking Technologies

Novell Administration

Novell Advanced Administration

Novell TCP/IP Transport

Novell Service and Support

Novell Installation and Configuration

Novell Design and Implementation

But Is It Computer Friendly?

Resume layout has long been a challenge to those who aren't desktop publishing wizards. It can take a dozen reprints to get the margins just right; settle on sharp, decent-sized fonts; and otherwise manipulate your resume so that it looks appealing. Today, that's only half the job. You also need a resume that's appealing to computers.

If you submit your beautifully designed masterpiece electronically, as is often required these days, it may arrive at the other end looking scrambled. Unless you're Picasso, that's not going to work in your favor. To get around this problem, you need a version of your resume that's computer readable.

The safest bet when transmitting resumes electronically is to use ASCII format. ASCII (American Standard Code for Information Interchange can be read by many different kinds of computers. Saving your resume in ASCII format will keep the text, tabs, and spacing but lose all other formatting, such as indents, special fonts, bold print, and underlining. But once you've created a reasonable ASCII resume, you'll be able to transmit it electronically and have it arrive looking the same as when you sent it.

To create an ASCII version of your resume, use your word processor and select a font that *isn't* proportionally spaced. Courier is a good choice. Don't apply any formatting as you input your resume information. You can still make it appear clean and appealing through the use of spaces and tabs to line things up. No line should be longer than 69 characters, or it may wrap in funny places on the recipient's screen.

To save your ASCII resume, chose **File | Save As** from your word processor's menu. Then look for one of the following options: DOS Text, Text Only, or ASCII. Select the option and save your file.

Before shipping your resume off to a potential employer, email it to yourself and see what shape it arrives in.

QUICK TIP

Another request you many encounter is one for a scannable resume. The employer will feed your resume through a scanner and convert it using OCR (optical character recognition) software into a text file for storage in a database. Although any resume can be scanned, results vary widely and illegible results are common. If you design your resume with scanning in mind, you can maximize the chances that yours will scan beautifully. To make your resume scanner friendly, follow these guidelines:

- Keep the format simple, standard, and free of borders.
- Avoid graphics.
- Use basic, sans serif fonts (such as Arial) that won't confuse scanning software.
- Select a font size between 10 and 14 point.
- Use light colored paper; white is best.
- Send an original. Photocopies may not be high enough quality.
- Send it in a flat 9x12 envelope so it arrives without folds or creases.

As you can see, you may need to create more than one version of your resume to meet employer requirements. But because the differences will be in formatting rather than in content, doing so shouldn't be excessively time consuming. And the beauty of electronic resumes lies in their accessibility. They can be searched and called up anytime from anywhere.

QUICK TIP

Rebecca Smith's eResumes & Resources (**www.eresumes.com**) is the **only** site you'll need to find out everything about electronic resumes. This wonderful resource covers everything from how to put your resume into formats that computers can handle to creating an online resume and finding places to post it. You can also browse a gallery of resumes that show how others are marketing themselves online, read loads of useful articles, and even grab a few laughs.

Keeping it Hush-Hush

There are many reasons why you might wish to keep your job search plans to yourself, the foremost being if your search ends without turning up a superior offer, the relationship with your current employer hasn't been damaged. But discretion has its price; you won't be able to network as extensively for fear of word getting back to your employer. Word of mouth can be a powerful job search tool, and giving it up can cramp your style considerably. You'll have to weigh the factors on both sides to decide whether a clandestine job search or a public one will serve you best.

If you do want to keep your plans to yourself, or at least be reasonably discreet, employ the following practices:

    ✐ Put only your home phone number on your resume, not your work number. Install an answering machine and check it daily to make sure it's operating properly. Call it throughout the day to check for messages so you can respond promptly.

    ✐ Don't return calls from your desk. Return calls from an empty conference room or, better yet, a phone away from your place of work.

    ✐ Don't use your employer's materials in your job search. Supply your own paper, and get your copies made at a copy shop.

    ✐ If you require the use of a fax machine, use one that's public (or one that belongs to a friend).

    ✐ Don't use your business email address for job search communications. Whether it's morally acceptable or not, it's legal for your boss to read your electronic mail.

    ✐ Make every effort to conduct your job search without impinging on your work hours. Utilize breaks, your lunch hour, and before- and after-hours options as frequently as possible.

If, despite your efforts, your boss does discover your job search, make the best of it. Explain why you were looking and that you were doing so on your own time. Reassure your employer that you will not leave him in a lurch and even offer to help find/train your replacement.

What if your current employer offers incentives to keep you from leaving? Consider carefully before accepting. You've already made up your mind to leave, and now that your boss knows that, it will linger as a question of your dedication and loyalty throughout your career with this employer. It may be best to not accept the inducements to stay and stick with your original plan to land that new job.

How to Find Job Openings

A primary activity of the job search is to find suitable job postings. Professionals in the computer field are currently enjoying a bountiful time, with more jobs than there are qualified people to fill them. This gap is projected to continue to widen.

A 1997 study by the Information Technology Association of America (ITAA) warns that the need for IT workers exceeds supply and will continue to do so until growth slows in both IT and non-IT industries.

According to the ITAA, "In a systematic survey of large- and midsize IT and non-IT companies, ITAA found that a weighted estimate reveals there are approximately 190,000 unfilled IT jobs in America today. This number actually understates the overall demand for such workers, because ITAA did not survey small companies, non-profit organizations, or local, state, and federal government agencies and, therefore, did not include those employers' needs for skilled IT workers in this study."

The study also found that among IT companies, 82% expected to increase the number of IT employees in the coming year and only 2% anticipated a reduction. Of companies that are outside the IT industry but still utilize IT workers, 56% expected to add to their IT staffing in the coming year, while only 3% anticipated reducing it.

All of this indicates that it's an IT worker's market out there, and you have plenty of opportunities to choose from. All you have to do is find the right ones. Thanks to the information technology boom, locating potential employment is easier than ever. You can connect with companies searching for skilled technology workers in many different ways, including:

- Headhunters and recruiting companies
- Print advertisements in newspapers and magazines
- Job fairs
- Internet and Web job banks
- Networking opportunities

To find your optimum position, you'll want to explore multiple avenues. Don't overlook opportunities to advance at your current place of employment. See Chapter 13 for help and advice on using your certification to get ahead right where you are.

Headhunters

Headhunters (also known as *recruiters*) are individuals who find people to fill jobs. Headhunters are hungry. They're always looking for resumes, because without resumes they can't fill positions. And they're always looking for positions to fill because they can't place people without jobs to put them in. Like a shark, they always have to keep moving, on the hunt. Like a shark, they've been known to bite the hand that feeds them.

A bad headhunter may send you on as many interviews as possible without performing adequate screening first, with the goal of getting you placed somewhere, anywhere, so they can get paid their fee. They've even been suspected, on occasion, of sending a candidate to a position that's a poor match because they want to get someone out there to look like they're doing something for the client company. Firms that practice these tactics are sometimes called *body shops*.

Working through a middleman has additional drawbacks. When communication has to pass through an additional layer, it's more likely to get muddled. When you work with a headhunter, communication between you and the potential employer passes through that extra layer.

Sometimes a headhunter will conceal the identity of the company behind a job opening until after they have your resume and have interviewed you. They do this for fear you'll go straight to the company yourself. Of course, if you did go to the company yourself, it might not do you much good because, in a large company, you'd have no idea who the hiring manger for the position in question is, and your resume might never reach the right person.

Like lawyers, headhunters are much maligned, often with good reason. And like lawyers, a good one can prove very valuable. Headhunters know the jobs that are out there. They have connections at corporations and relationships with hiring managers. Because of their relationship with hiring companies, headhunters are often aware of jobs that haven't been advertised. They can put you in for an excellent job you otherwise wouldn't have known existed. And they can negotiate money for you. That can be a big plus if you find negotiating compensation packages about as appealing as a severe case of stomach flu. Because the headhunter's payoff is a percentage of your first year's salary, they have a strong incentive to get you the biggest paycheck possible.

Given that headhunters can do so much for you, you may well decide to work with one or more. You'll find an extensive directory in the Resources section of this book and in the database on the companion Web site. You can also locate them online and through friends.

Before submitting your resume to a recruiter, find out as much as you can about them. Inquire about their procedures and insist that your resume won't be submitted anywhere, for any reason, without your prior approval. It's a small thing for the recruiter to call you up and say "I've got a position in East Osh Kosh doing C++ application development that I want to put you in for. Okay?" Insist on such courtesies.

It's also a good idea to ask other computer professionals what they know of the firm and whether their opinion of it is good or bad. You can also seek out such information online. Post an inquiry in a forum that computer professionals frequent, asking for opinions on the firm you're considering. The computer consultant's forum on CompuServe, for example, would be a suitable place.

Print Advertisements

One of the first places job hunters turn to is the Classified Section of a nearby newspaper. Because it's such a popular source of job leads, such advertisements trigger a ton of responses. Although that means you'll face a lot of competition, it's still worthwhile to respond to job announcements that interest you. Just don't be discouraged if you have a lower reply rate from potential employers you contact this way. They may be swamped with candidates and only take time to respond to the top applicants. Your goal, of course, is to be one of those top candidates.

Augment the listings in your local newspaper by picking up copies of (or subscribing to) national newspapers, such as the *Wall Street Journal*, the *New York Times*, and *National Business Employment Weekly*. As an alternative, you can also plan an evening at the library browsing these and other national publications, photocopying listings that interest you.

If you're planning a move to a new location, consider obtaining a subscription to the largest newspaper that serves the area. You can have it mailed to your current address.

Trade publications should be one of your key print sources of job postings. Because they're focused on the industry in question, you'll have fewer irrelevant ads to wade through. Good leads for computer jobs can be found in publications such as *Communications Week*, *Information Week*, or *Contract Professional*, among others.

When you come across a job advertisement that interests you, clip it and staple or tape it to a standard sized piece of paper to prevent it from getting mislaid. Each advertisement should have its own page, which will serve as a repository of notes regarding the particular ad. This method also enables you to easily store all of your advertisements in a folder or three-ring binder.

The first thing you should record on the page is the name and date of the publication you found the advertisement in. This will spare you the embarrassment of saying, "I don't know" when an employer asks where you encountered the ad, and it allows you to mention the ad source in your cover letter.

Next, read the advertisement carefully to identify the company that placed the ad and the qualifications sought. Record what you discover on your notes page. Figure 14-3 shows an example of what your page might look like so far.

Figure 14-3
Analyzing a Print
Advertisement

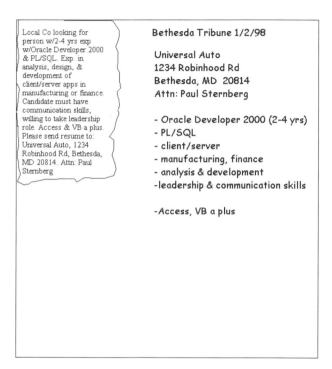

Local Co looking for person w/2-4 yrs exp w/Oracle Developer 2000 & PL/SQL. Exp. in analysis, design, & development of client/server apps in manufacturing or finance. Candidate must have communication skills, willing to take leadership role. Access & VB a plus. Please send resume to: Universal Auto, 1234 Robinhood Rd, Bethesda, MD 20814. Attn: Paul Sternberg

Bethesda Tribune 1/2/98

Universal Auto
1234 Robinhood Rd
Bethesda, MD 20814
Attn: Paul Sternberg

- Oracle Developer 2000 (2-4 yrs)
- PL/SQL
- client/server
- manufacturing, finance
- analysis & development
-leadership & communication skills

-Access, VB a plus

If the advertisement still looks appealing after your second read, it's time to find out something about the company. Some advertisements are blind, meaning they don't mention who the employer is, but most often the company offering the job is clearly identified. If you're already familiar with them, great. Otherwise, do a bit of research to find out the basics on their products, market, and size. A good resource is *Hoover's Handbook of American Companies*, which you can find at your library or access via the Internet at **www.hoovers.com**. Figure 14-4 shows the *Hoover's Web site*.

To actually respond to the advertisement, you're going to write a letter. And to do that, you'll need a name at the company. Human Resources Director isn't good enough. Call the company and ask the receptionist for the name and title of the proper person to send your resume to.

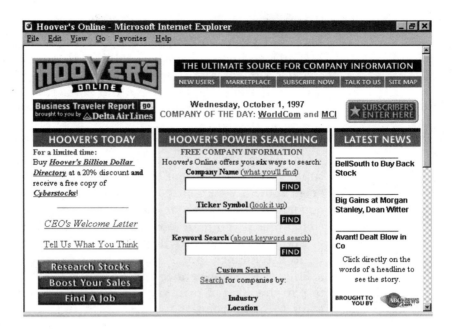

Figure 14-4
The Hoover's
Web Site

Your letter should be succinct, written on quality stationary, and intended to arouse interest in your abilities. As in a good novel, the first sentence is critical. Use it to grab your reader's attention by stating something that's important to them. One approach is to open with a mention of your strongest qualification for the job. As you continue, don't just mention your strengths, give examples of how you've applied them. Keep the letter short, two pages maximum. One page is better. Whoever is screening the replies will have many to go through and isn't going to appreciate long, rambling letters. Your closing sentence should be compelling, too. Use it to ask for a personal interview to further discuss the opportunity.

Staple a copy of your response letter to the page bearing the advertisement and your notes. If you're using more than one version of your resume, attach a copy of the version you sent with your letter as well. Then put everything in your "to follow up" file.

Job Fairs

A job fair offers the opportunity to meet dozens, if not hundreds, of employers in one place over the course of one or two days. It's a chance to do some efficient, condensed job hunting.

But job fairs can be intimidating, too. They can feel like meat markets and you're one piece of meat among hundreds. Nonetheless, attending them can prove well worth the temporary discomfort. Besides the obvious opportunity to connect with a specific job, you'll also be networking, creating and collecting contacts that you can come back to in the future. It's also a great place to learn about new companies, what they're doing, what they plan to do, and the types of jobs they have to fill.

Job fairs are usually advertised in local newspapers, and sometimes you can find them by searching the Internet. Choose one that's geographically compatible with your plans and focuses on technical opportunities. There's no use attending a job fair featuring only local companies if you plan to relocate to the opposite coast.

The advertisement will probably identify the companies slated to be in attendance, but if not, call the coordinating organization and ask for a list to be sent to you by mail or fax. This gives you a chance to plan hit lists of primary targets and second choice companies you want to make contact with. Do a little research on companies that interest you beforehand.

Your resume should be in tip-top shape, and it won't hurt to bring business cards, too. Make sure your certification is listed prominently on both. Consider preparing a second or third version of your resume that emphasizes different strengths. For example, one version might play up your mainframe skills while another underscores your expertise with personal computers.

In advance, create a three to five-minute spiel about yourself and your qualifications. Don't exceed five minutes. The recruiters and hiring managers will speak with hundreds of potential applicants and won't have the patience to listen to rambling, unfocused presentations. You want to say who you are, where your technical strengths lie, and what you've done with them. Include several examples of problems you've solved and how you've solved them. Practice your pitch in front of a mirror until you've got it down cold.

On the big day, dress as you would for an interview. It's unlikely that you'll be hired on the spot, but you need to look your professional best. Bring multiple copies of your resume and plenty of business cards, more than you think you'll need. It's also a good idea to bring a notepad for jotting down information on companies that interest you. And, of course, bring your list of target companies so you can make sure you visit the booths you've identified as most important.

Start with a company that's on your B list (or not on your list at all). That way you can fine-tune your spiel before connecting with the companies you're most interested in. When you're introducing yourself to a recruiter, watch his body language and wrap it up if he keeps glancing at his watch or gazing over your shoulder, signs that his interest isn't on you.

Collect business cards and company literature and pause between booths to take notes on what you talked about and with whom. Otherwise, it will be difficult to follow up effectively. Speaking of follow-up, do it within a day or so of the fair. Send a letter recapping your conversation, and include a fresh copy of your resume. Then, while you wait for the phone to start ringing with interview calls, continue your job search efforts on other fronts.

A job fair is an excellent place to get a feel for which technologies are hot and which skills are in demand. If you notice that many recruiters are searching for people with a particular skill, make a note of it so you can consider adding it to your repertoire.

QUICK TIP

Online Job Hunting

Job hunting via the Internet is efficient and fun, too. You get to browse all kinds of interesting Web sites, and you can take advantage of the incredibly rich supply of job hunting resources. If a particular company interests you, you can visit its Web site. Most will have a job opportunities section. In many cases, you'll be able to reply online.

The Web is also a huge repository of job postings. Many sites collect thousands of openings in databases, and you can search them by qualifications, salary, geographic location, or other specifications. Some of these sites will even let you register your preferences and then notify you by email if any postings are added that fit your specifications.

You can also utilize the Web to bring employers to you. It really is a worker's market in the computer industry, and recruiters are actively looking for bodies to fill open positions. If you post your resume on one of the many sites that allow you to do so, chances are your email box will soon hold inquiries for you to consider. The Acorn Career Counseling and Resume Writing Web site (**www1.mhv.net/~acorn/Acorn.html**) is an excellent resource containing links to dozens of places where you can post your resume electronically for free. Figure 14-5 shows the site.

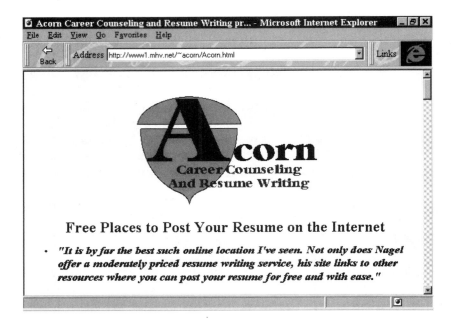

Figure 14-5
Acorn's Link List
to Free Places
to Post your
Electronic Resume

A Baker's Dozen: 13 Places to Find Computer Jobs Online

The Web as a medium is so conducive to job placement functions that the sheer quantity of job sites can, at times, become overwhelming. Although many of the giant job sites post openings in all industries and areas, others focus on particular job markets. The following Web sites cater to the high-tech job hunter. Most are specific to computer professionals. The others are more broadly based, but contain a high percentage of computer-related opportunities.

- **comp.jobs.offered** is a Usenet newsgroup of open computer positions.
- **computerwork.com** is the NACCB's (National Association of Computer Consultant Businesses) Online Job Board and Resume Bank, a database of technical jobs and contract opportunities and a potential place to post your resume.
- **www.cio.com/forums/wmf_job_posts.html** is *WebMaster Magazine*'s Webmaster Wanted site containing job postings for Web-related positions, including Webmasters, Web site managers, intranet managers, and others.

- **www.computerjobs.com** is the home page of The Computer-Jobs Store, which has job listings for Atlanta, Chicago, the Carolinas, and Texas.
- **www.datamation.com/PlugIn/jobs/itjobs.html** is Datamation's site that links to the recruitment pages of leading IT vendors.
- **www.dice.com** sends you to DICE (Data Processing Independent Consultant's Exchange), a monster collection of consulting and permanent computer-related job postings.
- **www.headhunter.net** is Headhunter.Net, and although it's not strictly limited to high-tech jobs, it includes many positions for computer professionals.
- **www.hotjobs.com** is a site that focuses on computer- and technology-related jobs in the Fortune 500 and other top technical firms across the country. You can also post your resume here.
- **www.occ.com** is the site for Online Career Center, which has a huge database of jobs from top companies. You can search by industry and geographic area or just browse the latest postings.
- **www.prgjobs.com** is the Jobs For Programmers site, an extensive job resource with full-time, contract, and telecommuting job listings. You can also post your qualifications blind (without your name) and have replies forwarded to you via email.
- **www.softwarejobs.com** is The Software Jobs home page. It lists positions available across the country and can be searched by keyword.
- **www.techweb.com/careers/careerdocs/findjob.html** allows you to search and apply for a job online through CMP Media. This site will email you when opportunities that meet your specifications are posted.
- **www.vjf.com/pub/links/hightech.html** is Westech's Virtual Job Fair—searchable databases of thousands of high-tech jobs.

When responding to an electronic job offering, follow the instructions mentioned in the posting. If a position identification number is mentioned, be sure to include it in your reply. If you are responding via email, be certain to spell check your message before sending it. Email is not an excuse for poor grammar and spelling.

QUICK TIP

If your electronic mail program doesn't incorporate spell checking, compose your message using your word processor instead. After you confirm that it's free from spelling errors, select the text of your message, then cut and paste it into the body of a new email message.

Networking

Don't underestimate the power of your connections to land your dream job. Tell relatives, coworkers, and friends that you're looking. If you're attempting to be covert, tell only those you can trust to be discrete. But keeping your job search confidential comes with a price because it will limit your options to some degree.

Successful networking largely consists of being visible. Attend professional functions and mingle. If you know someone who knows someone with connections to a place you want to work, don't be afraid to ask for an introduction. The worst they can do is say no, and they'll probably say yes.

Going Independent

If you've been on the brink of a career as an independent consultant, your certification may provide the impetus to make the move. But look carefully before you leap. The benefits of self-employment are potentially limitless, but there are plenty of drawbacks, too.

The independent contractor/consultant needs to be tenacious and organized. You'll have to find your own work, create and adhere to your own schedule, and perform the functions that accompany running your own business. Table 14-1 summarizes many of the pros and cons you'll encounter if you go independent.

Table 14-1
Pros and Cons of Going Independent

Pros	Cons
Manage your own career direction	Will have to manage fluctuations in income
Freedom from office politics and red tape	Work and leisure boundaries blur
Potential tax benefits via business tax deductions	You have to wear all the hats: accounting, sales, marketing, production, administration
More control over work/ life balance	No externally imposed structure to guide you
Direct responsibility for your income level and success	No corporate benefits

Drake Beam Morin, Inc., an outplacement and career management firm, has devoted a section of its Web site to information for people considering self-employment. Visit **www.dbm.com/career/employment/ reality.html** (shown in Figure 14-6) to explore your motivations for self-employment and the realities you're likely to face.

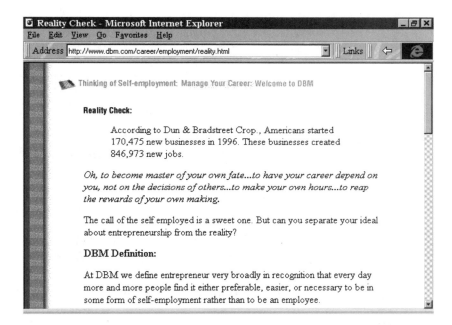

Figure 14-6
Self-Employment
Reality Check

To form a solid picture of the consulting life, there's no substitute for reports from the field. Seek out friends or coworkers who are self-employed or who have been in the past; take them to lunch so you can get the firsthand scoop. Visit forums and Web sites dedicated to computer contractors, and read, read, read. Professionals who frequent these sites are usually willing to share their advice and experiences and can be very helpful to the new consultant, and you'll find lots of articles to advise you. Some of the more helpful sites include:

✐ Janet Ruhl's Computer Consultant's Resource Page (**www.javanet.com/~technion**), which is shown in Figure 14-7, is a must-see site for anyone considering going independent. You'll find advice on the ins and outs of the consulting life, current billing rates around the country for various skill sets, suggestions on how to negotiate contracts, and lots more.

Figure 14-7
Janet Ruhl's
Computer
Consultant's Page

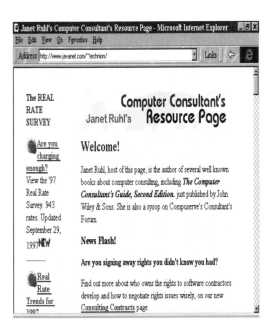

The discussion forums on the Web site of Contract Professional Forum (**www.contractpro.com/forum/forum.htm**), shown in Figure 14-8, is another good place to seek advice and interact with experienced contractors and consultants.

Figure 14-8
Contract
Professional's
Discussion Forums

If you decide to become an independent consultant, don't neglect to capitalize on your certification(s). They are credentials that will add to your credibility with potential clients, which will be especially useful when you're just starting out.

A Certified Advantage

These certifications have been tremendous for me. I've nearly quadrupled my hourly rate in less than a year. I also have much more confidence in myself and my abilities. My family and friends are very proud of me, and my certifications command respect from my peers and employees.

I'm now doing Network Engineering and Administration, which is what I was training for. My job is very challenging, but also very rewarding. I also am very happy in my new position, something I was lacking at other positions. The certifications have given me the knowledge to succeed. The abundance of readings from becoming certified and the hands-on experience I'm receiving are making the difference in my success.

Yes, I could have made it where I am now without certifications, but they accelerated my career. They've opened up so many doors in the job market. When I put out my resume to companies with the certifications I hold, nearly every company calls back, and sometimes the same day that I sent the resume!

—Cameron Brandon, MCSE, CNE, CNA,
A+ Certified, MCPS/Internet Systems

Follow Up

Whichever route you use to locate job listings, remember to follow up on opportunities you respond to. It's a basic task that's been stressed in every job hunting guide ever published, but it's often overlooked. Send that thank you letter after an interview, and you could distinguish yourself from all the other candidates who never get around to it. Make that follow-up phone call you promised in your cover letter, and you'll be demonstrating your ability to follow through. Yes, these are somewhat mundane tasks and they take up your time. But they could be just the step that clinches the interview, or the job, that you'd really like to call your own.

Spare Those Bridges

No matter how aggravating a position you are leaving has been, be careful of how you represent it. Don't knock your previous employer during interviews or to your new employer. Even if every word you say is true, you're conveying an image of yourself as a complainer and possibly even a backstabber. Those aren't good traits to have associated with your name. And if you've done it to a past employer, what's to keep you from badmouthing this one a year down the line?

Along the same lines, be wary of exit interviews. While it can be very satisfying to answer a question like: "Is there anything the company could have done to keep you from leaving?" with a retort like "Yes, treat me decently," don't do it. The future is unpredictable, and the day may come when you encounter your boss somewhere down the road. Such comments, however honest, may come back to haunt you. Although confidentiality may be promised during the exit interview process, don't count on it. It's probably not that hard for a manager to tie a particular exit interview with the individual who gave it, even without your name gracing the page.

Finally, throughout your job search, keep records of all your expenditures. You may be able to deduct some of your job search expenses on your tax return at the end of the year. Items such as resume printing, postage, unreimbursed travel for job-seeking purposes, and placement agency fees, are generally deductible as miscellaneous itemized deductions on Schedule A (Form 1040). As such, they are subject to the 2% limit, which means that they are deductible only to the extent that they exceed 2% of your adjusted gross income (AGI). Various and sundry other restrictions also apply. Consult a tax professional if your job search expenses are significant.

Although few people, if any, would consider a job hunt fun, the results can certainly justify the effort. By moving on to a new position, you may be able to boost your salary, increase your personal satisfaction, and land a job that offers an optimum blend of challenge, reward, and professional growth—the type of job you can look forward to undertaking each day.

CHAPTER **15**

Keeping Current

Once you've obtained your certification, it's important to pay attention to the currency of your skills. However you look at it, continuing professional education is a critical component of any successful career, especially in the computer industry. Many certifications, especially those that are vendor-independent, require continuing professional education as a condition of retaining certified status. Even if your sponsor doesn't insist on continuing requirements, the value of your certification will be enhanced by the fact that you've taken steps to update your skills to keep pace with technological changes.

Professional development efforts prove most valuable when undertaken in a planned, intentional manner. The requirements set forth by your certification program outline a minimum path for you to follow. Use it as a starting point, but keep in mind that sponsor requirements are geared to support the individual certification; if your certification is in a narrow area, they won't provide an adequate continuing education plan on their own. Choose courses and training events that will serve a particular purpose and add to your skills and/or knowledge in a meaningful way.

Your first step should be to determine what requirements, if any, have been set in place by your certification sponsor. You can do this by checking through the literature you have on hand and by visiting your sponsor's certification Web site. The Web site is likely to be more current than the printed materials, but don't count on either of these sources to supply complete and timely information. Continuing requirements are subject to change and can suddenly appear in programs where before there were none. It's best to verify your understanding of the requirements, or lack thereof, with the sponsor via phone, letter, or email.

Product-specific certifications are often version-specific. Although they don't require that you recertify on each new version, it's a good idea to do so. All it usually takes is passing an upgrade exam. You may or may not receive notice that a new version is imminent, but by keeping your eye on trade magazines and industry publications, you should catch wind of new releases before they hit the market. You can then inquire about certification upgrade requirements and be current and ready to go as the new release hits the streets.

Whether your certification(s) are vendor-specific, version-specific, or vendor-independent, tracking continuing requirements is entirely your responsibility; it's unlikely that you will receive any reminders from your sponsor. It's also up to you to remember that following the guidelines isn't enough—if you don't submit acceptable evidence that you've done so, it won't count. Figure 15-1 shows Microsoft's take on this issue.

As you delve into the world of continuing education requirements, you'll find that terminology varies between certification sponsors, training providers, and educational institutions. The most common monikers for this kind of ongoing career skill building are Continuing Professional Education (CPE), Continuing Education Units (CEUs), and Professional Development Credits (PDCs). You'll be required to complete a specific number of qualifying units of education. Exactly what activities qualify under a particular certification program will be spelled out. The requirements may be very specific or allow you quite a bit of latitude. You'll have to meet these requirements on an ongoing basis. You may have to complete the recertification cycle each year, or the cycle may extend over two or three years. Figure 15-2 shows the ICCP's explanation of their three-year recertification cycle.

Figure 15-1
A Microsoft
FAQ Makes Clear
Who's in Charge of
Keeping Current

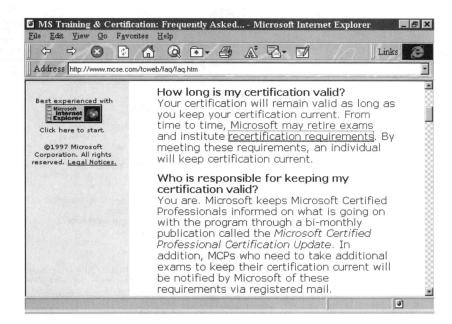

Once you've pinned down the details, calculate the deadlines and incorporate them into your schedule. Because these dates can be far into the future, it will help to circle them in red or mark them in some other prominent way. Remember that these dates are deadlines for completing the requirements, not for signing up for the necessary classes. If you're a procrastinator, consider moving your deadlines up a month; you'll have breathing room if a class should be canceled or some other circumstance interferes with your plans.

Where to Get Continuing Ed

Continuing education that meets recertification requirements can be obtained from many different sources, including:

Figure 15-2
The ICCP
Recertification Cycle

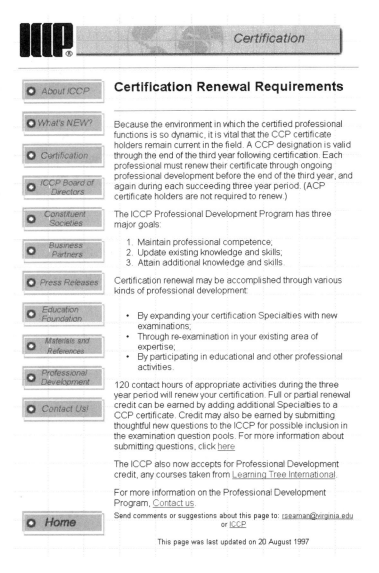

Certification Renewal Requirements

Because the environment in which the certified professional functions is so dynamic, it is vital that the CCP certificate holders remain current in the field. A CCP designation is valid through the end of the third year following certification. Each professional must renew their certificate through ongoing professional development before the end of the third year, and again during each succeeding three year period. (ACP certificate holders are not required to renew.)

The ICCP Professional Development Program has three major goals:

1. Maintain professional competence;
2. Update existing knowledge and skills;
3. Attain additional knowledge and skills.

Certification renewal may be accomplished through various kinds of professional development:

- By expanding your certification Specialties with new examinations;
- Through re-examination in your existing area of expertise;
- By participating in educational and other professional activities.

120 contact hours of appropriate activities during the three year period will renew your certification. Full or partial renewal credit can be earned by adding additional Specialties to a CCP certificate. Credit may also be earned by submitting thoughtful new questions to the ICCP for possible inclusion in the examination question pools. For more information about submitting questions, click here

The ICCP also now accepts for Professional Development credit, any courses taken from Learning Tree International.

For more information on the Professional Development Program, Contact us.

Send comments or suggestions about this page to: rsearnan@virginia.edu
or ICCP

This page was last updated on 20 August 1997

(Navigation buttons shown in figure: About ICCP, What's NEW?, Certification, ICCP Board of Directors, Constituent Societies, Business Partners, Press Releases, Education Foundation, Materials and References, Professional Development, Contact Us!, Home)

- ✐ Academic institutions, such as community colleges and technical schools
- ✐ Independent training companies
- ✐ Courses and seminars offered by your certification sponsor
- ✐ One-day seminars and conferences
- ✐ Employer-sponsored training
- ✐ Self-guided study programs

Some certification sponsors will accept training obtained through any of these outlets; others require that classes be taken through their authorized training network, or limit your choices in other ways. It's a good idea to double-check that a particular course will count toward the continuing requirements by consulting your sponsor before you enroll. Some certification vendors maintain a list of preapproved CEU options you can select from being assured they will qualify.

Academic Courses

One of the most common continuing education options is to take classes from a university, college, technical school, or other academic institution. In response to the demand for adult education alternatives, most academic institutions offer evening and weekend classes that will fit into your schedule. You'll also have a wide array of courses to choose from, which will make it easier to find something that will benefit you professionally, meet your recertification requirements, and be interesting. Because these are approved college courses, you'll also be able to apply the credits for classes you complete toward a degree program. That means you can get your continuing education to serve double duty: as recertification requirements and as requirements toward traditional educational goals, such as a master's degree.

The cost of college courses varies widely, depending on the school and level of the course. In general, you can expect to pay up to several hundred dollars per course. If you decide to take classes at one of the Ivy League colleges, you can, of course, expect your costs to be much higher. You may also have to pay administrative fees; however, these fees often entitle you to use other facilities on the campus, such as the library and computer lab. If you don't care about receiving a grade, you may be able to attend the course on an audit basis, which will remove test pressures and cut your costs.

It's a good idea to preview the computer lab if you'll be using it in your coursework. Despite their role as learning centers, many academic computer labs unfortunately lag behind the commercial sector when it comes to adopting modern technology. If lab work will be an important part of your training, find out before you enroll if the computer equipment is up to par.

Classes will meet two to three times a week for several months, following either the semester or term calendar. In many cases your classmates will be undergraduate students with less work and life experience than yourself. If you like being a mentor, this may appeal to you; if you prefer mixing with other experienced professionals, you may find a shortage of them in your class. One way to find out what your fellow students are apt to be like is to meet with the course's professor and ask.

Chapter 9 goes into detail on the features, benefits, and drawbacks of various learning options.

Independent Training Companies

Independent training companies offer many conveniences for working professionals. Their courses are compact and intense, often spanning just a few days. This makes it possible to complete continuing education requirements in a shorter time. Training companies are also more likely to offer up-to-the-minute curriculums, high-end computer equipment, and certified instructors with ongoing interaction in their areas of expertise. All of these can translate into an opportunity for you to learn a lot fast.

Courses and seminars offered by training companies run from one day to a week or more. Prices vary accordingly, and you can expect to pay up to several thousand dollars for a multiday, hands-on workshop. A one-day seminar will cost much less, possibly even under $100. Learning Tree International, which also sponsors its own certifications, is a large, independent trainer offering many different courses to computer professionals. Figure 15-3 shows the company's home page.

Increasingly, training businesses are bringing their courses to the Internet to make them accessible to more potential clients. These courses are often self-paced, include contact with an instructor, and offer interaction with other students via message boards and online conferences. Figure 15-4 shows one of these virtual classrooms.

Whether a course is offered over the Internet or in the classroom, it's important to investigate the quality of the facilities and trainers ahead of time. Although it's possible to complete an inferior course and use it to satisfy recertification requirements, doing so is really a waste of your money and time. The point of recertification is to continue to build your skills, and complying with the spirit of the requirements will serve you much better than just squeezing by.

Figure 15-3
Learning Tree
International
Technical Education

Figure 15-4
Learning Online

Training Offered by Certification Sponsors

Your certification sponsor will sometimes connect you with the educational opportunities necessary to maintain your certification. The sponsor will either offer the training itself or direct you to authorized training centers that do. If your sponsor operates an annual conference or trade show, attending it may earn some of the credits you need. You'll also get a chance to hobnob with other experts about the ins, outs, and job outlook of your field. In many cases, such conferences are free to individuals certified through the sponsor's program; you'll still have to pay for travel and lodging, though. You'll find sponsor-provided training listed on the certification program's Web page and in literature mailed to you.

One-Day Conferences and Seminars

You've probably received invitations to free seminars whose main purpose is selling a company's new product or new version release of an existing product. The seminars are given in major cities across the country, usually in hotel facilities.

Although these events are largely sales events, they do offer an opportunity to learn about new features and usually include demonstrations of many of the product functions. These can prove especially useful to holders of product-specific certifications. Generally, to update such certifications you are encouraged to take an upgrade exam. Attending one of these seminars can give you a feel for how extensive the changes are and may even provide the information you'll need to upgrade. If you're lucky, you might even win the traditional drawing for a free copy of the software.

Company Training

Employer-sponsored training can satisfy recertification requirements at no cost to you. Larger employers frequently offer courses led by in-house trainers. These are usually about the company products or software and hardware used within the organization. Even if you already know the material, attending one of these seminars may earn you credit toward recertification requirements.

Another way organizations provide training to employees is by bringing in outside trainers to provide instruction to a whole department. For example, one national corporation hired a local college instructor to present a weekly course on C programming to members of the technical support department. Participants were treated to a complete course curriculum and hands-on practice with the C language, all at no cost to themselves.

If there is a particular technology you want to learn about and think would also prove valuable to other members of your company, consider mounting a campaign to persuade your employer to provide the training. In a written proposal, explain exactly what training you're recommending is and how it would benefit the company (for example: through increased productivity, less down time, better product support, or increased employee retention). Your document should include a cost benefit analysis showing how the training will benefit the company's bottom line. You should also do some preliminary research exploring who might teach the course and how much it would cost, and include those results in your report, too. In addition to getting training for yourself, this route has the added benefit of demonstrating that you are concerned with ways the company can maintain or improve its competitive edge, which, on its own, will benefit how the higher-ups view you.

Do-It-Yourself Options

One of the most cost-effective routes to continuing education is self-study. In addition to affordability, this option has the advantages of being self-paced, widely available, and obtainable in a variety of formats. Unlike instructor-led options, you can also return to the material again for reference or review. Self-study options include:

- Books, manuals, and workbooks
- Video instruction
- Computer-based training (CBT) software
- Internet-based courses
- Hands-on exploration

You can find products in all of these categories by browsing the Internet using one of the popular search engines. Videos, books, and software can also be found in the computer section of major book stores or through advertisements in computer trade publications. The quality of self-study materials varies widely, so make every effort to try before you buy. You'll often be able to accomplish this by sampling trial versions of software or browsing through printed materials before purchasing. If not, verify that a return policy exists so you can get your money back if the materials don't meet your expectations. Ask friends and coworkers who have experience with self-study materials which vendors they recommend and if they've had any bad experiences with particular products or companies.

When evaluating self-study options, keep in mind that individual learning styles vary, so what works for someone else may be less effective for you, and vice versa. Chapter 10 explains how to analyze your personal learning style and determine which kind of training formats will suit you best.

Remember: certification training doesn't always have to be strictly computer-related—other business training may qualify.

QUICK TIP

Many certified professionals find that the best way to keep current with particular technologies is to obtain regular hands-on access to the software and/or hardware. When it comes to gaining proficiency with a particular type of application or programming language, the most efficient form of self-study is to purchase the software, install it, and practice using it with the manual or another reference guide nearby.

Individuals who work with technologies that require a platform other than a basic PC will find it worthwhile to uncover a way to get their hands on the particular environment on a regular, ongoing basis. This is easiest for those who have equipment at their place of employment and can work with it during breaks, lunch time, or after hours. Individuals who don't have suitable access through an employer sometimes set up a version of the platform and/or software at home. Doing so makes it possible to experiment with new options and technologies at your leisure without the risk of compromising a critical business computer system.

The types and amount of self-study that you can apply toward recertification requirements are likely to be limited by your certification sponsor. Figure 15-5 shows how the NPA makes these calculations. If you're counting on this route for continuing education, check into the limitations beforehand to make sure your self-study choices qualify and to find out what sort of documentation you'll need to provide as evidence you've completed the training.

Figure 15-5
The NPA's
Breakdown of
Continuing
Education Units for
Specific Activities

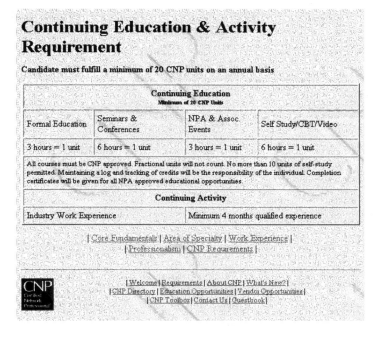

Continuing Education & Activity Requirement

Candidate must fulfill a minimum of 20 CNP units on an annual basis

Continuing Education			
Minimum of 20 CNP Units			
Formal Education	Seminars & Conferences	NPA & Assoc. Events	Self Study/CBT/Video
3 hours = 1 unit	6 hours = 1 unit	3 hours = 1 unit	6 hours = 1 unit

All courses must be CNP approved. Fractional units will not count. No more than 10 units of self-study permitted. Maintaining a log and tracking of credits will be the responsibility of the individual. Completion certificates will be given for all NPA approved educational opportunities.

Continuing Activity	
Industry Work Experience	Minimum 4 months qualified experience

| Core Fundamentals | Area of Specialty | Work Experience |
| Professionalism | CNP Requirements |

CNP
Certified
Network
Professional

Welcome	Requirements	About CNP	What's New?
CNP Directory	Education Opportunities	Vendor Opportunities
CNP Toolbox	Contact Us	Guestbook

QUOTE

Staying Certified

To be and to remain certified, it's up to the individual to seek out the information. Fortunately, the vendors themselves advertise to encourage individuals to become and stay certified. Vendors are generally very helpful and generous in the amount of time they provide you to become and stay certified. Each vendor is different. I prioritize based on perceived market value and my professional goals.

I have a local area network I've invested in and developed over the last few years. It's configured for maximum flexibility at minimum expense for me to run the latest software and emulate different environments. Without the hardware, it's extremely difficult to attain, much less remain certified.

As far as why I do it, it's all about becoming proficient and then marketing yourself. In the end, it translates to my continued livelihood.

—Matthew Chan, MCT, MCSE, MCNE, CNI,
IBM Lan Server Engineer, IBM Lan Server Instructor, and A+ Certified

Training Directories

As the need for continuing technical education has become more pronounced, a number of training resource clearinghouses, which connect students with learning resources, have appeared on the Web. These contain contact information and links to vendors that offer courses and training products. They are a good starting place when you're researching learning options for a particular topic. Two clearinghouses to check are:

- ✏ **www.crctraining.com/training/** is a page of The Computer Training Network site that provides an index of computer-related trainers and training companies organized by product.
- ✏ **www.trainingnet.com/index_new.cfm** includes computer and noncomputer training resources and covers a variety of training formats. Figure 15-6 shows the site's home page.

Yahoo!'s directory pages will also prove valuable in your search. Two useful Yahoo! pages are:

- ✏ **www.yahoo.com/Business_and_Economy/Companies/ Entertainment/Video/Tape_Sales/Specialty/Computers/** is Yahoo!'s directory of vendors for computer-training videos.
- ✏ **www.yahoo.com/Business_and_Economy/Companies/ Computers/Software/Training/** is Yahoo!'s index of computer-training software vendors.

Professional books can be purchased in traditional bookstores or through online outlets such as Amazon Books (**www.amazon.com books**) or Computer Book Express (**www.computerbookexpress.com**).

Don't forget to utilize any discounts that you received as perks of your certification program to reduce the price of publications or training you purchase.

QUICK TIP

Bonus Benefits

Besides maintaining your status as a certified professional, keeping up with recertification requirements provides other potential benefits. Completing continuing education requirements will often serve double duty by providing additional career boosting benefits not directly related to the certification.

Training venues are a prime networking opportunity. Through them you'll connect with other professionals in your field. By establishing relationships with these people, you'll build connections that can help you in many ways. When you meet another particularly

Figure 15-6
TrainingNet

The Web Site for Training and HR Solutions

Select from our list of solutions. Then press solve!   SOLVE

Need To Develop A CBT ... That Is Effective — We Can Help CLICK HERE...

The TrainingNet

Wed, November 05, 1997

Solutions

Directory

Event Finder

TeleForums

Job Finder

Magazine

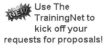

INSIDE The TrainingNet

Internet and Distance Learning

The TrainingNet in partnership with Coaching Success are pleased to present our next series of free TeleForums. On November 11th Judy Feld and Ernest Oriente of Coaching Success will be discussing TeleForums...A New Tool for Interactive Distance Learning. On November 12th Steve Glovsky of RKG Interactive will be presenting "Six Steps To Implementing Technology Delivered Training Programs" and Debbie Black of Databeam Corp. will be discussing "Internet Training - 'Tools of the Trade'".

Our October TeleForums were a great sucess and we hope that you will join us during November. Click here to register.

Use The TrainingNet to kick off your requests for proposals!

Our new Request for Information (RFI) system enables you to send your project details to leading Training and HR organizations and consultants from one single form.

Downloads, Demos, and Freebies!

The downloads and demos area of The TrainingNet provides quick access to FREE samples of the latest and best software for Training and Human Resources. If you are a developer and would to include your products in the section then please go to the downloads and demos page and follow the upload intsrcutions.

Organizational IQ Survey

An organization's I.Q. is the extent to which its systems, policies, and procedures result in behavior consistent with good reasoning. This survey, developed by Business Processes Inc, aims to assess people's perception of the level of intelligence achieved through their own organization's processes and systems. Click here to participate.

The TrainingNet Directory

The TrainingNet directory contains 11592 listings from 2433 companies.If you haven't taken advantage of a free listing in the directory then follow the links to the directory and create your listing today.

competent professional (whether online or in person), obtain their contact information and take note of their operating environment and other areas of expertise. Offer your information in return. When either of you encounters a technical dilemma, you'll be able to call on each other as problem-solving resources.

Connections you make through training forums will also build your career network in another important way: by extending your circle of professional acquaintances you'll build a web of personal connections that you may wish to draw on when seeking new employment in the future. Word-of-mouth is an often underestimated force when it comes to finding excellent job opportunities, and it's one you'll be able to use to great advantage if you know many other individuals in your field.

Continuing education courses can also serve double duty in other ways. If you decide to pursue an academic degree at a future time, you may be able to parlay the same courses that earned you recertification into credits applied toward your degree. Doing so has the potential to save you a great deal of time and money.

Going after an advanced degree isn't the only way to get your training to count twice. You may also be able to choose courses that maintain your current certification *and* apply toward obtaining another one. This trick, which requires careful planning and coordination, makes recertification especially painless.

Don't forget to incorporate significant training into your professional resume. It's an easy way to illustrate your abilities and the initiative you've taken to stay current in the industry, traits considered desirable by employers. A good way to include this information is to add a continuing education/continuing professional development heading under the education section of your resume and list the course or seminar titles there, along with the dates you completed them.

Record Keeping

When you investigate the details of the continuing education requirements for your certification, be sure to inquire about the details of submitting evidence that you've met them. Most often you'll need to submit supporting materials via standard mail, but some vendors offer online submission of continuing education details. (Figure 15-7 shows the ICCP online submission form.) Send only copies of your receipts, keeping the originals for your own files. Make sure all of your course documentation includes dates and descriptions. If you receive a simple, terse receipt, write the details on it yourself before filing it away.

Figure 15-7
ICCP's Electronic
Submission Form

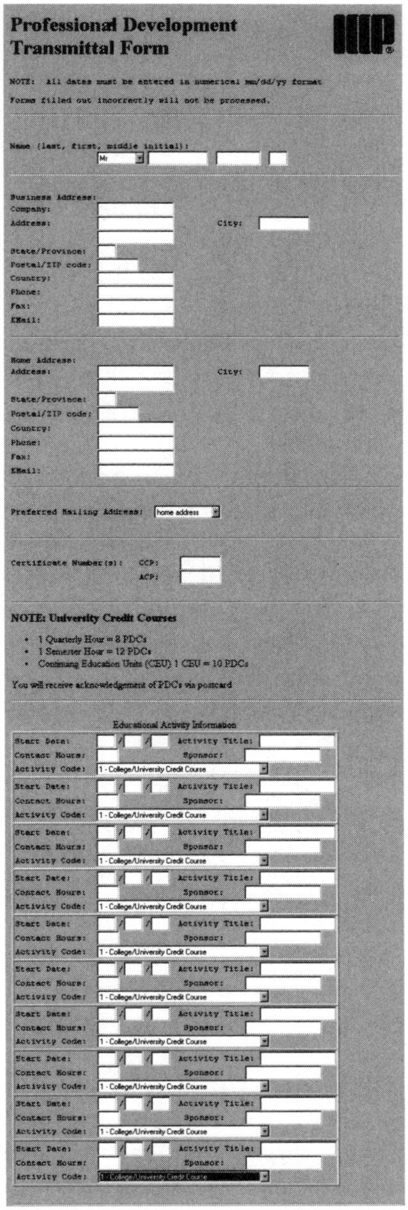

Once you've submitted your information, wait a few weeks before verifying that it's been recorded in your sponsor's certification records. Email and regular mail do sometimes go astray, and it won't take you much time or effort to confirm that yours has reached its intended target.

Besides providing evidence that you've met recertification requirements, there's another reason to be scrupulous about saving your receipts: tax time. Because this training is undertaken to further your skills in your current career, you may be able to deduct the costs as employee expenses (or, if you're self-employed, as business expenses).

To obtain any deductions you're entitled to, record every expense associated with your educational pursuits, including study materials, tuition charges, and even travel and lodging. If you drive to and from a course, record the mileage and dates, too. If you complete your own tax return, you'll need the information on file to support your claims. If you use a professional tax preparer you'll need to provide this information so he or she can obtain the deductions for you. Tax preparers don't always remember to ask every question they should, so be sure to bring up your education expenses yourself.

Completing recertification requirements is typically a simple process. These requirements provide a preplanned route for your continued professional development; all you have to do is follow it. Doing so will pay off in numerous ways, including bringing networking opportunities and adding to your sheaf of credentials. On the other hand, if you let your certification lapse because of inattention, you'll pay the price with increased hassle and costs.

CHAPTER 16

Taking Advantage of Perks and Privileges

Besides adding a credential to boost your marketing advantage, most certifications come with an array of benefits that can help you work more effectively. Even if a particular program doesn't spell out specific perks, it's fairly safe to assume that by becoming certified you've earned a privileged relationship with the certification sponsor. By taking advantage of your special status, you can gain access to resources that will make it possible to do your job more effectively and efficiently.

Before you can benefit from the perks associated with your certification, you have to know what they are. Don't count on what you read in printed materials you received at the outset; programs are revised frequently and defined benefits can change. The sponsor will probably notify you of such changes, but you can make sure you don't miss out by checking the sponsor's Web site regularly. Additions and modifications will often appear online before landing in your mailbox. Microsoft, for example, recently announced program changes that ranged from redesigned certification logos to the discontinuation of free telephone incident support.

Some of the larger sponsors maintain a special news page detailing certification program changes. These pages list testing changes, program alterations, and other news and announcements that may prove of interest to you. It's also a good idea to check the news pages for other certifications, to keep up on the latest news in the certification marketplace. Figure 16-1 shows a Microsoft benefits change announcement.

Figure 16-1
Microsoft Announces
Benefit Changes

News pages to visit include:

- IBM: **www.austin.ibm.com/pspinfo/pronews.htm**
- ICCP: **www.iccp.org/whatsnew.html**

📑 Microsoft: **www.microsoft.com/Train_Cert/mcp/default.htm**
📑 Novell: **education.novell.com/certinfo/certnews.htm**

QUOTE

Putting Perks to Work

The best perk I've gained through certification so far has been the subscription to Microsoft's TechNet. This is an invaluable tool, and I use it every day at my job. I also use it at home to study for more certification tests. I look forward to every month's issue. I was almost ready to pay for a subscription, but I just worked that much harder, faster, and smarter so I could get the free subscription upon becoming a certified engineer. I've also used a few priority tech-support calls when our company used up all of theirs. This was very convenient because one of our Exchange mail servers was down, and we needed immediate help.

The use of the logos has made my resume stand out and be noticed. I was very proud to have been able to display the logos, and interviewers are impressed to see such a diverse range of certifications. They even commented why other certified professionals have not used the logos in the past. The actual certification itself is great to frame and put by your desk at work to take pride in your accomplishments.

Novell certifications lack the year's subscription to the Network Support Connection CD, but they give you access to a password protected Web site that is exclusively for CNEs. Here you can download and order special offers and also talk with many other certified professionals like yourself.

—Cameron Brandon, MCSE, CNE, CNA, A+, MCPS/Internet Systems

Perks may arrive in the form of print or electronic subscriptions, admittance to focused technical forums, access to priority technical support, participation in referral programs that will funnel work your way, use of marketing aids, and other training and product money savers. Once you've identified the benefits specific to your certification program, it's time to put them to work for you.

About Those Subscriptions

You may receive two kinds of subscriptions from your certification sponsor: print and electronic. Print subscriptions typically include product announcements, bug reports, and training information. They may also include tips and tricks for handling product situations that may arise and offer a simple way for you to stay on top of new developments related to the product or specialty. This advance information will enable you to speak knowledgeably about what's pending in your field, an ability that will enhance your image as an expert.

Taming the Paper Pileup

If you receive multiple print publications, reading them all may be too time consuming to be worthwhile. However, don't just transfer them from your mailbox to the recycling bin: You may be tossing information that will bail you out of a sticky spot a month down the road. On the other hand, if you store every issue in a "reference" pile, you'll soon end up with a teetering mass that's more formidable than useful. To avoid these perils, scan each publication as it arrives to get a feel for what it contains. Read the table of contents, then quickly flip through the publication, scanning each page just long enough to identify the article titles, section headlines, illustrations, and sidebar subject matter. If you come across information that looks especially likely to be useful in the future, make a note of the topic and starting page number on the cover page of the publication. This will save you the trouble of thumbing through a dozen issues to locate the article later. Once you've completed your quick review (which you should do as soon as possible after the material arrives), file the publication either with your reference materials or in your "to read" folder, whichever seems more appropriate.

Electronic Issues

Electronic subscriptions typically arrive on CD-ROM. They contain much more information than their print counterparts and are often jam-packed with technical product information, software releases and trial versions, white papers, program patches, utilities, and other useful resources. Figure 16-2 shows the participating vendors of one Network Professional Association (NPA) Tech CD. Figure 16-3 shows the software it includes.

As with their print counterparts, CD-ROM subscriptions can pile up quickly. Although you can electronically search through the contents of a single disk, finding an item that you recall as having appeared "sometime in the recent past" can be time consuming. To avoid searching through a dozen disks to find the program or document you need, consider printing out a table of contents for each issue as you receive it. You may have to print out a separate table of contents for each section of the CD-ROM. You can then staple them together and file them in a folder dedicated to that subscription. File the disks in date order, and when you need to locate a particular resource, you'll be able to flip through your contents pages and pull out just the CD-ROM you need.

Figure 16-2
NPA Tech CD
Participating Vendors

NPA Technical Resource CD Second Quarter 97

Sponsors of this CD

 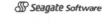 

Figure 16-3
NPA Tech CD
Software Freebies

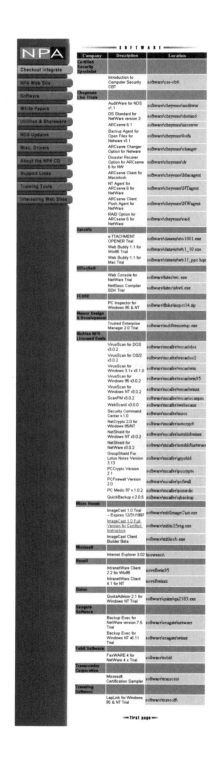

Becoming A Contributor

Your professional subscriptions offer another opportunity you should consider taking advantage of: a venue to establish your reputation as an expert. How can your subscriptions help you accomplish this? By publishing articles you write. Such articles will carry your byline, and each will convey to readers that you are enough of an expert to write intelligently on the subject at hand.

If the idea of writing for certification-related publications appeals to you, the first thing to do is study the format of one or more that interest you. Pay attention to who has written the articles—do the bylines belong to the people who edit the publication or are they outside writers? How long are the articles, and what topics do they cover? What tone are they written in—familiar or formal, technical or simplified? Contact the editorial offices via mail or email and request their writers' guidelines; they'll specify which areas are open to outside writers, pay rates, and other details of writing for the publication.

If your analysis reveals that the publication is one you'd like to write for, develop several ideas of your own that would fit well within the style and format you've identified. Write a short letter to the editor pitching your ideas and explaining why you're qualified to write about them. Be succinct, and keep your letter to a single page. Submit your ideas using the method specified in the writers' guidelines. If you don't receive a response within a few weeks, make a follow-up inquiry.

It may take a few tries before you hit on a combination of publication and topic that will win you an assignment. Be persistent, and you may end up with that byline, and your article in the hands of hundreds or thousands of readers. Then you'll also be able to add your article credits to the "professional publications" section of your resume, further enhancing your credentials.

Getting the Most from Restricted Forums

Another benefit that's becoming more common is the specialized, restricted-access forum. These areas are created by the sponsoring organization and are only accessible to individuals who've obtained the organization's certification. They're typically available via the Internet, using a password and sponsor-supplied identification number, but in some cases, the forum is only accessible by dial-up modem and isn't connected to the Internet. Figure 16-4 shows Novell's restricted CNE forum.

Figure 16-4
CNE Net

The utility of such forums varies widely, depending on the sponsor's commitment to them and the composition of the professionals who participate. Some forums will be closely monitored by the sponsoring organization's staff, which means they can personally respond to queries and participate in conversations. In other cases, participation is by the certified individuals, and the sponsor does little more than host the site.

These forums provide a number of opportunities for the certified professional. You can use them to solve problems, to network, and to identify ways to better perform common (and even unusual) tasks.

As problem resolution tools, restricted forums have advantages over both tech-support lines and unrestricted forums. First of all, you won't have to spend an extended period on hold, waiting your turn in a tech-support phone queue. When your need isn't urgent, you can post your question, go on to something else, and return a few hours (or a day or two) later and probably find several responses awaiting you. In addition, the forum participants will be other certified professionals like yourself. As such, they will be handling the technology in question in live environments on a daily basis.

Although telephone technical support people may have oodles of data and incident reports collected in a searchable database at their fingertips, when it comes to efficient and effective troubleshooting, there's nothing like interacting with a person who's actually handled the task you're facing. And because the forum is restricted to individuals certified through the same program as yourself, you're more likely to get accurate advice from a well-trained, experienced person who's kept up with the latest changes in the field.

You might wonder whether busy professionals, such as yourself, are really likely to take the time to assist you with your queries. The answer is yes, and the reason is simple: on these types of forums, the culture is one of information sharing and assistance. Someone helps you today, you help them tomorrow, and everyone is able to do their jobs better. That's one reason it's important for you to give advice in the forum setting as well as to seek it. A particular forum will only be as valuable as the participants make it. By doing what you can to create a quality professional environment, you'll encourage others to do the same.

When you post a question to the forum, make it as specific as possible. Provide as many relevant details as you can manage, starting with a succinct description of the information you're seeking. Include version numbers of the products/software in question and the hardware platform(s) in your operating environment. Include a brief summary of what you've already tried and the results you obtained. If error messages are involved, reiterate them exactly. The reason for including these details is expediency. If you leave them out, you may return to the forum only to find more questions (for example, "Which version of Windows NT are you running?") rather than solutions to your problem. Then you'll have to respond and wait some more before finding out what you really wanted to know.

Although it probably won't be your primary purpose for visiting restricted certification forums, they're also a reasonable place to do some professional networking. Every time you intervene to solve someone else's technical dilemma, you're advertising your own expertise. Over time, the repetition of your name at the end of your postings will become familiar to others who frequent the forum. This may come in handy if you choose to seek out a new position down the road, when you might decide to ask others in the forum for referrals and job leads. If you've been posting regularly, they'll know who you are and as a result will be more likely to share information about employment opportunities.

Don't participate in the more heated discussions (called *flame wars*) that break out from time to time on such forums. Online arguments tend to quickly deteriorate into emotional mudslinging events, and participating will only detract from your professional image.

QUICK TIP — There's a fail-safe way to prevent yourself from falling into a flame war in the heat of the moment: if you really want to reply, go ahead and compose your response, but don't send it right away. Instead, store it in your outbox for a few hours or overnight. When you come back later, you'll be better able to decide if posting your reply is in your best interest.

Keep in mind that sponsor-run, restricted forums aren't the only places you can seek out advice. Don't hesitate to turn to independent forums as well, where it's likely that more people (although possibly fewer experts) will read your postings. Wherever you post, take care to understand how the particular forum works, and follow the protocol. Doing so demonstrates respect for the other individuals who frequent the site.

How to Benefit from Priority Tech Support

As anyone who's been in a computer business for long knows first hand, obtaining technical support from a vendor can be a frustrating experience. Often, significant wait time is involved while your call is put on hold and a synthesized voice promises it will be handled "in the order it was received." At peak times, and especially after product upgrades, hold time can run up to an hour. Because vendor use of toll-free support phone numbers is dwindling, you (or your company) will be paying at peak phone rates for the privilege of listening to music or recorded messages until you make it to the front of the queue. Some product vendors charge for technical support on a per instance basis. All of this translates into stress and inconvenience. Priority technical-support privileges can significantly cut this hassle.

Priority technical-support privileges can come in several forms. They include:

- Access to a restricted technical-support system—You'll be able to utilize a support venue that has fewer people vying for access, which means a quicker response time. It's also likely to offer a higher level of support based on the assumptions that you (and others with access) are more technically able than the typical tech-support line caller and will not be calling for low-level help.

- ✐ A priority access code that moves you ahead in a telephone queue—This is basically authorization to "cut" to the front of the tech-support line.
- ✐ Automatic escalation to senior support staff—Support staffing is often organized in levels, with the first line (those that answer the calls) having the least expertise. The first-line staff can pass you on to more technically advanced support if needed. Because you've qualified for certification, you're likely to be able to solve minor product conflicts on your own. Some certification sponsors recognize this by providing a means for you to route your support call directly to a senior person, rather than having to pass through a vendor's first-line support analyst (who'll likely have to escalate your call to a senior support person anyway). This privilege may come in the shape of a special phone number or an access code.
- ✐ Free or reduced-cost incident calls—in a way, this is a direct financial reward for choosing a particular vendor's certification. It's also another confirmation that, as a certified individual, you're less likely to be making "frivolous" calls for help.

The first three priority support benefits can translate into significant time savings, and all of them have the potential to save money. To make the best use of your priority technical-support benefits, it's important to clarify what they are and how to use them. It's also critical to determine whether your priority privileges cover unlimited use or are only valid for a certain number of instances. You should nail down the details before you need to make your first call. If this information isn't included in your certification welcome kit, call the sponsoring organization and ask to have them faxed or mailed to you (that way you'll have them in writing).

QUICK TIP

As a certified professional, the priority technical-support privileges are assigned to **you**, not to your employer. If your employer already has a support agreement/contract, you'll probably want to use it most of the time, saving your own privileged access for special instances not otherwise covered. When you do need to use your special privileges, you can earn a few brownie points by mentioning to your employer that you did so, along with how it saved the company time and/or money. In cases where the number of incidents you can use your access for is limited, save them for a time when you really need them. That might be while working from home or on a project for a different client.

Putting Priority to Work

Priority technical-support privileges will only prove useful if your problem is clearly related to your certification sponsor's product or specialty. It can be tempting to use the priority access that you know won't keep you waiting as long, even if you're not certain your difficulty originates with that vendor's product. This is especially true when products from two separate vendors (such as an operating system and an application) interact. In such cases, it isn't always obvious which is at the root of the difficulties. If you give in to this temptation, you're likely to run into the "not our product" syndrome. For example, your application vendor may claim it's an operating system problem, while your operating system's manufacturer insists it's an application problem. Each tells you to call the other. To avoid wasting your time (and possibly your priority benefits) be prepared for this potential response and be ready to tell them why your situation should be handled by the technical-support line you're calling.

When you place the call, have the following information at hand:

- Your certification identification number, which will probably be required to obtain priority support. You may also be asked for your date of certification or certification renewal.
- A description of the problem, including the exact wording of any error messages, the steps necessary for the support person to reproduce the problem, and what you have already tried.
- Names and version numbers of all software and hardware involved.

Record the name and direct phone number (or extension) of the person who handles your call. If you have to call back, you'll be able to quickly reach the individual who's already familiar with your problem and assure that your follow-up call is recognized as a continuation of the same incident, rather than an additional occurrence. If the number of support incidents is limited, keep a list of what you called about and when you called so you'll know exactly how many covered calls you have remaining. A good place to record certification-related technical support calls is in a simple text or word processing file on your computer. Give it an easily recognizable name, such as "Novell incidents.doc."

Directory Assistance

Many certification sponsors offer some form of marketing assistance to their program graduates. One of the more common ways to do this is to create a directory of certified professionals and make it available to potential clients. Both vendor-specific and vendor-independent sponsors may provide this service. These directories are often incorporated into the sponsor's Web site (Figure 16-5 shows Centura's Web-based directory), but may be accessible in other ways as well. Some sponsors, for example, give out the name of their certified professionals when a customer calls and asks for a referral. Directories are sometimes created in the traditional print format as well.

Figure 16-5
Centura's Directory
of Certified
Professionals

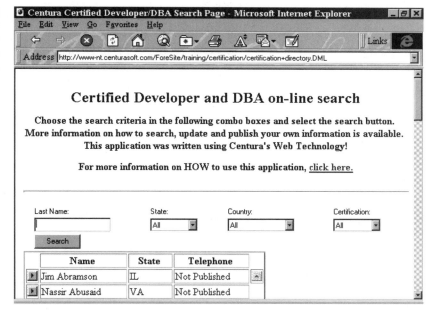

This is another benefit you should always ask about. Your sponsor may offer this service even if it isn't listed in your certification materials. This happens through simple oversight or sometimes because the materials haven't been reprinted since the directory benefit was initiated.

Inclusion in sponsor directories isn't automatic. It's your responsibility to request inclusion and provide the necessary information. You can often do this via the Internet by filling out a form on the sponsor's site. Figure 16-6 shows one such form.

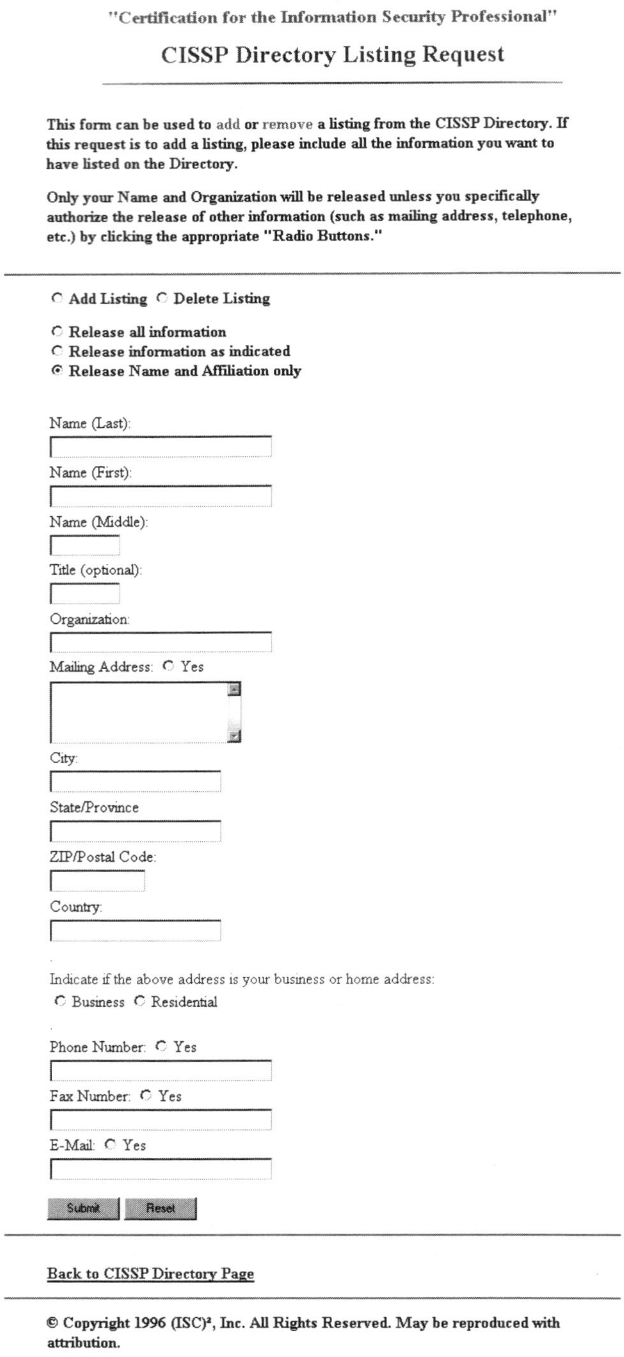

Figure 16-6
Getting Listed

"Certification for the Information Security Professional"

CISSP Directory Listing Request

This form can be used to add or remove a listing from the CISSP Directory. If this request is to add a listing, please include all the information you want to have listed on the Directory.

Only your Name and Organization will be released unless you specifically authorize the release of other information (such as mailing address, telephone, etc.) by clicking the appropriate "Radio Buttons."

○ Add Listing   ○ Delete Listing

○ Release all information
○ Release information as indicated
◉ Release Name and Affiliation only

Name (Last):

Name (First):

Name (Middle):

Title (optional):

Organization:

Mailing Address: ○ Yes

City:

State/Province:

ZIP/Postal Code:

Country:

Indicate if the above address is your business or home address:
○ Business   ○ Residential

Phone Number: ○ Yes

Fax Number: ○ Yes

E-Mail: ○ Yes

[Submit]   [Reset]

Back to CISSP Directory Page

© Copyright 1996 (ISC)², Inc. All Rights Reserved. May be reproduced with attribution.

A typical directory entry will include your name, qualification(s), email address, phone number, and sometimes a link to your personal Web site. Always double-check your directory listing to ensure accuracy; typos or other errors can prevent someone from selecting and contacting you. If you include your email address as a contact option, be sure to check your email regularly. Remember to update your listing if any of your information, such as your email address, changes.

Landing in the Spotlight

If you get yourself listed in a directory, you may also be able to become a "featured" professional. Some sponsors include a professional profile as a regular component of their directory resource or on another page of their Web site. These short articles summarize the qualifications and background of an individual and are placed prominently on the site. Anyone who views the page also views the profile, which demonstrates how the certification is being used for professional success, while at the same time promoting the services of the individual being profiled. Figure 16-7 shows a featured professional. Other sponsors sometimes include short blurbs on their Web site or in their print publications that describe the different ways individuals are capitalizing on their certified status.

To find out if your sponsor utilizes any of these "spotlight" techniques, visit its Web site and browse it thoroughly, looking for profiles. Watch the subscriptions you receive as well, for similar pieces. When you come across a profile, it will probably mention (at the bottom) how the individual was selected to be featured. If not, you can write or email the Webmaster or editor of the publication and inquire as to how you might get included.

If your sponsor doesn't publish professional profile pieces, consider suggesting the idea. It's fairly simple for the sponsor to add another article to an existing newsletter or Web site. By doing so, certification sponsors promote their programs and provide an extra service for their program graduates. You just might have the honor of becoming the first professional featured.

Figure 16-7
Profile of a
Featured CNP

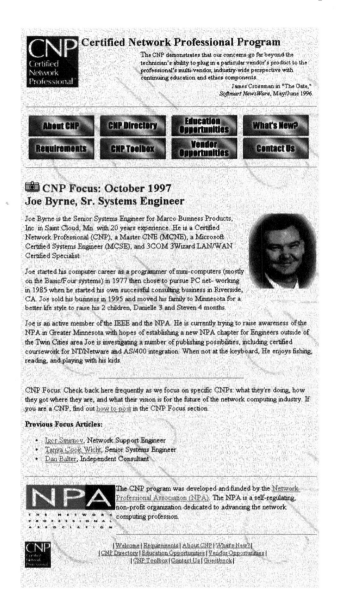

Image Enhancers

Certification logos are provided by most program sponsors. Use them to capitalize on the brand recognition they engender. Logos can be placed on resumes, Web sites, business cards, and marketing materials. Chapter 12 details how to use logos to advertise your professional status.

It doesn't happen often, but occasionally vendors redesign a certification's logo. In 1997, for example, Microsoft redesigned and reissued all of its certified professional program logos. Periodically check your vendor's Web site to keep abreast of such changes and to obtain the latest versions of logos.

If your certification agreement includes subscribing to a code of ethics/professional conduct, you can use that as a marketing tool, too. By including a copy of the standards with other promotional materials you provide to a potential employer or client, you can make a positive statement about your professionalism.

Using Your Certification to Save Money

Achieving certified status often entitles you to discounts on a slew of items that will prove useful in your career. These include free or reduced cost training, reduced or free admission to certain conferences, savings on technical books and publications, and deep discounts on software.

Tech Ed

Training discounts usually only apply to classes offered by the certification's sponsoring organization and/or authorized training partners. If your certification is vendor-sponsored, such discounts will probably only help you with classes related to that product. If that's the case, they may still prove useful, especially when new versions are released. Keep an eye out for training that demonstrates how to integrate the sponsor's products with products from other vendors, which can provide a way to expand your expertise.

Certification sponsors may also offer reduced or free admission to certain technical conferences and trade shows. Some sponsors even operate conferences just for their certified professionals. These can be a fun way to catch up on technological changes and to network with others in your field. The Building Industry Consulting Service International (BICSI), nonprofit sponsor of the Registered Communications Distribution Designer (RCDD) certification, holds educational conferences and technical seminars, and Bay Networks hosts an annual technical conference for its certified professionals. Many other sponsors hold similar events.

To avoid unpleasant surprises, always verify in advance (when you sign up for the course) that the discount applies. It would be disappointing to find out after the fact that a particular class was excluded from the discount program.

Discounts on books and training materials can add up. Adobe certified professionals, for example, receive discounts on Adobe Press books published by Macmillan Computer Publishing. Again, be sure to confirm at the time you place your order that the discount will apply.

QUICK TIP

When using your certification to obtain a discounted product or service, be sure to have your sponsor's name and your certification ID number handy. You'll need them to prove that you're eligible for the savings.

Deep Discounts

Perhaps the greatest cost-saving opportunity comes in the form of deep discounts on software or other products. Although most commonly offered by vendor certification sponsors, product discounts may be obtained from vendor-independent certification sponsors, too. Such discounts may apply to a single-copy purchase, or to as many copies as you wish to order.

Vendor sponsors typically offer reduced prices on their product line, as well as on materials created specifically for trainers to use when teaching about the product. Vendor-independent certification sponsors may not have their own products to offer at discounted prices, but that doesn't prevent them from participating in deals with outside vendors. As a certified professional, you're recognized as wielding influence over the marketplace, or at least your segment of it. For that reason, some product vendors want to simplify your access to their product. This makes it easier for you, in turn, to introduce and promote it throughout your workplace or client sites, thus encouraging the product's market penetration. To accomplish this, vendors sometimes offer their products through relevant certification sponsors for free or at a reduced cost. These deals won't be specifically stated in your certification materials but will appear from time to time in mailings you receive from your sponsor.

Your software/product discount savings may range from a few dollars to a few hundred or even more, depending on how frequently you purchase such items. For example, if you are an independent contractor who purchases software or hardware for your clients as part of your services, the savings over time can be quite substantial. Certainly your clients/boss will be pleased when you point out how you've saved them money. If you purchase software/hardware only occasionally for your own use, your savings will be less but still significant.

Beta Participation

Early access to new programs is another perk you may receive. By getting your hands on prerelease (beta) versions, you'll be able to try before you buy, as well as contribute suggestions as to what ought to be in a new program but isn't. If you're lucky, your suggestions will translate into a final product that better meets your needs. In any event, beta participation will give you a way to evaluate a product without having to purchase it.

Whether the menu of benefits that accompanies your certification is extensive or more limited, make sure you know what it includes. Take the time to scan mailings from your certification sponsor and periodically visit your sponsor's Web site to scout out any benefits that have been added or dropped. The perks and privileges that accompany a certification can prove to be valuable additions to your career tool chest—all you have to do is know about them and use them.

CHAPTER 17

Another Certification?

Now that you've completed your journey to certification, you face another important career decision: are you going to do it again? Just as some people obtain multiple academic degrees in the course of climbing the career ladder, you can combine various certifications to further boost your career. And earning certifications is typically faster and less expensive than obtaining academic degrees.

As part of a 1997 Gartner Group study sponsored by Sylvan Prometric, IBM, Microsoft, Novell, and Sybase, more than 7,000 certification candidates were asked about professional designations they already held. Two thirds of respondents reported already holding one or more certifications prior to the one they were currently pursuing. Less than one third (31%) were earning their first certification. In contrast, when the same question was asked back in 1994, more than half of respondents (56%) were in the process of earning their first certification. This data (illustrated in Figure 17-1) indicates a trend toward earning multiple certifications.

Figure 17-1
A Trend Toward
Multiple
Certifications

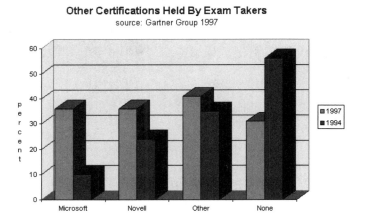

Other Certifications Held By Exam Takers
source: Gartner Group 1997

More Can Be Better

There are several reasons you might want to consider going after additional professional certifications. They include:

- Staying abreast of technological change
- Broadening your market
- Increasing your technical level
- Personal pride and a desire to excel

A few technologies endure for long periods, such as the COBOL programming language. But most fade almost as quickly as they become hot when, inevitably, something newer and better comes along. Professional certification programs can be used as tools for technical excellence. Although many in the computer field are skilled at self-instruction, it's difficult to know what you need to learn about a technology that's new to you. A certification program for that technology will outline the path to expertise; all you have to do is follow it.

If your first certification is version specific, you'll want to become certified on new releases as they come out. That way you'll be up to date on new features and functions. You'll also be clearly qualified to work at older installations as well as new ones.

Adding multiple certifications to your professional portfolio can significantly broaden your base of potential clients and employers. You'll be qualified for and able to choose from a wider range of positions and employers. Multiple certifications also tags you as a professional who takes initiative and someone who is a "go-getter." These traits are looked upon favorably by a large portion of potential clients and employers.

Some certifications are especially complementary. For example, people who are both Netware and NT certified will find plenty of employment opportunities. That's because computer environments today are blended, more often than not incorporating multiple vendors, products, and platforms. Individuals able to integrate the components of these environments are especially sought after.

QUOTE

Benefiting from Multiple Certifications

I had multiple certifications before I started teaching—partly because I gained a reputation for it and I wanted to open a business. Developers can certainly benefit from learning the other side of the business—the administration and engineering side. And those engineers or administrators that have an aptitude for programming can certainly benefit from learning the developer side of the business. A Microsoft person can benefit from knowing and certifying on Netware. They'll know better how to migrate people from Netware, for instance. Anybody involved with Microsoft or Netware at a high level could benefit from a Cisco certification, because there is more knowledge that they will gain—knowing more of the technical environment they're likely to be working in. With Microsoft, Netware, and/or Cisco certifications, you're more likely to be able to work in a high level environment.

—Herb Martin, MCSD, MCT, MCSEx2, and founder of LearnQuick.Com.

In addition to the more tangible benefits already mentioned, there's another reason people decide to earn numerous professional certifications: personal fulfillment. Holding professional certifications in more than one area can be a source of pride. It also feeds the appetite for excellence and urge to learn that many computer people possess. Figure 17-2 shows a Web page where certified pros boast of their accomplishments.

VICTOR DUBIN'S CERTIFICATION & NETWORKING PAGE

Certification Wall of Fame

And Current Champs Are:

Anders Gustafsson	6 (SIX) Novell tests a day
Ed Erichson	3 (I&C, D&I, AA) Novell tests a day
Pasha Pergamenchik	Possibly world's youngest CNE & MCPS (14 years old)
Herb Martin	All 6 MCSE tests in 11 days.
Michael Swisher	All 6 MCSE tests in one month, inc one beta
Undell Williams	4 tests in one day - 4.1 Admin, 4.1 I&C, NTS 3.51, NTW 3.51 6 more in three days - S&S, Access 95, D&I, SQL 6 IMP, TCPIP 3.51, Win95
Mark Spain	3 Novell tests in 20 (!!!) minutes - Can you beat it?
Jon Spencer	3 Novell tests(D&I, 3I&C, 3AA in 2 hours 15 minutes,
Pamela Forsyth	Largest number of certifications from different vendors: MCNE, CNX, CLP, CCIE, former CBS
Jens Stark	Fastest single test - Novell NT in 7 (seven) minutes.
Cameron Brandon	**Absolute** record so far: CNE, MCSE, A+ in FIVE!!! months. The guy claims he has personal life too. (G)

My sincere and to them

Your wanna be listed here too? Email me: 71660.117@compuserve.com

HOME

Ms scores | Novell scores | Other scores | Certification News | Preparation Tools | Resources |
Test Taking Rules | TS Tips & Facts | Links | Wall of Fame | Search Engines |
Links to Me | My CV

Last updated on Tue Aug 19 05:07:25 1997.
Your current time is Thu Nov 13 09:51:15 1997
Copyright © 1996,1997 Victor Dubin

Best viewed with

Broken links? Misprints? Wrong info? Questions? Please feel free to email me at
71660.117@compuserve.com

Drawbacks

Although adding more certifications to your professional credentials is largely a positive move, there are a few drawbacks you should be aware of. The most commonly encountered complication concerns logistics. Once you progress beyond your second certification, tracking the continuing education requirements requires more careful attention. You'll have more forms to complete and submit on time, and more requirements to comply with.

QUICK TIP

Individuals who hold multiple certifications may be able to get the education they complete to count double, or more, if it meets the qualifications for several of the programs. There aren't any rules that limit you to applying continuing education activity toward only one certification.

Because of the added complexity of managing several certifications on an ongoing basis, it becomes especially important to use a calendar to track and comply with continuing education deadlines.

Earning and maintaining multiple certifications will also add to your professional expenses. It's likely that at least some of the training options you employ to obtain and maintain the certifications will involve significant expense. Don't forget to apply the money-saving advice in Chapter 5 to earning additional certifications just as you did to earning the first one. That includes going after outside funding and remembering to take any tax deductions you are due.

A final potential drawback you should be aware of only applies when you top three certifications. It's the possibility that some people will look at your list of certifications and think that it's not possible for you to actually be technically competent in all of the areas you hold certifications for, and to then suspect that the certifications represent an ability to pass tests more than professional expertise. You can counteract this potential backlash by finding additional ways to demonstrate that your broad competencies are genuine. If you have plenty of diverse experience included on your resume, that should take care of it. Otherwise, you may have to do some additional convincing of potential clients.

One way around this potential image problem is to mention only those certifications which are especially relevant when applying for a particular job or contract. You don't have to list every one you hold if you think it will work against you. On the other hand, if you're after a senior position, having multiple certifications on your resume is likely to work in your favor rather than against you.

QUOTE

Maintaining Multiple Certifications

When you hold multiple certifications, employers expect you will be able to deliver on the promise of expertise that multiple certifications imply, which can be a good thing if you can manage it properly. I am finding that maintaining multiple certifications is difficult. Just keeping up with the continuing certification requirements takes a lot of effort. I lose my edge when I don't work with a technology for a certain period of time, so I'm rusty on a lot of specific knowledge that I used to have but don't use every day now.

I let the CBS lapse because of Banyan's diminishing presence in the market and because of the stringent continuing certification requirement. I would have had to spend about $2500 on additional Banyan training by the end of 1995, plus take a week of vacation, because my employer did not see a business need for me to maintain that certification. I spent the money on Network General training instead, which proved to be a good move.

I allowed the CNP to lapse because there wasn't any interest or recognition amongst prospective employers. One of my technical friends ridiculed me because CNP also stands for Certified Nurse Practitioner. Also, I am chronically bad at keeping track of paper (tree-bark and berry-juice, as one of my friends disparagingly calls it), so when it came time to recertify I wasn't able to put my hands on the documentation I needed in order to prove that I'd been to enough training over the preceding year.

I will probably allow the LCCS certification to lapse when the recertification requirement comes up because I don't want to work with applications any more.

On the other hand, people are really impressed when the list takes up half a page on your resume!

—Pamela Forsyth, CCSI, ECNE, MCSE, and other certifications

Selecting Additional Certifications

When choosing additional certifications to pursue, follow the same process that helped you decide which certification to make your first. You may need to redo the worksheets in Chapter 8 to reflect your situation, since your first certification has likely resulted in some changes.

You'll also need to decide on a strategy: do you want to obtain an array of complementary certifications or go for diversity? Each option has its benefits. Complementary certifications are those that are directly related and likely to prove useful within a single work site. For example, holding several networking certifications will make you attractive to the many organizations that operate heterogeneous networking environments. You can think of this as deepening your marketing options with in a particular market segment. Multiple complementary certifications often increases your level of expertise in a particular area to the extent where you can command premium rates as a senior person.

Choosing to go with a strategy of diversity, on the other hand, widens your customer base to include additional market segments. For example, if you hold a developer certification and decide to add a security-related certification, you will be increasing your access to additional segments of the computer job market. An added benefit of the diversity strategy is that it makes it possible for you to have more variety in your work, choosing different types of assignments that you find interesting.

Once you've settled on an overall strategy, start browsing through the available programs to determine which ones meet your qualifications and appeal to you in terms of cost and time factors. Places to check include:

- The resource listings included with this book
- The Web site of the sponsor of your first certification; this sponsor may have developed additional certifications that will work well for you
- Certification news pages for other sponsors: new certifications are being developed at a fairly fast rate, and if you want to be aware of all your options, you'll need to do your homework and keep up to date with certification news
- If you have professional acquaintances who hold certifications, ask them for opinions of the programs they have participated in
- Visit one or more of the certification discussion forums mentioned elsewhere in this book and post a message mentioning your current certification(s) and goals, and seeking advice and suggestions about which program to look into next

When you've settled on a certification that will enhance your portfolio of professional qualifications, remember to pursue it using the skills you have already learned. Choose learning options that cater to your learning styles and budget. Having already been through the process once, you should know what those are. Go back and do a quick review of the study tips and advice contained in Chapter 11 to refresh your memory on efficient study habits.

The Bottom Line

Certification can be a valuable career-boosting tool, or more accurately, set of tools. Like any other tools, certifications can be used properly or improperly. Using an adjustable wrench to pound in a nail may be somewhat effective, but using it to tighten a bolt will be infinitely more so. As with tools, the key to successful use of certifications is to match the tool to the job. This is true whether selecting your first certification or your fifth.

When you take the time to select and earn appropriate certifications, you're already advancing yourself toward the front of the pack. But if you stop there you're not getting all that you can out of the credentials. Take those certifications and put them to work for you. Advertise your professional status. Use them to land jobs. Employ them to keep your professional edge. And exploit them to launch your career to new heights.

SECTION 4

Resources

This section contains details for over 170 certifications along with many resources to help you reach your certification goals. Every effort has been made to ensure the accuracy of this information at the time of publication.

However, requirements, web addresses, and the like can change over time. Therefore, it's in your best interests to emulate those in the White House: trust but verify. Always double check significant details before basing important decisions on them.

Certification Programs

Sponsor:

3Com Corporation 3 Wizard Headquarters
PO Box 1610
Minneapolis, MN 55440 USA
Phone: 1-800-847-6972   **Fax:** 1-800-711-1384
Email: 3Wizard@3mail.3com.com
URL: www.3com.com

3Wizard Certification

At time of publication, 3Com's certification program was being completely restructured and redesigned. It's organized around 3Com's products.

Date Initiated: 1998   **# Granted:**   **Fees:**

Initial Requirements:
Contact 3Com for details of restructured program.

Continuing Requirements:

Perks:

Online Resources:
3Wizard Web Site: **www.3com.com/About/3Wizard/index.html**

Offline Resources:
CBT software is available from sponsor. To enroll, order materials, or to sign up for training, call 1-800-847-6972 (outside US: 621-820-3153).

Sponsor:

Adobe Systems Incorporated
345 Park Ave.
San Jose, CA 95110-2704 USA
Phone: 408-536-6000   **Fax:**
Email: certification@adobe.com
URL: www.adobe.com/supportservice/learningres/aceprogram.html

Adobe Certified Expert (ACE)

The ACE is for web designers, graphic designers, production artists, computer illustrators, business professionals, resellers, technical support people, and others who need to be an expert in Adobe products.

Date Initiated: June 1996   **# Granted:** 126   **Fees:** $150

Initial Requirements:
Must pass a 1–2 hour product proficiency exam.

Continuing Requirements:
none

Perks:
- use of Adobe logo
- certification card
- logo pin
- discount on one single user version of Adobe software
- discounts on Adobe Press books purchased from Macmillan Computer Publishing
- discounts on courses offered by Adobe Authorized Learning Providers
- discounts on Adobe certification preparation courses

Online Resources:
The Adobe Web site: **www.adobe.com**.
Start with the ACE Web page: **www.adobe.com/supportservice/ learningres/aceprogram.html**.
A test bulletin to help you prepare and study for the exam can be downloaded from **www.adobe.com/supportservice/learningres/ aceprogram.html**.
A database of third-party curriculum providers is available at **www.adobe.com/supportservice/training/cpinfo.html**.

Offline Resources:

Adobe user guide and Adobe technical notes from the Adobe automated fax (1-206-628-5737). Courseware and books are available from Adobe, and you can take courses from Adobe Authorized Learning Providers (AALPs). For information call the Adobe fax line listed above, or visit the Web site.

To register and take an Adobe product proficency exam, call 1-800-356-3926.

Adobe Certified Instructor (ACI)

This certification is for professional trainers, training businesses, consultants, instructors, academia, and others teaching Adobe products.

Date Initiated: June 1996   **# Granted:** 26   **Fees:** approx. $435

Initial Requirements:

Candidate must first become an Adobe ACE, then obtain a Certified Technical Trainer (CTT) certification. The CTT certification is not sponsored by Adobe, and is listed separately in this book. It includes a written exam and a video of your instructional skills.

Continuing Requirements:

None

Perks:

- use of certification logo
- promotion of your services to Adobe software users via fax and on the World Wide Web
- priority access to high level, free technical support for product you are certified on
- prerelease versions of software
- advertising discounts in Adobe Magazine
- discounts on Adobe mailing lists
- discounts on Adobe Press books purchased from Macmillan Computer Publishing

Online Resources:

Start with the ACI web page: **www.adobe.com/supportservice/acipinfo.html**.

A test bulletin to help you prepare and study for the exam can be downloaded from **www.adobe.com/supportservice/learningres/aceprogram.html**.

A database of third-party curriculum providers is available at **www.adobe.com/supportservice/training/cpinfo.html**. You can find additional resources for the CTT part of this certification under the CTT listing in this book.

The Adobe Web site is: **www.adobe.com**.

Offline Resources:

Adobe user guide and Adobe technical notes from the Adobe automated fax (1-206-628-5737). Courseware and books are available from Adobe, and you can take courses from Adobe Authorized Learning Providers (AALPs). For information call the Adobe fax line listed above, or visit the Web site.

To register and take an Adobe product proficiency exam, call 1-800-356-3926.

Sponsor:

Ascolta Training Company LLC
2351 McGaw Avenue
Irvine, CA 92614 USA
Phone: 714-477-2000   **Fax:** 714-477-2162
Email: training@ascoltatraining.com
URL: www.ascolta.com

Internet/Intranet Certified Engineer (I²CE)

For individuals who work with Internet and Intranet environments.

Date Initiated: 1997   **# Granted:**   **Fees:** $1,895+

Initial Requirements:

This program is just getting underway. Must complete three phases: an introductory course, a two- to four-week specialty concentration in design, security, applications, and servers; and then pass a written test and hands-on lab. Master certification requires successful completion of a comprehensive evaluation covering all four areas.

Continuing Requirements:

Perks:

Online Resources:

The Web page for this certification is **www.ascolta.com/ice.htm**.

Offline Resources:

Internet/Intranet Engineering Fundamentals (I2CE-101) $1,895 (4 days).

Sponsor:

Baan Company, The
4600 Bohannon Dr.
Menlo Park, CA 94025 USA
Phone: 1-415-462-4949   **Fax:** 1-415-462-4951
Email: training_info@baan.com
URL: www.baan.com/education/certify.htm

Baan Basic Certification

Baan basic certification recognizes that an individual has obtained a broad understanding of all the packages within the Baan enterprise resource planning (ERP) product. It is a prerequisite to any Baan advanced certification.

Date Initiated: **# Granted:**   **Fees:** $300

Initial Requirements:
Must pass the basic certification test.

Continuing Requirements:
Must re-certify with new releases.

Perks:
none

Online Resources:
The Baan certification page: www.baan.com/education/certify.htm

Offline Resources:
Contact Baan for information on MBT (multimedia based training) basic overview software, self study guides, and instructor-led training.

Baan Advanced Certification

Recognizes specific, functional understanding of a particular module within the Baan product. Modules are: Enterprise Modeler, Enterprise Logistics, Enterprise Finance, and Enterprise Tools.

Date Initiated: **# Granted:**   **Fees:** Exam $300

Initial Requirements:
Must hold Baan Basic Certification and pass advanced test.

Continuing Requirements:
Must re-certify with for new releases.

Perks:

Online Resources:
> The Baan certification page: **www.baan.com/education/certify.htm**

Offline Resources:
> Contact Baan for information on MBT (multimedia based training) basic overview software, self study guides, and instructor-led training.

Baan Expert Certification

> This certification recognizes comprehensive knowledge of Baan software.

Date Initiated: **# Granted:**   **Fees:**

Initial Requirements:
> Must hold advanced certification in a minumum of two Baan packages/modules. Proven Baan experience. Must deliver a presentation representing the candidate's integrated knowledge of Baan software.

Continuing Requirements:
> Re-certify with new releases.

Perks:

Online Resources:
> The Baan certification page: **www.baan.com/education/certify.htm**

Offline Resources:
> Contact Baan for information on MBT (multimedia based training) basic overview software, self study guides, and instructor-led training.

Baan Accredited Instructor

This is the ultimate Baan certification and is for Baan instructors. Individuals may become accredited in one course, or in the complete package.

Accredited individuals are recognized as part of the training resource base for Baan. For this reason, they require individuals enrolled in the Accreditation Program to commit a percentage of their time for the delivery of Baan training. This can be up to 50%.

Date Initiated: **# Granted:**   **Fees:**

Initial Requirements:

Must achieve Baan basic and advanced certification in the same product/module. Must demonstrate a minimum of one year training experience (or equivalent). Must also have a minimum one year practical experience in the relevant subject matter; employing Baan or other relevant software. Conceptual knowledge of systems and software applications.

After completing the above, the candidate must then participate in Education Excellence Program/Train the Trainer Session, which is a four day seminar offered approximately once a quarter, and team-teach or solo teach a Baan software course.

Continuing Requirements:

Must update certification with new releases.

Perks:

- certificate
- listing in Baan resource database
- eligibility for contracting for the delivery of Baan authorized training programs
- access to updated course materials
- instructor empowerment programs
- individual skill assessments and development plans
- product upgrade training
- assistance through the network of Accredited Instructors

Online Resources:

Baan accreditation Web page: **www.baan.com/education/acredit. htm**

Offline Resources:

Sponsor:

Banyan Systems Incorporated
120 Flanders Road
Westboro, MA 01581 USA
Phone: 800-832-4595 **Fax:** 508-898-1000
Email: jbernstein@banyan.com
URL: www.banyan.com/support/tcp97.html

Certified Banyan Specialist (CBS)

The CBS certification is for professionals working with Banyan VINES. A Windows NT track has recently been added.

Date Initiated: 1992 **# Granted:** **Fees:** $2175 –$5175

Initial Requirements:

Requires passing 3 exams: VINES Administration, Advanced VINES administration, and Problem Solving for VINES networks. Courses are available for all exams, but are only required for the Problem Solving component.

The NT track adds two additional courses and three additional exam requirements, including passing a test from the Microsoft Certified Product Specialist Curriculum. The additional courses are StreetTalk for Windows NT Administration and Support StreetTalk for Windows NT.

Continuing Requirements:

Must complete one course from the "recertification pool" during the year. The pool of qualified courses includes Banyan Education courses, workshops, ENA Training Institute workshops, and pre-product support workshops.

Perks:

- plaque
- copy of Banyan Knowledgebase (BKB) on CD-ROM
- 3 free incident calls to the Banyan Response Center during the year certification is achieved

Online Resources:

Study guides in MS WORD format can be downloaded from **www.banyan.com/support/studguid.html** for VINES Administration, Advanced VINES Administration, and Problem Solving for VINES Networks.

To find Banyan authorized course information visit: **oraweb1.banyan.com:1523/web_open/owa/pack_web_schedule.pro_web_schedsearch.** The Banyan company home page is at: **www.banyan.com**.

Offline Resources:

If you don't have Web access, you can call and request that copies of the exam study guides be sent to you.

Certified Banyan Expert (CBE)

The CBE designation is the expert-level Banyan VINES certification. It's designed for network and system engineers who provide advanced level support of Banyan networks including network design and performance tuning.

Date Initiated: 1991   **# Granted:**   **Fees:** $4750 + CBS

Initial Requirements:

Candidates must complete all requirements for Banyan CBS certification. You must also complete two courses: Supporting Network Services and Network Communications, and pass the associated exams. A Windows NT track is expected to be added in the near future.

Continuing Requirements:

Must complete one course from the "recertification pool" during the year. The pool of qualified courses includes Banyan Education courses, workshops, ENA Training Institute workshops, and pre-product support workshops.

Perks:

- plaque
- copy of Banyan Knowledgebase (BKB) on CD ROM
- priority technical support

Online Resources:

Study guides in MS WORD format can be downloaded from **www.banyan.com/support/studguid.html** for Supporting Network Services and Network Communications.

To find Banyan authorized course information, visit **oraweb1.banyan.com:1523/web_open/owa/pack_web_schedule.pro_web_schedsearch**. The Banyan company home page is at: **www.banyan.com**.

Offline Resources:

If you don't have Web access, you can call and request that copies of the exam study guides be sent to you.

Certified Banyan Instructor (CBI)

This certification is for professional trainers who desire to teach the Banyan Education curriculum. Successful candidates are authorized to teach the *VINES Administration* (EDU110) and *Advanced VINES Administration* (EDU210) courses. *Teaching Problem Solving for VINES Network*s is separately authorized, once a professional becomes a CBI.

Date Initiated: 1991   **# Granted:**   **Fees:** $1,800

Initial Requirements:

- Must be a current CBS professional.
- Candidate must demonstrate instructional skills. This requirement can be met if the candidate has attended an instructional presentation skills course that has been pre-approved by Banyan, he/she is a certified instructor for another vendor, or he/she is a Certified Technical Trainer (CTT).
- Technical competence must be demonstrated by obtaining adequate scores on the VINES Administration and Advanced VINES Administration tests.
- After completing previous requirements, candidate must register for and attend the Authorization Session, which will be offered two times a year in Westboro, MA. Cost of session is $1,800.
- Attending the authorization session for the additional *Problem Solving for VINES Networks* costs $1,200.

Continuing Requirements:

Perks:

- plaque
- briefcase bag
- access to instructor files on the instructor FTP site
- CBInsider quarterly newsletter

Online Resources:

CBI authorization program description: **www.banyan.com/support/cbi.htm** Banyan Web site: **www.banyan.com**.

Offline Resources:

If you don't have Web access, you can call and request that copies of the exam study guides be sent to you.

Sponsor:

Bay Networks Incorporated
USA
Phone: 800-252-6926   **Fax:**
Email:
URL: www.baynetworks.com

Bay Networks Certified Specialist—Network Mgmt (BNCS)

A Bay Networks Certified Network Management Specialist will have the knowledge to install, configure, and troubleshoot network topologies, create start-up, BootP, and TFTP files.

Date Initiated: **# Granted:**   **Fees:** $150

Initial Requirements:
- ✐ Must pass network specialist exam ($150).
- ✐ Recommended (not required) Instructor-led courses: *Optivity for Windows 6.x* course number AV0031171
- ✐ Recommended (not required) Self-paced courses are:
  Introduction to Network Management course number AX0000072
  Understanding SNMP course number AX0000011
  Understanding TCP/IP course number AX0000012
  Introduction into Internetworking course number AX0000013

Continuing Requirements:

Perks:
- ✐ certificate and plaque

Online Resources:
Network management specialist details, including exam breakdown, sample questions, and list of training resources, can be found at: **support.baynetworks.com/training/nwspc.html**.

A technical study guide can be downloaded from: **support. baynetworks.com/training/study.html**.

The Bay Networks Web site is at: **www.baynetworks.com**.

Offline Resources:

Bay Networks Certified Specialist—Hubs (BNCS)

A Certified Hub Specialist will have the knowledge to build, configure, and troubleshoot network problems where Bay Networks equipment is utilized.

Date Initiated: **# Granted:**   **Fees:** $125

Initial Requirements:

- Must pass the Hub Specialist exam ($125).

- Recommended (not required) Instructor-Led courses:
Hub Connectivity course number AV0029196
FDDI Connectivity course number AV0029031

- Recommended (not required) Self-Study courses:
Token Ring Basics course number AX0000076
Ethernet Basics course number AX0000075
Understanding FDDI Fundamentals course number AX0000056
Introduction to Internetworking course number AX0000113
Understanding SNMP course number AX0000011
Understanding TCP/IP course number AX0000012

Continuing Requirements:

Annual recertification is required. Continuing education is required periodically; certified professional will be notified by sponsor.

Perks:

- plaque

Online Resources:

Hub specialist details, including exam breakdown, sample questions, and list of training resources, can be found at: **support.baynetworks.com/training/hubspc.html**.

A technical study guide can be downloaded from: **support.baynetworks.com/training/study.html**.

The Bay Networks Web site is at: **www.baynetworks.com**.

Offline Resources:

Bay Networks Certified Specialist—Routers (BNCS)

A Certified Router Specialist will be able to install and configure the Bay Networks Router product family.

Date Initiated: **# Granted:**   **Fees:** $125

Initial Requirements:

    ✐ Must pass router specialist exam ($125).

    ✐ Recommended (not required) Instructor-led courses:
Accelerated Router Installation, Configuration and Management course number AV0025110 OR
Router Installation & Basic Configuration course number AV0030080
Router Configuration & Management course number AV0030090

    ✐ Recommended (not required) Self-Study courses:
Introduction into Internetworking course number AX0000113
Understanding TCP/IP course number AX0000012

Continuing Requirements:

Perks:

    ✐ certificate and plaque

Online Resources:

Router specialist details, including exam breakdown, sample questions, and list of training resources, can be found at: **support. baynetworks.com/training/rtrspc.html**.

A technical study guide can be downloaded from: **support. baynetworks.com/training/study.html**.

The Bay Networks Web site is at: **www.baynetworks.com**.

Offline Resources:

Bay Networks Certified Expert—Hubs (BNCE)

A Bay Networks Certified Hub Expert candidate, upon completing the electronic exam will have demonstrated knowledge to build, configure, and troubleshoot a hub network in a campus environment utilizing all products in the BayStack, 3000 Series, 5000 Series and D5000 concentrators.

Date Initiated: **# Granted:**   **Fees:** $550 +BNCS/hubs

Initial Requirements:

    ✐ Must posses the hub specialist (BNCS/hub) certification.

    ✐ Must pass the Hub Expert exam: $150.

    ✐ Must complete the Hands-on hub practical test: $400.

Continuing Requirements:

Perk:

    ✐ certificate and plaque

Online Resources:

Hub expert details, including exam breakdown, sample questions, and list of training resources, can be found at: **support.baynetworks.com/training/hubexp.html**.

Information about the practical exam can be found at: **support.baynetworks.com/training/13425.html**.

The Bay Networks Web site is at: **www.baynetworks.com**.

Offline Resources:

Bay Networks Certified Expert—Routers (BNCE)

A Bay Networks Certified Router Expert, candidate upon completing the electronic exam, will have demonstrated knowledge on installation and configuration procedures for the Router products with advanced protocols including: LAN-Advanced IP, VINES, and DECnet; as well as WAN-Frame Relay, SMDS, X.25, PPP, and Dial Services.

Date Initiated: **# Granted:**   **Fees:** $650 + BNCS

Initial Requirements:

    ✐ Must first complete specialist level (BNCS) for router technology.

    ✐ Must pass router expert exam ($150).

    ✐ Must complete hands-on practical test ($500).

    ✐ Recommended (not required) Instructor-led courses:
WAN Protocol Implementation course number AV0030131
Advanced IP Routing Technology course number AV0030160
LAN Protocol Implementation course number AV0030120

Continuing Requirements:

Perks:

    ✐ certificate and plaque

Online Resources:

Router expert details, including exam breakdown, sample questions, and list of training resources, can be found at: **support.baynetworks.com/training/rtrexp.html**.

Information about the practical exam can be found at: **support. baynetworks.com/training/13425.html**.

The Bay Networks Web site is at: **www.baynetworks.com**.

Offline Resources:

Bay Networks Certified Expert—Network Mgmt (BNCE)

A Bay Networks Certified Network Management Expert candidate will have the knowledge, upon completing the electronic exam, to install, configure, and troubleshoot virtual LAN/WAN networks including creation and analysis of data and event reports.

Date Initiated: **# Granted:**   **Fees:** $800 + BNCS

Initial Requirements:
- Must complete network management specialist level.
- Must pass network management expert exam ($150).
- Must pass hands-on practical exam ($650).
- Recommended (not required) Instructor-led course:
  Net Mngt—Optvity Enterprise for UNIX course number AV0025301

Continuing Requirements:

Perks:
- certificate and plaque

Online Resources:
Network management expert details, including exam breakdown, sample questions, and list of training resources, can be found at: **support.baynetworks.com/training/nwexp.html**.

Information about the practical exam can be found at: **support.baynetworks.com/training/13425.html**.

The Bay Networks Web site is at: **www.baynetworks.com**.

Offline Resources:

Sponsor:

Borland International
100 Borland Way
Scotts Valley, CA 95066 USA
Phone:408-431-4167 **Fax:** 704-824-1301
Email: kalderman@corp.borland.com
URL: www.borland.com

Certified JBuilder Trainer

Only Certified Trainers are qualified to purchase and teach Borland's official JBuilder Foundations courseware.

Date Initiated: 1997 **# Granted:** **Fees:** $1,500

Initial Requirements:

You must have the following prerequisites:
- A working knowledge of Java, C++, or Delphi
- A working knowledge of another database programming platform (e.g., Paradox for Windows, Dbase for Windows, Visual Basic, PowerBuilder). Development experience for one of the following SQL database servers: InterBase 3.3/4.0, Microsoft SQL Server, Sybase, Oracle, Informix, or an ODBC-supported server.

You must also participate in one of Borland's partner programs (see **www.borland.com/partner)**,which comes with its own fees (becoming a connections partner for one product costs $500). You are also required to attend either a Borland 2-1/2 day($1000) or a 5 day ($1000) train the trainer class. Fees include instructor materials.

Continuing Requirements:

Expect to re-certify with new releases.

Perks:
- use of logo
- directory listing

Online Resources:

The details of the Jbuilder program can be found at: **www.borland. com/programs/bsp/certify/traincert.html**.

Borland's Club Jbuilder site contains many resources that may prove useful: **www.borland.com/jbuilder/**.

Borland's home page is **www.borland.com**.

Offline Resources:

Certified Delphi 3 Client/Server Trainer

Certified Delphi 3 trainers are qualified to purchase and teach Borland's Delphi 3 courseware and are eligible to deliver training courses sold as part of Delphi 3 product and service bundles.

Date Initiated: 1995   **# Granted:**   **Fees:** $1,150

Initial Requirements:

You must meet the following prerequisites:

- A working knowledge of Windows
- A working knowledge of another Windows 4th generation database programming platform (e.g. Paradox for Windows, dBase for Windows, Visual Basic, PowerBuilder)
- Development experience for one of the following SQL database servers: InterBase 3.3/4.0, Microsoft SQL Server, Sybase, Oracle, Informix, or an ODBC supported server.
- Must pass Delphi exam ($150)

You must also participate in one of Borland's partner programs (see **www.borland.com/partner)**,which comes with its own fees (becoming a connections partner for one product costs $500). You are also required to attend either a Borland 2-1/2 day ($1000) or a 5 day ($1000) train the trainer class. Fees include instructor materials.

Continuing Requirements:

Re-certify with new releases.

Perks:

- use of logo
- directory listing

Online Resources:

Details of this program can be found at: **http://www.borland.com/programs/bsp/certify/traincert.html**.

The Delphi Developer Support site may prove helpful: **www.borland.com/devsupport/delphi/**.

The Borland home page is **www.borland.com**.

A study guide can be accessed at **www.borland.com/programs/bsp/certify/delphi3/d3sg.html**.

Offline Resources:

Certified Delphi 3 Client/Server Developer

For professional Delphi 3 developers.

Date Initiated: 1995   **# Granted:**   **Fees:** $150

Initial Requirements:
Must pass the Delphi 3 Client/Server certification exam ($150).

Continuing Requirements:
Re-certify with new releases.

Perks:
- use of logo
- directory listing

Online Resources:
Details of this program can be found at: **http://www.borland.com/programs/bsp/certify/devcert.html**.

A study guide can be downloaded from: **www.borland.com/programs/bsp/certify/d3sg.html**.

The Delphi Developer Support site may prove helpful: **www.borland.com/devsupport/delphi/**.

The Borland home page is **www.borland.com**.

Offline Resources:
A list of Delphi books can be found at: **www.borland.com/delphi/books**.

Additional Resources:
- Borland's Delphi C/S 3 Foundations Courseware Manual, which you receive when you take a Delphi 3 C/S Foundations training class. This cannot be purchased separately as a self-study guide. Borland's Delphi 3 Component Creation Courseware Manual which you receive when you take a Delphi 3 Component Creation training class. This cannot be purchased separately as a self-study guide.

Sponsor:

Building Industry Consulting Service International (BICSI)
10500 University Center Dr.
Suite 100
Tampa, FL 33612 USA
Phone: 800-242-7405   **Fax:** 813-971-4311
Email: bicsiadm@concentric.net
URL: www.bicsi.org/rcdd.html

Registered Communications Distribution Designer (RCDD)

The RCDD is for professionals in the field of telecommunications distribution design. You may wish to apply for the professional RCDD designation if you are an electrical engineer, telecommunications consultant, data network designer or other design industry specialist. A LAN specialty is available.

Date Initiated: **# Granted:**   **Fees:** $300

Initial Requirements:
- You must be a BICSI member ($100).
- You must submit an application fee ($100).
- You must take and pass the RCDD exam ($100).
- To sit for the exam you must first possess a minimum of two years distribution design experience including commercial, campus and multi-family buildings, and you'll also have to submit 3 letters of reference.

Continuing Requirements:
Certification lasts for 3 years, after which you must renew. To renew, BICSI requires a minimum of 45 hours of distribution design-related courses be completed during these three years. These credits can be obtained by attending BICSI conferences and courses. Some of them can come from technical continuing education requirements with non technical course work in a variety of areas—general engineering; business administration and finance; personal communication skills; personal growth courses such as speed reading, memory skills, listening skills and others.

Perks:
- certificate
- use of logo

Online Resources:

The BICSI home page is **www.bicsi.org**

Offline Resources:

The primary reference for the examination is BICSI's *Telecommunications Distribution Methods Manual*. Preparation courses are available from the BICSI Institute. Course information and manual order forms can be obtained from the BICSI Executive Offices.

Sponsor:

Centura Software
USA
Phone: **Fax:**
Email: nigel.chanter@centurasoft.com
URL: www.centurasoft.com/training/certification

Centura DBA Certification

The DBA certification is based on in-depth knowledge of server technology, including SQLBase advanced features, performance tuning, and database design.

Date Initiated: **# Granted:**   **Fees:** $120

Initial Requirements:
The only requirement is to pass the developer exam ($120).

Continuing Requirements:

Perk:
✐   listing in online Centura resource database

Online Resources:
The objectives for the developer exam and sample questions can be downloaded from Centura's Web site. **www.centurasoft.com**.

Offline Resources:

Centura Developer Certification

The Developer certification is based on in-depth knowledge of client technology, including SQL Windows advanced features, object-oriented programming, and application design.

Date Initiated: **# Granted:**   **Fees:** $120

Initial Requirements:
The only requirement is to pass the developer exam ($120).

Continuing Requirements:

Perks:
✐   listing in online Centura resource database

Online Resources:
The objectives for the developer exam can be found at: **www.centurasoft.com/training/certification/devob.html**.
You can take a sample exam at:**www-nt.centurasoft.com/ForeSite/training/certification/sample+certification+test.DM**.

Offline Resources:

Sponsor:

Chauncey Group, The (A subsidiary of Educational Testing Service [ETS])
PO Box 6541
Princeton, NJ 08541-6541 USA
Phone: 800-258-4914   **Fax:** 609-951-6767
Email: cttp@chauncey.com
URL: www.chauncey.com/itt/cttpool.html

Certified Technical Trainer (CTT)

The CTT examinations measure an individual's mastery of fundamental instructor knowledge and classroom performance as defined by the International Board of Standards for Training, Performance and Instruction (IBSTPI). It is vendor-independent.

Date Initiated: **# Granted:**   **Fees:** $285

Initial Requirements:

- Must pass exam ($150).
- Must submit a video demonstrating your teaching performance ($135), which will be judged to assess your competency.

Continuing Requirements:

Perks:

- certificate
- use of logo
- lapel pin
- opportunity to be included in CTT registry

Online Resources:

A summary of the standards you will be judged upon (IBSTPI) can be found at: **www.chauncey.com/itt/summary.html**.

Offline Resources:

To help prepare for the CTT Examination, candidates should be thoroughly familiar with the 14 competencies described in *Instructor Competencies: The Standards, Volume I*, also known as the *IBSTPI Standards*. To obtain copies of the Standards, contact IBSTPI Publications, 102 South Hager Avenue, Barrington, IL 60010 Phone: 800-236-4303 (toll free in the US) or 847-304-5571, FAX: 847-304-5553

Identify yourself as a CTT Candidate and request the certification version of the *Instructor Competencies: The Standards-Volume I*.

Sponsor:

Check Point Software Technologies Ltd
400 Seaport Court
Suite 105
Redwood City, CA 94063 USA
Phone: 800-429-4391   **Fax:** 650-562-0410
Email: info@checkpoint.com
URL: www.checkpoint.com/services/overview.html

Check Point Certified Security Engineer (CCSE)

This certification is for network and security adminstrators who need to implement and maintain air-tight security with CheckPoint's FireWall-1.

Date Initiated: 1996   **# Granted:**   **Fees:** $2100-$2500

Initial Requirements:
- Must hold CCSA.
- Must complete 2 day hands on course. Courses are offered through authorized training centers. Price varies by center.

Continuing Requirements:

Perks:

Online Resources:
The Check Point home page is at: **www.checkpoint.com**.
A listing of authorized training centers can be found at: **http://www.checkpoint.com/services/training.html**.
A Firewall-1 FAQ can be found at: **fw1.netrex.com/faq/**.

Offline Resources:

Check Point Certified Security Administrator (CCSA)

This certification is for end-users and re-sellers who need a good technical understanding of FireWall-1 and need to install and set up simple configurations.

Date Initiated: 1996   **# Granted:**   **Fees:** $2100-$2500

Initial Requirements:
Must complete a two day hands-on class ($2500). Classes are taught through authorized training centers. Price varies by center.

Continuing Requirements:

Perks:

Online Resources:
> The Check Point home page is at: **www.checkpoint.com**.
> A listing of authorized training centers can be found at: **http://www.checkpoint.com/services/training.html**.
> A Firewall-1 FAQ can be found at: **fw1.netrex.com/faq/**.

Offline Resources:

Check Point Certified Security Instructor (CCSI)

> This certification is for professionals interested in becoming a Check Point security trainer. Only certified individuals may teach authorized Check Point classes.

Date Initiated: **# Granted:**   **Fees: $1500**

Initial Requirements:
- Must hold CCSA and CCSE.
- Must complete CCSI course ($1500), which is only offered by Netrex (**www.netrex.com**). The course lasts 1 day.

Continuing Requirements:

Perks:

Online Resources:
> Visit the Netrex Web site (**nsec.netrex.com/schedules/ccsi.html**) to read about the CCSI course curriculum and scheduling. The Check Point home page is at: **www.checkpoint.com**.
> A Firewall-1 FAQ can be found at: **fw1.netrex.com/faq/**.

Offline Resources:

Sponsor:

Cisco Systems
170 West Tasman Drive
San Jose, CA 95134-1706 USA
Phone: 800-553-6387   **Fax:** 408-526-7117
Email: cs-rep@cisco.com
URL: www.cisco.com/warp/public/625/ccie/index.html

Cisco Certified Internetwork Expert (CCIE)

The program is designed to identify engineers with the internetworking expertise required in today's rapidly changing information systems environment. This certification tests people who work specifically with Cisco products.

Date Initiated: 1993   **# Granted:** 1850   **Fees** $1,200–$15,000

Initial Requirements:
- Must pass written test ($100).
- Must pass 2 day practical lab ($1000). Current CCIE lab exam sites are: San Jose, California; Raleigh, North Carolina; Halifax, Nova Scotia, Canada; Brussels, Belgium; Sydney, Australia; and Toyko, Japan.
- It is recommended (not required) that CCIE candidates complete the following Cisco training classes:
  Introduction to Internetworking Self-Study Guide
  Introduction to Cisco Router Configuration
  Installation and Maintenance of Cisco Routers
  Advanced Cisco Router Configuration
  SNA Configuration for Multiprotocol Administrators
  Cisco Internetwork Design
  Cisco Internetwork Troubleshooting
  Cisco Internetwork Implementation Lab (CIIL) (only available in the San Jose, California, CCIE lab)

Continuing Requirements:
Every two years after becoming certified, engineers must attend a CCIE technical seminar and also pass a written exam in one specialty area (IP, LAN/ATM, Dial, WAN switching).

Perks:
- participate in a "chat forum" and "open forum" that only CCIEs have access to.

Online Resources:

The certification page has additional resources. The Cisco home page is **www.cisco.com**.

Offline Resources:

- *CISCO CCIE Exam Guide*, Roosevelt Giles, McGraw-Hill, Inc.
- *Internetwork Technology Overview*, Cisco Systems
- *Local Area Networks*, John E. McNamara, Digital Press, Digital Equipment Corporation
- *LAN Protocol Handbook*, Mark Miller, M&T Press
- *Interconnections: Bridges & Routers*, Radia Perlman, Addison Wesley
- *Internetworking with TCP/IP, Vol. I*, Douglas Comer, Prentice Hall
- *Troubleshooting Internetworks*, Mark Miller, M&T Press
- *Troubleshooting Token Ring*, Daniel Nassar, New Riders Press
- *X.25 and Related Protocols*, Uyless Black, IEEE Computer Society Press
- *Troubleshooting Internetwork Systems*, Cisco Systems
- *Communications Server Configuration and Reference Guide* (all), Cisco Systems
- *Router Products Configuration and Reference Guide* (all), Cisco Systems

Sponsor:

CNX Consortium, The (sponsored by 8 companies)
Phone: **Fax:**
Email:
URL: www.cnx.org

Certified Network Expert (CNX)

For networking professionals. This is a multi-vendor certification that focuses on network analysis and troubleshooting.

Date Initiated: **# Granted:**   **Fees:** $1,000

Initial Requirements:
- Experience with a network analyzer is highly recommended.
- Must pass 4 exams ($1000). The exams are: Ethernet data link ($250), token ring data link ($250), FDDI data link ($250), and LAN cabling ($250). If you fail an exam, the retest fee is $100.

Continuing Requirements:

Perks:
- certificate

Online Resources:
An online pre-test guide can be found at: **www.optimized.com/cnx/**.

Offline Resources:
For an information guide, call Sylvan Prometric at 1-800-CNX-EXAM.

Sponsor:

Cognos Incorporated
3755 Riverside Dr.
Ottawa, ON K1G 4K9 Canada
Phone: 613-738-1440 **Fax:**
Email: ccpp@cognos.com
URL: www.cognos.com/busintell/ccpp.html

Technical Specialist—24 Ways

This certification is for certified resellers, services partners, and systems integrators.

Date Initiated: 6/1997 **# Granted:** 24 **Fees:** $100–$300

Initial Requirements:
- Must be certified on PowerPlay and Impromptu.
- Must pass exam ($100).
- Recommended study materials include the "24 Ways Implementation Kit" ($200).

Continuing Requirements:
Must upgrade certification with major new product releases.

Perks:
- use of logo

Online Resources:
Training courses and schedules: **http://www.cognos.com/suppserv/training.html**.
The Cognos home page: **www.cognos.com**.

Offline Resources:
To receive information and free study guides (complete program information and sample questions), send email with mailing address to **ccpp@cognos.com**.

Specialist I—PowerPlay v4

This certification is for certified resellers, users, PowerPlay administrators, partners, and systems integrators.

Date Initiated: 7/1996 **# Granted:** 93 **Fees:** $100

Initial Requirements:
- Must pass exam ($100).

✐ Recommended (not required) study includes product training courses & hands on experience, which can add approximately $1000 to the cost.

Continuing Requirements:

Must upgrade certification with major new product releases.

Perks:

✐ use of logo

Online Resources:

Training courses and schedules: **http://www.cognos.com/ suppserv/training.html**.

The Cognos home page: **www.cognos.com**.

Offline Resources:

To receive information and free study guides (complete program information and sample questions), send email with mailing address to **ccpp@cognos.com**.

Specialist II—Impromptu v3

This certification is for certified resellers, Impromptu administrators, services partners, and systems integrators.

Date Initiated: 1/1996   **# Granted:** 112   **Fees:** $100

Initial Requirements:

✐ Must hold Specialist I certification.

✐ Must pass exam ($100).

✐ Product training courses and hands on experience are recommended. Training can add $1000 to the cost, if you haven't already taking them for Specialist I.

Continuing Requirements:

Must upgrade certification with major new product releases.

Perks:

✐ use of logo

Online Resources:

Training courses and schedules: **http://www.cognos.com/ suppserv/training.html**.

The Cognos home page: **www.cognos.com**.

Offline Resources:

To receive information and free study guides (complete program information and sample questions), send email with mailing address to **ccpp@cognos.com**.

Specialist I—Impromptu v3

Date Initiated: 1/1996   **# Granted:** 257   **Fees:** $100

Initial Requirements:
- Must pass exam ($100).
- Product training courses and hands on experience are recommended. Training can add $1000 to the cost.

Continuing Requirements:
Must upgrade certification with major new product releases.

Perks:
- use of logo

Online Resources:
Training courses and schedules: **http://www.cognos.com/suppserv/training.html**.
The Cognos home page: **www.cognos.com**.

Offline Resources:
To receive information and free study guides (complete program information and sample questions), send email with mailing address to **ccpp@cognos.com**.

Sponsor:

Compaq Computer Corporation
Mail Stop 100103, P. O. Box 692000
Houston, TX 77269-2000 USA
Phone: 800-732-5741   **Fax:**
Email:
URL: www.compaq.com/ase/index.html

Compaq ASE

The Compaq ASE is an advanced-level accreditation of the ASE Program. ASEs have successfully demonstrated their knowledge and expertise in the integration of Compaq hardware and a specified operating system. Compaq ASEs must acquire and maintain the matching certification of a Compaq-approved operating system vendor.

Date Initiated: **# Granted:**   **Fees:** varies

Initial Requirements:
- Meet all requirements of the Associate ASE ($300).
- Obtain/Maintain matching certification from approved operating system (OS) vendor (i.e. Netware or Windows NT).

Continuing Requirements:
Periodic maintenance training is required by Compaq. The amount of maintenance training required throughout a year depends solely on Compaq product announcements, and whether Compaq determines that the new product training requires additional technical or presales training.

Perks:
- welcome kit
- access to every technical tool and subscription available from Compaq
- quarterly ASE Newsletter
- free subscription to Compaq SmartStart
- toll-free access to an exclusive Compaq ASE Forum
- may dial into Compaq's technical databases 24 hours a day, 7 days a week, free of charge
- free, priority access to Compaq technical support
- use of logo
- free advertising materials and brochures
- product discounts

Online Resources:

The Compaq home page is: **www.compaq.com**.

An ASE FAQ can be found at: **www.compaq.com/ase/lvl_3.html**.

Self-assessment guides for the tests can be found at: **www.compaq.com/training/ss-cto.html**.

Offline Resources:

The following documents are available from the Compaq automated fax system (1-800-345-1518, Option 1):

Doc#	Title
2037	*What is the Compaq Accredited Systems Engineer Program?*
2038	*Requirements for Becoming a Compaq ASE*
2007	*Compaq Training Overview & Registration Procedures*
2027	*Compaq Training Schedules*
2023	*Sylvan Prometric Testing Information*
2053	*Compaq ASE Application*

Compaq Associate ASE

Associate ASEs complete a curriculum that provides extensive training on the integration and configuration of Compaq hardware. The ASE certifications are targeted to Systems Engineers who are involved with the sales, support, planning, or optimization of Compaq platforms. Ideal candidates include Compaq Resellers, Consultants and Integration Specialists, Information Management personnel responsible for Compaq networks, etc.

Date Initiated: **# Granted:**   **Fees:** $300

Initial Requirements:

- Pass Compaq systems technologies test ($100).
- Pass Compaq integration & performance test (operating system specific) ($100).
- Pass Compaq systems management test ($100).
- If an ASE candidate chooses to complete the three preparatory courses (a total of 6 days), there is a total cost of $1800 for these courses.

Due to the privileged nature of the partnership between Compaq ASEs and Compaq, ASEs may not be employed by a competitor of Compaq.

Continuing Requirements:

Periodic maintenance training is required by Compaq. The amount of maintenance training required throughout a year depends solely on Compaq product announcements, and whether Compaq determines that the new product training requires additional technical or presales training.

Perks:

- welcome kit
- access to every technical tool and subscription available from Compaq
- quarterly ASE Newsletter
- toll-free access to an exclusive Compaq ASE Forum
- may dial into Compaq's technical databases 24 hours a day, 7 days a week, free of charge
- use of logo
- free advertising materials and brochures

Online Resources:

The Compaq home page is: **www.compaq.com**.

An ASE FAQ can be found at: **www.compaq.com/ase/lvl_3.html**.

Self-assessment guides for the tests can be found at: **www.compaq.com/training/ss-cto.html**.

Offline Resources:

The following documents are available from the Compaq automated fax system (1-800-345-1518, Option 1):

Doc#	Title
2037	*What is the Compaq Accredited Systems Engineer Program?*
2038	*Requirements for Becoming a Compaq ASE*
2007	*Compaq Training Overview & Registration Procedures*
2027	*Compaq Training Schedules*
2023	*Sylvan Prometric Testing Information*
2053	*Compaq ASE Application*

Sponsor:

Computing Technology Industry Association (CompTIA)
450 East 22nd St.
Suite 230
Lombard, IL 60148-6158 USA
Phone: 630-268-1818   **Fax:** 630-268-1384
Email info@comptia.org
URL: www.comptia.org

A+

This certification is for hardware technicians.

Date Initiated: 7/1993   **# Granted:** over 40,000 **Fees:** $190

Initial Requirements:

Must pass two test modules—the "Core," and either a WIN/DOS or MAC module. CompTIA members receive a discount. Training and preparation assistance are available from independent vendors.

Continuing Requirements:

Perks:

- use of logo
- certificate
- lapel pin
- wallet certification card

Online Resources:

Training is available from various market sources listed on the CompTIA Website at: **www.comptia.org/atraining.html**.

Offline Resources:

A+ Success Guide for Computer Technicians, Parks & Kalman, McGraw-Hill, Inc.

Certified Document Imaging Architech (CDIA)

CDIAs possess critical knowledge of all major areas and technologies used to plan, design and specify an imaging system. It is for system architects and designers, sales and sales support engineers, technical support professionals, technology evaluators and corporate buyers, system administrators, technology professionals, and consultants.

Date Initiated: 1/1996   **# Granted:** 300   **Fees:** $165

Initial Requirements:
- Must pass CDIA exam ($165).
- Training and preparation assistance are available from independent vendors.

Continuing Requirements:

Perks:
- use of logo
- certificate
- listing in online CDIA registry

Online Resources:
Training is available from various market sources listed on the CompTIA Website at: **www.comptia.org/cdiatraining.html**.

Offline Resources:

Network +

This certification was under development as this book was going to press. It is expected to go live in early 1998. The goal is to use the skills standards to design and publish a vendor neutral, product neutral certificate for network technicians.

Date Initiated: pending   **# Granted:**   **Fees:**

Initial Requirements:

Continuing Requirements:

Perks:

Online Resources:
The development of this new certification is detailed at: **www.comptia.org/itskills.html**.

Offline Resources:

Sponsor:

Corel Corporation
1600 Carling Ave.
Ottawa, ON K1Z 8R7 Canada
Phone: 613-728-8200   **Fax:**
Email: custserv2@corel.com
URL: www.corel.com/learning/training/certified_instructor/index.htm

Corel Certified Instructor (CCI)

Corel Certified Instructors are certified to teach CorelDraw 5, or Corel WordPerfect Suite 7. Lower level certifications are also available, but not included here because they are for end users.

Date Initiated: 1995   **# Granted:**   **Fees:** $100

Initial Requirements:
- Must pass exam ($100).

  Required prerequisites are:
- Minimum 6 months experience working with computer applications, particularly graphics based programs. Minimum 6 months teaching experience or equivalent, such as tutoring or hands-on consulting work.

  plus
- Proof of successful completion of a Certified Technical Trainer (CTT) Program or a industry recognized equivalent. Details of the CTT certification are listed under "Chauncey Group."

  or
- proof of current certification as a Certified Novell Instructor (CNI), WordPerfect Certified Instructor (CI), Lotus Notes Certified Instructor (LNCI), or Microsoft Certified Trainer (MCT).

Continuing Requirements:
Product knowledge updated and tested on a regular basis as determined by Corel.

Perks:
- product discount
- access to private Website for CTP/CBATPs & CCIs
- access to technical support on a toll line
- monthly newsletter direct from Corel's education division
- free first issue of Corel Magazine, with discount on full subscription

✎ certificate

✎ use of logo

Online Resources:

You'll find an outline of the exam at: **www.corel.com/ learning/training/certified_instructor/coreldraw5/exam.htm**.

Offline Resources:

A list of third party books, videos, and other training aids can be found at: **www.corel.com/learning/training/certified_ instructor/coreldraw5/preparing.htm**.

Sponsor:

Dialogic
1515 Route Ten
Parsippany, NJ 07054 USA
Phone: 800-755-4444   **Fax:** 973-993-3093
Email:
URL: www.dialogic.com/support/cti-edu/certify.htm

CT (Computer Telephony) Professional

For resellers and systems integrators who need to identify market opportunities and provide configuration solutions for CT applications.

Date Initiated: **# Granted:**   **Fees:**

Initial Requirements:
Must complete curriculum and pass certification exam ($).

Continuing Requirements:

Perks:

Online Resources:

Offline Resources:
Required courses are: *Telephony Fundamentals*, *Digital Telephony*, and *Installation and Configuration*. Core electives are: *Introduction to CT Opportunities 1* and *Introduction to CT Opportunities 2*. Specialization options are: *CT-Connect (Call Control) Solutions* and *Application Development Methods*.

CT (Computer Telephony) Solution Developer

For individuals who design, develop, and deploy CT applications using the Dialogic APIs.

Date Initiated: **# Granted:**   **Fees:**

Initial Requirements:
Must complete curriculum and pass certification exam ($).

Continuing Requirements:

Perks:

Online Resources:

Offline Resources:

Required courses are: *Telephony Fundamentals*, *Digital Telephony*, and *API Courses* (one or more—*MS-DOS Application Development for Business Communications Voice Products*, *Designing Call Processing Windows Applications*, *Designing Call Processing UNIX Applications*). Core electives are: *Installation and Configuration* and *Advanced Telephony*. Additional specialization options are: *CT-Connect Specialist*, *Technology / Resource Specialist*, or *CT Architect*.

Sponsor:

Digital Equipment Corporation (DEC) Accreditation and Certification Worldwide
PO Box 9091
Farmington, MI 48333-9091 USA
Phone: 800-233-2764   **Fax:** 800-488-2130
Email: digital@pmh.com
URL: www.networks.digital.com/dr/training/acp-mn.html

Digital Certified Salesperson

For individuals who sell DEC products.

Date Initiated: **# Granted:**   **Fees:**

Initial Requirements:
Must complete general curriculum and specialized training on hub, router, and switching products. Two levels of certification available. Must work for a Digital reseller.

Continuing Requirements:

Perks:

Online Resources:

Offline Resources:
For program details, call or email DEC.

Digital Certified Support Engineer

For individuals who support DEC products

Date Initiated: **# Granted:**   **Fees:**

Initial Requirements:
Must complete general curriculum and specialized training on hub, router, and switching products. Two levels of certification available. Must work for a Digital reseller.

Continuing Requirements:

Perks:

Online Resources:

Offline Resources:
For program details, call or email DEC.

Sponsor:

Disaster Recovery Institute (DRI) International
1810 Craig Rd.
Suite 125
St. Louis, MO 63146 USA
Phone: 314-434-2272   **Fax:** 314-434-1260
Email: billl@dr.org
URL: www.dr.org/certification.html

Certified Business Continuity Planner (CBCP)

Certified Business Continuity Planner (CBCP, formerly Certified Disaster Recovery Planner CDRP) is designed for the planner with a minimum of 2 years of experience as a business continuity / disaster recovery planner.

Date Initiated: 1989   **# Granted:**   **Fees:** $300

Initial Requirements:
- ✎ Must have at least 2 years of significant practical experience in business continuity or disaster recovery planning in three of the subject matter areas of the Common Body of Knowledge (CBK).
- ✎ Must pay application fee ($100).
- ✎ Must pass exam ($200).

Continuing Requirements:

Perks:

Online Resources:
The DRI home page is at: **www.dr.org**.

Offline Resources:
Classroom courses are available; see the organization's Web site.

Associate Business Continuity Planner (ABCP)

Associate Business Continuity Planner (ABCP, formerly ADRP) designation recognizes the individuals who have demonstrated their knowledge in business continuity planning, but have not yet acquired the necessary experience to become a CDRP (CBCP). This certification is also for individuals interested in the profession who have expertise in a related field. Examples are marketing, emergency response, or a field not directly related to business continuity planning.

Date Initiated: 1995   **# Granted:**   **Fees:** $300

Initial Requirements:
- Must pass exam ($200).
- Must pay application fee ($100).

Continuing Requirements:

Perks:

Online Resources:
> The DRI home page is at: **www.dr.org**.

Offline Resources:
> Classroom courses are available; see the organization's Web site.

Master Business Continuity Planner (MBCP)

> This certification is for the experienced, master level disaster recovery planner.

Date Initiated: 1995   **# Granted:**   **Fees:** $300

Initial Requirements:
- Must pass exam.
- Must complete either a case study examination or directed research.

Prerequisite:
- Must have acquired 5 years of significant practical experience in business continuity or disaster recovery planning within the last 10 years.

Continuing Requirements:
> Must complete continuing education credit on a two-year cycle to maintain certification.

Perks:

Online Resources:
> The DRI home page is at: **www.dr.org**.

Offline Resources:
> Classroom courses are available; see the organization's Web site.

Sponsor:

Folio Corporation
5072 North 300 West
Provo, UT 84604-5652 USA
Phone: 801-229-6700   **Fax:** 801-229-6787
Email: EdSrv@Folio.com
URL: www.folio.com/service/folio/edserv/incie/htm

Certified Infobase Engineer (CIE)

The CIE program is created to ensure a minimum skill set for professionals who create infobases and for individuals who support end-users in retrieving information from Folio infobases. In short, candidates are tested on the contents of Folio® Builder 4.x.

Date Initiated: **# Granted:**   **Fees:** $190

Initial Requirements:

Must pass 2 exams: exam I-Folio 4, Views Client Skills ($95), and exam II-Folio 4, Infobase Building Skills ($95). The Folio 4 *Views Client Skills* exam centers on supporting and using the Folio 4 Views client. The Folio 4 *Infobase Building Skills* exam centers around designing, building, and distributing Folio 4 infobases as well as supporting the Folio 4 Workbench.

Continuing Requirements:

Perks:

Online Resources:

www.folio.com/service/folio/edserv/4cie.htm details the elements of the exams. You can also download study guides from **www.folio.com/service/edserv/folio/4study.htm** (for exam I), and **www.folio.com/service/edserv/folio/4bstudy.htm** (for exam II).

Offline Resources:

You can find a list of Folio training partners at: **www.folio.com/service/edserv/folio/inaft.htm**, or, to locate the Authorized Folio Training Centers nearest you, please call Folio at (800) 228-1084.

Training and self-study manuals are listed at :**www. folio.com/service/edserv/folio/3ways.htm**. You can also obtain them by calling 1-800-543-6546.

Sponsor:

Hewlett-Packard
USA
Phone: 800-225-1451   **Fax:** 970-229-3647
Email: ovtraining@fc.hp.com
URL: hpcc920.external.hp.com/ovtelecom/ov/consult.html

HP OpenView Certified Consultant

The overall goal of the HP OpenView Certified Consultant Program is to ensure the technical competency needed for successfully delivering, supporting, training, and using HP OpenView products and services.

Date Initiated: **# Granted:**   **Fees:** $200

Initial Requirements:

Must pass 2 tests: Introduction to HP OpenView ($70) and NNM Fundamentals ($130).

Continuing Requirements:

Must recertify with major new releases.

Perks:

✑ use of logo

Online Resources:

A self assessment test is available at: **hpcc920.external.hp.com/ ovtelecom/ov/selfasmt.html**.

You can download "Introduction to HP OpenView," a self-study guide in pdf format, from **hpcc920.external.hp.com/openview/ training.html**.

Offline Resources:

Call the certification hotline (800-225-1451) to receive the self-paced training guide "Introduction to HP OpenView." For the NMM Fundamentals test, you can take the HP course "NMM Fundamentals for Technical Consultants" ($2,245). Other recommended reading includes "Guide for Distribution and Scalability," which you can also request via the hotline.

Sponsor:

IBM
11400 Burnet Road, Internal Zip 3013
Austin, TX 78758 USA
Phone: 800-426-8322   **Fax:**
Email:
URL: www.software.ibm.com/os/warp/pspinfo/profesnl.html

IBM Certified LAN Server Engineer

This certification verifies expertise in network design, performance tuning, and installation of OS/2 LAN server networks.

Date Initiated: **# Granted:**   **Fees: $600**

Initial Requirements:

You must pass 6 tests ($600). Five are core exams and one is an elective. The core exams are: *Installing OS/2* ($100), *OS/2 LAN Server Administration I* ($100), *OS/2 LAN Server Administration II* ($100), *OS/2 LAN Server Workstation Planning and Installation* ($100), and *OS/2 LAN Server Performance* ($100). The elective is chosen from the following: *Token-Ring Network Implementation and Management, An Introduction to Integrated Networking, Ethernet Implementation and Problem Determination, REXX for OS/2, IBM TCP/IP for Workstations, OS/2 LAN Server and NetWare: Client Co-existence, DSM: Remote Software Installation Using CID*, and *OS/2 Warp Connect*.

If you are a Certified Novell Engineer (CNE, ECNE, MCNE) or a Microsoft Certified Systems Engineer (MCSE) you only have to take 1 test ($), the LAN Server Engineer Advantage exam.

Continuing Requirements:

Perks:

Online Resources:

The IBM Web page for this certification is: **www.software.ibm.com/os/warp/pspinfo/prolse.htm**

You can access test objectives and sample questions here. Check out the IBM Education home page for additional course and testing information: **www.training.ibm.com/ibmedu/edushome.htm.**

Offline Resources:

IBM Certified DB2 Database Administrator

For individuals who support day-to-day DB2 administration and installation. This program validates the skills and expertise required to install and configure database servers/clients, implement database structures, and perform basic recovery and performance tuning procedures.

Date Initiated: **# Granted:**   **Fees:** $200

Initial Requirements:

You must pass 2 tests: DB2 Fundamentals($100), and DB2 Database Administration ($100). Experience with DB2 V2 and knowledge of SQL are recommended.

Continuing Requirements:

Perks:

Online Resources:

The web page for this certification's exam objectives and sample questions is: **www.software.ibm.com/os/warp/pspinfo/ prodb2a.htm.** Check out the IBM Education home page for additional course and testing information: **www.training.ibm.com/ ibmedu/edushome.htm.**

Offline Resources:

IBM Certified Specialist—AS/400 RPG Programmer

For RPG programmers implementing user requirements using AS/400 tools and techniques.

Date Initiated: **# Granted:**   **Fees:** $150

Initial Requirements:

- Must pass the AS/400 RPG Programmer exam ($150).
- AS/400 RPG programming experience is recommended.

Continuing Requirements:

Perks:

Online Resources:

The web page for this certification's exam objectives and sample questions is: **www.software.ibm.com/os/warp/pspinfo/ proa4rpg.htm**. Check out the IBM Education home page for additional course and testing information: **www.training.ibm.com/ ibmedu/edushome.htm.**

Offline Resources:

IBM offers several training classes you might want to take in preparation: the 5-day *AS/400 RPG IV Programming Workshop* ($) and
the 4-day A*S/400 RPG IV Programmer's Workshop—Advanced Topics* ($).

IBM Certified DB2 Application Developer

This certification validates the skills and expertise required to implement database structures, write DB2 programs using various application interfaces, and perform basic application performance tuning
procedures.

Date Initiated: **# Granted:**   **Fees:** $200

Initial Requirements:

    ✐ You must pass 2 tests: DB2 Fundamentals ($100), and DB2
       Application Development ($100).

    ✐ Experience with DB2 V2 and knowledge of SQL are recommend-
       ed.

Continuing Requirements:

Perks:

Online Resources:

The web page for this certification's exam objectives and
sample questions is: **www.software.ibm.com/os/warp/pspinfo/
prodb2ad.htm.** Check out the IBM Education home page for additional course and testing information: **www.training.ibm.com/
ibmedu/edushome.htm.**

Offline Resources:

IBM Certified AS/400 Professional Network
Administrator—Network/Multiple Systems Environment

This certification is for professionals who manage multiple, linked
AS/400 systems.

Date Initiated: **# Granted:**   **Fees:** $170

Initial Requirements:

Must have experience as an AS/400 System Administrator and proficiency in the administration of two or more networked AS/400 systems. Must pass AS/400 Professional Network Administrator exam
($170).

It will help to have familiarity with back-up and recovery, communications, topology, network configuration, and network security.

Continuing Requirements:

Perks:

Online Resources:

The IBM page for this certification is: **www.software.ibm.com/ os/warp/pspinfo/proa4pna.htm**.

You will find links to test objectives and sample questions there. Check out the IBM Education home page for additional course and testing information: **www.training.ibm.com/ibmedu/edushome. htm**.

Offline Resources:

IBM courses to help you prepare are available. Call 800-IBM-TEACH for course information.

Two recommended courses for this program are the 3-day *AS/400 Communications Introduction Workshop* ($), and the 5-day *AS/400 Peer Communication Workshop* ($).

IBM Certified Network Communications Engineer

For individuals who plan, install, configure, and support total client and server solutions using the IBM Enterprise Communications family of products (IBM Communications Server and IBM Personal Communications).

Date Initiated: **# Granted:**   **Fees:** $300

Initial Requirements:

You must pass 3 tests ($300): the Networking Concepts exam and 2 electives chosen from the following categories (no more than one per category):

- Network Operating System Electives: OS/2 LAN Server Administration 1, OS/2 Warp Server, or OS/2 Warp Server Administration. Candidates who are an IBM Certified LAN Server Administrator, IBM Certified OS/2 Warp Server Administrator, or an IBM Certified OS/2 Warp Server Engineer will receive credit for one test toward the elective requirement.
- Internet Electives: Internet Connection Server for OS/2 or Internet Connection Server for AIX. Enterprise Communications Electives: OS/2 Enterprise Communications, AIX Enterprise Communications, or Windows NT Enterprise Communications.

Candidates who are an IBM Certified Enterprise Communications Specialist will receive credit for one test toward the elective requirement.

Continuing Requirements:

Perks:

Online Resources:

The IBM Web page for this certification is: **www.software.ibm.com/os/warp/pspinfo/pronce.htm**.

You can access test objectives and sample questions here. Check out the IBM Education home page for additional course and testing information: **www.training.ibm.com/ibmedu/edushome.htm**.

Offline Resources:

IBM Certified Networking Solutions Engineer (NSE)

The Networking Solutions engineer (NSE) certification was developed to validate the skills necessary to successfully plan, install, and support IBM's Networking LAN Products.

Date Initiated: **# Granted:**   **Fees:** $200-$800

Initial Requirements:

This certification has 3 levels: I, II, and III, depending on the number of credits earned by passing exams.

- IBM Certified Networking Solutions Engineer—I: Requires 5 credits
- IBM Certified Networking Solutions Engineer—II: Requires 11 credits
- IBM Certified Networking Solutions Engineer—III: Requires 16 credits

The exams and credits for each are:

- IBM Ethernet Products—1 credit,
- IBM 8235 DIALS Server—2 credits,
- IBM ATM Products—3 credits,
- IBM 8271 and 8272 Switches—2 credits,
- IBM 8250 and 8260 Hubs—2 credits,
- IBM 8229 Bridge and 2210 Router—2 credits,
- IBM Token Ring Products—1 credit,
- IBM Nways Manager for Windows—3 credits, and
- IBM Nways 8273/8274 RouteSwitch—2 credits.

Each test you pass also earns you IBM certified specialist status on that product. Most exams cost $100.

Continuing Requirements:

Perks:

Online Resources:

The Web site for the NSE certification is: **www.networking.ibm.com/ntm/ntmcert.html.**

Sample networking tests can be downloaded in a variety of formats from: **www.networking.ibm.com/ntm/ntmsamp.html.**

Check out the IBM Education home page for additional course and testing information: **www.training.ibm.com/ibmedu/edushome.htm.**

Offline Resources:

For information on classes, call 800-IBM-TEACH.

IBM Certified OS/2 Warp Server Instructor

For individuals who wish to teach OS/2 Warp Server.

Date Initiated: # Granted: Fees: N/A

Initial Requirements:

- Must be a Certified OS/2 Warp Server Engineer.
- Must show proof of instructor experience or training, or submit evidence that you are a Certified Banyan Instructor, Microsoft Certified Trainer, or Certified Novell Instructor.
- Must supply 2 letters of reference.

Continuing Requirements:

Perks:

Online Resources:

IBM's Web page for this certification is: **www.software.ibm.com/os/warp/pspinfo/proins.htm**. Check out the IBM Education home page for additional course and testing information: **www.training.ibm.com/ibmedu/edushome.htm**.

Offline Resources:

Call 800-IBM-4FAX and request document #2331, the instructor certification application.

IBM Certified OS/2 Instructor

For individuals who wish to teach OS/2.

Date Initiated: **# Granted:**   **Fees:** N/A

Initial Requirements:
- Must be a Certified OS/2 Engineer.
- Must show proof of instructor experience or training, or submit evidence that you are a Certified Banyan Instructor, Microsoft Certified Trainer, or Certified Novell Instructor.
- Must supply 2 letters of reference.

Continuing Requirements:

Perks:

Online Resources:
IBM's Web page for this certification is: **www.software.ibm.com/os/warp/pspinfo/proins.htm**.
Check out the IBM Education home page for additional course and testing information: **www.training.ibm.com/ibmedu/edushome.htm**.

Offline Resources:
Call 800-IBM-4FAX and request document #2331, the instructor certification application.

IBM Certified Specialist—MQSeries

For specialists on the IBM MQSeries.

Date Initiated: **# Granted:**   **Fees:** $100

Initial Requirements:
- Must pass the MQSeries Installation and Configuration exam ($100).
- You will need experience with MQSeries machines and knowledge of basic communications (TCP/IP, SNA, etc., and should be familiar with Familiarity with MQSeries publications and manuals.

Continuing Requirements:

Perks:

Online Resources:
The web page for exam objectives and sample questions is: **www.software.ibm.com/os/warp/pspinfo/promqse.htm**. Check

out the IBM Education home page for additional course and testing information: **www.training.ibm.com/ibmedu/edushome. htm**.

Offline Resources:

IBM recommends that candidates attend the following seminar: *A Technical Introduction to MQSeries*, the *MQSeries Technical Workshop*, and the *MQSeries Pre-Certification Technical Review*. Call 1-800-IBM-TEACH for details.

To obtain MQSeries documentation and publications, call 800-879-2755 or visit IBM's publications Web site at: **www.elink.ibmlink. ibm.com/pbl/pbl**.

IBM Certified Solutions Expert—Firewall

This certification verifies the ability to install, configure and manage an IBM firewall.

Date Initiated: **# Granted:**   **Fees:** $100

Initial Requirements:

Must pass the Planning, Implementing and Supporting the IBM Firewall Version 3 Product exam ($100).

Continuing Requirements:

Perks:

Online Resources:

IBM's Web page for this certification is: **www.software.ibm.com/ os/warp/pspinfo/prosng.htm**. From here you can access test objectives and sample questions, as well as preparation advice. Self study guides for IBM Internet Connection Server, IBM Communications Server for AIX, and IBM AIX Server are available at: **www.software. ibm.com/sw-sell/besteam/studyguides/**.

Check out the IBM Education home page for additional course and testing information: **www.training.ibm.com/ibmedu/edushome. htm**.

Offline Resources:

IBM offers several courses relevant to this certification. Call 800-IBM-Teach. Several self-study guides are available from IBM. They are: *Building a Firewall with the IBM Internet Connection, Version 3.1, The Domino Defense, Security in Lotus Notes* and the *Internet, Self-Study Guide: IBM Internet Connection Server*. You can order these from IBM by calling 1-800-879-2755.

IBM Certified LAN Server Administrator

This is for individuals who are responsible for supporting day-to-day network operations on OS/2 LAN Server 4.0.

Date Initiated: **# Granted:**   **Fees:** $100

Initial Requirements:

You must pass the OS/2 LAN Server Administration I test ($100).

Continuing Requirements:

Perks:

Online Resources:

The IBM Web page for this certification is: **www.software.ibm. com/os/warp/pspinfo/prolsa.htm**.

You can access test objectives and sample questions here. Check out the IBM Education home page for additional course and testing information: **www.training.ibm.com/ibmedu/edushome.htm**.

Offline Resources:

IBM Certified Specialist—AIX V4.1 Support

This certification validates the AIX problem determination skills and problem resolution abilities of the support professional. The exam also tests the proficiency of the AIX system administrator to perform general software system maintenance.

Date Initiated: 1997   **# Granted:**   **Fees:** $100

Initial Requirements:

Must pass AIX Support Specialist Exam ($100).

Continuing Requirements:

Perks:

Online Resources:

The AIX professional certification page is: **www.rs6000.ibm.com/ support/aixcert/**. IBM's online self-testing system TOPCAT (**www.uk.ibm.com/topcat**) contains a suite of AIX self-assessment tests which are useful in preparing for AIX Professional Certification. Exam outline/objectives and a sample test can be viewed at: **www.rs6000.ibm.com/support/aixcert/Cert_97_Ann/169skills. html**.

Check out the IBM Education home page for additional course and testing information: **www.training.ibm.com/ibmedu/edushome. htm**.

Offline Resources:

IBM courses to help you prepare are available. Call 800-IBM-TEACH for course information.

IBM Certified Specialist—RS/6000 SP

This validates the skills required to plan an RS/6000 SP installation, to install & configure PSSP, and to perform the administrative and diagnostic activities needed to support multiple users in an SP environment.

Date Initiated: 1997   **# Granted:**   **Fees:** $200

Initial Requirements:

Must pass 2 tests ($200):
  🖉 AIX Systems Administration ($100) exam or AIX Support exam ($100) and RS/6000 SP & PSSP exam ($100).

Continuing Requirements:

Perks:

Online Resources:

The AIX professional certification page is: **www.rs6000.ibm. com/support/aixcert/**. IBM's online self-testing system TOPCAT (www.uk.ibm.com/topcat) contains a suite of AIX self-assessment tests which are useful in preparing for AIX Professional Certification. Exam outline/objectives and a sample test can be viewed at: **www.rs6000.ibm.com/support/aixcert/Cert_97_Ann/168_ skil.html**.

Check out the IBM Education home page for additional course and testing information: **www.training.ibm.com/ibmedu/edushome. htm**.

Offline Resources:

IBM courses to help you prepare are available. Call 800-IBM-TEACH for course information.

IBM Certified Advanced Technical Expert—RS/6000 AIX

Certifies an Advanced Level of AIX knowledge and understanding. Verifies the ability to perform in-depth analysis, apply complex AIX concepts, and provide resolution to critical problems.

Date Initiated: 1997   **# Granted:**   **Fees:** $400–$500

Initial Requirements:

Must pass 4 exams: Either AIX Systems Administration ($170) exam *or* AIX Support exam ($100), *and* three of the following elective exams:

- AIX Installation & System Recovery ($100)
- AIX Performance & System Tuning ($100)
- AIX Problem Determination Tools and Techniques ($100)
- AIX Communications ($100)
- RS/6000 SP & PSSP ($130)

Continuing Requirements:

Perks:

Online Resources:

The AIX professional certification page is: **www.rs6000.ibm.com/ support/aixcert/**. IBM's online self-testing system TOPCAT (**www.uk.ibm.com/topcat**) contains a suite of AIX self-assessment tests which are useful in preparing for AIX Professional Certification.

Check out the IBM Education home page for additional course and testing information: **www.training.ibm.com/ibmedu/edushome. htm**.

Offline Resources:

IBM courses to help you prepare are available. Call 800-IBM-TEACH for course information.

IBM Certified Specialist—AIX V 4.1 System Administration

This certification is for AIX administrators, and signifies the ability to apply the AIX skills and knowledge required to install AIX V4.1 and to perform a broad range of general system administration activities.

Date Initiated: 1997　　　**# Granted:**　　　**Fees:** $170

Initial Requirements:
Must pass AIX Systems Administrator Exam ($170).

Continuing Requirements:

Perks:

Online Resources:
The AIX professional certification page is: **www.rs6000.ibm. com/support/aixcert/**. IBM's online self-testing system TOPCAT (**www.uk.ibm.com/topcat**) contains a suite of AIX self-assessment tests which are useful in preparing for AIX Professional Certification.

Exam outline/objectives and a sample test can be viewed at: **www.rs6000.ibm.com/support/aixcert/Cert_97_Ann/161 skills.html**.

Check out the IBM Education home page for additional course and testing information: **www.training.ibm.com/ibmedu/edushome. htm**.

Offline Resources:
IBM courses to help you prepare are available. Call 800-IBM-TEACH for course information.

IBM Certified AIX V4 User

This certification evaluates the skills and knowledge of the AIX user, and the ability to effectively utilize an AIX System.

Date Initiated: 1997　　　**# Granted:**　　　**Fees:** $130

Initial Requirements:
Must pass AIX User exam ($130).

Continuing Requirements:

Perks:

Online Resources:
>   The AIX professional certification page is: **www.rs6000.ibm.com/ support/aixcert/**. IBM's online self-testing system TOPCAT (**www.uk.ibm.com/topcat**) contains a suite of AIX self-assessment tests which are useful in preparing for AIX Professional Certification. Exam outline/objectives and a sample test can be viewed at: **www.rs6000.ibm.com/support/aixcert/Cert_97_Ann/160skills. html.** Check out the IBM Education home page for additional course and testing information: **www.training.ibm.com/ibmedu/ edushome.htm**.

Offline Resources:
>   IBM courses to help you prepare are available. Call 800-IBM-TEACH for course information.

IBM Certified AS/400 Integrator for NetWare

>   Program verifies ability to integrate AS/400 and Netware.

Date Initiated: **# Granted:**   **Fees:** $150

Initial Requirements:
>   ✐ Must be a CNE certified on NetWare Version 4.X .
>   ✐ Must pass AS/400 Integrator for NetWare test ($150).

Continuing Requirements:

Perks:

Online Resources:
>   Test objectives and a sample test can be found at: **www.software. ibm.com/os/warp/pspinfo/proa4in.htm.** Check out the IBM Education home page for additional course and testing information: **www.training.ibm.com/ibmedu/edushome.htm**.

Offline Resources:
>   IBM courses to help you prepare are available. Call 800-IBM-TEACH for course information.

IBM Certified OS/2 Warp Server Administrator

This certification affirms your ability to install, configure, and manage LAN resources and users on OS/2 Warp Server.

Date Initiated: **# Granted:**   **Fees:** $100

Initial Requirements:

You must pass the OS/2 Warp Server Administration exam ($100). You should have fundamental DOS and Windows knowledge, familiarity with using and customizing OS/2 Warp, and experience as an OS/2 Warp Server administrator.

Continuing Requirements:

Perks:

Online Resources:

IBM's Web page for this certification is: **www.software. ibm.com/os/warp/pspinfo/prowsa4.htm**. It contains test objectives and a sample test. Check out the IBM Education home page for additional course and testing information: **www.training.ibm. com/ibmedu/edushome.htm**.

Offline Resources:

IBM Certified LAN Server Instructor

For individuals who wish to become a LAN server instructor.

Date Initiated: **# Granted:**   **Fees:** N/A

Initial Requirements:

- Must be a Certified LAN Server Engineer.
- Must show proof of instructor experience or training, or submit evidence that you are a Certified Banyan Instructor, Microsoft Certified Trainer, or Certified Novell Instructor.
- Must supply 2 letters of reference.

Continuing Requirements:

Perks:

Online Resources:

IBM's Web page for this certification is: **www.software.ibm. com/os/warp/pspinfo/proins.htm**. Check out the IBM Education home page for additional course and testing information: **www.training.ibm.com/ibmedu/edushome.htm**.

Offline Resources:

Call 800-IBM-4FAX and request document #2331, the instructor certification application.

IBM Certified Specialist—VisualAge Generator Configuration

For people who install and configure VisualAge Generator.

Date Initiated: 1997   **# Granted:**   **Fees:** $100

Initial Requirements:

Must pass VisualAge Generator Configuration Proficiency Test ($100).

Continuing Requirements:

Perks:

Online Resources:

The web page for this certification's exam objectives and sample questions is: **www.software.ibm.com/ad/certify/vag/index.html**. Check out the IBM Education home page for additional course and testing information: **www.training.ibm.com/ibmedu/edushome. htm**.

Offline Resources:

IBM Certified OS/2 Engineer (Warp 4)

This certification is for individuals who support OS/2 installations.

Date Initiated: **# Granted:**   **Fees:** $300

Initial Requirements:

You must pass 3 tests ($300). They are:

- ✐ OS/2 Warp 4 Fundamentals($100),
- ✐ OS/2 Warp 4 Connectivity($100), and
- ✐ OS/2 Warp 4 Advanced Concepts and Support($100).

If you're already certified on a previous version, you can just take the update exam: OS/2 Warp 4 Update for OS/2 Engineers.

Continuing Requirements:

Perks:

Online Resources:

IBM's Web page for this certification is: **www.software.ibm.com/ os/warp/pspinfo/proose4.htm**. From here you can access test objectives and sample questions. Check out the IBM Education home page for additional course and testing information: **www.training. ibm.com/ibmedu/edushome.htm**.

Offline Resources:
Relevant courses are available from IBM. Call 800-IBM-TEACH.

IBM Certified Developer/Developer Associate— Object-Oriented VisualAge for C++

This is for VisualAge for C++ developers.

Date Initiated: 8/1997   **# Granted:**   **Fees:** $3,300

Initial Requirements:
To obtain the associate level, you must pass 3 exams ($300). They are: *VisualAge Object-Oriented Analysis and Design Proficiency Test; C++ Language Proficiency Test*; and *Object-oriented VisualAge for Small Talk or COBOL*. To advance to the developer level, you must pass a 5 day practicum ($3000).

Continuing Requirements:

Perks:
- ⌀ Certificate
- ⌀ Lapel pin
- ⌀ Certification camera-ready logo (for use in advertising or in your business literature)
- ⌀ Access to technical literature in a private Technical Library on the Internet
- ⌀ Inclusion in the Directory of IBM Object Technology Certified Professionals published on the Object Technology Certification web site, **www.software.ibm.com/ad/certify/ot**
- ⌀ Recognition by the IBM BESTeam Program

Online Resources:
IBM's Web page for this certification is: **www.software.ibm. com/ad/certify/ot/rmc++.html**.

From here you can access test objectives and samples, as well as a bibliography of study materials. You'll find a practicum self-assessment at: **www.software.ibm.com/ad/certify/ot/casses1.html**.

Check out the IBM Education home page for additional course and testing information: **www.training.ibm.com/ibmedu/edushome. htm**.

Offline Resources:

Relevant courses are available from IBM. Call 800-IBM-TEACH.

IBM Certified Developer/Developer Associate— VisualAge for SmallTalk

This is for VisualAge for SmallTalk developers.

Date Initiated: 8/1997   **# Granted:**   **Fees:** $3,300

Initial Requirements:
- VisualAge Object-Oriented Analysis and Design Proficiency Test.
- To achieve the associate level, you must pass 3 tests ($300): VisualAge object-oriented analysis and design proficiency test, VisualAge for Smalltalk proficiency test, and the IBM Smalltalk language proficiency test.
- To advance to the developer level, you must pass a practicum ($3,000).

Continuing Requirements:

Perks:
- Certificate
- Lapel pin
- Certification logo
- Inclusion in the Directory of IBM Object Technology Certified Professionals published on the Object Technology Certification web site: **www.software.ibm.com/ad/certify/ot**.

Online Resources:

IBM's Web page for this certification is: **www.software. ibm.com/ad/certify/ot/rmst.html**.

From here you can access test objectives and samples, as well as a bibliography of study materials. Check out the IBM Education home page for additional course and testing information: **www.training. ibm.com/ibmedu/edushome.htm**.

Offline Resources:

Relevant courses are available from IBM. Call 800-IBM-TEACH.

IBM Certified Developer/Developer Associate—VisualAge for Java

This is for VisualAge for Java developers.

Date Initiated: 8/1997   **# Granted:**   **Fees:** $3,300

Initial Requirements:

- ✐ To obtain Developer Associate level, you must pass 3 exams ($300): *VisualAge Object-Oriented Analysis and Design Proficiency, VisualAge for Java Proficiency Test,* and *Sun Certified Java Programmer Test for JDK 1.1.*
- ✐ To advance to developer level individuals must pass a practicum ($3000).

Continuing Requirements:

Perks:

- ✐ Certificate
- ✐ Lapel pin
- ✐ Certification camera-ready logo (for use in advertising or in your business literature)
- ✐ Access to technical literature in a private Technical Library on the Internet
- ✐ Inclusion in the Directory of IBM Object Technology Certified Professionals published on the Object Technology Certification web site: **www.software.ibm.com/ad/certify/ot**
- ✐ Recognition by the IBM BESTeam Program

Online Resources:

IBM's Web page for this certification is: **www.software.ibm.com/ad/certify/ot/rmjav.html**.

From here you can access test objectives and samples, as well as a bibliography of study materials. You'll find a practicum self-assessment at: **www.software.ibm.com/ad/certify/ot/jasses1.html**. Check out the IBM Education home page for additional course and testing information: **www.training.ibm.com/ibmedu/edushome.htm**.

Offline Resources:

Relevant courses are available from IBM. Call 800-IBM-TEACH.

IBM Certified Developer/Developer Associate—VisualAge Generator

This is for professionals who are in the business of providing VisualAge application development services.

Date Initiated: 10/97   **# Granted:**   **Fees:**

Initial Requirements:

For the Developer Associate level, you must pass 2 exams ($): VisualAge Generator 3.0 environment test and the VisualAge Generator 3.0 language test. To advance to the developer level, you must must pass the VisualAge Generator Developer Practicum.

Continuing Requirements:

Perks:

- Certificate
- Lapel pin
- Certification Camera-ready logo (for use in advertising or in your business literature)
- Inclusion in the Directory of VisualAge Generator Certified Professionals published on the IBM VisualAge Generator Certification Web Site at: **www.software.ibm.com/ad/certify/vag**

Online Resources:

IBM's Web page for this certification is: **www.software. ibm.com/ad/certify/vag/index.html.** From here you can access test objectives and samples, as well as a bibliography of study materials. Check out the IBM Education home page for additional course and testing information: **www.training.ibm.com/ibmedu/ edushome.htm**.

Offline Resources:

Relevant courses are available from IBM. Call 800-IBM-TEACH.

IBM Certified Specialist— Networking Hardware Product Specific

This certification verifies an individual's expertise on a particular IBM Networking LAN hardware product. Multiple certifications can be obtained for different products. These certifications can be counted towards the IBM Certified Networking Solutions Engineer (NSE) certification.

Date Initiated: **# Granted:**   **Fees:** $100

Initial Requirements:

Must pass any 1 of the IBM Networking hardware exams ($100). They are: *IBM Ethernet Products, IBM 8235 DIALS Server, IBM ATM Products, IBM 8271 and 8272 Switches, IBM 8250 and 8260 Hubs, IBM 8229 Bridge and 2210 Router, IBM Token Ring Products, IBM Nways Manager for Windows*, and *IBM Nways 8273/8274 RouteSwitch*.

Continuing Requirements:

Perks:

Online Resources:

The Web site for the networking LAN specialist certifications is: **www.networking.ibm.com/ntm/ntmcert.html**. Sample networking tests can be downloaded in a variety of formats from: www.net-**working.ibm.com/ntm/ntmsamp.html.** Check out the IBM Education home page for additional course and testing information: **www.training.ibm.com/ibmedu/edushome.htm**.

Offline Resources:

For information on classes call 800-IBM-TEACH.

IBM Certified OS/2 Warp Server Engineer

For individuals who plan and support OS/2 Warp Server networks, and establish stagies for disaster recovery, systems management, remote LAN access, or software distribution.

Date Initiated: **# Granted:**   **Fees:** $300

Initial Requirements:

Must pass 3 exams ($300): OS/2 Warp ($100), OS/2 Warp Connect ($100), and OS/2 Warp Server ($100). Individuals who are already an IBM Certified OS/2 Engineer don't have to take the Server test. Individuals who are already a Certified Novell Engineer (CNE, ECNE,

MCNE) or a Microsoft Certified Systems Engineer (MCSE) can get this certification by taking only the OS/2 Warp Server Advantage for CNEs and MCSEs exam. IBM Certified LAN Server Engineers also only have 1 exam to pass, the OS/2 Warp Server Advantage for LAN Server Engineers.

Continuing Requirements:

Perks:

Online Resources:

IBM's Web page for this certification is: **www.software. ibm.com/os/warp/pspinfo/prowse4.htm.** From here you can access test objectives and samples, as well as a bibliography of study materials. Check out the IBM Education home page for additional course and testing information: **www.training.ibm.com/ibmedu/ edushome.htm**.

Offline Resources:

IBM Certified Network Communications Engineer

This program is for individuals who plan, install, configure, and support total client and server solutions using the IBM Communications Server and IBM Personal Communications.

Date Initiated: **# Granted:**   **Fees:** $300

Initial Requirements:

Must already be an IBM Certified Specialist—eNetwork Software.
Must pass 3 exams ($300): a core (Networking Concepts) and 2 electives.

Electives are chosen from the following (not more than one per category):

- Network Operating System Electives: OS/2 LAN Server Administration 1, OS/2 Warp Server, or OS/2 Warp Server Administration. Candidates who are an IBM Certified LAN Server Administrator, IBM Certified OS/2 Warp Server Administrator, or an IBM Certified OS/2 Warp Server Engineer will receive credit for one test toward the elective requirement.
- Internet Electives: Internet Connection Server for OS/2 or Internet Connection Server for AIX.
- Enterprise Communications Electives: OS/2 Enterprise Communications, AIX Enterprise Communications, or Windows NT Enterprise Communications. Candidates who are an IBM Certi-

fied Enterprise Communications Specialist will receive credit for one test toward the elective requirement.

Continuing Requirements:

Perks:

Online Resources:

Exam outline/objectives and a sample test can be accessed from **www.software.ibm.com/os/warp/pspinfo/pronce.htm.** Check out the IBM Education home page for additional course and testing information: **www.training.ibm.com/ibmedu/edushome.htm.**

Offline Resources:

IBM Certified Developer/Developer Associate— Object-Oriented VisualAge for COBOL

This is for VisualAge for COBOL developers.

Date Initiated: 7/1997   **# Granted:**   **Fees:** $3,200

Initial Requirements:

To obtain the associate level, you must pass 2 tests ($200): *VisualAge Object-Oriented Analysis and Design Proficiency Test* and the Object-*Oriented VisualAge for COBOL Proficiency Test.* To advance to the developer level you must pass a practicum ($3000).

Continuing Requirements:

Perks:

- Certificate
- Lapel pin
- Certification camera-ready logo (for use in advertising or in your business literature)
- Access to technical literature in a private Technical Library on the Internet
- Inclusion in the Directory of IBM Object Technology Certified Professionals published on the Object Technology Certification web site, **www.software.ibm.com/ad/certify/ot**
- Recognition by the IBM BESTeam Program

Online Resources:

IBM's Web page for this certification is: **www.software. ibm.com/ad/certify/ot/rmcob.html.** From here you can access test objectives and samples, as well as a bibliography of study materials. Check out the IBM Education home page for additional course and testing information: **www.training.ibm.com/ibmedu/edushome. htm**.

Offline Resources:
Relevant courses are available from IBM. Call 800-IBM-TEACH.

IBM Certified Specialist—ADSM

This is for individuals who are responsible for implementing and supporting ADSM.

Date Initiated: **# Granted:**   **Fees:** $100

Initial Requirements:
Must pass 1 exam ($100): ADSM Solution Development and Implementation.

Continuing Requirements:

Perks:

Online Resources:
The IBM Web page for this certification is: **www.software. ibm.com/os/warp/pspinfo/prosadsm.htm**. From here you can access test objectives and sample questions. Check out the IBM Education home page for additional course and testing information: **www.training.ibm.com/ibmedu/edushome.htm**.

Offline Resources:
Relevant courses are available from IBM. Call 800-IBM-TEACH.

IBM Certified OS/2 Warp Developer

This certification is for individuals who design and develop OS/2 Warp applications and are proficient in a programming language.

Date Initiated: **# Granted:**   **Fees:** $300

Initial Requirements:
You must pass 3 exams ($300). One is a core exam—OS/2 Warp Kernel, the other two are electives. Electives include a programming language elective (C, C++, REXX for OS/2), and an application development elective. (VisualAge for Smalltalk Proficiency, VisualAge for C++ Object-Oriented Proficiency, VisualAge for COBOL Object-Oriented Proficiency, OS/2 Warp Problem Determination/ Application Trap Analysis, OS/2 Presentation Manager for C, DB2 Application Development). The C Language and C++ Language tests are owned by ICCP.

Continuing Requirements:

Perks:

Online Resources:

IBM's Web page for this certification is: **www.software. ibm.com/os/warp/pspinfo/proosd.htm.**

From here you can access test objectives and sample questions (except for the C/C++ tests). The ICCP Web site address is **www.iccp.org.** Check out the IBM Education home page for additional course and testing information: **www.training.ibm.com/ ibmedu/edushome.htm.**

Offline Resources:

Relevant courses are available from IBM. Call 800-IBM-TEACH. Objectives and a sample test for the C and C++ language exams are available from the Institute for Certification of Computer Professionals (ICCP). Call 708-299-4227.

IBM Certified AS/400 Associate or Professional System Administrator

For IBM AS/400 system administrators.

Date Initiated: **# Granted:**   **Fees:** $170/$340

Initial Requirements:

- ✐ To obtain the associate certification you must pass the AS/400 Associate System Administrator exam ($170). To obtain the professional certification you must pass the AS/400 Professional System Operator exam ($170).
- ✐ Experience as an AS/400 System Administrator is recommended.

Continuing Requirements:

Perks:

Online Resources:

The web page for the associate certification exam objectives and sample is: **www.software.ibm.com/os/warp/pspinfo/proa4asa. htm.** The web page for the professional exam objectives and sample is: **www.software.ibm.com/os/warp/pspinfo/proa4psa.htm.**

Check the IBM Education home page for additional course and testing information: **www.training.ibm.com/ibmedu/edushome.htm.**

Offline Resources:

IBM Certified AS/400 Associate or Professional System Operator

For IBM AS/400 system operators.

Date Initiated: **# Granted:**   **Fees:** $170/$340

Initial Requirements:

To obtain the associate certification you must pass the AS/400 Associate System Operator exam ($170). To obtain the professional certification you must pass the AS/400 System Operator exam ($170). Experience as an AS/400 System Operator is recommended.

Continuing Requirements:

Perks:

Online Resources:

The web page for the associate certification exam objectives and sample is: **www.software.ibm.com/os/warp/pspinfo/proa4aso. htm.** The web page for the professional exam objectives and sample is: **www.software.ibm.com/os/warp/ pspinfo/proa4pso.htm.**

Check the IBM Education home page for additional course and testing information: **www.training.ibm.com/ibmedu/edushome.htm.**

Offline Resources:

IBM Certified Specialist—AS/400 Client Access

This certification is for individuals who plan, assess and implement client access solutions. You should be able to install and support client access by adjusting both the AS/400 and PC environment.

Date Initiated: **# Granted:**   **Fees:** $150

Initial Requirements:

- Must pass the AS/400 Client Access exam ($150).
- Experience with CA/400 implementation is recommended.

Continuing Requirements:

Perks:

Online Resources:

The web page for this certification's exam objectives and sample questions is: **www.software.ibm.com/os/warp/pspinfo/proa4sca.htm.** Check the IBM Education home page for additional course and testing information: **www.training.ibm.com/ ibmedu/edushome.htm.**

Offline Resources:

IBM Certified Solutions Expert—Net.Commerce

This certification is for individuals who will plan, implement and support the IBM Net.Commerce Version 2 Product.

Date Initiated: **# Granted:**   **Fees:** $100

Initial Requirements:

    ✐ Must pass 1 exam ($100): Planning, Implementing and Supporting the IBM Net.Commerce Version 2 Product.

You should also have the following knowledge:

    ✐ General skills in Windows NT and/or AIX operating system commands

    ✐ Working knowledge of Secure Sockets Layer (SSL)

    ✐ HyperText Transfer Protocol (HTTP)

    ✐ HyperText Transfer Protocol Secured (HTTPS)

    ✐ Working knowledge of IBM Net.Data and TCP/IP

Continuing Requirements:

Perks:

Online Resources:

The IBM Web page for this certification is: **www.software.ibm.com/os/warp/pspinfo/prosnc.htm.** You can access test objectives and sample questions here. Review the IBM Internet Connection Server Study Guide, the IBM AIX Server Study Guide, and the IBM Database Server Study Guide, which you will find at: **www.software.ibm.com/sw-sell/besteam/studyguides/.** Check out the IBM Education home page for additional course and testing information: **www.Training.ibm.com/ibmedu/ edushome.htm**.

Offline Resources:

If you have limited TCP/IP experience, IBM recommends that you take the 2 day TCP/IP Architecture class. For info, call 800-IBM-TEACH.

IBM Certified Systems Expert—VisualAge Generator

For people who install and configure VisualAge Generator.

Date Initiated: 1998   **# Granted:**   **Fees:** $3,000

Initial Requirements:

Must first be an IBM Certified Specialist—VisualAge Generator Configuration. Must then complete the Expert practicum. Practicum was under development at time of press, but other IBM practicums cost $3,000.

Continuing Requirements:

Perks:

Online Resources:

The web page for this certification's exam objectives and sample questions is: **www.software.ibm.com/ad/certify/vag/index.html**. Check out the IBM Education home page for additional course and testing information: **www.training.ibm.com/ibmedu/edushome.htm**.

Offline Resources:

IBM Certified Specialist—Transaction Server

Certification of operating system specific expertise on IBM's Transaction Server.

Date Initiated: **# Granted:**   **Fees:** $100

Initial Requirements:

Must pass one of the operating system specific Transaction Server exams ($100). Exams exist for AIX, OS/2, and Windows NT. You should know CICS fundamentals, basic communications (TCP/IP, SNA, etc.), and DCE and ENCINA .

Continuing Requirements:

Perks:

Online Resources:

The web page for this certification is: **www.software.ibm.com/os/warp/pspinfo/prots.htm**

From here you can jump to test objectives and sample questions. Check the IBM Education home page for additional course and testing information: **www.training.ibm.com/ibmedu/edushome.htm**.

Offline Resources:

Publications and classes are available for each of the exams. Call 800-IBM-TEACH, or visit the following Web sites:

✐ For OS/2: **www.software.ibm.com/os/warp/pspinfo/ edu520v1.htm**

✐ For AIX: **www.software.ibm.com/os/warp/pspinfo/ edu521v1.htm**

✐ For Windows NT: **www.software.ibm.com/os/warp/pspinfo/ edu522v1.htm**

IBM Certified Networking Solutions Instructor

The IBM Certified Networking Solutions Instructor program is designed to equip instructors to provide quality consistent training on IBM networking products.

Date Initiated: **# Granted:**   **Fees:** $100

Initial Requirements:

You must have 2 to 3 years experience in networking and have at least 1 year training experience or have completed a recognized technical instructor program and attend the IBM Instructor Training course on the product you want to teach AND pass the IBM Certified Specialist (networking hardware product) exam ($100) for the product you want to teach at the Instructor-eligible Level (85%).

Continuing Requirements:

Perks:

Online Resources:

The IBM Web page for this certification is: **www.networking. ibm.com/ntm/ntmnsi.html.** Check out the IBM Education home page for additional course and testing information: **www.training. ibm.com/ibmedu/edushome.htm**.

Offline Resources:

You can obtain an IBM Certified Instructor application and instructions from IBM's faxback system at 1-800-IBM-4FAX (document 2331).

IBM Certified Specialist—eNetwork Software

For individuals who are responsible for the planning, implementation and support of the IBM eNetwork Software products.

Date Initiated: **# Granted:**   **Fees:** $100

Initial Requirements:

Must pass the AIX, OS/2, or Windows NT Enterprise Communications exam ($100).

Continuing Requirements:

Perks:

Online Resources:

The web page for this certification is: **www.software. ibm.com/os/warp/pspinfo/prosens.htm**. From here you can jump to test objectives and sample questions for each of the exams. Check out the IBM Education home page for additional course and testing information: **www.training.ibm.com/ibmedu/edushome.htm**.

Offline Resources:

IBM Professional Server Specialist/Expert (PSS/PSE)

This certification is for networking or server technical specialists working with IBM PC Server. This is part of IBM's TechConnect program.

Date Initiated: 1995   **# Granted:**   **Fees:** $1,450

Initial Requirements:

To obtain the specialist certification you must attend the IBM PC Server Technical Training class ($750) and pass the associated exam ($600). Expert certifications are available for Novell Netware, OS/2 Warp Server, and Windows NT Server. To obtain expert certification you must attend the installation and performance class related to the operating system of your chosen certification ($), and pass the associated exam ($100). You must also be certified by that vendor (MCSE, CNE, or OS/2 Warp Engineer).

Continuing Requirements:

Perks:

- quarterly CD-ROM set containing technical articles, news, white papers and drivers and fixes.
- access to the TechConnect forum.

    ✐ certificaton Kit, with a certificate, a frame, and thank you gifts from IBM.

PSEs receive, in addition:

    ✐ priority access to the IBM HelpCenter.

    ✐ electronic access to the IBM Support systems.

    ✐ access to interactive forums on the IBM PC Company BBS.

    ✐ invitiation to an annual PSE Briefing conference.

Lastly, the PSE has an opportunity to participate in the annual PSE Briefing, a combination of technical updates and relaxation hosted by IBM.

Online Resources:

The IBM Web page for this certification is: **www.pc.ibm.com/ techconnect/program/certification.html**. The home page of the PC Institute is at: **www.pc.ibm.com/techconnect/program/ institute.html**. It contains information on training classes.

Offline Resources:

For FAX information call 1-800-IBM-4FAX (1-800-426-4329) and request index document number 3211.

Sponsor:

Information Systems Audit and Control Association (ISACA)
3701 Algonquin Rd
Suite 100
Rolling Meadows, IL 60008 USA
Phone: 847-253-1545   **Fax:** 847-253-1443
Email: certification@isaca.org
URL: www.isaca.org

Certified Information Systems Auditor (CISA)

This certification is for individuals who work in the Information Systems audit, control and security profession.

Date Initiated: 1978   **# Granted:** 10,500   **Fees:** $355.00

Initial Requirements:
- Must pass CISA examination ($275/ISACA members, $355/non-members).
- Must also provide verification of a minimum of five years of experience in the IS audit, control or security profession. There are experience substitutions or waivers for a bachelor degree and working as a full-time college instructor in the field.

Continuing Requirements:
Once certified, a CISA must comply with the Continuing Education requirements annually. Those requirements are: a minimum of 20 continuing professional education (CPE) hours earned that year, pay the continuing education maintenance fee, comply with the ISACA Code of Professional Ethics. In the third year of the fixed three-year certification cycle, you must also have completed a minimum of 120 CPE hours earned within that fixed three-year certification cycle.

Perks:

Online Resources:

Offline Resources:
1997 CISA exam study aids are available from the ISACA: CISA Candidates Guide $5 members/ $15 nonmembers; CISA Review Manual $90 members/ $105 nonmembers; Sample Test $45 members/$55 nonmembers. Many of the 145 local chapters offer CISA Review Courses which vary in length and cost.

Sponsor:

Informix
4100 Bohannon Dr.
Menlo Park, CA 94025 USA
Phone: 650-926-6300   **Fax:**
Email:
URL: www.informix.com/informix/services/certific/csbrch2.htm

Informix Certified Database Specialist

This certification is for professionals who work with Informix databases.

Date Initiated: 1980   **# Granted:** "thousands"   **Fees:** $500

Initial Requirements:

Must complete 2 exams ($500): Database Fundamentals ($250), and Managing and Optimizing INFORMIX-OnLine Dynamic Server Databases ($250).

Continuing Requirements:

Must recertify on new versions.

Perks:

- ✎ certificate of achievement
- ✎ use of logo
- ✎ lapel pin
- ✎ access to the InformixLink TechInfo Center
- ✎ subscriptions to TechNotes (quarterly Technical Support journal), and CS Times (Customer Services newsletter)

Online Resources:

The company's home page is: **www.informix.com**. A complete program brochure, including study guide, can be downloaded in PDF format from the certification Web site. Online documentation for Informix products can be found at: **www.informix.com/answers**.

Offline Resources:

Informix offers training classes. For class availability and enrollment, contact Informix Education Services at 800-331-1763. Course information is also available on the web at: **www.informix.com/training/**.

Informix Certified System Administrator

This certification is designed for system administrators, database administrators, and technical support personnel currently working with INFORMIX-OnLine Dynamic Server 7.x.

Date Initiated: 1980   **# Granted:** "thousands"   **Fees:** $500

Initial Requirements:

Must pass 2 exams ($500): INFORMIX-OnLine Dynamic Server System Administration ($250), and INFORMIX-OnLine Dynamic Server Performance Tuning Exam ($250).

Continuing Requirements:

Must recertify on new versions.

Perks:

- certificate of achievement
- use of logo
- lapel pin
- access to the InformixLink TechInfo Center
- subscriptions to TechNotes (quarterly Technical Support journal), and CS Times (Customer Services newsletter)

Online Resources:

The company's home page is: **www.informix.com**. A complete program brochure, including study guide, can be downloaded in PDF format from the certification Web site. Online documentation for Informix products can be found at: **www.informix.com/answers**.

Offline Resources:

Informix offers training classes. For class availability and enrollment, contact Informix Education Services at 800-331-1763. Course information is also available on the web at: **www.informix.com/training/**.

Sponsor:

Institute for Certification of Computing Professionals (ICCP)
2200 East Devon Avenue
Suite 247
Des Plaines, IL 60018 USA
Phone: 800-843-8227   **Fax:** 847-299-4280
Email: 74040.3722@compuserve.com
URL: www.iccp.org

Associate Computing Professional (ACP)

This certification is for the person new to the computing industry or for the recent college graduate who wishes to gain professional credentials substantiating their level of computing knowledge.

Date Initiated: 1973   **# Granted:**   **Fees:** $228

Initial Requirements:

Must pass 2 exams: a core ($149) and one language exam ($79). Must ascribe to the ICCP Code of Ethics and Code of Conduct.

Continuing Requirements:

Perks:

- educational discounts
- college credits
- job matching and relocation program
- peer networking
- quarterly newsletter

Online Resources:

The ICCP Web page contains further information on the certification program, including exam subject outlines: **www.iccp.org**.

Offline Resources:

The ICCP offers an Official Exam Review Outline ($63.50) and exam textbooks. Approved third-party preparation suppliers also exist and can be found listed on the ICCP Web site. Contact the ICCP and request the Guide to Certification as a Computing Professional.

Certified Computing Professional (CCP)

This vendor-independent certification is suitable for most IS professionals (programmers, analysts, etc. to IT managers and CIOs).

Date Initiated: 1973   **# Granted:** 50,000   **Fees:** $475

Initial Requirements:

Must have four years of documented experience in the computing industry. Up to 24 months of credit is given for Bachelor degrees in related fields. Must pass at 70% or better a core ($) and two elected specialty exams($). Must ascribe to the ICCP Code of Ethics and Code of Conduct.

Continuing Requirements:

Must complete 120 hours of approved continuing education over a three year revolving period and payment of annual maintenance fees of $50.

Perks:

- educational discounts
- college credits
- job matching and relocation program
- peer networking
- quarterly newsletter

Online Resources:

The ICCP Web page contains further information on the certification program, including exam subject outlines: **www.iccp.org**.

Offline Resources:

The ICCP offers an Official Exam Review Outline ($63.50) and exam textbooks. Approved 3rd party preparation suppliers also exist and can be found listed on the ICCP Web site. Contact the ICCP and request the Guide to Certification as a Computing Professional.

Sponsor:

**International Information Systems Security
Certification Consortium, Inc. (ISC²)**
Park View Office Tower, 255 Park Avenue
Suite 1000
Worcester, MA 01609-1946 USA
Phone: 508-842-0452   **Fax:** 508-842-6461
Email: info@isc2.org
URL: www.isc2.org

Certified Information Systems Security Professional (CISSP)

For experienced professionals in the computer security field.

Date Initiated: **# Granted:**   **Fees:** $250

Initial Requirements:

Must have three years of direct work experience in one or more of the ten test domains of the information systems security Common Body of Knowledge (CBK). You must also subscribe to the (ISC)² code of ethics, and pass the CISSP exam ($250).

Continuing Requirements:

Recertification is required at three year intervals by earning 120 Continuing Professional Education (CPE) credits.

Perks:

- inclusion in online directory
- career opportunity listings

Online Resources:

Offline Resources:

ISC² will provide certain program information and materials only in hardcopy. A draft Study Guide containing a description of the ten test domains, sample test questions, and a list of reference materials, is available to candidates at cost (for copying and shipping), on a limited, individually-requested basis. Request information from them via the organization via mail, email or phone.

Sponsor:

International Programmers Guild (IPG) Society
6535 Millcreek Drive, Unit 44
Mississauga, ON L5N 2M2 Canada
Phone: 800-318-0745   **Fax**: 905-812-1953
Email: webmaster@ipgnet.com
URL: www.ipgnet.com/certify.htm

Certified Programmer (fellow/senior/master)

This is a vendor-independent certification for programmers.

Date Initiated: 1991   **# Granted:**   **Fees:** $505–$755

Initial Requirements:
- Must be a member of the IPG (registration $14.85, annual membership $60). Must have work experience as a programmer.
- Must pay certification fee ($250).
- Must pass Guild evaluation conducted via personal interview, and will be scored using a point system. You must proceed through the levels in order: fellow ($180), senior ($250), master. Master level does not require a fee or further evaluation. You must also ascribe to the Guild's code of ethics.

Continuing Requirements:

Perks:

Online Resources:
Details and applications for each level are contained on the IPG Web site: **www.ipgnet.com/certify.htm**.

Offline Resources:

Sponsor:

Learning Tree International
1805 Library Street
Renton, VA 20190-5630 USA
Phone: 800-843-8733   **Fax:** 613-748-0479
Email: cncourses@learningtree.com
URL: www.learningtree.com

Learning Tree certification programs are recommended for up to 10 semester hours by the American Council on Education (ACE).

Cisco Router Certified Professional

For individuals who design, configure, troubleshoot or manage internetworks with Cisco routers, including network managers, technicians, consultants and designers.

Date Initiated: late 1997   **# Granted:**   **Fees:** $10,899

Initial Requirements:

You must succesfully complete four core courses and one elective course, along with their associated examinations. Core courses are: *Introduction to Internetworking: Bridges, Switches and Routers* (4 days/$2,595), *Cisco Routers: A Comprehensive Hands-On Introduction* (4 days/$2,076), *Configuring Cisco Routers: Advanced Hands-On Workshop* (4 days/$2,076), and *IP Routing With OSPF and BGP: Hands-On* (4 days/$2,076). Electives include: *Hands-On Internetworking With TCP/IP* (4 Days/$2,076), *Migrating to IPv6: Hands-On* (4 days/$2,076) *Hands-On SNMP: From Workgroup to Enterprise Networks* (4 days/$2,076), *Hands-On Introduction to TCP/IP* (4 days/ $2,076), *Data Network Design and Performance Optimization* (4 days/$2,076) *Deploying Internet and Intranet Firewalls: Hands-On* (4 days/$2,076), *Internet and System Security: Attacks and Countermeasures* (4 days/$2,076), *Fast LAN Technologies* (4 days/$2,076), *Hands-On High-Performance Ethernet: Switched, Fast and Traditional* (4 days/$2,076).

Continuing Requirements:

Perks:

     ✎ certificate

Online Resources:
The Web page for this certification is **http://www.learningtree. com/cn/certific/785.htm**.

Offline Resources:

Software Development Certified Professional

Date Initiated: **# Granted:**   **Fees:** $10,499–
                                                                  $11,219

Initial Requirements:
You must successfully complete four core courses ($8,823), one elective course ($1,676–$2,396) and their associated examinations. The core courses are: *Software Project Planning and Management* (4 days/$2,595), *Identifying and Confirming User Requirements* (4 days/$2,076), *Software Quality Assurance* (4 days/$2,076), and *Software Configuration Management* (4 days/$2,076). Electives include: *Practical Software Testing Methods* (4 days/$2,076), *Software Systems Analysis and Design* (4 days/$2,076), *Introduction to Object Technology* (4 days/$2,076), *Object-Oriented Analysis and Design* (5 days/$2,396), *Implementing the Year 2000 Conversion: Hands-on* (3 days/$1,676), *Business Process Re-engineering* (4 days/$2,076), *Hands-on Project Management: Skills for Success* (4 days/$2,076), *Management Skills for IT Professionals* (4 days/$2,076).

Course costs may vary depending on whether you take them all within 1 year, and other factors.

Continuing Requirements:

Perks:
   ✏ certificate

Online Resources:
The Web page for this certification is **www.learningtree.com/ cn/certific/740.htm**. From here you can view detailed course outlines.

Offline Resources:
Course materials are provided at each course.

Client/Server Systems Certified Professional

This certification is for individuals involved in the design, development, implementation and support of client/server systems.

Date Initiated: **# Granted:**   **Fees:** $10,899–
                                              $11,219

Initial Requirements:

You must successfully complete four core courses ($8,823), one elective course ($2,076–$2,396) and their associated examinations. The core courses are: *Introduction to Client/Server Computing* (4 days/$2,595), *Client/Server Systems: Analysis and Design* (4 days/$2,076), *Distributing Data in Client/Server Systems* (4 days/$2,076) *Client/Server Applications: A Hands-on Development Workshop* (4 days/$2,076). *Elective options are: Relational Databases* (4 days/$2,076), *UNIX* (4 days/$2,076), *Oracle7 Introduction* (5 days/$2,396), *Microsoft SQL Server 6* (4 days/$2,076), *PowerBuilder 5 and Oracle7* (4 days/$2,076), *Windows NT 4.0* (5 days/$2,396), *Managing & Supporting Client/Server Systems* (4 days/$2,076), *Oracle Developer/2000* (5 days/$2,396), *Oracle WebServer Applications Development* (4 days/$2,076).

Course costs may vary depending on whether you take them all within 1 year, and other factors.

Continuing Requirements:

Perks:

✍ certificate

Online Resources:

The Web page for this certification is **www.learningtree.com/cn/ certific/769.htm.** From here you can view detailed course outlines.

Offline Resources:

Course materials are provided at each course.

Telecommunications Certified Professional

For individuals who specify, design, evaluate, install, operate or maintain telecommunications services, including telecommunications specialists, PBX administrators, technical support staff, network designers, network managers and administrators, and project managers.

Date Initiated: late 1997   **# Granted:**   **Fees:** $10,499–
                                                                      $10,899

Initial Requirements:

You must complete four core courses($8,823), one elective course($1,676-$2,076), and pass the associated examinations. Core courses are: *Wide Area Networking and Telecommunications* (4 days/$2,595), *Implementing Computer Telephony Integration* (4 days/$2,076), *ISDN for Telecommunications* (4 days/$2,076), and *High-Speed Wide Area Networks* (4 days/$2,076). Electives include: *Deploying T1 and T3 Services* (3 days/$1,676), *Utilizing Frame Relay Networks* (3 days/$1,676) *Implementing ATM* (3 days/$1,676), *Mobile Communications and Wireless Networks* (4 days/$2,076), *Introduction to Internetworking: Bridges, Switches and Routers* (4 days/$2,076), *Hands-On Introduction to TCP/IP* (4 days/$2,076), *Implementing Fiber-Optic Communications* (4 days/$2,076), *Computer Network Architectures and Protocols* (4 days/$2,076) *Implementing ISDN Data Networks: Hands-On* (4 days/$2,076), and *Hands-On X.25* (4 days/$2,076).

Continuing Requirements:

Perks:

✑ certificate

Online Resources:

The Web page for this certification is: **http://www.learningtree.com/cn/certific/786.htm**.

Offline Resources:

Oracle8 Application Development Certified Professional

For application developers, designers, programmers, Web developers, database and Web administrators, analysts and others involved in developing and maintaining client/server and Web-based applications that access enterprise data stored in Oracle databases.

Date Initiated: late 1997   **# Granted:**   **Fees:** $12,039–
                                                                   $12,359

Initial Requirements:

Must successfully complete four core courses($9,963), one elective course($2,076-$2,396), and associated examinations. Core courses are: *Oracle8: A Comprehensive Hands-On Introduction* (5 days/$2,995), *Oracle8 Applications Development and Tuning: Hands-On* (5 days/$2,396), *Oracle Developer/2000: Hands-On* (5 days/$2,396), and *Building Oracle WebServer Applications: Hands-On* (4 days/$2,076). Electives include: *Relational Databases: Design, Tools and Techniques* (4 days/$2,076) *Introduction to Object Technology* (4 days), *Object-Oriented Analysis and Design* (5 days/$2,396), *Developing SQL Queries for Oracle7: Hands-On* (3 days), *Building a Data Warehouse: Hands-On* (5 days/$2,396), *Oracle8 Database Administration: Hands-On* (5 days/$2,396) *Developing Client/Server Applications: Hands-On* (4 days/$2,076), *Distributing Data in Client/Server Systems* (4 days/$2,076), *Hands-On PowerBuilder* (4 days/$2,076), and *Developing Applications With PowerBuilder 5 and Oracle7: Hands-On* (4 days/$2,076).

Continuing Requirements:

Perks:

⌀ certificate

Online Resources:

The Web page for this certification is **http://www.learningtree.com/cn/certific/790.htm**.

Offline Resources:

PC Service and Support Certified Professional

Date Initiated: **# Granted:**   **Fees:** $11,219–
$11,539

Initial Requirements:

You must successfully complete four core courses ($9,143), one elective course ($2,095–$2,396) and their associated examinations. The core courses are: *Hands-on PC Configuration and Troubleshooting* (4 days/$2,595), *Advanced PC Configuration, Troubleshooting and Data Recovery: Hands-on* (4 days/$2,076), *Windows 95 Support and Networking: Hands-on* (5 Days/$2,396), and *Hands-on PC Networking* (4 days/$2,076). Electives include: *Integrating Microsoft Office 97: Hands-on* (4 days/$2,076), *Hands-on LAN Troubleshooting* (4 days/$2,076), *UNIX: A Hands-on Introduction* (4 days/$2,076), *Windows NT 4 Workstation and Server: Hands-on* (5 Days/$2,396), *Hands-on IntranetWare: NetWare 4.x Administration* (5 Days/ $2,396), *Hands-on NetWare Service and Support* (4 days/$2,076), *Windows 95/NT/3.11 Multiplatform Networking: Hands-on* (4 days/ $2,076), *UNIX and Windows NT Integration: Hands-on* (4 days/ $2,076), *NetWare to Windows NT Integration and Migration: Hands-on* (4 days/$2,076).

Course costs may vary depending on whether you take them all within 1 year, and other factors.

Continuing Requirements:

Perks:

✐ certificate

Online Resources:

The Web page for this certification is **www.learningtree.com/ cn/certific/753.htm**. From here you can view detailed course outlines.

Offline Resources:

Course materials are provided at each course.

TCP/IP Certified Professional

Date Initiated: **# Granted:**   **Fees:** $10,899

Initial Requirements:

You must successfully complete four core courses ($8,823), one elective course ($2,076) and their associated examinations. The core courses are: *Hands-on Introduction to TCP/IP* (4 days/$2,595), *Hands-on Internetworking With TCP/IP* (4 days/$2,076), *Hands-on SNMP: From Workgroup to Enterprise Networks* (4 days/$2,076), and *Internet and System Security: Attacks and Countermeasures* (4 days/$2,076). *Electives include: Introduction to Internetworking: Bridges, Switches and Routers* (4 days/$2,076), *Introduction to the Internet and Intranets for Business: Hands-on* (4 days/$2,076), *Computer Network Architectures and Protocols* (4 days/ $2,076), *Hands-on TCP/IP Programming* (4 days/$2,076), *Cisco Routers: A Comprehensive Hands-on Introduction* (4 days/$2,076), *Hands-on TCP/IP Internetworking on Windows NT* (4 days/$1995), *UNIX and Windows NT Integration: Hands-on* (4 days/$2,076), *IP Routing With OSPF and BGP: Hands-on Deploying Internet and Intranet Firewalls: Hands-on* (4 days/$2,076), *Migrating to IPv6:Hands-on* (4 days/$2,076).

Course costs may vary depending on whether you take them all within 1 year, and other factors.

Continuing Requirements:

Perks:

✎ certificate

Online Resources:

The Web page for this certification is **www.learningtree.com/ cn/certific/767.htm**. From here you can view detailed course outlines.

Offline Resources:

Course materials are provided at each course.

Internetworking Certified Professional

Date Initiated: **# Granted:**   **Fees:** $10,899

Initial Requirements:

You must successfully complete four core courses ($8,823), one elective course ($2,076) and their associated examinations. The core courses are: *Introduction to Internetworking: Bridges, Switches and Routers* (4 days/$2,595), *Hands-on Introduction to TCP/IP* (4 days/$2,076), *IP Routing With OSPF and BGP: Hands-on* (4 days/$2,076), and *Data Network Design and Performance Optimization* (4 days/$2,076). Electives include: *Hands-on Internetworking With TCP/IP* (4 days/$2,076), *Migrating to IPv6: Hands-on* (4 days/$2,076), *Hands-on SNMP: From Workgroup to Enterprise Networks* (4 days/$2,076), *Computer Network Architectures and Protocols* (4 days/$2,076), *Cisco Routers: A Comprehensive Hands-on Introduction* (4 days/$2,076), *Configuring Cisco Routers: Advanced Hands-on Workshop* (4 days/$2,076), *Internet and System Security: Attacks and Countermeasures* (4 days/$2,076), *Hands-on TCP/IP Internetworking on Windows NT* (4 days/$2,076), *UNIX and Windows NT Integration: Hands-on* (4 days/$2,076), *Deploying Internet and Intranet Firewalls: Hands-on* (4 days/$2,076).

Course costs may vary depending on whether you take them all within 1 year, and other factors.

Continuing Requirements:

Perks:

✐ certificate

Online Resources:

The Web page for this certification is **www.learningtree.com/cn/certific/781.htm**. From here you can view detailed course outlines.

Offline Resources:

Course materials are provided at each course.

Wide Area Networks Certified Professional

Date Initiated: **# Granted:**   **Fees:** $10,099–
                                                                         $10,499

Initial Requirements:

You must successfully complete four core courses ($8,423), one elective course ($1,676–$2,076) and their associated examinations. The core courses are: *Introduction to Datacomm and Networks* (4 days/$2,595), *Utilizing Frame Relay Networks* (3 days/$1,676), *Hands-on Wide Area Network Troubleshooting* (4 days/$2,076), and *High-Speed Wide Area Networks* (4 days/$2,076). Electives include: *Deploying T1 and T3 Services* (3 days/$1,676), *Wide Area Networking and Telecommunications* (4 days/$2,076), *Implementing ATM* (3 days/$1,676) *Mobile Communications and Wireless Networks* (4 days/$2,076), *Introduction to Internetworking: Bridges, Switches and Routers* (4 days/$2,076), *Hands-on Introduction to TCP/IP* (4 days/$2,076), *Implementing ISDN Data Networks: Hands-on* (4 days/$2,076), *Cisco Routers: A Comprehensive Hands-on Introduction* (4 days/$2,076), *Internet and System Security: Attacks and Counter-measures* (4 days/$2,076), *Hands-on SNMP: From Workgroup to Enterprise Networks* (4 days/$1995).

Course costs may vary depending on whether you take them all within 1 year, and other factors.

Continuing Requirements:

Perks:

    🖉 certificate

Online Resources:

The Web page for this certification is **www.learningtree.com/ cn/certific/780.htm**. From here you can view detailed course outlines.

Offline Resources:

Course materials are provided at each course.

Local Area Network Certified Professional

Date Initiated: **# Granted:**   **Fees:** $10,899–
                                                                    $11,219

Initial Requirements:

You must successfully complete four core courses ($8,823), one elective course ($2,076–$2,396) and their associated examinations. The core courses are: *Local Area Networks: Implementation and Configuration* (4 days/$2,595), *Hands-on High-Performance Ethernet: Switched, Fast and Traditional* (4 days/$2,076), *Hands-on LAN Troubleshooting* (4 days/$2,076), and *Fast LAN Technologies* (4 days/$2,076). Electives include: *Designing and Implementing High-Performance Cabling Systems* (4 days/$2,076), *Hands-on PC Networking* (4 days/$2,076), *Windows 95 Support and Networking: Hands-on* (5 Days/$2,396), *Hands-on Introduction to TCP/IP* (4 days/$2,076), *Hands-on Internetworking With TCP/IP* (4 days/$2,076), *Introduction to Internetworking: Bridges, Switches and Routers* (4 Days/$2,076), *Hands-on IntranetWare: NetWare 4.x Administration* (5 Days/$2,396), *Windows 95/NT/3.11 Multiplatform Networking: Hands-on* (4 days/$2,076), *NetWare to Windows NT Integration and Migration: Hands-on* (4 days/$2,076), *Cisco Routers: A Comprehensive Hands-on Introduction* (4 days/$2,076).

Course costs may vary depending on whether you take them all within 1 year, and other factors.

Continuing Requirements:

Perks:

  ✎ certificate

Online Resources:

The Web page for this certification is **www.learningtree.com/cn/certific/758.htm.** From here you can view detailed course outlines.

Offline Resources:

Course materials are provided at each course.

System and Network Security Certified Professional

Date Initiated: **# Granted:**   **Fees:** $11,219–
                                                                    $11,539

Initial Requirements:

You must successfully complete four core courses ($9,143), one elective course ($2,076–$2,396) and their associated examinations. The core courses are: *Internet and System Security: Attacks and Counter-measures* (4 days/$2,595), *Implementing Windows NT Security: Hands-on* (5 Days/$2,396), *UNIX System and Network Security: Hands-on* (4 days/$2,076), and *Deploying Internet and Intranet Firewalls: Hands-on* (4 days/$2,076). Electives include: *Windows 95 Support and Networking: Hands-on* (5 Days/$2,396), *Hands-on Microsoft Exchange 5* (4 days/$2,076), *Lotus Notes and Domino System Administration: Hands-on* (4 days/$2,076), *Hands-on Microsoft Systems Management Server* (4 days/$2,076), *Hands-on IntranetWare: Net-Ware 4.x Administration* (5 Days/$2,396), *UNIX: A Hands-on Introduction* (4 days/$2,076), *UNIX Server Administration: Hands-on* (4 days/$2,076), *Data Network Design and Performance Optimization* (4 days/$2,076), *Windows NT 4 Workstation and Server: Hands-on* (5 days/$2,396), *Developing a Web Site: Hands-on* (4 days/ $2,076).

Course costs may vary depending on whether you take them all within 1 year, and other factors.

Continuing Requirements:

Perks:

✐ certificate

Online Resources:

The Web page for this certification is **www.learningtree.com/cn/certific/768.htm**. From here you can view detailed course outlines.

Offline Resources:

Course materials are provided at each course.

Lotus Notes Domino Certified Professional

For individuals who implement, administer, and supporting Notes applications and Domino Web sites.

Date Initiated: late 1997   **# Granted:**   **Fees:** $10,899–
                                                                      $11,219

Initial Requirements:

You must successfully complete four core courses ($8,823), one elective course ($2,076-$2,396) and their associated exams. Core courses are: *Lotus Notes and Domino: A Comprehensive Hands-On Introduction* (4 days/$2,595), *Lotus Notes Applications Development: Hands-On* (4 days/$2,076), *Lotus Notes and Domino System Administration: Hands-On* (4 days/$2,076), and *Lotus Domino Web Site Development: Hands-On* (4 days/$2,076). Electives include: *Developing a Web Site: Hands-On* (4 days/$2,076), *Internet and System Security: Attacks and Countermeasures* (4 days/$2,076), *Deploying Internet and Intranet Firewalls: Hands-On* (4 days/$2,076), *Hands-On Java Programming* (4 days/$2,076), *Java for Enterprise Systems Development: Hands-On* (4 days/$2,076), *Windows NT 4 Workstation and Server: Hands-On* (5 days/$2,396), *Hands-On TCP/IP Internetworking on Windows NT* (4 days/$2,076), *Hands-On Internetworking With TCP/IP* (4 days/$2,076), *Introduction to Client/Server Computing* (4 days/$2,076), and *Local Area Networks: Implementation and Configuration* (4 days/$2,076).

Continuing Requirements:

Perks:

✐   certificate

Online Resources:

Offline Resources:

Java Programming Certified Professional

Date Initiated: **# Granted:**   **Fees:** $10,899–
                                                                      $11,219

Initial Requirements:

You must successfully complete three core courses ($6,747), two elective course ($4,152–$4,472) and their associated examinations. The core courses are: *Hands-on Java Programming* (4 days/$2,595), *Hands-on Advanced Java Programming* (4 days/$2,076), and *Java for Multimedia Applications Development: Hands-on* (4 days/$2,076). Electives include: *C++ for Non-C Programmers* (4 days/$2,076), *C++ Object-Oriented Programming* (4 days/$2,076), *Introduction to Programming* (4 days/$2,076), *Visual J++ Workshop* (4 days/$1995), *Perl Programming* (4 days/$2,076), *Object-Oriented Analysis and Design* (5 days/$2315), *Internet and System Security* (4 days/$2,076), *Internet/Intranet for Business Applications* (4 days/$2,076), *Developing a Web Site* (5 days/$2,396), *Designing an Intranet* (4 days/$2,076).

Course costs may vary depending on whether you take them all within 1 year, and other factors.

Continuing Requirements:

Perks:
- certificate

Online Resources:
The Web page for this certification is **www.learningtree.com/cn/ certific/772.htm**. From here you can view detailed course outlines.

Offline Resources:
Course materials are provided at each course.

SQL Server DBA Certified Professional

This certification is for database administrators (DBAs) and others with database administration responsibilities who are working in a SQL Server environment.

Date Initiated: 1997   **# Granted:**   **Fees: $11,619–$11,939**

Initial Requirements:
You must successfully complete four core courses ($9,543), one elective course ($2,076–$2,396) and their associated examinations. The core courses are: *Windows NT 4 Workstation and Server: Hands-on* (5 days/$2,995), *Microsoft SQL Server: A Comprehensive Hands-on Introduction* (4 days/$2,076), *Hands-on Microsoft SQL Server System Administration* (5 days/$2,396), *Optimizing SQL Server Database and Application Performance: Hands-on* (4 days/$2,076). *Elective options include: Developing SQL Server Applications with VB 5* (4 days/$2,076) *Relational Databases* (4 days/$2,076) *Visual Basic 5 & ActiveX for Enterprise Applications* (5 days/$2,396), *Windows NT*

Optimization and Troubleshooting (5 days/$2,396), *Microsoft Internet Information Server* (4 days/$2,076), *Microsoft Systems Management Server* (4 days/$2,076), *Microsoft Access for Database Applications* (4 days/$2,076), *Client / Server Application Development* (4 days/ $2,076), *Visual Basic 5 for Business Solutions* (4 days/$2,076), *Microsoft Access Programming* (4 days/$2,076).

Course costs may vary depending on whether you take them all within 1 year, and other factors.

Continuing Requirements:

Perks:
✎ certificate

Online Resources:
The Web page for this certification is **www.learningtree.com/cn/ certific/726.htm.** From here you can view detailed course outlines.

Offline Resources:
Course materials are provided at each course.

C++ Object-Oriented Programming Certified Professional

Date Initiated: **# Granted:**   **Fees:** $11,219–
                                                                                   $11,539

Initial Requirements:
You must successfully complete four core courses ($9,143), one elective course ($2,076–$2,396) and their associated examinations. The core courses are: *Hands-on Introduction to C++ for Non-C Programmers* (4 days/$2,595), *Object-Oriented Analysis and Design* (5 days/ $2,396), *C++ Hands-on Object-Oriented Programming* (4 days/ $2,076), and *Hands-on Advanced C++ Programming* (4 days/$2,076). Electives include: *Introduction to Programming: Hands-on* (4 days/$2,076), *Introduction to Object Technology* (4 days/$2,076), *Hands-on C Programming* (4 days/$1995), *Hands-on Java Programming* (4 days/$2,076), *Java for C++ Programmers: Hands-on* (4 days/ $2,076), *Java for Enterprise Systems Development: Hands-on* (4 days/ $2,076), *Hands-on Visual C++: Windows Programming With MFC for C Programmers* (5 Days/$2,396), *Windows Programming With Visual C++ and MFC for C++ Programmers: Hands-on* (4 days/$2,076), *Pro-*

gramming ActiveX With Microsoft Foundation Classes: Hands-on (4 days/$2,076), *COM and ActiveX Programming With C++: Hands-on* (4 days/$2,076).

Course costs may vary depending on whether you take them all within 1 year, and other factors.

Continuing Requirements:

Perks:

    ✎ certificate

Online Resources:

The Web page for this certification is **www.learningtree.com/cn/ certific/797.htm**. From here you can view detailed course outlines.

Offline Resources:

Course materials are provided at each course.

C and C++ Programming Certified Professional

Date Initiated: 1997   **# Granted:**   **Fees:** $10,899– $11,219

Initial Requirements:

You must successfully complete four core courses ($8,823), one elective course ($2,076–$2,396) and their associated examinations. The core courses are: *Hands-on C Programming* (4 days/$2,595), *C++ Hands-on Object-Oriented Programming* (4 days/$2,076), *Hands-on C Advanced Programming: Techniques and Data Structures* (4 days/ $2,076), and *Hands-on Advanced C++ Programming* (4 days/$2,076). Electives include: *Introduction to Programming: Hands-on* (4 days/$2,076), *Win32 GUI Programming: Hands-on* (4 days/$2,076), *Win32 Systems and Network Programming: Hands-on* (4 days/$2,076), *Hands-on Visual C++: Windows Programming With MFC for C Programmers* (5 days/$2,396), *Windows Programming With Visual C++ and MFC for C++ Programmers: Hands-on* (4 days/$2,076), *Hands-on Java Programming* (4 days/$2,076), *Java for C++ Programmers: Hands-on* (4 days/$2,076), *Object-Oriented Analysis and Design* (5 Days/$2,396), *Hands-on X Window System Programming* (4 days/$2,076), *Hands-on UNIX Programming* (4 days/ $2,076).

Course costs may vary depending on whether you take them all within 1 year, and other factors.

Continuing Requirements:

Perks:
    ✐ certificate

Online Resources:
The Web page for this certification is **www.learningtree.com/cn/ certific/763.htm**. From here you can view detailed course outlines.

Offline Resources:
Course materials are provided at each course.

Windows Programming Certified Professional

Date Initiated: 1997   **# Granted:**   **Fees:** $11,219–$11,539

Initial Requirements:
You must successfully complete four core courses ($9,143), one elective course ($2,076–$2,396) and their associated examinations. The core courses are: *Win32 GUI Programming: Hands-on* (4 days/ $2,595), *Win32 Systems and Network Programming: Hands-on* (4 days/$2,076), *Hands-on Visual C++: Windows Programming With MFC for C Programmers* (5 days/$2,396), and *Programming ActiveX With Microsoft Foundation Classes: Hands-on* (4 days/ $2,076). Electives include: *Windows Programming With Visual C++ and MFC for C++ Programmers: Hands-on* (4 days/$2,076), *COM and ActiveX Programming With C++: Hands-on* (4 days/$2,076), *C++ Hands-on Object-Oriented Programming* (4 days/$2,076), *Windows Open Services Architecture* (4 days/$2,076), *Porting Applications from UNIX to Windows NT: Hands-on* (4 days/$2,076), *Hands-on TCP/IP Programming* (4 days/$2,076), *Hands-on Visual J++* (4 days/$2,076), *Visual Basic 5 and ActiveX for Enterprise Applications: Hands-on* (5 days /$2,396), *Introduction to Visual InterDev: Hands-on* (4 days/ $2,076), *Visual InterDev for Enterprise Applications: Hands-on* (4 days/ $2,076).

Course costs may vary depending on whether you take them all within 1 year, and other factors.

Continuing Requirements:

Perks:

✎ certificate

Online Resources:

The Web page for this certification is **www.learningtree.com/cn/ certific/798.htm**. From here you can view detailed course outlines.

Offline Resources:

Course materials are provided at each course.

Windows Application Development Certified Professional

For individuals who develop applications for the Windows environment.

Date Initiated: **# Granted:**   **Fees:** $11,219

Initial Requirements:

You must successfully complete four core courses ($9,143), one elective course($2,076) and their associated examinations. The core courses are: *Hands-on Visual Basic 5* (4 days/$2,595), *Visual Basic 5 and ActiveX for Enterprise Applications: Hands-on* (5 Days/$2,396), *Microsoft Access Programming: Hands-on* (4 days/$2,076), and *Building Office 97 Intranet Applications: Hands-on* (4 days/$2,076). Electives include: *Win32 GUI Programming: Hands-on* (4 days/ $2,076), *Win32 Systems and Network Programming: Hands-on* (4 days/$2,076), *Hands-on Visual C++: Windows Programming With MFC for C Programmers* (Course 301—5 Days), *Programming ActiveX With Microsoft Foundation Classes: Hands-on* (4 days/ $2,076), *Introduction to Visual InterDev: Hands-on* (4 days/$19,95), *Visual InterDev for Enterprise Applications: Hands-on* (4 days/ $2,076), *Developing SQL Server Applications With Visual Basic 5: Hands-on* (4 days/$2,076), *Microsoft Exchange Applications Development: Hands-on* (4 days/$2,076), *Windows Open Services Architecture* (4 days/$2,076), *Hands-on Visual J++* (4 days/$2,076).

Course costs may vary depending on whether you take them all within 1 year, and other factors.

Continuing Requirements:

Perks:
    ✎ certificate

Online Resources:
The Web page for this certification is **www.learningtree.com/cn/ certific/776.htm.** From here you can view detailed course outlines.

Offline Resources:
Course materials are provided at each course.

Microsoft BackOffice Certified Professional

This certification is for individuals who implement and support the BackOffice family of products.

Date Initiated: **# Granted:**   **Fees:** $11,219

Initial Requirements:
You must successfully complete four core courses ($9,223), one elective course ($2,076) and their associated examinations. The core courses are: *Windows NT4 Workstation and Server* (5 Days/$2,995), *Hands-on Microsoft Exchange* (4 days/$2,076), *Microsoft SQL Server: A Comprehensive Hands-on Introduction* (4 days/$2,076), and *Hands-on Microsoft Systems Management Server* (4 days/$2,076). Electives include: *Microsoft SQL Server System Administration* (4 days/$2,076), *Windows NT Optimization and Troubleshooting* (5 days/$2,396), *TCP/IP Internetworking on Windows NT* (4 days/ $2,076), *Windows NT Security* (4 days/$2,076), *Implementing SNA Server 3* (4 days/$2,076), *Exchange Server Administration* (4 days/ $2,076), *Microsoft Internet Information Server* (4 days/$2,076), *Developing SQL Server System Administration* (4 days/$2,076), *Optimizing SQL Server Performance* (4 days/$2,076), *Visual Basic 4 for Enterprise Applications* (4 days/$2,076).

Course costs may vary depending on whether you take them all within 1 year, and other factors.

Continuing Requirements:

Perks:

    ✍ certificate

Online Resources:

The Web page for this certification is **www.learningtree.com/cn/ certific/757.htm**. From here you can view detailed course outlines.

Offline Resources:

Course materials are provided at each course.

Windows NT Systems and Networks Certified Professional

This is for individuals who implement and integrate the Windows NT family of desktop and network operating systems.

Date Initiated:	**# Granted:**	**Fees:** $11,939– $12,259

Initial Requirements:

You must successfully complete four core courses ($9,863), one elective course ($2,076–$2,396) and their associated examinations. The core courses are: *Windows NT 4 Workstation and Server: Hands-on* (5 Days/$2,995), *Windows NT Optimization and Troubleshooting: Hands-on* (5 Days/$2,396), *Hands-on TCP/IP Internetworking on Windows NT* (4 days/$2,076), and *Implementing Windows NT Security: Hands-on* (5 Days/$2,396). Electives include: *Windows 95 Support and Networking: Hands-on* (5 Days/$2,396), *Hands-on Microsoft Systems Management Server* (4 days/$2,076), *Microsoft SQL Server : A Comprehensive Hands-on Introduction* (4 days/$2,076), *Hands-on Microsoft Exchange 5* (4 days/$2,076), *Microsoft Exchange 5 Server Administration: Hands-on* (4 days/$2,076), *Implementing Microsoft SNA Server 3: Hands-on* (4 days/$2,076), *Hands-on Microsoft Internet Information Server* (4 days/$2,076), *Windows 95/NT/3.11 Multiplatform Networking: Hands-on* (4 days/$2,076), *UNIX and Windows NT Integration: Hands-on* (4 days/$2,076), *NetWare to Windows NT Integration and Migration: Hands-on* (4 days/$2,076).

Course costs may vary depending on whether you take them all within 1 year, and other factors.

Continuing Requirements:

Perks:

✐ certificate

Online Resources:

The Web page for this certification is **www.learningtree.com/cn/certific/756.htm.** From here you can view detailed course outlines.

Offline Resources:

Course materials are provided at each course.

UNIX Programming Certified Professional

This is for individuals who develop and maintain programs for UNIX based systems.

Date Initiated: **# Granted:**   **Fees:** $10,899

Initial Requirements:

You must successfully complete four core courses (8,823), one elective course ($2,076) and their associated examinations. The core courses are: *UNIX Hands-on Workshop* (4 days/$2,595), *C Programming Hands-on Workshop* (4 days/$2,076), *Hands-on UNIX Programming* (4 days/$2,076), *Hands-on TCP/IP Programming* (4 days/$2,076). Electives include: *Introduction to Programming* (4 days/$2,076), *UNIX Tools and Utilities* (4 days/$2,076), *X Window System Programming* (4 days/$2,076), *C Advanced Programming* (4 days/$2,076), *KornShell Programming* (4 days/$2,076), *UNIX Workstation Administration* (4 days/$2,076), *UNIX Server Administration* (4 days/$2,076), *Perl Programming* (4 days/$2,076), *Porting from UNIX to Windows NT* (4 days/$2,076), *UNIX System and Network Security* (4 days/ $2,076).

Course costs may vary depending on whether you take them all within 1 year, and other factors.

Continuing Requirements:

Perks:

✐ certificate

Online Resources:

The Web page for this certification is **www.learningtree.com/cn/certific/733.htm.** From here you can view detailed course outlines.

Offline Resources:

Course materials are provided at each course.

UNIX Systems Certified Professional

This certification program is for individuals involved in the day-to-day operation of UNIX-based systems and networks.

Date Initiated: **# Granted:**   **Fees:** $10,899

Initial Requirements:

You must successfully complete four core courses ($8,823), one elective course ($2,076) and their associated examinations. The core courses are: *UNIX Hands-on Workshop* (4 days/$2,595), *UNIX Workstation Administration: Hands-on* (4 days/$2,076), *UNIX Server Administration: Hands-on* (4 days/$2,076), *UNIX Tools and Utilities: Hands-on Workshop* (4 days/$2,076). Electives include: *UNIX Programming* (4 days/$2,076), *TCP/IP Programming* (4 days/$2,076), *KornShell Programming* (4 days/$2,076), *Introduction to TCP/IP* (4 days/$2,076), *Internetworking With TCP/IP* (4 days/$2,076), *UNIX and Windows NT Integration* (4 days/$2,076), *Internet and System Security* (4 days/$2,076), *C Programming Workshop* (4 days/$2,076), *UNIX System and Network Security* (4 days/$2,076), *Deploying Internet and Intranet Firewalls* (4 days/$2,076).

Course costs may vary depending on whether you take them all within 1 year, and other factors.

Continuing Requirements:

Perks:

🖍 certificate

Online Resources:

The Web page for this certification is **www.learningtree.com/cn/certific/735.htm**. From here you can view detailed course outlines.

Offline Resources:

Course materials are provided at each course.

Oracle7 Application Development Certified Professional

This certification program is for application developers, analysts, designers and others who will be developing applications within an Oracle7 environment.

Date Initiated: **# Granted:**   **Fees:** $9,299

Initial Requirements:

You must successfully complete four core courses ($7,223), one elective course ($2,076) and their associated examinations. The core courses are: *Oracle7: A Comprehensive Hands-on Introduction* (5 days/$2,995), *Oracle7 for Application Developers: Hands-on* (3 days/ $1,676), *Tuning Oracle7 Applications: Hands-on* (2 days/$1,276), *Complex SQL Queries: Hands-on* (2 days/$1,276). Electives include: *Visual C++: Windows Programming With MFC* (4 days/$2,076), *Visual Basic 4* (4 days/$2,076), *Microsoft Access* (4 days/$2,076), *Power-Builder* (4 days/ $2,076), *Client/Server Application Development* (4 days/$2,076), *Building a Data Warehouse* (4 days/$2,076), *Power-Builder 5 and Oracle7* (4 days/$2,076), *Distributing Data in Client/ Server Systems* (4 days/$2,076), *Oracle Developer/2000* (4 days/ $2,076), *Building Oracle WebServer Applications* (4 days/$2,076).

Course costs may vary depending on whether you take them all within 1 year, and other factors.

Continuing Requirements:

Perks:

   ✐ certificate

Online Resources:

The Web page for this certification is **www.learningtree.com/cn/ certific/730.htm.** From here you can view detailed course outlines.

Offline Resources:

Course materials are provided at each course.

Oracle7 DBA Certified Professional

Date Initiated: **# Granted:**   **Fees:** $9,939–
$11,859

Initial Requirements:
You must successfully complete three core courses ($7,387), two elective courses ($2,552–$4,472) and their associated examinations. The core courses are: *Relational Databases: Design, Tools and Techniques* (4 days/$2,595), *Oracle7: A Comprehensive Hands-on Introduction* (5 days/$2,396), *Oracle7 for Database Administrators: Hands-on* (5 days/$2,396). Electives include: *Tuning Oracle7 Applications* (2 days/ $1,276), *Complex SQL Queries* (2 days/$1,276), *UNIX Course* (4 days/$2,076), *Distributing Data in Client / Server Systems* (4 days/ $2,076), *Building a Data Warehouse* (4 days/$2,076), *PowerBuilder 5 and Oracle7* (4 days/$2,076), *Windows NT 4.0* (5 days/$2,396).

Course costs may vary depending on whether you take them all within 1 year, and other factors.

Continuing Requirements:

Perks:
    ✐ certificate

Online Resources:
The Web page for this certification is **www.learningtree.com/cn/ certific/731.htm.** From here you can view detailed course outlines.

Offline Resources:
Course materials are provided at each course.

Internet/Intranet Certified Professional

Date Initiated: **# Granted:**   **Fees:** $10,899

Initial Requirements:
You must successfully complete four core courses ($8,823), one elective course ($2,076) and their associated examinations. The core courses are: *Introduction to the Internet and Intranets for Business: Hands-on* (4 days/$2,595), *Developing a Web Site: Hands-on* (4 days/ $2,076), *Designing an Intranet: Hands-on* (4 days/$2,076), and *Internet and System Security: Attacks and Countermeasures* (4

days/$2,076). Electives include: *Hands-on Microsoft Internet Information Server* (4 days/$2,076), *Netscape Servers for Intranet Development: Hands-on* (4 days/$2,076), *Lotus Domino Web Site Development: Hands-on* (4 days/$2,076), *Building Oracle WebServer Applications: Hands-on* (4 days/$2,076), *Building Office 97 Intranet Applications: Hands-on* (4 days/ $2,076), *Hands-on Java Programming* (4 days/$2,076), *Perl Programming: Hands-on* (4 days/$2,076), *Deploying Internet and Intranet Firewalls: Hands-on* (4 days/ $2,076), *Hands-on Introduction to TCP/IP* (4 days/$2,076), *Implementing ISDN Data Networks: Hands-on* (4 days/$2,076).

Course costs may vary depending on whether you take them all within 1 year, and other factors.

Continuing Requirements:

Perks:
✐ certificate

Online Resources:
The Web page for this certification is **www.learningtree.com/cn/ certific/754.htm**. From here you can view detailed course outlines.

Offline Resources:
Course materials are provided at each course.

Sponsor:

Lotus Development Corporation—Education and Certification
400 Riverpark Drive
North Reading, MA 01864 USA
Phone: 800-346-6409   **Fax:**
Email:
URL: www.lotus.com/education.nsf

Certified Lotus Professional (CLP)—Application Developer

This certification is for individuals responsible for building multiple database Notes applications that automate workflow between several departments. Principle Application Developer level certifies enterprise-wide level expertise.

Date Initiated: 1995   **# Granted: 2000 (all CLP)**   **Fees:** $270/$360

Initial Requirements:

Must pass 3 Lotus Notes Release 4 exams for application developer level: Application Development 1 ($90), Systems Administration 1 ($90), Application Development 2 ($90). Principle application developer level requires an additional elective exam, such as LotusScript in Notes for Advanced Developers ($90).

Continuing Requirements:

Certifications are release specific. Upgrades with new releases are encouraged.

Perks:

- certificate
- use of logo
- wallet id card
- lapel pin
- subscription to Knowledge Base
- access to private Web area
- free 5 pack of support incidents + discount on additional incidents
- subscription to CLiPpings newsletter
- Lotus and IBM conference, exam, and special event discounts and free invitations
- beta participation
- training and education discounts on continuing education courses and products

Online Resources:

Lotus exam guides and practice tests are available for download from the Web site.

Offline Resources:

Lotus exam guides are available on the Web site or by calling 800-346-6409. Third party preparation software is available through Self Test Software. Lotus offers CBT courses as well through CBT Systems 800-929-9050. Training courses are also available through authorized vendors, and cost between $1,500–$3,500. The *Lotus Notes Certification Exam Guide: Application Development and System Administration* from McGraw-Hill is an excellent resource.

Certified Lotus Professional (CLP)—System Administrator

This certification is for individuals experienced in Notes server install and configuration, server monitoring and statistics, server maintenance and operations, certification, and managing multiple Notes domains and controlling Notes communications. The principal systems administrator level requires additional expertise in integrating other communication product technology.

Date Initiated: 1995   **# Granted:** 2000 (all CLP)   **Fees:** $270/$360

Initial Requirements:

Must pass 3 Lotus Notes Release 4 exams for system administrator level: Application Development 1 ($90), Systems Administration 1 ($90), System Administration 2 ($90). Principle system administrator level requires an additional elective exam, such as cc: Mail System Administration ($90).

Continuing Requirements:

Certifications are release specific. Upgrades with new releases are encouraged.

Perks:

- certificate
- use of logo
- wallet id card
- lapel pin
- subscription to Knowledge Base
- access to private Web area
- free 5 pack of support incidents + discount on additional incidents
- subscription to CLiPpings newsletter

- Lotus and IBM conference, exam, and special event discounts and free invitations
- beta participation
- training and education discounts on continuing education courses and products

Online Resources:

Lotus exam guides and practice tests are available for download from the Web site.

Offline Resources:

Lotus exam guides are available on the Web site or by calling 800-346-6409. Third party preparation software is available through Self Test Software. Lotus offers CBT courses as well through CBT Systems 800-929-9050. Training courses are also available through authorized vendors, and cost between $1,500–$3,500.

Certified Lotus Professional (CLP)— cc:Mail System Administrator

This certification is for individuals who are responsible for the organization-wide deployment, installation, and configuration of cc:Mail across multiple networks and platforms.

Date Initiated: 1995   **# Granted:** 2000 (all CLP)   **Fees:** $180

Initial Requirements:

Must pass 2 cc:Mail exams: System Administration 1 ($90) and Systems Administration 2 ($90).

Continuing Requirements:

Certifications are release specific. Upgrades with new releases are encouraged.

Perks:

- certificate
- use of logo
- wallet id card
- lapel pin
- subscription to Knowledge Base
- access to private Web area
- free 5 pack of support incidents + discount on additional incidents
- subscription to CLiPpings newsletter
- Lotus and IBM conference, exam, and special event discounts and free invitations

- beta participation
- training and education discounts on continuing education courses and products

Online Resources:

Lotus exam guides and practice tests are available for download from the Web site.

Offline Resources:

Lotus exam guides are available on the Web site or by calling 800-346-6409. Third party preparation software is available through Self Test Software. Lotus offers CBT courses as well through CBT Systems 800-929-9050. Training courses are also available through authorized vendors, and cost between $1,500–$3,500.

Certified Lotus Specialist (CLS)—Domino Web Development & Administration

This certification is for individuals responsible for developing and deploying Web sites using Domino 4.5.

Date Initiated: 7/1997   **# Granted:** 4,000 (all CLS)   **Fees:** $90

Initial Requirements:

Must pass the Domino Web Development exam ($90).

Continuing Requirements:

Certifications are release specific. Upgrades with new releases are encouraged.

Perks:

- certificate
- use of logo
- subscription to Knowledge Base
- access to private Web area
- subscription to CLiPpings newsletter
- Lotus and IBM conference, exam, and special event discounts and free invitations
- training and education discounts on continuing education courses and products

Online Resources:

Lotus exam guides and practice tests are available for download from the Web site.

Offline Resources:

Lotus exam guides are available on the Web site or by calling 800-346-6409. Third party preparation software is available through Self Test Software. Lotus offers CBT courses as well through CBT Systems 800-929-9050. Training courses are also available through authorized vendors, and cost between $100–$700.

Certified Lotus Specialist (CLS)—SmartSuite Developer

This certification is for individuals responsible for coding, managing, and troubleshooting LotusScript Solutions for 1-2-3 applications.

Date Initiated: 7/1997   **# Granted:** 4,000 (all CLS)   **Fees:** $90

Initial Requirements:

Must pass the LotusScript Development in 1-2-3 exam ($90).

Continuing Requirements:

Certifications are release specific. Upgrades with new releases are encouraged.

Perks:

- certificate
- use of logo
- subscription to Knowledge Base
- access to private Web area
- subscription to CLiPpings newsletter
- Lotus and IBM conference, exam, and special event discounts and free invitations
- training and education discounts on continuing education courses and products

Online Resources:

Lotus exam guides and practice tests are available for download from the Web site.

Offline Resources:

Lotus exam guides are available on the Web site or by calling 800-346-6409. Third party preparation software is available through Self Test Software. Lotus offers CBT courses as well through CBT Systems 800-929-9050. Training courses are also available through authorized vendors, and cost between $100–$700.

Certified Lotus Specialist (CLS)—Notes R4 Developer

This certification is for individuals responsible for building a single Notes database application.

Date Initiated: 7/1997   **# Granted:** 4,000 (all CLS)   **Fees:** $90

Initial Requirements:

Must pass the Notes R4 Application Development 1 exam ($90).

Continuing Requirements:

Certifications are release specific. Upgrades with new releases are encouraged.

Perks:

- certificate
- use of logo
- subscription to Knowledge Base
- access to private Web area
- subscription to CLiPpings newsletter
- Lotus and IBM conference, exam, and special event discounts and free invitations
- training and education discounts on continuing education courses and products

Online Resources:

Lotus exam guides and practice tests are available for download from the Web site.

Offline Resources:

Lotus exam guides are available on the Web site or by calling 800-346-6409. Third party preparation software is available through Self Test Software. Lotus offers CBT courses as well through CBT Systems 800-929-9050. Training courses are also available through authorized vendors, and cost between $100–$700.

Certified Lotus Specialist (CLS)— cc:Mail R6 System Administrator

This certification is for individuals who are responsible for small site deployment, installation, and configuration of cc:Mail across multiple networks and platforms.

Date Initiated: 7/1997   **# Granted:** 4,000 (all CLS)   **Fees:** $90

Initial Requirements:

Must pass the cc:Mail R6 System Administration 1 exam ($90).

Continuing Requirements:
Certifications are release specific. Upgrades with new releases are encouraged.

Perks:
- certificate
- use of logo
- subscription to Knowledge Base
- access to private Web area
- subscription to CLiPpings newsletter
- Lotus and IBM conference, exam, and special event discounts and free invitations
- training and education discounts on continuing education courses and products

Online Resources:
Lotus exam guides and practice tests are available for download from the Web site.

Offline Resources:
Lotus exam guides are available on the Web site or by calling 800-346-6409. Third party preparation software is available through Self Test Software. Lotus offers CBT courses as well through CBT Systems 800-929-9050. Training courses are also available through authorized vendors, and cost between $100–$700.

Certified Lotus Specialist (CLS)—Notes R4 System Administrator

This certification is for individuals who set up, operating, and maintain Notes/Domino servers and client workstations.

Date Initiated: 7/1997   **# Granted:** 4,000 (all CLS)   **Fees:** $90

Initial Requirements:
Must pass the Notes R4 System Administration 1 exam ($90).

Continuing Requirements:
Certifications are release specific. Upgrades with new releases are encouraged.

Perks:
- certificate
- use of logo
- subscription to Knowledge Base
- access to private Web area

- subscription to CLiPpings newsletter
- Lotus and IBM conference, exam, and special event discounts and free invitations
- training and education discounts on continuing education courses and products

Online Resources:

Lotus exam guides and practice tests are available for download from the Web site.

Offline Resources:

Lotus exam guides are available on the Web site or by calling 800-346-6409. Third party preparation software is available through Self Test Software. Lotus offers CBT courses as well through CBT Systems 800-929-9050. Training courses are also available through authorized vendors, and cost between $100–$700.

Sponsor:

McAfee Associates
Mcafee University, 4099 McEwen
Dallas, TX 75244 USA
Phone: 972-855-2634   **Fax:** 972-855-2716
Email: profserv@mail.mcafee.com
URL: www.mcafee.com/university/cert_.asp

McAfee Certified Anti-Virus Administrator—Workstation (MCAVA)

For individuals who manage McAfee products, including VirusShield DOS, and VirusScan (DOS, Win 3.x, Wind95, NT), on workstations.

Date Initiated: 1995   **# Granted:**   **Fees:** $85

Initial Requirements:
Must pass associated test ($85), which you download and take at your own site, and mail in once you obtain a passing (80%) score.

Continuing Requirements:
Must recertify with new releases.

Perks:
- 10% discount on 1 McAfee training class
- 15% discount on purchase of Enterprise Support service
- 50% discount on any 1 course curricula
- 3 free calls to Enterprise Support

Online Resources:
Courseware can be purchased online from the McAfee University Web site **http://www.mcafee.com/university/university.asp**.

Offline Resources:
Study guides and classroom training are available from McAfee University. Call 800-972-2634.

McAfee Certified Anti-Virus Administrator—LAN (MCAVA)

For individuals who manage McAfee products, including VirusShield DOS, and VirusScan (DOS, Win 3.x, Wind95, NT), and NetShield, in a LAN environment.

Date Initiated: 1995   **# Granted:**   **Fees:** $85

Initial Requirements:

Recommended that you hold NetWare or NT server certification. Must pass associated test ($85), which you download and take at your own site, and mail in once you obtain a passing (80%) score.

Continuing Requirements:

Must recertify with new releases.

Perks:
- 10% discount on 1 McAfee training class
- 15% discount on purchase of Enterprise Support service
- 50% discount on any 1 course curricula
- 3 free calls to Enterprise Support

Online Resources:

Courseware can be purchased online from the McAfee University Web site **http://www.mcafee.com/university/university.asp**.

Offline Resources:

Study guides and classroom training are available from McAfee University. Call 800-972-2634.

McAfee Certified Help Desk Administrator—LAN (MCHDA)

For individuals who use McAfee products DP Umbrella, Vycor Web, Orchestrator, Crystal Reports, Casepoint, Rescue in a LAN environment.

Date Initiated: 1995   **# Granted:**   **Fees:** $85

Initial Requirements:

Must pass associated test ($85), which you download and take at your own site, and mail in once you obtain a passing (80%) score. SQL, Sybase, or Oracle certification recommended.

Continuing Requirements:

Must recertify with new releases.

Perks:
- 10% discount on 1 McAfee training class
- 15% discount on purchase of Enterprise Support service

      ✎ 50% discount on any 1 course curricula
      ✎ 3 free calls to Enterprise Support

Online Resources:

Courseware can be purchased online from the McAfee University Web site **http://www.mcafee.com/university/university.asp**.

Offline Resources:

Study guides and classroom training are available from McAfee University. Call 800-972-2634.

McAfee Certified Anti-Virus Administrator— Enterprise (MCAVA)

For individuals who manage McAfee products, including VirusShield DOS, VirusScan (DOS, Win 3.x, Wind95, NT), NetShield (NT, Netware),Group Scan, WebShield, in a network environment.

Date Initiated: 1995   **# Granted:**   **Fees:** $85

Initial Requirements:

Recommended that you hold NetWare or NT server certification and be knowledgeable about Lotus Notes administration. Must pass associated test ($85), which you download and take at your own site, and mail in once you obtain a passing (80%) score.

Continuing Requirements:

Must recertify with new releases.

Perks:

      ✎ 10% discount on 1 McAfee training class
      ✎ 15% discount on purchase of Enterprise Support service
      ✎ 50% discount on any 1 course curricula
      ✎ 3 free calls to Enterprise Support

Online Resources:

Courseware can be purchased online from the McAfee University Web site **http://www.mcafee.com/university/university.asp**.

Offline Resources:

Study guides and classroom training are available from McAfee University. Call 800-972-2634.

McAfee Certified Network Management—Administrator (MCNMA)

For individuals who manage McAfee products on a network.

Date Initiated: 1995   **# Granted:**   **Fees:** $240

Initial Requirements:

Recommended that you hold NetWare or NT server certification. Must pass associated test ($240), which you download and take at your own site, and mail in once you obtain a passing score.

Continuing Requirements:

Must re-certify with new releases.

Perks:

- 10% discount on 1 McAfee training class
- 15% discount on purchase of Enterprise Support service
- 50% discount on any 1 course curricula
- 3 free calls to Enterprise Support

Online Resources:

Courseware can be purchased online from the McAfee University Web site **http://www.mcafee.com/university/university.asp**.

Offline Resources:

Study guides and classroom training are available from McAfee University. Call 800-972-2634.

McAfee Certified Help Desk Administrator–Workstation (MCHDA)

For individuals who use McAfee products DP Umbrella, Vycor Web, Orchestrator, Crystal Reports, Casepoint, Rescue in a workstation environment.

Date Initiated: 1995   **# Granted:**   **Fees:** $85

Initial Requirements:

Must pass associated test ($85), which you download and take at your own site, and mail in once you obtain a passing (80%) score.

Continuing Requirements:

Must re-certify with new releases.

Perks:

- 10% discount on 1 McAfee training class
- 15% discount on purchase of Enterprise Support service

    ✎ 50% discount on any 1 course curricula

    ✎ 3 free calls to Enterprise Support

Online Resources:

Courseware can be purchased online from the McAfee University Web site **http://www.mcafee.com/university/university.asp**.

Offline Resources:

Study guides and classroom training are available from McAfee University. Call 800-972-2634.

Sponsor:

Microsoft Corporation
Redmond, WA USA
Phone: 800-636-7544   **Fax:**
Email:
URL: http://www.mcse.com/tcweb/cert/certif.htm

Microsoft Certified Trainer (MCT)

For individuals who want to be qualified instructionally and certified technically by Microsoft to deliver Microsoft Official Curriculum instructor-led courses for Microsoft Authorized Technical Education Centers.

Date Initiated: **# Granted:** 9,024   **Fees:** $1,135–
                                                                         $3,600

Initial Requirements:

Must pass the Certified Technical Trainer exam ($285/see listing under Chaucey Group) or show instructional skills by showing a Novell or Banyan Trainer Certificate. You must also take a Microsoft Certified Professional course ($850-$2750 -varies widely) through an Authorized Technical Education Center and pass the corresponding exam or exams.

Continuing Requirements:

Perks:

Online Resources:

The MCT home page is: **www.mcse.com/tcweb/cert/mctint.htm**.
   www.mcse.com/tcweb/cert/assessex.htm contains practice tests to help you prepare.
   www.moli.com is the Microsoft Online Institute.
   You can find an authorized training provider by searching the online database at: **www.mcse.com/tcweb/provider/provide. htm**.

Offline Resources:

To request an MCT application kit, call Microsoft at 1-800-688-0496 or use the Microsoft Fax-back Service: phone number 800-727-3351, document number 1000-0310.

Microsoft Certified Solution Developer (MCSD)

For developers who design and develop custom business solutions with Microsoft development tools, technologies and platforms, including Microsoft Office and Microsoft BackOffice.

Date Initiated: **# Granted:** 5,056   **Fees:** $400

Initial Requirements:

Must pass two core technology exams ($200) and two elective exams ($200). The core exams are: Microsoft Windows Operating Systems and Services Architecture I and Microsoft Windows Operating Systems and Services Architecture II. Electives include: Microsoft SQL Server 4.2 Database Implementation, Developing Applications with C++ Using the Microsoft Foundation Class Library, Implementing a Database Design on Microsoft SQL Server 6, Microsoft Visual Basic 3.0 for Windows-Application Development, Microsoft Access 2.0 for Windows-Application Development, Developing Applications with Microsoft Excel 5.0 Using Visual Basic for Applications, Programming in Microsoft Visual FoxPro 3.0 for Windows, Programming with Microsoft Visual Basic 4.0, Microsoft Access for Windows 95 and the Microsoft Access Developer's Toolkit, and Implementing OLE in Microsoft Foundation Class Applications.

Continuing Requirements:

If one of the exams is retired, you will need to pass the replacement exam.

Perks:

- discount on Microsoft Developer Network subscription
- free Ten-pack of Priority Development with Desktop support incidents
- 1 year subscription to the Microsoft Beta Evaluation program
- subscription to Microsoft Certified Professional Magazine
- use of MCSD logos
- access to restricted forum
- certification update newsletter
- invitations to Microsoft conferences, technical training sessions, and special events

Online Resources:

The MCSD home page is: **www.mcse.com/tcweb/cert/mcsd.htm**. **www.mcse.com/tcweb/cert/assessex.htm** contains practice tests to help you prepare.

www.moli.com is the Microsoft Online Institute.

You can find an authorized training provider by searching the online database at: **www.mcse.com/tcweb/provider/provide. htm**.

Offline Resources:

Both Microsoft and many independent vendors offer training products.

Microsoft Certified Product Specialist (MCPS)

For individuals who would like to demonstrate their expertise with a particular Microsoft product.

Date Initiated: 1992   **# Granted:** 106,933   **Fees:** $100

Initial Requirements:

Must pass one operating system exam ($100). Choices are: Implementing and Supporting Microsoft Windows NT Workstation 4.02, Implementing and Supporting Microsoft Windows NT Workstation 3.51, Implementing and Supporting Microsoft Windows NT Server 4.0, Implementing and Supporting Microsoft Windows NT Server 3.5, Microsoft Windows 3.1, Microsoft Windows for Workgroups 3.11-Desktop, Implementing and Supporting Microsoft Windows 95, Microsoft Windows Operating Systems and Services Architecture I, or Microsoft Windows Operating Systems and Services Architecture II.

Continuing Requirements:

If the exam is retired, you will need to pass the replacement exam.

Perks:

- 1 year subscription to Microsoft's TechNet Technical Information Network
- 1 year subscription to the Microsoft Beta Evaluation program
- subscription to Microsoft Certified Professional Magazine
- use of MCPS logos
- access to restricted forum
- certification update newsletter
- invitations to Microsoft conferences, technical training sessions, and special events

Online Resources:

The MCPS home page is: **www.mcse.com/tcweb/cert/mcpsint.htm**.

www.mcse.com/tcweb/cert/assessex.htm contains practice tests to help you prepare.**www.moli.com** is the Microsoft Online Institute.

You can find an authorized training provider by searching the online database at: **www.mcse.com/tcweb/ provider/provide. htm.**

Offline Resources:

Both Microsoft and many independent vendors offer training products.

Microsoft Certified Systems Engineer (MCSE)

For individuals who plan, implement, and support business solutions with Microsoft Windows NT and Microsoft BackOffice.

Date Initiated: **# Granted:** 25,756   **Fees:** $600

Initial Requirements:

Must pass four operating system (core) exams ($400) and two elective exams ($200). There are two tracks: Windows NT 3.51 and Windows NT 4.0.

Exams for 3.51 are: Implementing and Supporting Microsoft Windows NT Server 3.51; Implementing and Supporting Microsoft Windows NT Workstation 3.51; 1 of Microsoft Windows 3.1, Microsoft Windows for Workgroups 3.11-Desktop, Implementing and Supporting Microsoft Windows 95; and 1 of Networking with Microsoft Windows for Workgroups 3.11, Networking with Microsoft Windows 3.1 Networking Essentials.

The 4.0 core exam list is largely similar, with the obvious NT version variations. Electives include: Microsoft SNA Server, Implementing and Supporting Microsoft Systems Management Server 1.0, Microsoft SQL Server 4.2 Database Implementation, Microsoft SQL Server 4.2 Database Administration for Microsoft Windows NT, System Administration for Microsoft SQL Server 6, Implementing a Database Design on Microsoft SQL Server 6, Microsoft Mail for PC Networks 3.2-Enterprise, Internetworking Microsoft TCP/IP on Microsoft Windows NT (3.5-3.51), Internetworking Microsoft TCP/IP on Microsoft Windows NT 4.0, Implementing and Supporting Microsoft Exchange Server 4.0, Implementing and Supporting Microsoft Internet Information Server, and Implementing and Supporting Microsoft Proxy Server 1.0. Individuals already certified by Novell and Banyan may be able to get some exams waived.

Continuing Requirements:

If one of the exams is retired, you will need to pass the replacement exam.

Perks:

- 1 yr subscription to Microsoft's TechNet Technical Information Network
- free Priority Comprehensive support Ten Pack from Microsoft
- 1 yr subscription to the Microsoft Beta Evaluation program
- subscription to Microsoft Certified Professional Magazine
- use of MCSE logos
- access to restricted forum
- certification update newsletter
- invitations to Microsoft conferences, technical training sessions, and special events

Online Resources:

www.mcse.com/tcweb/cert/mcse.htm is Microsoft's MCSE page. From here you can link to exam preparation materials and study guides. **www.mcse.com/tcweb/cert/assessex.htm** contains practice tests to help you prepare, and an NT 4.0 assessment guide. **www.moli.com** is the Microsoft Online Institute.

You can find an authorized training provider by searching the online database at: **www.mcse.com/tcweb/provider/provide.htm**

Offline Resources:

Both Microsoft and many independent vendors offer training products. Also, try *MCSE NT Certification Exam Guide* from McGraw-Hill, May 1998.

Sponsor:

Motorola Information Systems Group (ISG)
USA
Phone: 800-446-0144   **Fax:**
Email:
URL: www.mot.com/MIMS/ISG/Training/cert/index.html

Motorola ISG Certification

For Motorola channel partners who want to become certified to design and sell Motorola networks. There are several tests you can take.

Date Initiated: **# Granted:**   **Fees:** $0

Initial Requirements:
Must pass free tests that you download from company Web site.

Continuing Requirements:

Perks:
✐ access to restricted forum

Online Resources:
Motorola CBTs can be downloaded from: **www.mot.com/MIMS/ISG/Training/cert/925_cbts.html**. The tests are available online from: **http://www.mot.com/MIMS/ISG/Training/cert/dload.html**.

Offline Resources:
Call ISG at 1-800-261-4111 to register for courses.

Sponsor:

Net Guru Technologies
2625 Butterfield Rd.
Suite 312E
Oak Brook, IL 60523 USA
Phone: 800-566-9648   **Fax:** 630-990-9635
Email: info@nirvana.ngt.com
URL: www.ngt.com

Certified Internet Webmaster Administrator

For web administrators and professionals in IT management. This program emphasizes how to administer, secure, and manage critical Internet server systems.

Date Initiated: 1997   **# Granted:**   **Fees:** $2440

Initial Requirements:

Must complete 2 courses ($2,290) and pass exam ($150). The courses are: *Internet Infrastructure & Security* ($995/2 days) and *Internet Network Administration* ($1,295/3 days).

Continuing Requirements:

Perks:

✐ use of logo

Online Resources:

The home page for this certification is: **www.ngt.com/certification/admin.html.** It contains course information including curriculum, objectives, and locations.

Offline Resources:

The books *Webmaster Administrator Certification Exam Guide* and *Managing Internet Information Services* are used as reference material for this course.

Certified Internet Webmaster Designer

For individuals who access the Web and build Web sites. Vendor independent.

Date Initiated: 1997   **# Granted:**   **Fees:** $1225

Initial Requirements:

Must complete 3 courses ($1,075) and pass exam ($150). The courses are: *Internet Basics* ($285/1 day), *Planning & Building a Web Site* ($395/1 day) and *Web Development Using HTML* ($395/1 day).

Continuing Requirements:

Perks:

    ✐ use of logo

Online Resources:

The home page for this certification is: **www.ngt.com/certification/designer.html**. It contains course information including curriculum, objectives, and locations.

Offline Resources:

The book *The Whole Internet* is used as reference material in this course.

Certified Internet Webmaster Network Professional

For technical professionals and management with the need to design, manage, upgrade and secure IP networks.

Date Initiated: 1997   **# Granted:**   **Fees:** $2,440

Initial Requirements:

Must complete 2 courses ($2,290) and pass exam ($150). The courses are: *TCP/IP Internetworking* ($995/ 2 days) and *Advanced TCP/IP Concepts* ($1,295/3 days).

Continuing Requirements:

Perks:

    ✐ use of logo

Online Resources:

The home page for this certification is: **www.ngt.com/certification/netprof.html**. It contains course information including curriculum, objectives, and locations.

Offline Resources:

Uday O. Pabrai's text on *UNIX Internetworking, 2nd Edition*, is used as a reference.

Certified Internet Webmaster Developer I

For individuals who develop web applications using HTML, CGI and PERL, Java and Javascript.

Date Initiated: 1997   **# Granted:**   **Fees:** $2,440

Initial Requirements:

Must complete 2 courses ($2,290) and pass exam ($150). The courses are: *Web Scripting* ($995/2 days) and *Java Programming Fundamentals* ($1,295/3 days).

Continuing Requirements:

Perks:

✐ use of logo

Online Resources:

The home page for this certification is: **www.ngt.com/certification/ dev1.html**. It contains course information including curriculum, objectives, and locations.

Offline Resources:

Programming Perl is used as reference material for the course Web Scripting. *Java in a Nutshell* is used as reference material for the course Java Programming Fundamentals.

Certified Internet Webmaster Developer II

For individuals who want to develop smart, interactive web pages that interface with the back-end database system using technologies and standards such as Java, JDBC, CORBA, and ORB.

Date Initiated: 1997   **# Granted:**   **Fees:** $2,140

Initial Requirements:

Must complete 2 courses ($1,990) and pass exam ($150). The courses are: *CORBA & ORB Concepts & Fundamentals* ($995/2 days) and *Java & JDBC* ($995/2 days).

Continuing Requirements:

Perks:

✐ use of logo

Online Resources:

The home page for this certification is: **www.ngt.com/certification/ dev2.html**. It contains course information including curriculum, objectives, and locations.

Offline Resources:

Certified Internet Webmaster Security Professional

For individuals who handle Internet security issues.

Date Initiated: 1997   **# Granted:**   **Fees:** $4,730

Initial Requirements:

Must complete 4 courses ($4,580) and pass exam ($150). The courses are: *Windows NT System & Network Administration* (3 days) or *UNIX System & Network Administration* (3 days), *TCP/IP Internetworking* ($995/2 days), *Advanced TCP/IP Concepts* ($1,295/3 days) and *Internet Security & Firewall* ($995/2 days).

Continuing Requirements:

Perks:

✎ use of logo

Online Resources:

The home page for this certification is: **www.ngt.com/certification/secprof.html.** It contains course information including curriculum, objectives, and locations.

Offline Resources:

NGT Certified Internet Web Developer Instructor

For individuals who want to teach NGT Internet Web Developer courses.

Date Initiated: 1997   **# Granted:**   **Fees:** $6,645

Initial Requirements:

Must have proven hands-on experience and expertise in HTML, Perl, CGI, Java, C and object-oriented programming. Must attend 3 courses and pass associated tests with overall score of 90%. Courses are: *Hands-on Internet Webmaster Designer Program* (3 days), *Hands-on Internet Webmaster Developer I Program* (5 days), and *Hands-on Internet Webmaster Developer II Program* (5 days).

Continuing Requirements:

Perks:

✎ email technical support
✎ use of logos
✎ NGT may consider you for teaching NGT-sponsored courses, or make your name available to licensees in your area

Online Resources:

> The Web page for all of the NGT instructor certifications is: **www.ngt.com/instruct.html**. It contains course information including curriculum, objectives, and locations.

Offline Resources:

Certified Internet Webmaster ECommerce Professional

> For technical professionals with a need to implement and support electronic commerce systems.

Date Initiated: 1997   **# Granted:**   **Fees:** $1,445

Initial Requirements:

> Must complete the *Certified Internet Webmaster ECommerce Professional* course ($1,295.00/ 3 days) and pass associated test ($150).

Continuing Requirements:

Perks:

> ✎ use of logo

Online Resources:

> The home page for this certification is: **http://www.ngt.com/certification/ecommerce.html**. It contains course information including curriculum, objectives, and locations.

Offline Resources:

Certified UNIX Administrator

> For individuals getting started with UNIX, and wishing to effectively manage UNIX systems on a TCP/IP network.

Date Initiated: 1997   **# Granted:**   **Fees:** $2,440

Initial Requirements:

> Must complete 2 courses ($2,290) and pass exam ($150). The courses are: *UNIX Fundamentals* ($995/2 days) and *UNIX System & Networking Administration* ($1,295/ 3 days).

Continuing Requirements:

Perks:

> ✎ use of logo

Online Resources:

> The home page for this certification is: **www.ngt.com/certification/ unixadmin.html.** It contains course information including curriculum, objectives, and locations.

Offline Resources:

> *UNIX in a Nutshell* and *Learning the vi Editor* are used as reference materials in these courses.

NGT Certified Windows NT Instructor

> For individuals who want to teach NGT Windows NT courses.

Date Initiated: 1997   **# Granted:**   **Fees:** $3,425

Initial Requirements:

> Must have Microsoft Certified Windows NT Professional status with demonstrated hands on experience. Must attend 2 courses and pass associated tests with overall score of 90%. Courses are: *Hands-on Windows NT System and Network Administration* (3 days) and *Hands-on Windows NT and TCP/IP Internetworking* (2 days). Finally, NGT Certified Instructor candidates will spend one day co-teaching with an NGT mentor and be evaluated at that time.

Continuing Requirements:

Perks:

> - email technical support
> - use of logos
> - NGT may consider you for teaching NGT-sponsored courses, or make your name available to licensees in your area

Online Resources:

> The Web page for all of the NGT instructor certifications is: **www.ngt.com/instruct.html**. It contains course information including curriculum, objectives, and locations.

Offline Resources:

NGT Certified Network Professional Instructor

For individuals who want to teach NGT Network Professional courses.

Date Initiated: 1997   **# Granted:**   **Fees:** $5,700

Initial Requirements:

Must have Hands-on experience and expertise in designing and managing TCP/IP networks. Must attend 4 courses and pass associated tests with overall score of 90%. Courses are: *Hands-on Windows NT System & Network Administration* (3 days) or *Hands-on UNIX System & Network Administration* (3 days), *Hands-on TCP/IP Internetworking* (2 days), *Advanced TCP/IP Concepts & Practices* (3 days), and *Hands-on Windows NT & TCP/IP Internetworking* (2 days).

Continuing Requirements:

Perks:

- email technical support
- use of logos
- NGT may consider you for teaching NGT-sponsored courses, or make your name available to licensees in your area

Online Resources:

The Web page for all of the NGT instructor certifications is: **www.ngt.com/instruct.html**. It contains course information including curriculum, objectives, and locations.

Offline Resources:

NGT Certified Security Professional Instructor

For individuals who want to teach NGT Security Professional courses.

Date Initiated: 1997   **# Granted:**   **Fees:** $7,775

Initial Requirements:

Must have demonstrated Hands-on experience and expertise in TCP/IP networks, managing UNIX systems, security concepts, practices and firewall systems. Must attend 3 courses and pass associated tests with overall score of 90%. Courses are: *Hands-on UNIX System and Network Administration* (3 days), *Hands-on Internet Webmaster Administrator Program* (5 days) , *Hands-on Certified Internet Webmaster Network Professional Program* (5 days), and *Hands-on Internet Security & Firewall Systems* (2 days).

Continuing Requirements:

Perks:
- email technical support
- use of logos
- NGT may consider you for teaching NGT-sponsored courses, or make your name available to licensees in your area

Online Resources:

The Web page for all of the NGT instructor certifications is: **www.ngt.com/instruct.html.** It contains course information including curriculum, objectives, and locations.

Offline Resources:

Sponsor:

Network Professional Association (NPA)
401 N. Michigan Ave.
Chicago, IL 60611 USA
Phone: 801-379-0288   **Fax:**
Email: lhatch@npa.org
URL: www.npa.org/cnp_frameset.htm

Certified Network Professional (CNP)

For experienced network professionals.

Date Initiated: 1995   **# Granted:** 160   **Fees:** $400

Initial Requirements:

- Must pass a core fundamentals exam ($100). Must pay application fee ($300/nonmembers $200/NPA members). Must hold 2 specialty certifications. Specialty areas and qualifying certifications are: Network Operating Systems (Novell CNE/ECNE/ MCNE, Microsoft MCSE, Banyan CBE/CBS, IBM CLSE, CWSE, AS/400, SCO ACE), Groupware (Lotus CLP), Internetworking (Cisco CCIE), Network Analysis (CNX), and Networked Hardware (Compaq ASE, IBM PSE).
- Must demonstrate 24 months of related work experience. Formal educational achievements can substitute for up to 12 months.
- Must also ascribe to the CNP code of ethics.

Continuing Requirements:

Must complete continuing education (20 CNP units as defined by the NPA) on an annual basis. Qualifying activities include self-study, NPA events, formal education, and conferences. Must also demonstrate at least 4 months of continuing work experience.

Perks:

- CNP ID card
- lapel pin
- CNP shirt
- CNP resource kit
- inclusion in a referral directory

Online Resources:

A master objectives list and study guide for the core exam are available from the CNP web site: **www.npa.org/cnp–frameset.htm**.

Offline Resources:

Sponsor:

Newbridge Networks Corporation
593 Herndon Parkway
Herndon, VA 22070 USA
Phone: 703-834-3600   **Fax:** 703-471-7080
Email:
URL: www.newbridge.com/mainstreet/96july/wisenf.html

Newbridge Wise for ATM Specialist

For individuals who work with Newbridge ATM products.

Date Initiated: 1997   **# Granted:**   **Fees:** $980

Initial Requirements:
Must pass 4 exams ($480) and a job simulation test ($500). The exams are: ATM Technology ($120), MainStreetXpress 36150 ($120), MainStreetXpress 36170 ($120), and ATM Network Management ($120). The job simulation test is Newbridge Wise for ATM ($500).

Continuing Requirements:
Must update with new product releases.

Perks:
- priority technical support
- plaque

Online Resources:

Offline Resources:
Training courses are available, though not required, through Newbridge.

Newbridge Wise for VIVID Specialist

For individuals who work with Newbridge VIVID.

Date Initiated: 1997   **# Granted:**   **Fees:** $740

Initial Requirements:
Must pass 2 Exams ($240) and a job simulation test ($500). The exams are: *ATM Technology* ($120) and *VIVID* ($120). The job simulation test is *Newbridge Wise for VIVID* ($500).

Continuing Requirements:
Must update with new product releases.

Perks:
- priority technical support
- plaque

Online Resources:

Offline Resources:
Training courses are available, although not required, through Newbridge.

Newbridge Wise for WAN Network Administrator

For individuals who administer a Newbridge WAN.

Date Initiated: 1997   **# Granted:**   **Fees:** $500

Initial Requirements:
Must be a Newbridge WAN Network Management Specialist and pass 46020 MainStreet Systems Administrator job simulation ($500).

Continuing Requirements:
Must update with new product releases.

Perks:
- priority technical support
- plaque

Online Resources:

Offline Resources:
Training courses are available, although not required, through Newbridge.

Newbridge Wise for ATM Network Administrator

For individuals who administer ATM products and systems.

Date Initiated: 1997   **# Granted:**   **Fees:** $500

Initial Requirements:
Must hold Newbridge Wise for ATM Specialist certification. Must pass 46020 MainStreet Systems Administrator job simulation ($500).

Continuing Requirements:
Must update with new product releases.

Perks:
- priority technical support
- plaque

Online Resources:

Offline Resources:
Training courses are available, though not required, through Newbridge.

Newbridge Wise for WANs Specialist

For individuals who work with Newbridge WAN products.

Date Initiated: 1997   **# Granted:**   **Fees:** $1,220

Initial Requirements:
Must pass 6 Exams ($720) and a job simulation test ($500). The exams are: MainStreet Voice and Data Commissioning ($120), MainStreet Voice and Data Configuration ($120), MainStreet Frame Relay ($120), MainStreet ISDN ($120), MainStreet Small Mux ($120), and WAN Network Management ($120). The job simulation test is Newbridge Wise for WANs ($500).

Continuing Requirements:
Must update with new product releases.

Perks:
- priority technical support
- plaque

Online Resources:

Offline Resources:
Training courses are available, though not required, through Newbridge.

Sponsor:

Novell Corporation
1555 North Technology Way
Orem, UT 84097 USA
Phone: 800-233-3382   **Fax:**
Email: EDCUSTOMER@novell.com
URL: education.novell.com

Certified Internet Professional (CIP)— Internet Business Strategist

For IT managers, strategic planners, MIS managers, operating division business managers, communication managers, Web publishers, and anyone who makes recommendations on networking and Internet strategy. This is not limited to Novell products.

Date Initiated: 1997   **# Granted:**   **Fees:** $85

Initial Requirements:

Must pass Internet Business Strategies exam ($85).

Continuing Requirements:

Perks:

- access to the Certified Internet Professional benefits home page with current technology and program information
- free 2-user version of IntranetWare
- discount on Corel's Web Graphics Suite
- discounts on Novell Press books and AppNotes
- discounts and free passes to top industry events

Online Resources:

The Web page for this designation is: **www.netboss.com/strategi.htm**. The CIP training locater is at: **www.netboss.com/trngctrs.htm**.

Offline Resources:

Recommended courses are: *Mastering the Net with Netscape Navigator* and *Internet Business Strategies*. They are available through Novell Authorized Education Centers.

Certified Novell Instructor (CNI)

For individuals who want to teach Novell curriculums.

Date Initiated: **# Granted:**   **Fees:** $1,285

Initial Requirements:

Prerequisites:

- ✐ You must have an in-depth, working knowledge of microcomputer concepts, including hardware and operating systems. Networking and Interoperability candidates must have at least 1 year of hands-on experience in the area you want to specialize in as an instructor, and 1 year of experience teaching adults in a classroom setting is required for all Networking and Interoperability candidates.

To certify:

- ✐ Must attend the Novell courses ($700 and up) you want to be certified to teach and pass the associated exams ($85 each) at the instructor level. CNA or CNE exams you already passed will automatically apply toward CNI certification if passed at the current CNI level.
- ✐ You must also successfully complete an Instructor Performance Evaluation (IPE) ($500). During a standard two-day IPE, you will be required to set-up a classroom or lab and then teach a section of your target course.

CNI certification is not required to teach Novell's CIP curriculum. CTT certification is acceptable instead (available from the Chauncey Group).

Continuing Requirements:

Perks:

- ✐ instructor kit updates
- ✐ CNI update training
- ✐ free copies of Novell's Support Connection CD
- ✐ CNI 40% discount for a one-year monthly subscription to Novell's Support Connection CD
- ✐ CNI support on NetWire on Compuserve
- ✐ CNI support on the web
- ✐ monthly issues of NetWare Application Notes (AppNotes)
- ✐ program communications and update information sent directly to your email address
- ✐ use of logo

Online Resources:

You may send your CNI questions via email to: **cniadmin@novell.com**

The CNI page is: **http://education.novell.com/cni/**. You can download a 50-page CNI guide there. You'll also have to download the proprietary Envoy viewer to read it.

Offline Resources:

Call Novell FaxBack at 1-800-233-3382 or 1-801-429-5363 to request the current CNI Certification Requirements and CNI Categories and Course Classifications charts, document number 1452.

Certified Internet Professional (CIP)—Internet Architect

For CNEs, network integrators, system engineers, consultants, and other IT professionals who want to specialize in Internet integration.

Date Initiated: 1997   **# Granted:**   **Fees:** $425

Initial Requirements:

Must pass 5 exams ($425). Exams are: Fundamentals of Internetworking ($85), NetWare TCP/IP Transport ($85), Web Server Management ($85), DNS & FTP Server Installation and Configuration ($85), and Securing Intranets with BorderManager ($85).

Continuing Requirements:

Perks:

- access to the Certified Internet Professional benefits home page with current technology and program information
- free 2-user version of IntranetWare
- discount on Corel's Web Graphics Suite
- discounts on Novell Press books and AppNotes
- discounts and free passes to top industry events

Online Resources:

The Web page for this designation is: **www.netboss.com/architec.htm**. The CIP training locater is at: **www.netboss.com/supportp.htm**.

Offline Resources:

Recommended courses are: *CNE Certification, Fundamentals of Internetworking, NetWare TCP/IP Transport, Web Server Management, DNS and FTP Server Installation and Configuration*, and *Securing Intranets with BorderManager*. They are available through Novell Authorized Education Centers.

Certified Internet Professional (CIP)—Intranet Manager

For existing CNAs, network integrators, system administrators, system engineers, consultants, and anyone who want to deploy an intranet. This CIP track is currently based on Novell's IntranetWare product.

Date Initiated: 1997   **# Granted:**   **Fees:** $510

Initial Requirements:

Must pass 6 exams ($510). They are: Web Authoring and Publishing ($85), Internet Business Strategies ($85), Advanced Web Authoring ($85), NetWare TCP/IP Transport ($85), Web Server Management ($85), and IntranetWare: NetWare 4.11 Administration ($85).

Continuing Requirements:

Perks:

- access to the Certified Internet Professional benefits home page with current technology and program information
- free 2-user version of IntranetWare
- discount on Corel's Web Graphics Suite
- discounts on Novell Press books and AppNotes
- discounts and free passes to top industry events

Online Resources:

The Web page for this designation is: **www.netboss.com/supportp.htm**.

The CIP training locater is at: **www.netboss.com/supportp.htm**.

Offline Resources:

Recommended courses are: *Internet Business Strategies, Web Authoring and Publishing, Advanced Web Authoring, IntranetWare: NetWare 4.11 Administration, NetWare TCP/IP Transport*, and *Web Server Management*. They are available through Novell Authorized Education Centers.

Certified Internet Professional (CIP)—Web Designer

For marketing professionals, corporate communication professionals, artists, desktop publishers, graphic designers, writers, editors, librarians, researchers, administrative assistants, and any other professional who needs to design and manage Web sites.

Date Initiated: 1997   **# Granted:**   **Fees:** $340

Initial Requirements:

Must pass 4 exams ($340). They are: Internet Business Strategies ($85), Web Authoring and Publishing ($85), Advanced Web Authoring ($85), and Designing an Effective Web Site ($85).

Continuing Requirements:

Perks:

- access to the Certified Internet Professional benefits home page with current technology and program information
- free 2-user version of IntranetWare
- discount on Corel's Web Graphics Suite
- discounts on Novell Press books and AppNotes
- discounts and free passes to top industry events

Online Resources:

The Web page for this designation is: **www.netboss.com/webdesig.htm**.

The CIP training locater is at: **www.netboss.com/trngctrs.htm**.

Offline Resources:

Recommended courses are: *Internet Business Strategies, Web Authoring and Publishing, Advanced Web Authoring*, and *Designing an Effective Web Site*. They are available through Novell Authorized Education Centers.

Certified Internet Professional (CIP)—Web Developer

For systems programmers, graphics programmers, object-orient programmers, C++ programmers, VisualBasic programmers, and other application developers who program in Java.

Date Initiated: 1997   **# Granted:**   **Fees:** $85

Initial Requirements:

Must pass associated exam ($85). Exam title not avaliable at time of publication.

Continuing Requirements:

Perks:

- access to the Certified Internet Professional benefits home page with current technology and program information
- free 2-user version of IntranetWare
- discount on Corel's Web Graphics Suite
- discounts on Novell Press books and AppNotes
- discounts and free passes to top industry events

Online Resources:

The Web page for this designation is: **www.netboss.com/webdevel.htm**.

The CIP training locater is at: **www.netboss.com/trngctrs.htm**.

Offline Resources:

Recommended courses are: *Internet Business Strategies, Web Authoring and Publishing, Advanced Web Authoring, Designing an Effective Web Site, Introduction to Java Programming*, and *Java Advanced Topics*. They are available through Novell Authorized Education Centers. Additional Java courses may be added.

Certified Novell Engineer (CNE)

For individuals who provide high-end, solutions-based technical support for Novell products.

Date Initiated: **# Granted:**   **Fees:** $170

Initial Requirements:

Must pass 2 core exams ($170): Networking Technologies ($85) and Service and Support ($85). Must complete exams affiliated with chosen track. Tracks and exams are:

- IntranetWare (IntranetWare Netware 4.11 Administration, IntranetWare NetWare 4.11 Adv. Administration, IntranetWare NetWare 4.11 Installation & Configuration Workshop, IntranetWare NetWare 4.11 Design & Implementation, and Building Intranets with IntranetWare);
- NetWare 3 (NetWare 3.1x Administration, NetWare 3.1x Advanced Administration, NetWare 3 Installation & Configuration Workshop, and IntranetWare Netware 3 to NetWare 4.11 Update);
- GroupWise 5 (IntranetWare NetWare 4.11 Administration, GroupWise 5 Administration, GroupWise 5 Advanced Administration, and GroupWise 5 Connectivity); or

✐ GroupWise 4 (IntranetWare Netware 4.11 Administration, GroupWise 4 Administration, GroupWise 4 Async Gateway & GroupWise Remote, and GroupWise 4 Advanced Administration).

All tracks except the IntranetWare track also require passing 2 elective tests ($). Electives include: Fundamentals of Network Mgmt, InForms 4 Admin and Form Design, SoftSolutions 4 Adv Admin, Printing with NetWare, Printing in an Integrated NetWare Environment, NetWare Navigator, NetWare TCP/IP Transport, NetWare NFS Services: MGT & Printing-NetWare 4 Ed, NetWare NFS Services: File Sharing, NetWare 4 Ed, Extending Enterprise Access with NetWare Connect, NetWare for SAA: Install & Troubleshooting, and LANalyzer for WIN.

Passing any of the administration tests earns automatic CNA certification for that track.

Continuing Requirements:

CNEs must periodically meet Continuing Certification Requirements (CCRs). You can get CCR information by visiting the Certification Headline News (education.novell.com/certinfo/certnews.htm) or by going to CNE Net.

Perks:

✐ access to restricted CNE Web site which includes beta releases, patches, and technical info
✐ use of logo
✐ 50% off technical support calls and online incidents
✐ free subscription to NetWare Connection
✐ free and discounted technical seminars and programs
✐ receive two-user versions of the latest products from Novell every quarter for a nominal fee
✐ discount on tech training videos
✐ Novell Power Partner CD containing technical info and demo software
✐ discounts on Novell Applications Notes, Novell Support Connection CD, NCS Tool Kit and Novell Press books.

Online Resources:

The CNE page is: **education.novell.com/cne/**.

To find an authorized training center near you, visit the training locater at: **db.netpub.com/nov_edu/x/naecloc**.

Offline Resources:

Self-study products are available through participating NAECs and Novell resellers. For more information on CBT courseware, contact CBT Systems at 1-800-929-9050 or 1-415-737-9050. For more information on video courses, contact Gartner Group Learning Corporation at 1-800-532-7672 or 1-612-930-0330. For more information on NETG courses, contact NETG at 1-800-263-1900 or 1-708-369-3000. Also check out the *CNA / CNE Study Guide* from McGraw-Hill.

Master CNE (MCNE)

For individuals who provide solutions to complex networking problems that may span across several different platforms. Focused on Novell products.

Date Initiated: **# Granted:**   **Fees:** $255–$340

Initial Requirements:

Must already be a CNE. Must choose one or more areas of specialty and pass associated exams. Specialties (and exams) are: Management (Network Management Using NetWare ManageWise ($85), plus 4 credits from MCNE management elective pool); Connectivity (Internetworking with NetWare MultiProtocol Router ($85), plus 4 credits from connectivity elective pool); Messaging (6 credits from messaging elective pool); Internet/Intranet Solutions (NetWare TCP/IP Transport, Web Server Management ($85), DNS & FTP Server Install & Configuration ($85), and an Internet/Intranet elective); or Client/Network Solutions (AS/400, UNIX, or Windows NT specific exams totalling 8 credits). All specialties must pass the Fundamentals of Internetworking exam.

Continuing Requirements:

Master CNEs must meet periodic Continuing Certification Requirements (CCRs). CCR information will be available in CNE Net and will also be announced via Certification Headline News.

Perks:

- certificate
- use of logo
- all CNE benefits

Online Resources:

The MCNE page is: **education.novell.com/mcne/**.

To find an authorized training center near you, visit the training locator at: **db.netpub.com/nov_edu/x/naecloc**.

Offline Resources:

Self-study products are available through participating NAECs and Novell resellers. For more information on CBT courseware, contact CBT Systems at 1-800-929-9050 or 1-415-737-9050. For more information on video courses, contact Gartner Group Learning Corporation at 1-800-532-7672 or 1-612-930-0330. For more information on NETG courses, contact NETG at 1-800-263-1900 or 1-708-369-3000.

Certified Novell Administrator (CNA)

For individuals who handle the day-to-day administration of an installed Novell networking product.

Date Initiated: **# Granted:**   **Fees:** $85

Initial Requirements:

Must pass exam for chosen CNA track ($85). Tracks are: *IntranetWare: NetWare 4.11 Administration, NetWare 3.1x Administration, GroupWise 5 Administration*, and *GroupWise 4 Administration*.

Continuing Requirements:

Perks:

- access to restricted CNA Web site which includes beta releases, patches, and technical info.
- use of logo

Online Resources:

The CNA page is: **education.novell.com/cna/**

To find an authorized training center near you, visit the training locater at: **db.netpub.com/nov_edu/x/naecloc**

Offline Resources:

Self-study products are available through participating NAECs and Novell resellers. For more information on CBT courseware, contact CBT Systems at 1-800-929-9050 or 1-415-737-9050. For more information on video courses, contact Gartner Group Learning Corporation at 1-800-532-7672 or 1-612-930-0330. For more information on NETG courses, contact NETG at 1-800-263-1900 or 1-708-369-3000. Also check out the *CNA/CNE Study Guide* from McGraw-Hill.

Certified Novell Salesperson (CNS)

For individuals who create sales proposals for Novell products.

Date Initiated: 1997   **# Granted:**   **Fees:** $85

Initial Requirements:
Must pass CNS test ($85).

Continuing Requirements:

Perks:

Online Resources:
The CNS page is: **education.novell.com/powersell**.

Introductory self-study course ($0) is available online or by calling Novell.

To request information via email send a message to **powersell@novell.com**.

Offline Resources:
A 2 day training PowerSell session is recommended (not required). Price ranges from $250–$300 depending on location. Call Novell for information (800-235-4779).

Sponsor:

ObjectShare, Inc. (formerly ParcPlace-Digitalk, Inc.)
999 E. Arques Ave.
Sunnyvale, CA 94086 USA
Phone: 800-888-6892   **Fax:**
Email:
URL: www.parcplace.com/about/press/certify1.htm

Certified Smalltalk Developer (CSD)

For Smalltalk developers.

Date Initiated: **# Granted:**   **Fees:**

Initial Requirements:

For basic certification you must pass 3 exams ($). They are: *Intro-level Smalltalk* ($), *Intermediate-level Smalltalk* ($), and *OOD* ($). Senior level certification also requires completion of a five-day design and prototyping practicum ($) where students prototype a solution to a case study. The practicum includes a performance-based assessment.

Continuing Requirements:

Perks:

✏ use of logo
✏ listing in resource directory
✏ certificate

Online Resources:

The company home page is **www.parcplace.com**, but since they have recently changed their name, they have also created a new Web site at **www.objectshare.com**. Training course information can be found at: **www.parcplace.com/training/cnt_trng.htm**.

Offline Resources:

A complete curriculum is available from the sponsor. Call 800-888-6892, x213 for information.

Sponsor:

Open Software Foundation (OSF)
11 Cambridge Center
Cambridge, MA 02142-1405 USA
Phone: 800-268-5424   **Fax:** 617-621-0306
Email: direct@opengroup.org
URL: www.osf.org/service/skillsindex.html

DCE Administrator

Date Initiated: 1996   **# Granted:** 300   **Fees:** $300

Initial Requirements:
Must pass 2 OSF exams ($300).

Continuing Requirements:

Perks:

Online Resources:
Test objectives and sample questions are available on the Web site.

Offline Resources:
Suggested study references are: *OSF DCE Introduction to Administration*, *OSF DCE Administration Guide—Core Components*, and *OSF DCE Command Reference*. Study kits including these materials and others can be purchased for $75 from OSF by calling 800-268-5245. OSF also offers DCE courses.

Sponsor:

Oracle Corporation
500 Oracle Parkway
Redwood Shores, CA 94065 USA
Phone: 800-633-0575   **Fax:** 650-506-7200
Email:
URL: education.oracle.com/education/certification/

Oracle7 Certified Database Administrator

For Oracle DBAs.

Date Initiated: 1997   **# Granted:**   **Fees:** $500

Initial Requirements:
Must have at least 6 months of on-the-job experience. Must pass 4 exams ($500). The exams are: *Introduction to Oracle: SQL and PL/SQL Using Procedure Builder* ($125), *Oracle7 Database Administration* ($125), *Oracle7: Backup and Recovery Workshop* ($125), and *Oracle7: Performance Tuning Workshop* ($125).

Continuing Requirements:
Recertification is required for new releases.

Perks:
✐ certificate

Online Resources:
Sample self-assessment tests can be downloaded from: **education. oracle.com/education/cgi-bin/certform.cgi**.

Offline Resources:
Oracle offers many training courses and classes, both instructor-led and self-paced. Contact Oracle Education for details.

Sponsor:

PC DOCS Group
25 Burlington Mall Road
Burlington, MA 01803 USA
Phone: 617-273-3800   **Fax:** 617-272-3693
Email: danm@pcdocs.com
URL: www.pcdocs.com

Certified DOCS Professional

For individuals who wish to sell or train DOCS Open.

Date Initiated: **# Granted:**   **Fees:** $150

Initial Requirements:

Must pass PC DOCS exam ($150). Prospective resellers and training centers must also attend a 5 day training class ($1,900).

Continuing Requirements:

Perks:

Online Resources:

The Web page for this certification is **www.pcdocs.com/training/ subtrain.htm**.

Offline Resources:

Sponsor:

Project Management Institute (PMI)
130 South State Rd
Upper Darby, PA 19082 USA
Phone: 610-734-3330   **Fax:** 610-734-3266
Email: cert@pmi.org
URL: www.pmi.org/cert/cert.html

Project Management Professional (PMP)

For project management professionals.

Date Initiated: 1984   **# Granted:** 5,960   **Fees:** $555

Initial Requirements:

Must have 7 years post/high school work experience, or a 4-year college degree plus 2 years graduate education or 2 years work experience. Must pass 8 section PMP exam. Certification fees are $555 for non PMI members and $405 for members. Individual PMI membership costs $100.

This program is being revised and new requirements are likely to be in effect as of 12/1998.

Continuing Requirements:

7.5 Professional Development Units of continuing education per 3 year cycle.

Perks:

Online Resources:

The *Project Management Body Of Knowledge (PMBOK) Guide* is available on line at: **www.pmi.org/publictn/pmboktoc.htm**. Many other links and resources are available from the PMI Web site.

Offline Resources:

Request a PMP brochure by calling 610-734-3330.

Sponsor:

Quality Assurance Institute (QAI)
7575 Dr. Phillips Blvd.
Suite 350
Orlando, FL 32819 USA
Phone: 407-363-1111   **Fax:** 407-363-1112
Email: qaiadmin@qaiusa.com
URL: www.qaiusa.com

Certified Software Test Engineer (CSTE)

For software testing professionals.

Date Initiated: 1995   **# Granted:** 400   **Fees:** $175

Initial Requirements:

Must demonstrate two years of test work experience and show proficiency in six skill dimensions. This is accomplished by filling out and submitting forms ($175) *not* by taking an exam. Must subscribe to the Professional Code of Conduct.

Continuing Requirements:

Requires forty hours per year of continuing professional education as specified by the certification board.

Perks:

Online Resources:

www.csst-technologies.com/certapp.htm contains all the details for this certification, as well as the skills proficiency form and application form.

Offline Resources:

Sponsor:

Santa Cruz Operation, The (SCO)
400 Encinal Street, P.O. Box 1900
Santa Cruz, CA 95061-1900 USA
Phone: 800-726-8649   **Fax:** 408-458-4227
Email:
URL: www.sco.com/Training/ace/acenotes.html

SCO ACE—SCO OpenServer Rel 5

For individuals who support and administer SCO OpenServer
Release 5 installations.

Date Initiated: 1996   **# Granted:**   **Fees:** $430

Initial Requirements:

Must pass 3 exams ($430). They are: SCO OpenServer Release 5
Administration ($180), Shell Programming for System Administra-
tors ($125), and SCO OpenServer Release 5 Network Administration
($125).

Continuing Requirements:

It is recommended that you recertify every year by taking a 2-hour
comprehensive exam ($180).

Perks:

- certificate
- lapel pin
- desk trophy
- stickers
- discount on technical support for your organization
- free copy of the SCO Support Library on CD-ROM, which
  includes the SCO Online Support System (SOS), the knowledge
  base used by SCO's own support engineers.
- access to SCO Online Support (SOS) the SCO bulletin board.

Online Resources:

Sample exam questions can be found at: **www.sco.com/Training/
ace/exam.html**.

Offline Resources:

For a print copy of the certification guidelines call 1-800-SCO-UNIX.
Courses related to this certification are also available through SCO
authorized education centers.

SCO ACE—SCO UnixWare 2.1

For individuals who support and administer SCO UnixWare 2.1 installations.

Date Initiated: 1996   **# Granted:**   **Fees:** $430

Initial Requirements:

Must pass 3 exams ($430). They are: SCO UnixWare 2.1 Administration ($180), Shell Programming for System Administrators ($125), and SCO OpenServer Release 5 Network Administration ($125).

Continuing Requirements:

It is recommended that you recertify every year by taking a 2-hour comprehensive exam ($180).

Perks:

- certificate
- lapel pin
- desk trophy
- stickers
- discount on technical support for your organization
- free copy of the SCO Support Library on CD-ROM, which includes the SCO Online Support System (SOS), the knowledge base used by SCO's own support engineers.
- access to SCO Online Support (SOS) the SCO bulletin board.

Online Resources:

Sample exam questions can be found at: **www.sco.com/Training/ace/exam.html**.

Offline Resources:

For a print copy of the certification guidelines call 1-800-SCO-UNIX. Courses related to this certification are also available through SCO authorized education centers.

SCO ACE—SCO Server

For individuals who support and administer SCO Server installations.

Date Initiated: 1996   **# Granted:**   **Fees:** $500

Initial Requirements:

Must pass 4 exams ($500). They are: SCO UNIX System Administration ($125), Basic Communications: UUCP Administration ($125), Shell Programming for System Administrators ($125), and SCO TCP/IP and SCO NFS: Administration & Configuration ($125).

Continuing Requirements:

It is recommended that you recertify every year by taking a 2-hour comprehensive exam ($180).

Perks:

- certificate
- lapel pin
- desk trophy
- stickers
- discount on technical support for your organization
- free copy of the SCO Support Library on CD-ROM, which includes the SCO Online Support System (SOS), the knowledge base used by SCO's own support engineers.
- access to SCO Online Support (SOS) the SCO bulletin board.

Online Resources:

Sample exam questions can be found at: **www.sco.com/Training/ace/exam.html**.

Offline Resources:

For a print copy of the certification guidelines call 1-800-SCO-UNIX. Courses related to this certification are also available through SCO authorized education centers.

Sponsor:

SAP Partner Academy
950 Winter Street
Waltham, MA 02154 USA
Phone: 612-376-7750   **Fax:** 612-376-7755
Email:
URL: www.sap.com

SAP R/3 Certified Consultant

For SAP professionals who work with various modules.

Date Initiated: 1994   **# Granted:** 5,000   **Fees:**

Initial Requirements:

Must pass SAP test in desired module ($). Certifications available include: Accounting and Controlling, Handling of Customer Orders, Materials Management, Production and Production Planning, Human Resources, Development of Applications with ABAP/4, and R/3 System Support.

Continuing Requirements:

Continued training is encouraged by SAP. Certification is release specific.

Perks:

- access to SAP R/3 information network
- certificate

Online Resources:

The SAP site is **www.sap.com.** Use the search function with the keyword "certification" to locate the certification guidelines. You can download them in .PDF format for viewing with the Adobe Acrobat reader.

Offline Resources:

You may need to attend extensive SAP training that lasts about 5 weeks. Extensive experience with SAP is needed to pass the test. Contact the SAP Partner Academy in your country for details.

Sponsor:

Software Publishers Association (SPA)
PO Box 79237
Baltimore, MD 21279-0237 USA
Phone: 800-388-7478   **Fax:** 202-223-8756
Email: csminfo@spa.org
URL: www.spa.org/csm/csmbroch.htm

Certified Software Manager (CSM)

For individuals who need to optimize the use of software for maximum productivity, as well as ensure compliance with license agreements.

Date Initiated: **# Granted:**   **Fees:** $295–$495

Initial Requirements:

Must pass exam ($100). You will need to either attend the CSM seminar ($395) or purchase the self-study materials ($195) in order to pass the exam.

Continuing Requirements:

Perks:

   ✐ inclusion in CSM networking directory
   ✐ invitations to educational events

Online Resources:

Registration forms, scheduling information, and additional materials are available on the CSM Web site.

Offline Resources:

A six-hour CSM training seminar is offered throughout the United States and Canada. The seminar fee ($395) includes the student manual and lunch. Self-study materials are available for is $195.

Sponsor:

Solomon Software
USA
Phone: 800-476-5666   **Fax:**
Email:
URL: www.solomon.com/cert.htm

Solomon IV Certified Application Developer (SCAD)

For individuals who want to become Solomon Software Developers. Certification includes licensing rights.

Date Initiated: 12/1993   **# Granted:** 110   **Fees:** $2,020–
                                                                              $3,020

Initial Requirements:

Must pay fee ($3,020 if not already a Solomon consultant, $2020 if a Solomon Certified Consultant. Price includes recommended course listed in offline resources). Must pass SCAD exam ($100, included in fee).

Continuing Requirements:

Recertification may be required for new releases. Annual renewal fee $995.

Perks:

- access to independent developer Web and ftp site
- access to online technical support knowledgebase
- license rights

Online Resources:

A sample certification exam can be downloaded from the Solomon Web site.

Offline Resources:

Recommended courses include: *Solomon IV Tools for Visual Basic* and *Advanced Customization Manager* ($1,025). You can obtain an exam preparation outline from Solomon's faxback system by calling 419-424-5060 and requesting document 3072.

Solomon IV Certified Systems Engineer (SCSE)

For individuals who want to become Solomon Software Consultants.

Date Initiated: 12/1993   **# Granted:** 270   **Fees:** $2,795

Initial Requirements:

Must pay fee of $2,695. Must pass SCSE exam ($100, included in first fee). Must pass Microsoft's *Implementing and Supporting Microsoft Windows NT Server* exam ($100).

Continuing Requirements:

Recertification may be required for new releases.

Perks:

  ✐ access to independent developer Web and ftp site
  ✐ access to online technical support knowledgebase

Online Resources:

A sample certification exam can be downloaded from the Solomon Web site.

Offline Resources:

Recommended courses include: *Implementation & System Administration* ($325), *Customization Manager* ($325), *Platform Strategies* ($325), *Training on Scalable SQL for NetWare* ($) or *Platform Strategies and Training on Scalable SQL for NT* ($325). You can obtain an exam preparation outline from Solomon's faxback system by calling 419-424-5060 and requesting document 2786.

Sponsor:

Sun Microsystems
901 San Antonio Rd.
Palo Alto, CA 94043 USA
Phone: 800-422-8020   **Fax:**
Email: teched1@teched1.ebay.sun.com
URL: suned.sun.com.suned/index.html

Sun Certified Java Developer

For Java developers.

Date Initiated: **# Granted:**   **Fees:** $400

Initial Requirements:
Must be a Sun Certified Java Programmer. Must pass the Sun Certified Java Developer exam ($150). Must complete a Sun Developer Assessment, which is a programming assignment ($250).

Continuing Requirements:

Perks:
- certificate
- lapel pin
- use of logo

Online Resources:
java.sun.com is Sun's Java Web site.

Offline Resources:
Instructor-led courses are available from Sun. Check out the *Java 1.1 Certification Exam Guide* from McGraw-Hill.

Sun Certified Java Programmer

For Java programmers. Certifications are available for different versions of the JDK.

Date Initiated: **# Granted:**   **Fees:** $150

Initial Requirements:
Must pass 1 exam ($150)—The Sun Certified Java Programmer for JDK 1.1 exam. Separate versions are available for IBM and non-IBM candidates.

Continuing Requirements:

Perks:
- certificate
- lapel pin
- use of logo

Online Resources:

Offline Resources:

Instructor-led courses are available from Sun. Check out the *Java 1.1 Certification Exam Guide* from McGraw-Hill.

Certified Solaris Administrator (CSA)

For individuals who administer Solaris systems.

Date Initiated: **# Granted:**   **Fees:** $300

Initial Requirements:

Must pass 2 exams ($300). They are Solaris 2.5 System Administrator Exam: Part I ($150), and Solaris 2.5 System Administrator Exam: Part II ($150).

Continuing Requirements:

Perks:
- certificate

Online Resources:

Exam objectives and other details are available from the Sun education page.

Offline Resources:

Both instructor-led and CBT courses are available from Sun. To receive information on this certification call Sun's faxback system at 800-564-4341 and request document #250.

Sun Certified Network Administrator

For experienced Solaris 2.X or UNIX System V administrators who want to add to their Sun credentials.

Date Initiated: 1997   **# Granted:**   **Fees:** $150

Initial Requirements:

Must already be a SUN CSA. Must pass The Sun Certified Network Administrator Exam for Solaris 2.5 exam ($150).

Continuing Requirements:

Perks:

✐ certificate

Online Resources:

Offline Resources:

Both instructor-led and CBT courses are available from Sun.

Sponsor:

Sybase
6475 Christie Ave.
Emeryville, CA 94608 USA
Phone: 800-879-2273   **Fax:**
Email:
URL: www.sybase.com

Certified Sybase Professional—Database Administrator (CSP-DBA)

For individuals who design, administer, and support Sybase SQL Server databases.

Date Initiated: **# Granted:**   **Fees:** $300

Initial Requirements:
Must pass 2 exams ($300). They are: SQL Server System 11: Fast-Track ($150) and SQL Server System 11: Server Administration ($150).

Continuing Requirements:
Upgrade exams are available with new releases.

Perks:
- CSP-DBA identification card
- CSP-DBA certificate
- use of logo
- a CSP logo-branded gift
- subscription to Sybase Magazine

Online Resources:
The Web page for this certification is: **www.sybase.com/services/ education/cspdba.html.** You can use the Sybase Learning Connection **www.sybase.com/services/education/slc/index.html** to find training near you.

Offline Resources:
Recommended (*not* required) classes are: *Introduction to SQL* ($/1 day), *FastTrack to SQL Server* ($/4 days), and *SQL Server Administration* ($/5 days). *SKILS Suite for System 11* is a self-paced study package for this certification. It is available from Sybase.

Certified Sybase Professional—
Open Interface Developer (CSP-IFD)

For individuals who design and develop application interfaces using Sybase Open Client and Open Server software.

Date Initiated: **# Granted:**   **Fees:** $450

Initial Requirements:

Must pass 3 exams ($450). They are: SQL Server System 11: Fast-Track ($150), Open Client/Client Library ($150), and Open Server ($150).

Continuing Requirements:

Upgrade exams are available with new releases.

Perks:

- CSP-IFD identification card
- CSP-IFD certificate
- use of logo
- a CSP logo-branded gift
- subscription to Sybase Magazine

Online Resources:

The Web page for this certification is: **www.sybase.com/services/ education/cspifd.html.** You can use the Sybase Learning Connection **www.sybase.com/services/education/slc/index.html** to find training near you.

Offline Resources:

Recommended (not required) classes are: *Introduction to SQL* ($/1 day), *FastTrack to SQL Server* ($/4 days), *Open Client Programming Using Client Library* ($/3 days), and *Open Server Programming* ($/2 days).

Certified Sybase Professional—Performance
And Tuning Specialist (CSP-PTS)

For individuals who want to be recognized as skilled at fine-tuning Sybase database systems to achieve maximum efficiency.

Date Initiated: **# Granted:**   **Fees:** $150 + CSP-
                                                                   DBA

Initial Requirements:

Must hold CSP-DBA. Must pass 1 exam ($150), the SQL Server System 11: Performance and Tuning exam.

Continuing Requirements:

Upgrade exams are available with new releases.

Perks:

- CSP-PTS identification card
- CSP-PTS certificate
- use of logo
- a CSP logo-branded gift
- subscription to Sybase Magazine

Online Resources:

The Web page for this certification is: **www.sybase.com/services/education/csppts.html.** You can use the Sybase Learning Connection **www.sybase.com/services/education/slc/index.html** to find training near you.

Offline Resources:

The recommended (*not* required) class is: *Performance and Tuning for System 11* ($/5 days).

Certified Powerbuilder Developer (CPD)

For PowerBuilder developers.

Date Initiated: 1993   # Granted: 3,000   Fees: $550

Initial Requirements:

Associate level requires passing 2 exams ($300). They are: PowerBuilder Fundamentals ($150) and PowerBuilder Advanced Concepts ($150). To obtain the full CPD professional certification, you must also pass the CPD hands on Professional Application exam ($250).

Continuing Requirements:

Must pass an update test with new releases.

Perks:

- certificate
- use of logo
- listing in CPD resource directory
- discount on technical support

Online Resources:

The Web page for this certification is: **www.sybase.com/services/education/sle/plan/cpdpro.html**. Study guidelines are available at this site. go powersoft on Compuserve to visit the Powersoft forum. You can also email questions to **education@powersoft.com**.

Offline Resources:

For Powerbuilder certification information call 888-769-7338. You can also call 508-287-1600 and order FaxLine catalog number 2 for a list of education and certification FaxLine documents. Sybase/Power-soft offers instructor-led and CBT training options.

Sponsor:

Symantec
10201 Torre Avenue
Cupertino, CA 95014 USA
Phone: 888-827-7962   **Fax:**
Email:
URL: www.symantec.com/var/varconsult.html

Certified ACT! Consultant

For individuals who administer Symantec's ACT!.

Date Initiated: **# Granted:**   **Fees:** $100

Initial Requirements:
Must pass ACT! exam ($100).

Continuing Requirements:

Perks:
- use of logo
- access to restricted Symantec Web site
- listing in Symantec's consultant directory

Online Resources:
Test objectives, information, and practice exams are available at: **www.symantec.com/var/vartest.html.** Symantec's ACT! Web site is: **www.symantec.com/act/.**

Offline Resources:
Preparation materials are available online and from Symantec. Suggested self study materials include: *ACT! Course 601 Instructor Guide* ($398) and the *ACT! Course 601 Student Guide* ($36). To order courseware, contact Symantec Education at 1-800-786-8620.

Certified Norton AntiVirus Consultant

For individuals who deal with virus protection.

Date Initiated: **# Granted:**   **Fees:** $100

Initial Requirements:

Must pass AntiVirus exam ($100).

Continuing Requirements:

Perks:

- use of logo
- access to restricted Symantec Web site
- listing in Symantec's consultant directory

Online Resources:

The Web site for this certification is: **http://www.symantec.com/ var/vartest.html**. Test objectives, information, and practice exams are available there. Symantec's Norton AntiVirus Web site is: **www.symantec.com/nav/**.

Offline Resources:

Preparation materials are available online and from Symantec. Suggested self-study guides include: *Norton AntiVirus Participant Pack* ($30) and *Norton AntiVirus Leader's Guide* ($175). To order courseware, contact Symantec Education at 1-800-786-8620.

Sponsor:

USWeb
2880 Lakeside Dr.
Suite 350
Santa Clara, CA 95054 USA
Phone: **Fax:**
Email:
URL: www.usweb.com/certification

USWeb Certified Architect (USWeb C/A)

For Internet Architects, project managers and team leaders who are responsible for defining and designing the development environment and who evaluate tools, products and resources needed for Internet and Intranet projects.

Date Initiated: 1997   **# Granted:**   **Fees:** $8,000

Initial Requirements:
Must complete 10 courses and pass 7 exams. Program cost is approximately $8,000.

Continuing Requirements:

Perks:

Online Resources:

Offline Resources:
Recommended courses are: *Web Development, Web Site Logistics, Programming & Database Principles, Internet Networking & Security Principles, Web Graphics & Multimedia Principles, Web Administration Principles, Web Project Management Principles*, and *Specialization Courses*.

USWeb Certified Programming & Development Specialist (USWeb C/S)

For the programmer responsible for key aspects of the production and deployment process.

Date Initiated: 1997   **# Granted:**   **Fees:** $5,000

Initial Requirements:
Must complete 5 courses and 3 exams ($). Approximate total cost is $5,000.

Continuing Requirements:

Perks:

Online Resources:

Offline Resources:
Courses are: *Web Development, Web Site Logistics, Programming & Database Principles*, and *Specialization Courses*.

USWeb Certified Web Administration Specialist (USWeb C/S)

For Web administrators.

Date Initiated: 1997   **# Granted:**   **Fees:** $5,000

Initial Requirements:
Must complete 5 courses and 3 exams ($). Approximate total cost is $5,000.

Continuing Requirements:

Perks:

Online Resources:

Offline Resources:
Courses are: *Web Development, Web Site Logistics, Web Administration Principles*, and *Specialization Courses*.

USWeb Certified Internet Security Specialist (USWeb C/S)

For individuals responsible for Internet security issues.

Date Initiated: 1997   **# Granted:**   **Fees:** $5,000

Initial Requirements:
Must complete 5 courses and 3 exams ($). Approximate total cost is $5,000.

Continuing Requirements:

Perks:

Online Resources:

Offline Resources:
Courses are: *Web Development, Web Site Logistics, Internet Networking & Security Principles*, and *Specialization Courses*.

USWeb Certified Web Graphics & Multimedia Specialist (USWeb C/S)

For individuals responsible for Web site design.

Date Initiated: 1997   **# Granted:**   **Fees:** $5,000

Initial Requirements:

Must complete 5 courses and 3 exams ($). Approximate total cost is $5,000.

Continuing Requirements:

Perks:

Online Resources:

Offline Resources:

Courses are: Web Development, *Web Site Logistics, Web Graphics & Multimedia Principles*, and *Specialization Courses*.

Sponsor:

Xplor International, The Electronic Document Systems Association
24238 Hawthorne Blvd.
Torrance, CA 90505-6505 USA
Phone: 800-669-7567   **Fax:** 310-375-4240
Email: info@explor.org
URL: www.xplor.org/edpp.html

Electronic Document & Printing Professional (EDPP)

For individuals who use and manage electronic document and printing systems.

Date Initiated: 1990   **# Granted:**   **Fees:** $365

Initial Requirements:

Must pay application fee ($35). Must submit portfolio supporting your qualifications and pay evaluation fee ($330/nonmembers, $200/members). You must be employed in the field of electronic document systems, and spend the majority of your time in one of the disciplines identified by the body of knowledge. You must also have five years of experience in the field of electronic document systems or at least three years in the field coupled with four years' experience in a field specifically related to the body of knowledge. You must also agree to accept the Electronic Document & Printing Professional Code of Ethics.

Continuing Requirements:

Must complete maintenance educational and professional activities on a 5 year cycle. Must pay maintenance fee of $25 per year.

Perks:

Online Resources:

An application and program details are available at the organization's Web site. To join a Listserv for this certification, send an email message to **LISTSERV@services.web.aol.com** with **SUBSCRIBE edppnews firstname lastname** in the body of the message.

Offline Resources:

Helpful Resources

Books & Magazines

General

The Computer Consultant's Guide, Second Edition
By Janet Ruhl
ISBN: 0471176494   Additional Media:
John Wiley & Sons; 1997; $24.95; 250 pages
Book URL: **javanet.com/~technion/faq.htm**

The Computer Consultant's Workbook
By Janet Ruhl
ISBN: 0964711605   Additional Media:
Janet Ruhl/Technion Books; 1996; $36.00; 276 pages
Book URL: **javanet.com/~technion/faq.htm**

A+

A+ Certification Success Guide
By Sarah T. Parks, Bob Kalman
ISBN: 0070485968   Additional Media:
McGraw-Hill, Inc.; 9/1996; $29.95; 304 pages

IBM

DB2 Certification Guide
By Grant Hutchinson, Calene Janacek, Dwayne Snow
ISBN: 0130796611   Additional Media: CD ROM
Prentice-Hall; 12/1997; $50.00; 600 pages

Java

Sun Java 1.2 Certification Exam Guide Book
By Cary Jardin
ISBN: 078971390X   Additional Media: CD ROM
Que; 1/1998; $69.99; 650 pages

Java 1.1 Certification for Programmers and Developers
By Barry Boone
ISBN: 0079136575   Additional Media: CD ROM
McGraw-Hill, Inc.; 7/1997; $54.95; 758 pages
URL: **www.pbg.mcgraw-hill.com./java-updates/**

Java 1.1 Certification Study Guide
By Simon Roberts, Philip Heller
ISBN: 0782120695   Additional Media: CD ROM
Sybex; 9/97; $44.99; 448 pages

Lotus

Lotus Notes Certification: Application Development and System Administration
By Scott L. Thomas, Amy E. Peasley
ISBN: 0079136745   Additional Media: CD ROM
McGraw-Hill, Inc.; 10/1997; $54.95; 624 pages

Microsoft

MCSE Career Microsoft!
By William C. Jeansonne
ISBN: 0764531417   Additional Media:
IDG Books Worldwide; $24.99; 352 pages

MCSE NT 4 Certification Exam Guide
By Brian Langan and Mark Cates
ISBN: 0079137393   Additional Media: CD ROM
McGraw-Hill, Inc; 5/98; $99.95; 1,200 pages

The Complete Microsoft Certification Success Guide
By Anthony Gatlin
ISBN: 007913176X   Additional Media: CD ROM
McGraw-Hill, Inc; 5/97; $39.95; 908 pages

Microsoft Certified Professional Magazine
Publisher: QuickStart Technologies/ MCP Magazine
Subscription: $34.95   Newstand Price: $3.95/issue/monthly
URL: **www.mcpmag.com**

Novell

The CNA / CNE Study Guide: Intranetware Edition
By Robert A. Williams, John Paul Mueller
ISBN: 0079136192   Additional Media: CD ROM
McGraw-Hill, Inc.; 9/1997; $59.95; 752 pages

The CNE-4 Study Guide
By James Chellis (Editor), et al
ISBN: 0782117546   Additional Media: CD ROM
Sybex; 1/1996; $89.99; 1563 pages

Novell's CNA Study Guide for Netware 4.1
By David James, et al.
ISBN: 0764545000   Additional Media:
IDG Books Worldwide; 6/96; $38.49; 848 pages

The Novell Certification Handbook
By Robert Williams, John P. Mueller
ISBN: 0070443653   Additional Media:
McGraw-Hill, Inc.; 7/96; $24.95; 320 pages

PowerBuilder

PowerBuilder Essentials: A Guide to the CPD
By James Clifford, Ralph DiVito, Eric Pearson & Kent Marsh
ISBN: 1-886141-09-6   Additional Media: disk
SYS-CON Publications; 1997; $44.95
Book URL: **www.sys-con.com/books/essentoc.htm**

Prosoft

Webmaster Administrator Certification Handbook
By Net Guru Technologies
ISBN: 0079132871   Additional Media: CD ROM
McGraw-Hill, Inc.; 12/97; $74.95; 960 pages

Study

How To Study, 4th Edition
By Ron Fry
ISBN: 1564142299   Additional Media:
Career Press; 5/1996; $9.99; 224 pages

Becoming a Master Student, 8th Edition
By David B. Ellis
ISBN: 0395830540   Additional Media:
College Survival (Houghton Mifflin); 9/1996; $27.96; 346 pages

Visual Basic

Visual Basic 5 Bootcamp Certification Exam Guide
By New Technology Solutions
ISBN: 0079136710   Additional Media: CD ROM
McGraw-Hill, Inc.; 1/1998; $54.95; 512 pages

Web Sites

URL: 128.32.89.153/CalRENHP.html
Sponsor: University of California, Berkeley
Contents: The CalREN Project
Summary:
A series of tips and exercises to help develop better study strategies and habits. Topics include a seven day plan to beat procrastination and tips for taking different types of tests.

URL: javanet.com/~technion/
Sponsor: Janet Ruhl/Technion Books
Contents: Janet Ruhl's Computer Consultant's Resource Page
Summary:
This is an excellent place to research what computer professionals with various skills really earn. You can also network with others about certification and consulting issues, and find out the ins and outs of working as a consultant.

URL: members.aol.com/jfloy/index.html
Sponsor: J Floy
Contents: J Floy's Certification Resource Page
Summary:
This site focuses on "How To Get Certified Without Paying An Arm And Two Legs." It includes self-study advice and links, and exam tool and study group information.

URL: www.1digitalsolutions.com/
Sponsor: Digital Solutions
Contents: Microsoft Press
Summary:
Order Microsoft Press books here. Over 290 titles available.

URL: www.arrowweb.com/Echarbon/cert.html
Sponsor: Eric Charbonneau
Contents: Eric Charbonneau's Computer Professional Certification Site
Summary:
This site is for technicians and computer professionals working toward professional certification. It contains links to certification resources, salary surveys, and exam preparation advice and products.

URL: www.bnla.baynet.de/bnla01/members/robsch19/index.htm
Sponsor: Robert Schmid
Contents: MCSE MCP Braindump Heaven
Summary:
After taking MCP tests, people come to this site and share the details of what the test was like. Find out what people who've already taken the tests you're facing say you should know.

URL: www.certify.com
Sponsor: Cyber Pass Inc
Contents: CNEQUIZR Resource Page/ Book Swap
Summary:
While it focuses on Novell and Microsoft test preparation, this site also contains Bookswap, where you can trade in your certification books/kits for someone else's.

URL: www.certpro.com/
Sponsor: Ben Simpson
Contents: CertPro Link Page
Summary:
Here's a place you can advertise yourself once you've obtained certifi-caiton. This site contains links to certified professionals, organized by state.

URL: www.dartmouth.edu/admin/acskills/
Sponsor: Dartmouth College Academic Skills Center
Contents: Dartmouth College Academic Skills Center
Summary:
Dartmouth college has posted on the Web a useful collection of articles on study habits articles. Topics covered range from coping with test anxiety to managing time. You can also purchase short learning skills videos to help you improve your study efficiency. A set of 4 costs $100.

URL: www.diac.com/~wlin/cpcert.html
Sponsor: Wayne Lindimore
Contents: Wayne's Comprehensive Computer Professional Certification Resource
Summary:
This Web site contains links to various certification programs, certi-fication news, and links to resources for people pursuing Novell, Microsoft, and IBM certifications. You'll also be able to connect to relevant newsgroups and study aids.

URL: www.elink.ibmlink.ibm.com/pbl/pbl
Sponsor: IBM - Publications
Contents: IBM Publications Online Catalog
Summary:
Many publications can be read online at this site, and still more can be ordered. Books and manuals here are not limited to IBM products. You can get CD ROMs here too.

URL: www.gamoba.sk/APTC/TESTS/AP9K0.HTM
Sponsor: Sylvan Prometric
Contents: Sylvan Prometric Certification Test Details
Summary:
This site lists all of the technical certification exams administered by Sylvan Prometric, along with testing rules, number of questions, and estimated length of exam.

URL: www.mcp.com/personal/
Sponsor: Macmillan Computer Publishing
Contents: MCP Personal Bookshelf
Summary:
You can choose five titles from the more than 100 available to include on your personal "electronic bookshelf." You can read these books at your leisure. Many technical topics are available. This service is free.

URL: www.mindtools.com
Sponsor: Mind Tools Ltd.
Contents: Memory Techniques and Mnemonics
Summary:
This is a veritable goldmine of memory techniques and other mental skills that will help you learn more and remember more of what you learn.

URL: www.ncres.com/COW/
Sponsor: NetCent Communications
Contents: ChatterNet Forum
Summary:
The ChatterNet Forum hosted by NetCent contains a section devoted to certification issues. This isn't a heavily trafficked forum, but you can discuss certification questions here.

URL: www.pcwebopedia.com/index.html
Sponsor: Sandy Bay Software
Contents: PC Webopaedia
Summary:
Any time you want to learn more about a particular computer technology or term, visit this site. It's a constantly evolving encyclopedia of computer information. You'll find up-to-the-minute definitions of the latest terminology, along with links to additional information on the topic.

URL: www.saluki.com/mcp/
Sponsor: Tim Sneath
Contents: MCP Online
Summary:
Tim Sneath's MCP Online site is an excellent resource for individuals pursuing Microsoft certifications. You can join an ongoing discus-

sion, find out which Microsoft certification is best for you, learn what the passing exam marks are, and ask your own questions. You'll also find an MCP FAQ to review.

URL: www.sharat.co.il/vvv/index.html
Sponsor: Victor Dubin
Contents: Victor Dubin's Certification and Networking Page
Summary:
This site contains computer professional certification program info, Novell and Microsoft test details, including passing scores, tests preparation tools and vendors, and other information. You'll also find the Certification Wall of Fame here.

URL: www.utexas.edu/student/lsc/handouts.html
Sponsor: University of Texas - Austin
Contents: Study Skills Handouts from The University of Texas
Summary:
These handouts from the University of Texas - Austin come from the school's Study Strategies class. Topics include improving motivation and increasing concentration while studying, among many others.

Training Tools

4D Corp
2207 Concord Pike #310
Wilmington, DE.19803 USA
Phone: 800-514-9226   **Fax:** 302 234-7697
Email: sales@4dcorp.com
URL: www.4dcorp.com
Summary:
Sells training packages and software for A+, Microsoft, Novell, and other certification programs.

Automated Training Systems (ATS)
21250 Califa St. Suite 107
Woodland Hills, CA 91367 USA
Phone: 800-426-8737   **Fax:**
Email:
URL: www.ibmuser.com
Summary:
Sells CBT courses for for AS/400, Novell, Microsoft, OS/2 and others.

B & C Data Systems
3 Fall Ln., P.O. Box 430
Gorham, ME 04038 USA
Phone: 207-839-7322   **Fax:**
Email: info@bcdata.com
URL: www.bcdata.com/tools1.htm
Summary:
Sells self study kits for certification programs incuding Novell, A+, and Microsoft.

Bird Publications
HC76-2465 Scriver Bluff Rd.
Garden Valley, ID 84622 USA
Phone: 208-462-3138   **Fax:** 208-462-3100
Email: bird@micron.net
URL: www.bird.boise.id.us/
Summary:
Sells ICCP exam preparation materials including audiocassettes and workbooks, and exam simulation software.

CBT Systems

1005 Hamilton Ct.
Menlo Park, CA 94025-1422 USA
Phone: 800-387-0932   **Fax:** 650-614-5901
Email: salesinfo@cbtsys.com
URL: www.cbtsys.com/
Summary:
Courseware for Cisco, INFORMIX, Java, Lotus, Microsoft, Novell,
Oracle, SAP, Sybase, Internet and Intranet Skills, UNIX, and Centu-
ra. Demos available. Also runs scholars.com, an Internet-based
online Microsoft and Novell "learning community."

CDi Communications

50 Yorkshire Dr.
Suffern, NY 10901 USA
Phone: 800-617-5586   **Fax:** 914-368-2472
Email: webmaster@netwind.com
URL: www.netwind.com
Summary:
Sells certification training packages for A+, Java, Novell, Microsoft,
Oracle, and others.

ComputerPREP

410 N 44th St., Suite 600
Phoenix, AZ 85008 USA
Phone: 800-228-1027   **Fax:** 602-275-1603
Email: vcorral@computerprep.com
URL: www.computerprep.com
Summary:
Sells computer training software for individuals and organizations.
Certification training programs for A+, Microsoft, Novell,
Client/Server, Lotus, IBM, and Internet.

Cyber Pass Inc

Minto Place, P.O. Box 56060
Ottowa, ON K1R Canada
Phone: 613-237-4991   **Fax:** 613-230-5279
Email: support@certify.com
URL: www.certify.com
Summary:
Sellers of CNEQUIZR software. Shareware downloads available
from Web site.

CyberState University

25 Orinda Way, Suite 301
Orinda, CA 94563-4022 USA
Phone: 888-438-3382   **Fax:** 510-253-8152
Email: admissions@cyberstateu.com
URL: www.cyberstateu.com
Summary:
Internet-based training courses for Microsoft and Novell certification
candidates.

D.O.C. Software

27 Glendale Dr.
Danbury, CT 06811 USA
Phone: 203-790-1769   **Fax:** 203-778-5093
Email: sales@docsoftware.com
URL: www.docsoftware.com
Summary:
Sells PowerBuilder, Oracle, and Sybase certification test preparation
software. Demo available.

Data-Tech Institute

PO Box 2429
Clifton, NJ 07015 USA
Phone: 973-478-5400   **Fax:** 973-478-3344
Email:
URL: www.datatech.com
Summary:
Sells many self-study courses on video and CBT. Programs covered
include Microsoft, Novell, Informix, Sybase, Oracle, PowerBuilder,
Java, Lotus, Bay Networks, Cisco, Sun, UNIX, and general technolo-
gy topics.

DigitalThink

1000 Brannan Street Suite 501
San Francisco, CA 94103 USA
Phone: 415-437-2800   **Fax:** 415-437-3877
Email: info@digitalthink.com
URL: www.digitalthink.com
Summary:
Provides Internet-based courses. Offerings include certification-spe-
cific curriculums for Java certifications.

ForeFront Group, The
1360 Post Oak Blvd., Suite 2050
Houston, TX 77056 USA
Phone: 800-475-5831   **Fax:**
Email: webmaster@ffg.com
URL: www.ffg.com
Summary:
Sells certification preparation software for A+, Microsoft, and Novell.
Trial versions available on Web site.

Franklin College
2400 Louisiana N, Suite 200
Albuquerque, NM 87110 USA
Phone: 800-467-2378   **Fax:** 505-881-3226
Email:
URL: www.franklinet.com/html/distance_education.html
Summary:
Offers one-on-one Internet-based training for A+ and Microsoft certi-
fications.

Free Academy of Career Training (FACT)
London, ON Canada
Phone: **Fax:**
Email: freeinfo@freeacademy.london.on.ca
URL: www.freeacademy.london.on.ca/FACT-HP.HTM
Summary:
Offers absolutely FREE (except for enduring some advertising) train-
ing courses via the Internet. Certification programs include A+,
Microsoft, Novell, and Net Guru.

Heathkit Educational Systems
455 Riverview Dr.
Benton Harbor, MI 49022 USA
Phone: 800-253-0570   **Fax:**
Email: heathkit@heathkit.com
URL: www.heathkit.com
Summary:
Sells a self-study kit and reference library for A+ certification.

International Business and Institutional Development Corporation (IBID)

16301 N.E. 8th St., Suite 205
Bellevue, WA 98008 USA
Phone: 800-852-9816   **Fax:** 425-401-0460
Email: jpfotzer@mail.ibidpub.com
URL: www.ibidpub.com
Summary:
Sells preparation software for A+ and Microsoft.

KeyStone Learning Systems

2241 Larsen Parkway
Provo, UT 84606 USA
Phone: 800-748-4838   **Fax:** 801-373-6872
Email: keystone@klscorp.com
URL: www.keylearnsys.com
Summary:
Video training for Microsoft, Novell, Java, Oracle, PowerBuilder, and other topics.

Lantell

16250 Ventura Blvd, #202
Encino, CA 91436 USA
Phone: 800-526-8355   **Fax:** 818-905-1292
Email: info@lantell.com
URL: www.lantell.com
Summary:
Sells videos and CD ROMs for A+, Microsoft, and Novell.

LearnKey

1845 W. Sunset Blvd
St. George, UT 84770 USA
Phone: 800-865-0165   **Fax:** 435-674-9734
Email: sales@learnkey.com
URL: www.learnkey.com
Summary:
LearnKey sells certification Videos, CD ROMs, and Study Guides for A+, Microsoft, Novell, and Lotus certifications.

Mastering Computers

11000 N. Scottsdale Rd., Suite 260
Scottsdale, AZ 85254 USA
Phone: 800-800-9686   **Fax:**
Email:
URL: www.masteringcomputers.com
Summary:
Sells training aids for Microsoft, Novell, Sun, Lotus, Web site development, and other curriculums. Some are on video; most are on CD ROM.

MaxIT

2771-25 Monument Rd., MS 355
Jacksonville, FL 32225 USA
Phone: 800-868-8039   **Fax:** 904-998-0221
Email: info@maxit.com
URL: www.maxit.com/
Summary:
Develops and distributes preparation materials and assistance for certification training including A+, CNE, Informix, Lotus, Internet, Networking, Oracle, OS/2, Mainframe (AIX, UNIX), and others.

Microhard Technologies

300 West Adams, Suite 825
Chicago, IL 60606 USA
Phone: 800-266-7648   **Fax:** 312-368-9530
Email: mti@mcs.com
URL: www.microhard.com/cbt
Summary:
Sells self-study kits for Microsoft, Novell, PowerBuilder, and Visual Basic programs.

Microsoft Online Institute (MOLI)

Redmond, WA USA
Phone: **Fax:**
Email:
URL: moli.microsoft.com
Summary:
Internet-based training for Microsoft certification candidates and others.

MindWorks

1525 N. Hayden, Suite F7
Scottsdale, AZ 85257 USA
Phone: 800-874-1516   **Fax:**
Email: info@mindwork.com
URL: www.mindwork.com
Summary:
Sells self study manuals and CBT kits for A+, Microsoft, and Novell
certification programs.

NETg

1751 West Diehl Rd., Second Floor
Naperville, IL 60563-9099 USA
Phone: 800-265-1900   **Fax:** 630-983-4518
Email: info@netg.com
URL: www.netg.com
Summary:
Sells training courses and courseware. Certification areas include
Microsoft, Novell, PowerBuilder, Lotus Notes, and others.

On With Learning (OWL)

131-A Bridge Street
Arroyo Grande, CA 93420 USA
Phone: 800-272-0887   **Fax:** 800-508-0487
Email: owl@execpc.com
URL: www.execpc.com/~owl/index.html
Summary:
Video instruction for Microsoft, Novell, Unix, Oracle, IBM AS/400
and others.

Open Window Software

6175 Garlock Way
Colorado Springs, CO 80918 USA
Phone: 719-531-0403   **Fax:** 719-531-0403
Email: DickBryant@compuserve.com
URL: www.openwindow.com/pages/winflash.htm
Summary:
This is the maker of the WinFlash shareware program, a software
package that lets you create your own study flashcards, which you
can view on screen or print out and carry with you.

OraWorld, A Division of Animated Learning
P.O. Box 345
Aptos, CA 95001 USA
Phone: 800-235-3030   **Fax:** 408-427-2949
Email:
URL: www.oraworld.com/index.htm
Summary:
Multimedia Oracle training. Test drive a course at the company Web site.

Page One Design
Unit 24 - 5380 Smith Dr.
Richmond, BC V6V 2K8 Canada
Phone: 800-668-2511   **Fax:** 604-522-1159
Email: info@pageone.com
URL: www.islandnet.com/pageone/
Summary:
Sells video and CD ROM training products. Courses include Novell, Microsoft, programming languages, Lotus, UNIX, project management, and other titles.

PC Age
20 Audrey Place
Fairfield, NJ 07004 USA
Phone: 800-722-4360   **Fax:** 732-287-4511
Email: wb@pcage.com
URL: www.pcage.com
Summary:
Sells self study kits for Microsoft and Novell certification programs. Products include a Windows NT simulator.

PC Technology
The Woodlands, TX 77387 USA
Phone: 281-362-1728   **Fax:** 281-362-1882
Email: pct@hia.net
URL: www.pct-nas.com/
Summary:
Sells NetWare Administrator Simulator (NAS) ($50), a training tool that allows a person to train in a NetWare 4.11 environment without being attached to a network. Also sells Novell NDS Simulator ($25).

PowerConcepts
11600 Meridian Dr.
Frisc, TX 75035 USA
Phone: 972-335-8878   **Fax:** 972-335-7530
Email: info@powerconcepts.com
URL: www.powerconcepts.com
Summary:
Specializes in PowerBuilder tools and certification training. Sells books, videos, and CD ROMs.

QuickStart
CA USA
Phone: 800-326-1044   **Fax:**
Email: info@quickstart.com
URL: www.quickstart.com
Summary:
This company sells Microsoft training aids including audio tapes and study guides, as well as instructor-led training.

Self Test Software
4651 Woodstock Road, Suite 203, M/S 384
Roswell, GA 30075 USA
Phone: 800-244-7330   **Fax:** 770-641-9719
Email:
URL: www.stsware.com/
Summary:
Sells certification practice testing and training software for Novell, Microsoft, Lotus, and A+. Demos available.

Specialized Solutions
31 W. Tarpon Ave, Suite B
Tarpon Springs, FL 34689 USA
Phone: 800-942-1660   **Fax:** 813-943-9683
Email: sales@specializedsolutions.com
URL: www.specializedsolutions.com
Summary:
Sells training study kits that include study guides, video tapes and CD ROMs for A+, Microsoft, and Novell certification programs.

Startext Computing Services Ltd.
105 Scarboro Avenue SW
Calgary, AB T3C 2H2 Canada
Phone: 403-244-9636   **Fax:** 403-244-7349
Email: service@flashcards.com
URL: www.flashcards.com
Summary:
Sells electronic flashcards for Microsoft and Novell test preparation.

Transcender
621 Mainstream Dr., Suite 270
Nashville, TN 37228 USA
Phone: 615-726-8779   **Fax:** 615-726-8884
Email: sales@transcender.com
URL: www.transcender.com
Summary:
Sells an extensive selection of Microsoft exam preparation software titles.

Trier Software
4139 W. 123rd, Suite 3350
Alsip, IL 60803 USA
Phone: 708-239-3311   **Fax:** 708-489-2469
Email: trierexams@aol.com
URL: trierexams.com
Summary:
Sells practice exams for Microsoft certification candidates.

United Education Centers
50 S. Main St.
Pleasant Grove, UT 84062 USA
Phone: 800-877-4889   **Fax:** 801-785-0575
Email: sales@uec.com
URL: www.uec.com
Summary:
Sells preparation materials for Microsoft and Novell. Media include audio and video tapes, printed study guides, and software programs. Demo available.

Virtual Training Company, The
2086 Walsh Ave, Suite A/B
Santa Clara, CA 95050 USA
Phone: 888-872-4623   **Fax:** 408-492-1851
Email: mark@vtco.com
URL: www.vtco.com
Summary:
Sells training CD ROMs on various topics including Adobe.

Wave Technologies International
10845 Olive Blvd, Suite 250
St. Louis, MO 63141 USA
Phone: 888-204-6143   **Fax:**
Email: webmaster@wavetech.com
URL: www.wavetech.com
Summary:
Sells A+, Microsoft, and Novell certification study kits. Recently initiated WaveU, an Internet-based training environment.

ZDNet University (ZDU)
USA
Phone: **Fax:**
Email:
URL: www.zdu.com
Summary:
This is Ziff-Davis's Internet-based training center. Study all you want for $4.95 a month. Courses cover many different technical topics.

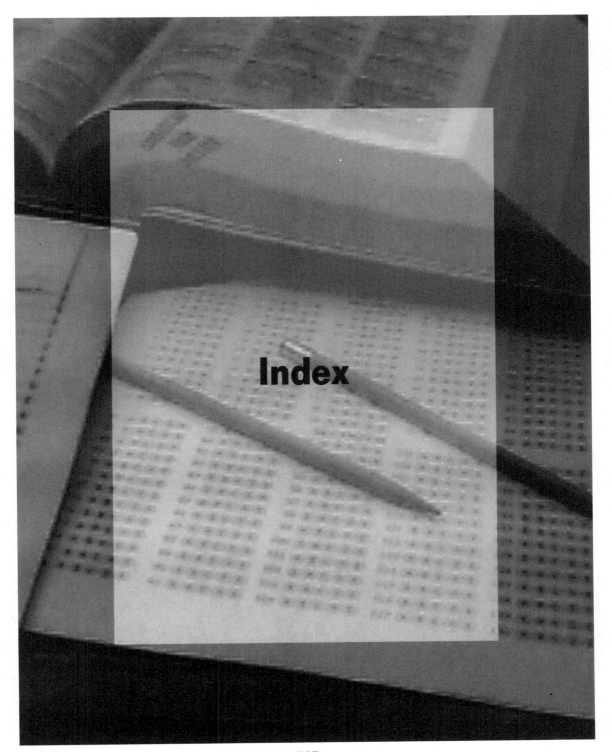

Index

Index

About the Author

Anne Martinez is a respected computing writer and regular contributor to *Contract Professional*. Her work has also appeared in *Small Business Builder* and many other publications. She holds a degree in computer science and previously worked in the MIS department of a major corporation. She lives in Winston-Salem, North Carolina.